WHY BELIEVE? GOD EXISTS!

Rethinking The Case For God And Christianity

Dr. Terry L. Miethe
Dr. Gary R. Habermas

WHY BELIEVE? GOD EXISTS!

Rethinking The Case For God And Christianity

Dr. Terry L. Miethe
Dr. Gary R. Habermas

**COLLEGE PRESS
PUBLISHING COMPANY**
Joplin, Missouri

Scripture quotations are from the *New American Standard Bible*, Copyright ©
1960, 1962, 1963, 1968, 1972, 1973, 1975, and 1977 by the Lockman
Foundation, and are used by permission; and, The HOLY BIBLE, *New
International Version*®. Copyright © 1973,1978, 1984 by International Bible
Society. Used by permission of Zondervan Publishing House. All rights
reserved.

Printed and Bound in the United States of America

Library of Congress Catalog Card Number 92-75787
International Standard Book Number: 0-89900-608-6

God is not in need of anything,
But all things are in need of Him.
– Marcianus Aristides (530?468? B.C.)

Revelation 15:3-4

"Let all the world in ev'ry corner sing
My God and King."
– George Herbert (1593-1633)

"God is and all is well."
– John Greenleaf Whittier (1807-1892)

"God's in his heaven –
All's right with the world."
– Robert Browning (1812-1889)

Psalm 145:3

"Truth – is as old as God –
His Twin identity
And will endure as long as He
a Co-Eternity – ."
–Emily Dickinson (1830-1886)

"For since the creation of the world His invisible attributes, His
eternal power and divine nature, have been clearly seen, being
understood through what has been made, so that they are without
excuse."
Romans 1:20 (NASB)

CONTENTS

PREFACE

Have you ever heard someone say: "If there is such a 'thing' as 'God', why don't intelligent people believe in Him?" Of course, this is stated in such a way as to say "*de facto*" (from the fact, as a matter of fact) that no intelligent people believe in God.[1] A statement like this prejudices the case even before an answer can be given. By implication, if *you* believe in God you are *not* intelligent.

A more angry – and bigoted way – of saying it is: "Only idiots believe in God!" There are many angry people in the world – some of whom, it must be admitted, have been abused by a person who claimed to be a Christian, or by a church full of them. Another, perhaps more subtle, way of really saying the same thing is: "Christianity is only for women and little children." When we were both in full-time ministry in the local church, it was quite common to hear a non-believing husband or other male make such a statement. This implies there is really no necessary truth (God does not exist, or is really irrelevant) in it (Christianity) but it *may* have a good social effect on women[2] and children.

"Does God exist?" is the *most important question* a person can ask. The whole of the history of philosophy "speaks out" – almost screams out – to affirm the importance of this question. But, the importance of this question is in no way confined to philosophy as an academic discipline. The whole history of humanity as such can be written as a search for a meaningful answer to the question of the existence of God. Almost everyone agrees on the

---

1. In the discipline of logic this is an error referred to as "Begging the Question," (*Petitio Principii*). If one assumes as a premise for an argument, the very conclusion it is intended to prove this fallacy is committed.
2. Not to mention being incredibly sexist.

importance of the question.[3] Unfortunately, not everyone agrees on the answer.

We, the authors, believe that the evidence is rather clear and very convincing. Yet, it must certainly be admitted at the beginning that this is a very complex question, the importance of which demands much study. It is most unfortunate that people – both in the church and outside of it – are often not happy with even simple answers unless they are at the same time simplistic. Very complex concepts, ideas, or truths can often be presented in a "simple way" in an attempt to make them widely understandable, but without denying their true complexity.

We have tried to write this book on a "popular" level, to the "layman" (when it comes to philosophy or science). Yet, it must be pointed out that many are the issues which must be addressed in this book for which there is no way to deal with them, that is, at the same time, both simple and really responsible to their complexity. We have no delusions that this book is complete or exhaustive in any way. Every attempt will be made to encourage further study and to give resources for it.[4]

Additionally, we have also attempted to remain within our own areas of specialization, as well as pursuing a few other interests. Dr. Miethe penned Parts One and Two of this work, along with the appendices. Dr. Habermas wrote Parts Three and Four. The first two Parts were purposely written in a style that would encourage the reader to stretch for a *deeper* level of knowledge. Intermittently these sections are followed by lighter material in order to give the reader a "mental reprieve." Our intent is to prepare our case intellectually to defend Christianity *intelligently* with the non-believing scholars of our day. Throughout the book, the term "atheist" is defined in the classic sense of a "non-believer" in God. By the term "theist" is meant those who hold a "belief in a personal God who created and rules the world. All Christians are theists, though not all theists are Christians."[5]

But if this is true – that the evidence for God's existence is clear and very convincing – why don't all people believe? The answer to this question would

---

3. Not *everyone* agrees that the question, "Does God exist?" is important. In chapter one, we relate the story of a "philosopher" who says that it is a meaningless question to which one should answer: "Who cares?" See chapter 1, pp. 19-22.

4. See the important bibliography at the end of this book.

5. Terry L. Miethe, *The Compact Dictionary of Doctrinal Words* (Minneapolis: Bethany House, 1988), p. 203.

be another book.[6] There are dozens, maybe even hundreds of reasons why people do not so believe. Still, the fact that people choose not to believe may have nothing to do with a lack of good evidence.[7] Evidence is not coercive. In other words, evidence – no matter how strong – does not, simply cannot, force people to believe. People have to accept evidence only if they want to come to grips with facts and the implication(s) of those facts with regard to how they live their daily lives. The old adage, "You can lead a horse to water, but you cannot make him drink," is forever true in this case.

The purpose of this book is to defend the position that God exists and that His existence makes a difference to each person, everyday. We hope to show at the very least that: (1) The questions cannot be ruled out of court without a fair hearing. This is not intellectually or historically honest. Ronald Nash has rightly said:

> Human beings are never neutral with regard to God. Either we worship God as Creator and Lord, or we turn away from God. Because the heart is directed either toward God or against him, theoretical thinking is never so pure or autonomous as many would like to think.[8]

(2) The question cannot just be simply "ignored." For to "ignore" it is to answer it in the negative. This reminds us of Pascal's famous statement that every man has a god-shaped vacuum in his heart which is, in fact, filled by something. (3) There are good reasons for believing in God and Christianity as the revelation of His will for our lives. Intellectual honesty demands that all of these reasons be examined closely and fairly. (4) Far from being a burden, belief in God – and the relationship with Him which is possible through His son, Jesus – not only frees people to live to the fullest, but is the source to true joy in life.

–Oxford, England

11 April 1993

The Festival of the Resurrection of Jesus

---

6. This would then be a book, perhaps, on "the psychology of belief or disbelief." Some of the reasons why people do not believe will, however, be addressed directly or indirectly, e.g., the problem of evil which is one of the most common reasons for rejecting the existence of the Christian God, is addressed in chapter 18, "So Much Pain and Evil."

7. See chapter 4: "God: A Psychological Crutch?"

8. Ronald H. Nash, *Worldviews in Conflict: Choosing Christianity in a World of Ideas* (Grand Rapids: Zondervan, 1992), p. 24.

PART ONE

Evidence
from Philosophy

Chapter One
GOD'S EXISTENCE:
IMPORTANCE OF THE QUESTION

Introduction: Importance of the Question
God's Existence & Experience
God's Existence & Scripture
God's Existence: Personal Importance

INTRODUCTION: THE IMPORTANCE OF THE QUESTION

Since the beginnings of the discipline of philosophy, whether we start with Socrates (circa. 470-399 B.C.) or Plato (427-347 B.C.) and move down through the ages to modern times by way of Aristotle (384-322 B.C.), Augustine of Hippo (A.D. 354-430), Thomas Aquinas (1224/5-1274), John Locke (1632-1704), Immanuel Kant (1724-1804), or dozens of other thinkers, philosophy has sought to discern the existence of extra-physical reality.[1] The question of God's existence and what we can "know" of it has motivated, even inspired, thinkers for thousands of years. "Does God exist?" is by far the most important question we can ask both in terms of its relationship to the nature of *ultimate* reality and to our personal *everyday* lives.

Except for the period of the last two hundred years (philosophy after Kant), the story of philosophy as a record of thought was motivated by much the same type of question that motivated theology. The whole history of philo-

---

1. Extra-physical reality is reality not limited by the physical, i.e., the spiritual. For some excellent resources on God in the history of philosophy see Frederick Copleston's multivolumed set *A History of Philosophy* (New York: Doubleday, 1946) which is generally regarded as the best available. See also James Collins, *God in Modern Philosophy* (Chicago: Henry Regnery, 1959); Charles Hartshorne and William L. Reese, *Philosophers Speak of God* (Chicago: University of Chicago Press, 1953); and Terry L. Miethe, *The Metaphysics of Leonard James Eslick: His Philosophy of God* (Ann Arbor: University Microfilms, Inc., 1976).

sophical thought "speaks out" in support of the importance of this question. Even Friedrich Nietzsche (1844-1900, famous as the father of the modern death of God movement) prophetically envisages himself as a madman: to have lost God equals madness.[2] When mankind discovers that it has lost God, universal madness will break out. Much of Nietzsche's philosophy is involved with a forceful denial of what philosophy had for thousands of years considered the Truth.[3] Sometimes it seems, when we watch the evening news, that our society *is* getting perilously close to that predicted madness.

GOD'S EXISTENCE & EXPERIENCE

In recent years it has *not* been fashionable to talk as if one could "prove" the existence of God.[4] Many good Christians, even Christian philosophers, have mistakenly been willing to place the total burden of "proof" for God on religious experience alone. This is most unfortunate for both Christian philosophy and for practical ministry/evangelism for several reasons: (1) Experience alone is not an adequate test for truth claims. Experience is not self-interpreting. It must be interpreted/understood in a certain context, i.e., that of the facts about reality surrounding the claims inferred from a parfacts about reality surrounding the claims inferred from a particular experience. (2) Experience can be so easily misinterpreted according to one's emotional state at the time. (3) When people base their religious beliefs primarily on experience their "staying power" in the faith does not seem at all strong. We know one widely-recognized philosopher who bases his belief in the validity of Christianity on personal religious experience and claims to have been converted three times. He joked with us that perhaps this time it would "stick." Regardless of one's theology about such matters, his example shows clearly that religious experience alone cannot claim to rationally verify or maintain the Christian life.

---

2. Nietzsche's parable of *The Madman* can be found in Walter Kaufmann, *Nietzsche: Philosopher, Psychologist, Antichrist* (New York: Meridian Books, 1966), p. 81.

3. See Terry L. Miethe, "Atheism: Nietzsche" chapter six in *Biblical Errancy: An Analysis of Its Philosophical Roots* edited by N. L. Geisler (Grand Rapids: Zondervan, 1981), pp. 131-160.

4. Of course this depends in large part on what one means by the word "prove." See Terry L. Miethe, *Living Your Faith: Closing the Gap Between Mind and Heart* (Joplin, MO: College Press Publishing, 1993), pp. 49-51.

A view of faith that is totally "subjective" – totally personal – cannot answer the questions of an intelligent skeptic or meet such a person's needs in relation to the serious problems we face in everyday life.[5] Richard L. Purtill says:

> Thus we showed that it is not unreasonable to believe in Christianity. Some Christians seem to feel that this is all reason can be expected to do in this area, and that then faith must take over. That this is not the biblical view nor the traditional Christian view is, I think, clear from a study of the scriptures and a study of history. It is also, I believe, based on a misunderstanding of the nature of faith. *Faith must be based on reasons, and the reasons must be good ones.* [emphasis added][6]

This view that "my experience/belief is just as good as yours" (and that is all I have to show) is the "Mexican standoff" view of faith, that is: it is good enough to show that my religious experience is not unreasonable. This may be fine for the Christian who is arguing for his experience and is already convinced, but it is not very likely to impress (or certainly not help "convert") the unbeliever who wants to know why he should accept Christianity. In history, most Christian philosophers have been rather reluctant to rest the case for the existence and/or reality of God on the level of experience alone for several reasons.

> First, at best the conceptual content of the Transcendent (God) is minimal. For not much if anything is known via unanalyzed experience about the nature of such a reality. Second, it seems to them that only reason can transcend the subjectivity of pure experience. Third, the argument from experience is not a rational demonstration such as many theists offer for their belief in God. For these reasons, theists have offered rational proofs for their belief that there is an objective basis for their religious experience.[7]

Though religious experience has a place in the discussion, it too must be based on reason, analysis, and factual evidence for the claims made regarding the importance, validity, and relevance of the experience in question.[8]

---

5. See chapter 1, "What Is Faith Really?" in Miethe, *Living Your Faith*, pp. 15-25.

6. Richard L. Purtill, *Reason to Believe* (Grand Rapids: Eerdmans, 1974), pp. 71-75.

7. Norman L. Geisler, *Philosophy of Religion* (Grand Rapids: Zondervan, 1974), p. 87.

8. See chapter 29 of this book: "Our Personal God."

GOD'S EXISTENCE & SCRIPTURE

One of the arguments often given as to why one does not need to – in fact, should not – try to prove the existence of God is that: "The Scripture does not argue for God's existence. The Bible just assumes God's existence." This assertion (that the Bible does not argue for the existence of God) must be answered in three ways: (1) Even if it is true that the Bible does not argue for the existence of God, this does not mean we should not. After all the Bible was written primarily as revelation *about God* to a believing community which already believed *in God*. They did not need to be argued into belief. But it is still quite appropriate to support the existence of God to those outside the believing community. (2) You cannot just rule "argumentation" out of hand because there is argument presented throughout the Bible when something was disputed (see for example: 1 Pet 3:15, 2 Pet 1:16). "So it would seem appropriate that those who follow in the biblical tradition should argue, when the supreme belief that there is a God becomes the subject of dispute."[9]

(3) Though this is not the Bible's primary purpose, the assertion that it does not argue for the existence of God is just plain false. Certainly the Bible indicates that man has a "natural knowledge of God." Romans 1:18-23 says:

> For the wrath of God is revealed from heaven against all ungodliness and unrighteousness of men, who suppress the truth in unrighteousness, because that which is known about God is evident within them; for God made it evident to them. For since the creation of the world *His invisible attributes, His eternal power and divine nature, have been clearly seen*, [emphasis added] being understood through what has been made, so that they are without excuse. For even though they knew God, they did not honor Him as God, or give thanks; but they became futile in their speculations, and their foolish heart was darkened. Professing to be wise, they became fools, and exchanged the glory of the incorruptible God for an image in the form of corruptible man and of birds and four-footed animals and crawling creatures. (NASB)

Thus it is clear – if one accepts the authority of Scripture – that men knew through nature God's attributes, power and nature.[10] "It will not do to say that in such passages the author is only arguing to God's nature . . . and not his existence. For arguing that a god is good and powerful is arguing that there is a god who is God (i.e., omnipotent, omniscient, etc.), and so that there is a God."[11]

---

9. See Richard Swinburne, *Faith and Reason* (Oxford: Clarendon Press, 1981), p. 86.

10. See also Romans 2:14-15.

11. Swinburne, *Faith and Reason,* p. 86.

GOD'S EXISTENCE: PERSONAL IMPORTANCE

As we begin this section, a statement in support of the importance of *serious* Christian education is appropriate here. Very often, even in larger churches with good resources, the education program is all too weak! We lose so many during the years of high school and early years of college needlessly. Very early on in the first semester my freshman year at the university, I was the only one of the seven of us there from my graduating class who was still attending church. We all attended church in high school. We all were active members in a fairly good and conservative Bible preaching church. If we could only realize that our youth need more than "a fun and games" approach to the faith and the church, or a legalistic approach to the "do's and don'ts of life." Intelligent young people always see through mindless legalism. While they are playing games in Sunday School and church, they are working, learning and being challenged (often regarding their faith) in high school and college. They are forced to answer some very important questions about life, morality, the world in which they live, God, etc. These are questions that all too often they have not been prepared to answer by the church. It must be stated that these answers must be more than a catechism type approach, or quick, often memorized, "pat" answers to life's most difficult problems. They need sound answers, but above all they *need to be taught to be able to think* through the issues, the quick answers, and the problems. They need serious Christian education! Only then will we be able to keep them and see them grow in wisdom and stature, and in favor with God and man (as did Jesus according to Luke 2:52).

When I was a freshman in the School of Science of a major university in the Midwest, I learned – even before I knew what philosophy was – that philosophers were certainly right in saying the most important question a person could ask was: "Is there a God?" This was in 1966, during the Viet Nam War, when universities were trying to "flunk out" students as quickly as they could. The university I attended reportedly had the highest suicide rate of any of the "Big Ten" universities.

The pressure on students was great indeed. The normal first year pressures and adjustment problems were compounded by the war and the time in which we lived. It was a very hard year for a young man with big ideas from a small town in Indiana. It was quite an experience for a boy whose high school had less than 150 students to be thrown into a university with over 35,000 students. How could a boy with such big dreams have such adjustment problems and feel so lonely with so many people concentrated around him?

I was supposed to be a Christian. I knew Christianity was supposed to have answers to problems like I was experiencing. *But what were the answers*? By the end of that first semester in university, I realized any meaningful answers to the problems of daily living could not be separated from questions like: "What is truth?" "What is reality?" and "What is God's will for my life?" I realized that the most important question one could ask was indeed: "Is there a God?" And just as importantly, I realized that if I answered: "Yes, there is a God," then that answer should have an important effect on me and on how I lived my life. I also realized that if I answered: "No, there isn't a God," then that answer as well would affect how I lived my life.

Further, I knew I needed to answer the question very thoughtfully and carefully because personal integrity demanded that my life be lived out according to the answer. I set out on what ended up being an eighteen year educational quest. A quest not just to answer the question (for I came to realize that an intelligent answer could be achieved much sooner than that) but also to learn as much as I could about the God I said I believed in and His will for my life.[12] It also became obvious somewhere in this long process that we must be willing to constantly reexamine the question as we grow. C. S. Lewis' famous statement that faith is " . . . assent to a proposition which we think so overwhelmingly probable that there is a psychological exclusion of doubt although not a logic exclusion of dispute," is most important.[13]

Earlier, in the "Preface" I indicated that "almost everyone" agreed on the importance of the question. In the past I would have said that "everyone agreed on the importance of the question, atheist and theist alike," though they obviously disagree on the answer. But I found that this assertion was not true. A few years back, we were asked by several groups to debate a fellow philosopher on the question of the "existence of God" (Miethe) and to make a presentation on the "Resurrection" (Habermas) at a state university in the Washington, D.C. area. The debate was to be jointly sponsored by several

---

12. Two excellent resources on the will of God are: Paul E. Little, *Affirming the Will of God* (Downer's Grove: InterVarsity Press, 1971), 34 pages; and Garry Friesen, *Decision Making & the Will of God: A Biblical Alternative to the Traditional View* (Portland: Multnomah Press, 1980), 452 pages.
13. C. S. Lewis, "On Obstinacy in Belief," in *The World's Last Night and Other Essays* (New York: Brace Jovanovich, 1955), p. 16.

Christian groups and an area chapter of a national atheist organization.

We had a couple of colleagues and some students with us. Arriving for the debate early, we decided to walk around and see the campus. All over the campus were posters announcing the debate. When we entered the student union the posters were plastered everywhere. Interestingly enough, across one of the posters announcing the debate on: "Does God exist?" a person had written: "Who cares?" I started my presentation in the debate that night by relating the historical importance of the question and then what was written on the poster and added that I assumed everyone there that night – atheist or theist – agreed on the importance of the question or they would not have been there. In response to my comments, when my opponent started to speak, he said: "Whoever wrote 'Who cares?' on the poster got it absolutely right. That's the right answer. Those who know the truth know that that's the right answer."

You see, to my opponent the question had little or no importance. This certainly became obvious by his actions later that night. He was there, by his own admission, to "teach another Christian a lesson." It became very clear, very quickly that he was not there to engage in serious dialogue on a very important issue, but "show up" another "stupid" believer. Almost unbelievably, after the debate the president of the D.C. chapter atheist organization took the microphone and apologized to the entire audience for the atheist's action. In fact, the atheist philosopher's mother who was in the audience personally apologized to me for her son's behavior!

My opponent made two very serious mistakes: (1) He did not think the question important enough to seriously prepare for the debate, and (2) he assumed that "anyone who believed in God today must be mentally deficient." But it became clear, again, very quickly who was living in a rather unreal and sheltered world, and who was guilty of escapism. In this case, fortunately it was not the believer. "Is Christian belief escapism, running away from reality? Or are the escapists really those who won't face up to the evidence for Christian belief?"[14] Certainly, if one has personal integrity, (atheist and theist alike) he must admit the importance of the question, take it seriously, and attempt to answer it with sound reason and good evidence (either way). It is easy to see that how we live, how we react to grief, how we treat life's great problems and challenges depends on the answer!

---

14. See Michael Green's excellent little book: *Runaway World* (Downers Grove: InterVarsity Press, 1968).

We challenge you – theist and atheist alike – to take the question seriously, to see its obvious importance, and not to think that the issue should be settled (certainly not fully or finally) by reading this one book. We challenge all with intellectual integrity to search for the truth, *to search for an answer that they can live with*, and to be willing to always reexamine the evidence in light of all the information available. Certainly, the personal, practical importance of the question demands it! It is never good enough to live as if the question is unimportant, as that atheist opponent did, for to do so is to have decided by default, to do so is to lack the wisdom or integrity to see the personal implications of the question, to do so is most assuredly to have answered in the negative and to bear the burdens of life alone, and ultimately the consequences of your decision.

Chapter Two
GOD'S EXISTENCE:
HISTORICAL IMPORTANCE

INTRODUCTION: IMPORTANCE OF THE QUESTION

As we said in the beginning of the first chapter, since the beginnings of philosophical thought philosophers have sought to discern the existence of extra-physical reality. For thousands of years, the question "Does God exist?" has been and still is by far the most important question we can ask both in terms of the nature of reality and to our personal lives. It is important here to look at four very important philosophers to see what they said about God. For in looking at their thought we will be able to get a glimpse of why the question is important historically.

GOD AND PLOTINUS

The *term* "Neoplatonism" dates only from the nineteenth century. Neoplatonism is considered by many to be the last great effort of ancient pagan philosophy. The movement was thought to be a direct continuation of Plato's thought by its defenders. Plotinus (A.D. 204/5 to 270) is considered the founder of Neoplatonism.[1] A biography written by his student Porphyry

---

1. Miethe, *The Metaphysics of Leonard James Eslick*, pp. 60-70.

tells us almost all we know of Plotinus.

Neoplatonism is not at all "Platonic" when judged by Plato's own theology. This is true both of pagan and Christian Neoplatonism. The Neoplatonic theologies all identify the ultimate God or Godhead with the "One" or the "Good" – a principle which not only transcends the physical world (as Aristotle's God did), but transcends being itself. It – the "Good" or the "One" – is beyond being, essence, and knowledge.

Plato does have a principle which he calls the "One" or the "Good" which is the "Form" of all the Forms and is the first principle of the whole of reality, but Plato never identifies this with God. Such a principle could hardly be an efficient cause of the sort that Plato needs in order to account for the motions of the world. Plato's divinity is the "World Soul" and is immanent (present or in-dwelling) in the world. It is a self-moving mover which causes all moved movers.

Neoplatonic theology is really loosely based on an interpretation of two texts in Plato: (1) The first hypothesis of the second part of the *Parmenides* of Plato.[2] But in this hypothesis for Plato what follows is that nothing whatever can be predicated (said of or) about the "Good" or the "One." Plato intended this as a *failure* of the hypothesis. Plato was looking for a world of being which is intelligible. (2) A text from the *Republic* where Plato is talking about the "Good." He says that the "Good" is beyond being, essence, and knowledge.[3] It is the cause of these things. Plato was not a mystic.

Plotinus, on the other hand, supposedly had a number of mystical experiences. In the last six years of his life, Porphyry reports that Plotinus had four ecstatic experiences of union with the "One." Thus the keystone of Neoplatonic theology is the utterly transcendent One which is beyond being itself. It is beyond any activity of any kind, even will or creation. The "One" is beyond being, essence, and knowledge; but this is not to say for Plotinus that it is nonexistent.[4] It is non-being in the sense that it is beyond being. It is not less than being but more than being, at least as understood by Plotinus. But, obviously, what can be said of this "more" is a great problem.

The "One" of Plotinus transcends all being of which we have any experience. It is a unity without any multiplicity, division, or distinction. Plotinus'

---

2. *Ibid.*, pp. 36-47, 191-193.

3. Plato, *Republic*, p. 740; Miethe, *Ibid.*, p. 45.

4. Plotinus, "Eighth Tractate: Nature, Contemplation, and the One," in *Plotinus: The Enneads*, pp. 239ff.

"One" is strictly speaking beyond anything that can be predicated of it. If the "X" – Plotinus' "One" – is so transcendent it is not meaningful to even talk about it. In fact, it would be a principle that is utterly unknown. Plotinus' divinity can only be spoken about negatively. It is the "Good" in terms of effects which it produces. But how can this "Principle" produce *any* effects if it is "beyond being, essence, and knowledge"? It is called the "One" in terms negatively of not having any plurality or multiplicity whatever. There are *many* serious problems for so-called "Christian" Neoplatonism. For example, there will always be a tension for Christian Neoplatonism in accounting for a Trinity.

The only process that Plotinus can use to account for plurality is a mysterious one called emanation. Much of what Plotinus says about the process of emanation is metaphorical. The primary metaphor is the light which streams from the sun. This light in no way diminishes the sun. The sun remains unchanged. This is the way in which the lower proceeds from the "One" itself.[5] The first emanation from the "One" is *nous* which is thought or mind. Matter itself is evil, not the physical world as such.[6]

Almost amazingly, it is rather easy to find the roots of most of the great problems of the history of theology in this misunderstanding of Plato, by Plotinus. Here we see an absolute division between the ultimate, the "One" or the "Good," and the rest of everything that exists.[7] If the one is so utterly transcendent as to be beyond being, essence, or knowledge, then it is beyond any activity of any kind.

If we accept this totally "static" view of God (some might even call this the "sovereignty of God," but wrongly so) then God cannot change or be related to us in any meaningfully way. How can we possibly have a Trinity, the Incarnation, prayer, or fellowship with this "God"? Of course, these are the problems that occur time and again in the history of theology, until (as we will shortly see) we are finally told by Kant that we can't know anything about ultimate reality in our world of experience. Some philosophers think that this absolutely "wooden" view of transcendence, taken really from Plotinus, has contributed to most every problem in the theology of God.

---

5 Plotinus, "Fourth Tractate: How the Secondaries Rise from the First and on the One," *Ibid.*, pp. 400ff.

6. Plotinus, "Eighth Tractate: The Nature and Source of Evil," *Ibid.*, pp. 66ff.

7. Here we have a preview of Kant's absolute categories of the *phenomena* and the *noumena*.

GOD AND AUGUSTINE

Vernon J. Bourke (born 1907), the world famous Augustinian scholar, has said of the great Augustine whose wisdom is among the most profound the Western World has ever known:

> Augustine of Hippo was the source of much that is most characteristic in western Christianity. His career covered the last decade of the fourth and the first third of the fifth centuries. Yet he was called the "first modern man" by Adolf Harnack. Augustine's times were much like our own: threats and realities of war faced the political establishments; a new spirit was developing in the religions of the post-classical period; daring men were exploring the earth; tradition confronted innovation on many fronts. Into this seething cauldron of human struggle and puzzlement, a young scholar from North Africa threw his remarkable intellectual and moral talents.[8]

Time even called Augustine "The Second Founder of the Faith."[9]

It is certainly true that though Augustine died 1,563 years ago, his influence is still very much felt today. He was born at Tagaste in North Africa in A.D. 354 and studied and taught rhetoric in Carthage and Rome. As a young man he was attracted philosophically to Manichaeism, Skepticism, and Neoplatonism. At age thirty-four he became a Christian and a priest in 395. Little in his family background would suggest to the historical psychologist that he would become one of the foremost defenders of the faith. In his many works one finds the nuclei of most of the ethical thought from his time to our own. After forty years of literary productivity, he died in A.D. 430.[10]

Augustine lived in an interesting turbulent time. The year 410 ushered in a very disturbed and troubled age. Rome, the "Eternal City," had been captured and sacked by the barbarians. Impossible! Unthinkable! Yet sadly true. During this crisis, which must have seemed like the end of the world, the Church –

---

8. See "Foreword" by Vernon J. Bourke in Terry L. Miethe's *Augustinian Bibliography, 1970-1980: With Essays on the Fundamentals of Augustinian Scholarship* (Westport, Ct: Greenwood Press, 1982), pp. xi-xiii.

9. See Richard N. Ostling, "The Second Founder of the Faith." *Time* 29 Sep., 1986, p.76.

10 See Terry L. Miethe, *Augustinian Bibliography*. Though Augustine had died over 1,500 years before, in the ten years between 1970 and 1980 over 1400 scholarly articles and books were written on his thought. This included over 218 doctoral dissertations from the 1890's to the early 1980's. Certainly, his influence is still very much alive.

through Augustine – responded with an answer for all time. Augustine said the true cause of the calamity was to be found in the moral decay of Roman society. The theater, the temples, and the public games reeked with violence and moral sickness.

Much to his credit, Augustine was not satisfied with criticism of the evils of the situation in which he found himself. Rather he attempted a Christian world view (*weltänschauung*),[11] with hope for reconstructing the very fabric of the civilized world. Thus, his literary classic, the *City of God*[12] was born. Man's city was ruled by passion and pride. It was a city that lacked a true foundation (Heb 13:14). Augustine believed the city of God and Christ was marked by purity, love, and true life. It shall never pass away because it has a sure foundation, "whose architect and builder is God" (Heb 11:10). These two cities are radically different yet they share to a large extent a common lot, Christians and pagans. In the end, the Living God shall forever separate the two cities.

Until that time it was up to the people of Augustine's day (and to us in our own) to make the two cities overlap as closely as possible. This was Augustine's grand apologetic task, *as it must be ours as well*. That was Augustine's answer to the problems of the world: the actual, factual existence of God and His relevance to daily living. Augustine's whole life was a quest for wisdom.[13] For Augustine, God is He who is, i.e., Supreme Being. His whole approach to philosophy was a highly personal one as is seen by reading his *Confessions*.[14] Philosophy for St. Augustine is inseparable from religion. There is no real distinction between the two.

Augustine was concerned with his own unhappiness which he thought was

---

11. A "*weltänschauung*" is a comprehensive conception or apprehension of the world especially from a specific standpoint, world view.

12. This book of Augustine's is one of the great literary works of all time and a spiritual classic. One should not be allowed to graduate from an accredited undergraduate school without having read this most important work.

13. Vernon J. Bourke, *Augustine's Quest for Wisdom: Life and Philosophy of the Bishop of Hippo* (Milwaukee: Bruce Publishing Co., 1945) is certainly one of the very best biographies of Augustine ever published. See also Bourke's new book: *Augustine's Love of Wisdom: An Introspective Philosophy* (West Lafayette, IN: Purdue University Press, 1992); and Terry L. Miethe, "The Writings of Vernon J. Bourke" in *The Modern Schoolman* (March/May 1992), pp. 499-509 which details Bourke's 60 years of writing.

14. Augustine, *The Confessions*, ed. by J. M. Lelen (New York: Catholic Book Publishing Co., 1952).

the fruit of disordered thought and his moral life. His struggle to bring order into his mind leads him to God as the source of all order and happiness. This has obvious importance to us in terms of the question of the existence of God which we will build on throughout this book. If God exists, then He must bring all order (intellectual and moral) into the world and happiness into our lives. If God does not exist, we are very hard pressed to find any real order or personal meaning, let alone true happiness, in a world that would finally be naturalistic, mechanistic, and deterministic.

For Augustine, only Christians can know man's true happiness. Christians alone possess the means to achieve that happiness. His famous statement is that one believes in order to understand.[15] All of the resources of reason and philosophy should go into the task of understanding what is believed in, that is, revealed truth believed in, because God exists and has communicated to us. There should be no opposition between faith and reason, but reason should be the servant of faith. A faith which is not understood does not reach its full-ness.[16]

"One cannot bracket the problem of divine existence and go on first to study psychology, physics or history. All order, all events, all meanings, stem from God." The very fact that we know certain truths which are absolutely necessary, eternal, and immutable is the evidence of the existence of God.

> Essentially, Augustine says this: we start with a fact of human consciousness (I make a judgment that is eternally and immutably true, say, seven plus three equals ten); then we ask what is the ground or justification for such a judgment. He thinks that it cannot rest on any feature of bodies, for they are neither eternal nor immutable. But this judgment is. Nor can it be grounded on man's soul: the soul is not eternal, nor is it wholly immutable. There must then be some reality above the soul which will guarantee, account for, the eternity and immutable truth of such judgments. This eternal and immutable being, higher than the soul, either is God – or, if there be a still higher being, then He is God.[17]

For Augustine, to prove the existence of truth in our minds is at the same time to prove the existence of God. God is Truth with a capital "T." Man turns inward into himself where he discovers truth. The sole sufficient reason for

---

15. The source of Augustine's view on faith and reason is a text from Isaiah (7:9 in the Septuagint), which reads: "Unless you will have believed, you will not under-stand" (*nisi credideritis non intelligentis*).

16. See Miethe, *Living Your Faith*, 1993.

17. Vernon J. Bourke, *The Essential Augustine* (Indianapolis: Hackett Publishing, 1974), pp. 121-122.

the presence of truth of this sort is to be found in a transcendent God. The way to God leads from the exterior to the interior and from the interior to the superior. This is how Augustine proves God's existence.[18] For Augustine we *must* approach God through understanding.

GOD AND THOMAS AQUINAS

Aquinas was born at Roccasecca in Italy late in 1224 or early in 1225. In 1239 he began studying liberal arts at the University of Naples. Thomas entered the Order of Preachers in 1244. He studied under Albert the Great at Colone from 1248-1252. In 1256, Thomas received the magistrate in theology at the University of Paris and joined the faculty in 1257. Thomas was well-known by his early thirties as a scholar and teacher. He received a second professorate at Paris from 1269 to 1272. In 1272, he returned to southern Italy as master of theology at the University of Naples. He died on March 7, 1274, not far from the place of his birth.[19]

The very idea of a "natural theology" (knowledge of God from that which is revealed in the natural world) in Thomas Aquinas is an indication of a shift in thinking about God which is of great significance. During the thirteenth century, for the first time in the Latin West, substantial translations of Aristotle were made. This brought about a revolution in terms of European philosophy. Thomas was given the job, historically, of assimilating Aristotle, i.e., of "baptizing" Aristotle to make his philosophy compatible with Christian doctrine.

For the first time in history, Thomas proposes a supreme metaphysical (the study of ultimate reality, a philosophy of God) principle of actuality which is known as the "real distinction," that is a real distinction of existence and essence (its nature considered independently of its existence). God has for His

---

18. See Terry L. Miethe, *The Metaphysics of Leonard James Eslick: His Philosophy of God* (Ann Arbor: University Microfilms, Inc., 1976), pp. 70-79.

19. Three important works for anyone interested in Aquinas are: Vernon J. Bourke's two books, *Aquinas' Search for Wisdom*, (Milwaukee: Bruce Publishing Co., 1965) and *The Pocket Aquinas* (New York: Washington Square Press, 1960); also Terry L. Miethe and Vernon J. Bourke, *Thomistic Bibliography, 1940-1978* (Westport, CT.: Greenwood Press, 1980) which lists 4,097 scholarly articles and books written on Aquinas' thought during those years.

proper effect existence itself. For Thomas, God is a being who is capable of producing the very existence of His creatures. He is pure Existence itself which is superior to essence or Form. God contains within Himself all perfections and can produce the total creature or effect.

God's existence is self-evident in itself, but not to us; or self-evident in itself, and to us. Because we do not know the essence of God, the proposition is not self-evident to us.[20] But the existence of God, insofar as it is not self-evident to us, can be shown through His effects which are known to us. The existence of God can be known by natural reason and by Revelation. The question of what a thing is comes after the question of whether it is. The names given to God will be derived from His effects.

Thomas was famous for his "five ways" to know that God exists. In the first of these, the meaning of the name God is God as first unmoved mover. In the second, the meaning of the name of God is first efficient cause.[21] The meaning of the name of God is an uncaused necessary Being who is the cause of caused necessary beings (angels) and of contingent beings in the third way. In the fourth way, the meaning of the name God is maximal Being, Goodness, and Truth, who causes finite beings, goods, and truths. In the fifth way, God is the cause of the existence of things as ordered to ends. Thomas says that we can know God from His effects, but we cannot know Him perfectly only through His effects.[22]

It is radically impossible, according to Thomas Aquinas, that anything should be the cause of itself.[23] To cause itself it would have to pre-exist itself which is an impossibility. Without a first cause there would be no terminal effect, intermediate causes, or any efficient cause anywhere. The fact from the world of our experience that we start with is the existence of contingent beings, i.e., ourselves. Contingent beings are defined as those which are possible to be and not to be. A contingent being comes into being by generation and passes out of being by perishing. Such beings cannot have the reason for

---

20. Thomas Aquinas, *Summa Theologica*, literally translated by Fathers of the English Dominican Province (Chicago: Benziger Brothers, 1947), Pt. 1, Q. 2, Art. 1, 2, pp. 11-12.

21. This "efficient causality of existence itself" is in every one of the five ways, but explicit only in the second way. The sculptor who makes a statue is the efficient cause of the statue.

22. Thomas Aquinas, *Summa Theologica*, pp. 11-12.

23. See chapter 7.

their existence in themselves.[24]

But contingent beings do exist, thus there must be an eternal first cause of all caused existence. Ultimately, there are only two possibilities for the identity of this first uncaused cause: an eternal material universe or an eternal God. In the last chapter of part one and the chapters of part two of this book it is shown that the best of modern thought and of modern science indicate that the physical, material world is *not* eternal. If this is true, then one must conclude that the eternal first cause of all caused existence is what the Christian's have always called God. "Aquinas thinks that man can know, by careful discursive reasoning, that God exists."[25]

GOD AND KANT

Until Immanuel Kant comes on the historical scene, using reason to prove the existence of God was an important and legitimate enterprise. Kant was born in 1724 at Königsberg, Germany, and died there in 1804. In his whole lifetime, Kant did not travel forty miles from his home. One could supposedly set the tower clock by his methodic schedule. In 1770 Kant obtained the chair of logic and metaphysics at the University of Königsberg. Kant's effect in philosophy was of the magnitude of the Copernican revolution in astronomy. There are three main questions in philosophy according to Kant. He addresses himself to these in the *Critique of Pure Reason*, the first critique.[26] He wants to know (1) What makes mathematics possible, (2) what makes physics possible, and (3) what makes metaphysics possible. He answers that metaphysics (a philosophy of God) is not possible.

Metaphysics deals with three basic types of ideas: (1) the idea of the world in its unconditioned totality, (2) the idea of freedom, and (3) the idea of God.[27] Kant systematically attempts to show that it is not possible for the pure intellect working with such ideas to achieve positive knowledge of any of these ideas. It is not a question for Kant of regarding them as meaningless.

---

24. Miethe, *The Metaphysics of Leonard James Eslick: His Philosophy of God*, pp. 85-102.

25. Bourke, *The Pocket Aquinas*, p. 6.

26. Immanuel Kant, *Critique of Pure Reason*, trans. by Norman Kemp Smith (London: Macmillan, St. Martin's Press, 1933).

27. *Ibid*, pp. 495ff.

Metaphysical questions have meaning all right. Kant is not holding that such ideas have no intelligibility whatever. Such ideas have an importance which is regulative, but they do not constitute positive knowledge. The mind, when it attempts to work with them establishing their existence or positive truth, falls into a situation in which equally strong arguments can be given on either of two sides.

This is because for Kant the mind has to know ultimate reality (reality outside the mind) by way of sense knowledge. Thus the mind is divided from the external (the real world outside the mind) by an impenetrable gulf. The mind only knows appearances, images of the real world. We can only know images of reality (the *phenomena*), but never the thing in itself (the *noumena*). Experience for Kant can never disclose the thing in itself. Since God must be a Necessary Being and we cannot know by way of the senses ultimate reality, obviously (reasons Kant) we cannot know God by way of the senses. Because the only knowledge we have is knowledge from the senses, there is no way we can use reason to prove God exists.

Kant thinks he is doing Christianity a favor. It is not that there is no God for Kant, but only that we cannot prove that God exists by the use of pure reason. This is not the fault of Christianity, but the fault of the nature of pure reason. We are all in the same boat in this regard, atheists and theists alike. No one can know anything for sure, that is with positive knowledge because no one can know any "thing" in itself, its ultimate reality. Remember, we can only know images of the actual entity.

But says Kant, what pure reason cannot prove, practical reason must affirm.[28] The only way we can make sense of, give any real meaning to, the world we experience is to act as if (believe in three postulates of practical reason) there is (1) freedom of the will, (2) immortality of the soul, and (3) the existence of God. These three are consequences of the reality of moral being for Kant. The fact of the existence of moral duty implies as a consequence the postulate of God. The ought implies the can. The can implies the existence of God.

Kant is not an atheist, but he is in terms of pure reason an *agnostic*. One can neither prove or disprove the existence of this necessary being. But this is true only if Kant's peculiar assumptions about the nature of knowledge are

---

28. Immanuel Kant, *Critique of Practical Reason* (New York: The Liberal Arts Press, 1965).

true. Even in Kant there is some seeming implication of some kind of causal relation between *phenomena* and *noumena*, though we are never told what that is. Certainly, for Kant a phenomenon has the meaning of an appearance of a reality which underlies it. Kant seems to simply take it for granted that appearance implies reality. How can Kant be sure of the precise boundaries between the phenomenal reality and the noumenal (the thing in itself) without knowing something about the noumenal?

There is no way in Kant to put together the schism into two worlds; a world which is that of nineteenth-century science, mechanistic in nature; and a world of spiritual value, freedom, moral value, the immortal soul, and God. This gives one mechanism on the one hand and freedom on the other and never the two will meet. Yet, Kant thinks that they do meet somehow mysteriously in man.

Kant's assertions were accepted rather uncritically by most philosophers after him. It was not long after that philosophers said, "Kant, you are right about pure reason and about the gulf between appearance and the thing in itself (actual external existence, ultimate reality). But because this is true we cannot therefore accept your postulates of practical reason. Metaphysics is dead. Any meaningful philosophy of God is impossible. God is dead!" Thus the great favor Kant thought he was doing for Christianity, metaphysics/philosophy of God, was really a death blow – if you accept his assumptions.[29]

---

29. Miethe, *The Metaphysics of Leonard James Eslick*, pp. 102-114.

Chapter Three
THE NATURAL VERSUS THE SUPERNATURAL

INTRODUCTION: IMPORTANCE OF THE QUESTION

Before actually, or formally, arguing for the existence of God, more needs to be said about what is at stake in the issue in general. As we will see throughout this book, there are really only two options. Either the universe and all that exists within it can be explained by some materialistic, naturalistic, or mechanistic principle,[1] i.e., the physical universe as we know it is eternal; *or* there is a first uncaused cause, i.e., what theists call God who is eternal, behind the physical universe.

Some may reply that this either/or is rather simplistic. What about "emergent evolutionists" (vitalists) who hold a variant of teleology (or meaning and direction in the universe) by accepting a "Power" or "Force" guiding nature like Bergson or Whitehead? Two things can be said immediately about such emergent evolutionists: (1) either they are really in the naturalistic tradition because the "force" is an impersonal part of nature itself, or (2) if this "force" is distinct from nature, then the legitimate question arises: "How does this "Force" differ from what Christians call God?"

If one holds to a mechanistic world view, reality is a great and complicated machine, like a tractor or airplane though much more intricate. All that we

---

1. In this case the three are used almost as synonyms.

experience in the world can be explained in terms of how this physical/chemical machine works. Such a view reduces all physical and living processes to the natural functioning of this intricate machine. What we view as having purpose, meaning, and existing in nature, but not being reducible to nature, such as spirit, are just concepts imposed by the human mind on the structure of reality. As we will see, anything that is not strictly material is either said to be reducible to the merely material, or it is arbitrarily defined out of existence by naturalists who reject the supernatural out of hand, as a matter of course.

A theist thinks that while a mechanistic process can explain part of reality, it cannot explain all. There are laws of nature, but these have purpose behind them. As our good friend Antony G. N. Flew, the famous atheist philosopher, so aptly pointed out:

> . . . both (atheists and theists alike) have a vested interest in insisting on strong notions of natural necessity and natural impossibility, because only if you have a strong idea of a natural order can you suggest that this natural order, if it's overridden, is in this overriding evidence of a supernatural power at work.[2]

Theists believe reality has a purposeful end and that the processes in the universe are grounded in an Eternal Being. It is only this Eternal Being (God) who can account for life, intelligence, and the creative powers of humankind. Thus it is the atheist who must present a very convincing case that all life, intelligence, and creativity can be explained on and by naturalistic principles alone. Theists are not in any way rejecting "empiricism." They are, however, calling for a much more rigorous empiricism than that of David Hume.[3]

THE EXISTENCE OF LIFE

The first question which must be discussed is: "Can we account for life on the basis of matter alone?"

> Currently accepted scenarios concerning the origin of life are based on the Darwin-Oparin-Haldane 'warm little pond' concept in which nucleotides, amino acids and the basic compounds necessary to life are thought to have been formed by chemical and physical processes during a period of chemical evolution."[4]

---

2. See Gary Habermas and Antony Flew, *Did Jesus Rise From the Dead? The Resurrection Debate*, edited by Terry L. Miethe (San Francisco: Harper & Row, Publishers, 1987), p. 34.

3. See "A More Rigorous Empiricism" in chapter 4.

4. See M. Calvin in *Evolutionary Biology,* edited by T. Dobzhansky, M.K. Hecht

As early as 1977, at the end of an excellent article on Information Theory and Spontaneous Biogenesis, Hubert P. Yockey said of this "warm little pond":

> The "warm little pond" scenario was invented *ad hoc* as a materialistic reductionist explanation of the origin of life. It is unsupported by any other evidence and it will remain *ad hoc* until such evidence is found. Even if it existed, as described in the scenario, it nevertheless falls very far short indeed of achieving the purpose of its authors even with the aid of a *deus ex machina*. One must conclude that, contrary to the established and current wisdom a scenario describing the genesis of life on earth by chance and natural causes which can be accepted on the basis of fact and not faith has not yet been written.[5]

Life is to some extent dependent on matter but not reducible to it. Even a *deus ex machina*[6] (any unconvincing character or event brought artificially into the plot of a story to settle an involved situation) cannot account for life.

In fact, when a student studies chemistry at the university he or she finds the field divided into two parts: inorganic, that is being or composed of matter other than plant or animal, that which is nonliving matter; and organic, i.e., of, related to, or derived from, living organisms. Why is this? Because there is a fundamental difference between the two. You see, the general theory of evolution[7] has not one, but *seven* basic assumptions in it: (1) that nonliving things gave rise to living material, i.e., that spontaneous generation occurred; (2) that spontaneous generation occurred only once; (3) that viruses, bacteria, plants, and animals are all interrelated; (4) that the protozoa gave rise to the metazoa; (5) that the various invertebrate phyla are interrelated; (6) that the invertebrates gave rise to the vertebrates; (7) that the vertebrates and fish gave rise to the amphibia, the amphibia to the reptiles, and the reptiles to the birds and

---

and W.C. Steere, Vol. 1 (New York: Appleton Croft, 1967); J.B.S. Haldane in the *Rationalist Annual* 148 (1928), p. 3; and A. Oparin, *Proiskhozhdenie Zhizni. Izd* (Moskovsky Rabochy, 1924) and *The Origin of Life* (New York: Academic Press, 1957).

5. Hubert P. Yockey, "A Calculation of the Probability of Spontaneous Biogenesis by Information Theory," *Journal of Theoretical Biology* 67 (1977), pp. 377, 396.

6. In ancient Greek and Roman plays, a deity brought in by stage machinery to intervene in the action.

7. Really there are many theories of evolution. In recent years many scientists have quietly changed the theory of general evolution, i.e., from basic origins evolving to man and beyond, and/or have rejected a general theory and have adopted a much more refined and restricted special theory of evolution involving some form of speciation, i.e., change within species, rather than evolution of one species into another. See chapter 17, "The Limits of Science" in this book.

mammals. In the past, many evolutionists ignored the first six and considered only the seventh. These are all assumptions that cannot be proven. Actually, instead of there being one "missing link" on the evolutionary trail, there are actually thousands upon thousands of missing links.[8] G. A. Kerkut, an evolutionist, says regarding these seven assumptions which form the general theory of evolution: "The first point that I should like to make is that the seven assumptions by their nature are not capable of experimental verification. They assume that a certain series of events has occurred in the past."[9]

But for our discussion here, it is the first two assumptions that are most important. It is pure conjecture that nonliving things gave rise to living things. We accept it so readily because we have a high sounding scientific term for this supposed fact which we are taught as proven "beyond a shadow of a doubt" from late grade school or early high school on, that "spontaneous generation" occurred.[10]

What is "spontaneous generation?" The idea that life came from matter, which had no living properties, that life "spontaneously" generated, or came into being, that is immediately and without cause, self-acting, developed without apparent external influence, force, cause, or treatment. "Spontaneous generation" is the theory that matter, having none of the properties of life, all of a sudden on its own without any outside influence of any kind developed the properties of life, in fact became alive. Now who is making the bigger "leap of faith?" Surely, it is the atheist. Certainly the theist who says that living things must come from living things is the one being truly "scientific" here.

But listen to what prominent evolutionists, nontheists, say about so called evolution and/or "spontaneous generation." Charles Darwin (1809-1882) himself said on the eve of the publication of his *Origin of Species* in a letter to

---

8. There is a wealth of good material currently available on the problems with evolution. You might wish to start with: Robert T. Clark and James D. Bales, *Why Scientists Accept Evolution* (Grand Rapids: Baker Book House, 1966), Norman Macbeth, *Darwin Retried: An Appeal to Reason* (Ipswich, MA.: Gambit, 1971), Henry M. Morris and Gary E. Parker, *What is Creation Science?* (San Diego: Creation-Life Publishers, Inc., 1982), Evan Shute, *Flaws in the Theory of Evolution* (Nutley, N.J.: Craig Press, 1961), and A. E. Wilder Smith, *Man's Origin, Man's Destiny* (Minneapolis: Bethany House Publishers, 1968).

9. G. A. Kerkut, "Implications of Evolution," *International Series on Monographs on Pure and Applied Biology* (New York: Pergamon Press, 1960), Vol. 4, p. 3.

10 Another term for this is "*abiogenesis*" which means "the origination of living from lifeless matter."

Charles Lyell, a geologist: "Often a cold shudder runs through me, and I have asked myself whether I may not have devoted my life to a phantasy." George Wald, then a Harvard professor of Biology, said: "One has only to contemplate the magnitude of this task of bringing together complex organisms in this manner to concede that spontaneous generation of a living organism is impossible. Yet, here we are, as a result, I believe, of spontaneous generation." Sir Arthur Keith, a famous Anthropologist, has said: "Evolution is unproved and unprovable. We believe it because the only alternative is special creation, and that is clearly unthinkable."

The second assumption is that "spontaneous generation" has occurred only once. Why do we say that it happened only once? It must have happened at least once, that is if one is going to accept the explanation given in atheistic evolutionary theory for this is the only way one can account for life. But there is absolutely *no evidence* that it has ever happened, certainly not since recorded history.

Also, as we will see later, life is far too complicated to have come about by accident.

> For example, if we see a tossed coin come up heads ten times, either we have witnessed a very rare event (probability $2^{-10} = 1/1024$), or the event is expected because the coin is two headed. If the test is successful 32 times we may be the ecstatic witnesses of an event whose probability is 2.33×10^{-9}. All scientists and other practical men, except for a set of very small probability, would, however, be virtually certain that the coin is two headed even without examining it. By the same token the conclusion that life arose by a very lucky accident only once in the universe, on earth about 4×10^9 years ago (Monod, 1971) begs the question and must be rejected as a scientific explanation of the origin of life. A rationalist will hardly use standards of credibility for scenarios dealing with the origin of life less critical than those used to test other scientific hypotheses.[11]

There are just too many factors that would have to have come into being by chance evolution to believe this, for example: the world is in just the right relation to the sun; the crust of the earth is just the right thickness to support life; the depth of the ocean is just right for the presence of oxygen; the rotation of the earth at just the right speed; the size, density, temperature of the sun and our distance from it are just right for life, etc.

---

11. Hubert P. Yockey, "A Calculation of the Probability of Spontaneous Biogenesis by Information Theory," in the *Journal of Theoretical Biology* 67 (1977), pp. 378-379.

Immediately someone will say, "This is just the old Teleological Argument." It is very interesting that at a recent national conference where panels of atheists and theists debated (in philosophy, natural science, social sciences, theology, culture and morality) several of the scientists on the natural science panel defending the theistic position were converts to Christianity within the last few years because of what they thought was the validity of teleological arguments, i.e., the order and complexity of the physical universe supports the existence of God. When we asked them why they thought these teleological arguments supported the Christian God, they answered because the scientific evidence points not only to a "God," but to a Personality, a Personal Being behind the physical universe.[12]

> A. Cressy Morrison in his . . . book, *Man Does Not Stand Alone*, . . . says: "so many essential conditions are necessary for life to exist on our earth that it is mathematically impossible that all of them could exist in proper relationship by chance on any one earth at one time. Therefore, there must be in nature some form of intelligent direction." . . . The chance of any one of these factors (and others not mentioned) occurring would be one in a million; the chance that they would all occur is too great to be calculated. The evidence, then, says Dr. Morrison, is conclusively in favor of the existence of a Supreme Intelligence.[13]

Water just happened. This is extremely hard to accept as water is the universal solvent. Water dissolves acids, bases and salts. There are numerous other arguments, e.g., the complexity of the human body, etc.

THE EXISTENCE OF INTELLIGENT LIFE

One not only has to account for life itself on the basis of matter alone, but also for intelligent life. Perhaps, they are not the same thing. Humor aside, certainly intelligent life is more than just life. Again the question is: Can the more complex come from the less complex? Can we believe that simple living things over millions of years simply developed intelligence? Is man merely the most sophisticated of machines, or is he essentially different from any conceivable feedback mechanism? Does man's knowledge of the brain support the claim

---

12. For a fuller development of this argument see chapter 12, "Order in the Universe."

13. Warren C. Young, *A Christian Approach to Philosophy* (Grand Rapids: Baker Book House, 1954), p. 146. Quoted from A. Cressy Morrison, *Man Does Not Stand Alone*, rev. (New York: Revell & Co., 1944), p. 13.

that human reasoning corresponds to mechanical processes?[14]

There are many aspects of the mind, or intelligence, which are very hard to account for on the basis of a pure mechanism: (1) Our minds can work with the material world without being controlled by it. We have free will.[15] (2) Morals must be integrated with a material world as well. We act as if some things are right and some are wrong. (3) Human beings have values which are not man-made. (4) Human beings have an aesthetic experience which also separates us from the animal world. (5) Human beings have religious experience which confirms meaning and purpose in the universe. God makes Himself known both in the natural order and in human experience.

To just explain these away as a result of a mechanistic evolutionary process is to reduce these experiences to much less than they are in reality. How does a purely naturalistic, mechanistic system develop "purpose" or design or such complicated order, let alone the intricacies of freedom, morality, aesthetics, or religion? We are reminded of the scholar who admitted that the alternative to a mechanistic atheism is special creation (God) "and that is clearly unthinkable." Talk about a "leap of faith" or "blind faith." A simple materialistic explanation for all that man is and does will not fit with human experience or with what is known about the human brain.

THE EXISTENCE OF CREATIVITY

There is yet another level, qualitatively different from the first two, which we must also be able to account for as the sole product of a naturalistic or mechanistic universe. For life and intelligence are not all that we experience in this "material" world. If intelligence is not reducible to life, then certainly creativity is not reducible to mere intelligence. We have to somehow be able to account for creativity on this mechanistic model.

---

14. Stanley Jaki, professor of the history and philosophy of physics, gives a thoroughly documented rebuttal of contemporary claims about the existence of, or possibility of man-made minds. His book, *Brain, Mind and Computers* (New York: Herder and Herder, 1969), poses a serious challenge to philosophies of physicalistic reductionism. He argues convincingly the conviction that man, precisely because of his mind, is not a machine, but a marvel.

15. See Miethe, *Living Your Faith* (1993), pp. 42-47; and Samuel M. Thompson, *A Modern Philosophy of Religion* (Chicago: Henry Regnery Co., 1955), pp. 181-5, 458-9, 479-82, 501-4.

Philosophers sometimes refer to creativity as "radical novelty." For the totality of the universe – all that exists within it – to be a product of pure chance and mechanistic evolution, as the atheist claims, creativity must be explained on and by naturalistic principles alone. What is creativity, this "radical novelty" of the philosopher? It is the bringing about of something entirely new, something that never existed before. This is certainly a possibility in the realm of ideas. Because we are limited by physical existence, our freedom and creativity are always qualified. If we look at the physical laws of nature, it seems that all are "perishing." The universe is running down.[16] Energy is being lost. The perishing is inseparable from physical time and change.

If this is true, then one cannot account for radical novelty on the basis of a mechanistic universe that is constantly losing energy. Creativity can only be accounted for if there is something outside of the physical process, a "spiritual" motion or energy. It is the "spirit" that endures and creates. The mind must be different from the brain.[17] Ultimately, the mind must be seated in the spirit of man, not in the material part of man. The mental pole has to have priority over the physical pole for humans and this mental pole cannot be derived from the physical. This is the root of creative freedom. *We argue that creativity cannot have any real meaning in a deterministic, mechanistic, naturalistic universe.* And yet, we do experience creativity.

How can one preserve a vital and continuing selfhood, a continuing and growing self-identity, in terms of a merely static formal content that never changes in which accidental forms come to exist and perish? Only a spiritual reality can account for a continuing and growing self. But it is true that our creativity is qualified and subject always to material conditions, so that it cannot be a creativity precisely of existence itself. An absolute creativity can only be found in a Being whose very essence is existence and, as such, is unique and transcendent.

The essence of God is existence which is unlimited and unreceived. His perfection is not a matter of any measurement by any finite capacity. It is only in God that creativity is not limited.

The life of God is eternity in the famous formula of Boethius, "the simultaneous

---

16. For a more detailed explanation see chapter 13 on "The Second Law of Thermodynamics." Some will claim that there are possibilities for recovering energy in the universe as we know it, but there is no evidence for this.

17. See chapter 16 on "The Nature of the Brain and of Thought."

and total possession of life everlasting without beginning or end." Such a life is neither static nor inefficacious. God wills us, His creatures, from eternity and He has known us from eternity. In this sense we make a difference to God, because of God's creative power and not because of ours.[18]

Thus, it would seem that the only way to account for creativity in the world of our experience is to ground that creativity in the Being of God whose essence is existence itself. Only a Being such as this can be totally creative and delegate freedom, i.e., creativity, to the beings created in His image.

There are two analogies from experience of the creative power of God: (1) In literary art the writer has always been thought of as creating a fictional world of his own. But there are two kinds of literary creativity: (a) the bad literary craftsman who manipulates lifeless puppets in a predetermined pattern with no room for surprise (like most television writers today); and (b) writers like Shakespeare or Cervantes whose creatures like Falstaff or Don Quixote exhibit a mysterious life and freedom of their own. We suspect that even their creators could not always have predicted in advance what these two would do. (2) In the relationship of teacher and student, we believe that the teacher who only produces carbon copies of himself or herself and of his opinions has the least "power" or ability of teaching. The students are not given any independent power of judgment. Teaching as indoctrination is a betrayal or failure of the true power of the art. Plato was at his height in producing an Aristotle who so disagreed with his teacher.

God by unlimited authentic power can produce independently existing creatures who share in the liberty of deity, and who can become co-creators with Him in their own measure. This is true *power* for God! God's divine creative power is synonymous with the Divine Names of Freedom and Love. God is Freedom and Love and He imparts these to His creatures because it is His very nature to do so. *We believe that existence in freedom is itself the gift of Divine power.*

---

18. Miethe, *The Metaphysics of Leonard James Eslick: His Philosophy of God*, p. 161.

Chapter Four
FUNDAMENTAL
LAWS OF HUMAN BELIEF

INTRODUCTION: IMPORTANCE OF THE QUESTION

From the very beginnings of philosophy, philosophers have sought to identify a substance or principle which unified reality and accounted for existence,
for example: in Thales (6th Cent. B.C.) this was water, in Anaximander (6th
Cent. B.C.) it was "the infinite," in Anaximenes (6th Cent. B.C.) the basic
substance was air.[1] Plato thought philosophy was an attempt to grasp essence
or reality when others grasped only shadows or appearances. Philosophers
have always been about, and will probably always be about, trying to understand reality in terms of its "lowest common denominator/s." The simple is
not (actually of necessity) the same as the simplistic!

What is the basic substance, principle, or truth of all existence? Rene
Descartes (1596-1650), a French philosopher founded the modern school of
thought known as Rationalism. He taught that truth can be discovered simply
by pure reasoning. Descartes started with universal doubt. If something can be
doubted then it must not be true. Thus by doubting everything that could be
doubted, Descartes thought he came up with three basic things that could not
be doubted: (1) I exist. His famous statement was *cogito ergo sum*, "I think,
therefore I exist." One cannot doubt his own existence without involving him-

---

1. These ancient philosophers were members of what has been called the
"Milesian school" from the name of the Greek city Miletus. They were active in
Greece around the 7th or 6th century B.C.

self in a contradiction. Obviously, one must exist to think or to doubt (Augustine said: *si fallor sum*, "If I make a mistake in thinking, I exist."[2]) (2) God must exist. Since Descartes was finite, he could not have the idea of Infinite being unless a Perfect Being put the idea in his mind.[3] (3) The external world must exist because God, by His nature, would not deceive him.

Thus the attempt of philosophers to come up with "fundamental laws of human belief" is basic for two very important reasons: (1) It is an attempt to help us understand the nature of reality as such, for example questions like: "Does God exist?" How can we make pronouncements about what exists or does not exist, and the effect of such on everyday life, if we have not first examined and understood the most basic elements of reality, those which unify and explain. (2) It helps us to avoid philosophical skepticism, which amounts to an "intellectual dead-end". It is nothing more than an intellectual "cop-out" to say – and be satisfied with – a statement like: "We cannot know anything for sure." Except, of course, the skeptic who knows that much. In reality, such a statement is a contradiction because it purports to be a statement about something – denying certain knowledge – but is in fact claiming what it is actually denying.

Actually, the term "fundamental laws of human belief" comes historically from the thinkers known as "Scottish Common Sense" philosophers, principally Thomas Reid (1710-1796) and his student Dugald Stewart (1753-1828).[4] This philosophy was an attempt to save, from the skepticism of David Hume (1711-1776), the certainty of moral judgments and progress.[5] Americans, wanting to believe in both scientific progress *and* in unchanging moral principles, turned to Scotland's philosophers of Common Sense. These were their only acceptable European teachers at the time.

---

2. Many scholars have noted the resemblance of Descartes' statement to Augustine's. When a Father Arnauld (who knew Augustine's works well) first drew Descartes' attention to the similarity of thought and expression of the two sayings, the French thinker merely said that he was happy to have so great a thinker for his patron. See Vernon Bourke, *The Essential Augustine*, p. 20.

3. See chapter 7 of this book.

4. See Terry L. Miethe, *The Philosophy and Ethics of Alexander Campbell: From the Context of American Religious Thought, 1800-1866* (Ann Arbor: University Microfilms, Inc., 1984), pp. 73-79.

5. *Ibid.*, "The Enlightenment," pp. 29-34. There were four forms of the Enlightenment. America was influenced by the first and the fourth. The first is known as the "Moderate Enlightenment," or as the "Rational Enlightenment," which

Thomas Reid was the founder and leader of Common Sense philosophy. It was David Hume's skepticism which entered "into the domain of morals and religion that called forth the opposition" of Thomas Reid. Thus Common Sense philosophers "became the champions of religion and morality as over against skepticism and materialism." Reid said, "to every man who believes in the existence, the perfections and the providence of God, the veneration and submission we owe him are self-evident."[6]

Reid started from the problem set by George Berkeley (1685-1753), and particularly Hume, that it was impossible rationally to demonstrate any identity between the ideas in our minds and external reality. Reid was in many ways sympathetic to Hume. Little could be "proved" by reasoning – not the existence of matter or our own (or others) minds. Reid asked, are we "to admit nothing but what can be proved by reasoning? Then we must be skeptics indeed and believe nothing at all," he says in his *An Inquiry into the Human Mind* (p. 109). Reid wanted, he claimed, to be more of a skeptic than Hume. He asked why we should reject the beliefs common to mankind, and still accept the arguments of the minds of philosophers. Reid said the assumption that we have no trustworthy knowledge about anything is absurd. The skeptic's assertion that he has positive knowledge that he has no positive knowledge at all is contradictory and self-refuting.

On the grounds of experience, consensus, and necessity, Reid argued we can assume what most people always have assumed: Our minds *can* know actual objects, and not mere images or ideas of them. Hume felt that actions relying on moral and sensory impressions – rather than reason – was reasoning psychologically. Reid declared that it was rationally justifiable as well. Reid was making this sort of intuitive certainty the center of his argument. Reid developed three principal themes: (1) egalitarian epistemology, (2) a humble empiricism, and (3) a communitarian morality. These affected

---

preached balance, order and religious compromise, and was dominant in England from the time of Newton and Locke until about the middle of the eighteenth century. This form of the Enlightenment became deeply embedded in the institutions of America. The fourth is called the "Didactic Enlightenment" and it tried to save from what it saw as the debacle of the Enlightenment, the intelligible universe, clear and certain moral judgments, and progress. It was mainly centered in Scotland and began before the middle of the eighteenth century, but its principal triumphs in America took place in the first quarter of the nineteenth.

6. Clarence R. Athearn, *The Religious Education of Alexander Campbell* (St. Louis: The Bethany Press, 1928), p. 170.

Thomas Jefferson (1743-1826) as well as Alexander Campbell (1788-1866).[7]

Reid argues in the *Inquiry into the Human Mind* principally for the existential grasp of *simple perception*. Common sense is the exercise of what Reid calls "the inductive principle" upon perceptions. Reid observed that the rule of cause and effect is so universally believed that there is not a prudent man who does not act from this opinion, including David Hume. Reid maintained that such popular opinion stands on a higher authority than philosophy.[8] Common sense philosophy has been defined as "the power of knowledge in general, as it is possessed and employed by a man of ordinary development and opportunities." Common sense philosophies affirm that the ordinary person has the power to know the external world and its relations through his senses.

A MORE RIGOROUS EMPIRICISM

What is really needed here is a more rigorous empiricism than the empiricism of Hume and later skeptics, i.e., an empiricism that looks more critically at reality itself and does not define out of existence broad ranges of reality (for example the spiritual) before a very careful examination. Metaphysics is the science of being *qua* (as) being, the study of existence as such. The very word "metaphysics," therefore, implies a consideration of causes and principles in some way transcending the physical order of explanation. The metaphysician is seeking a more ultimate explanation of real things than can be provided by natural sciences dealing only with material entities subject to becoming and change. Thus, a science of metaphysics depends on establishing the existence of a kind of being which is spiritual or immaterial. This has been the problem of all metaphysicians in history.

For Aristotle and Thomas Aquinas, metaphysics was a science in the

---

7. Campbell was one of the most famous ministers of his day. He is one of the early leaders of the Christian Church/Church of Christ, the Christian Church (Disciples of Christ) and also of Bethany College in West Virginia. See Terry L. Miethe's *The Philosophy and Ethics of Alexander Campbell: From the Context of American Religious Thought, 1800-1866* (Ann Arbor: University Microfilms, Inc., 1984, 302 pages.

8. See *The Encyclopedia of Philosophy*, "Thomas Reid," vol. 7, pp. 118-21; also *Works of Thomas Reid*, Sir William Hamilton, ed., 2 vols. (Edinburgh, 1846-63). Contains Dugald Stewart's *Life of Reid*, and a long dissertation on common sense by Hamilton.

strictest sense, i.e., of that which cannot be other than it is. For Thomas, what is separated and known as analogically common to all beings is the act of existence itself. This has become known as the "negative judgment of separation;" or, that to exist is not the same as to exist in a material way. But to ground this "negative judgment of separation" in order to have a science of metaphysics, compelling evidence must be found in our experience of sensible things.

If there is to be any valid starting point at all for the journey into metaphysical wisdom, it can only be in our integral experience, perceptual and intellectual, of the world of sensible, material beings. Far too long we have accepted uncritically the empirical theory that experience is purely physical. It is not purely physical. Physical existence does not exhaust what it is to exist in the world. Man is not just physical as we saw in the last chapter. Man has *nous*, mind. It is ultimately absurd to deny the existence of the spiritual in the physical world. To reduce all experience to a narrow mechanistic materialism, as atheism must, is ultimately a *reductio ad absurdum* (reduction to absurdity).[9]

A narrower type of empiricism cannot account for life, intelligent life, or radical novelty (creativity) in the world of our experience. We do have direct experience of the spiritual in the real world, in the three areas we have just mentioned. It is absurd to claim that these can be explained on the basis of mechanistic materialism. A reexamination of the data of experience which is more searching, more profound, and above all more *empirical* than that which was made by the empiricists of modern philosophy is called for today.

In Book XII of the *Metaphysics*, Aristotle tries to go far beyond that which his maxim – there is nothing in the intellect which is not first in sense – will allow. As we will see later in the book, there is much evidence that points to the fact that existence is unrestricted, unlimited, and unconfined of itself. Thomas Aquinas' insight was in the primacy of *esse* (to be). Existence is never the function of the material reception and limitation of form. The aspect of entities that is physical exists only in the temporal mode of perpetual perishing. As a consequence the physical can only exist in a subject other than itself, and such an entity which exists in its own right, which endures dynamically through time as a center of spontaneity and freedom, can be nothing but spirit. The primacy of the living spirit is a metaphysical trait analogically

---

9. This is a disproof of a principle or proposition by showing that it leads to an absurdity when followed to its logical conclusion.

common to all that exists. From this we can move analogically, from this experience to the Divine Creativity, i.e., to the existence of God.

"What, precisely, are our empirical contacts with the spiritual?" By putting the question this way one has already misunderstood the ultimate nature of our existence *and* of our experience. *There is no experience of the merely physical as such*! All of our experience is of living continuity of memory, i.e., a physical encounter with values objectively realized by spiritual agencies in the past, and guided by our own spirits for new fulfillment. The very nature of our experience of time and memory, that is the living mind reflexively knowing, reveals contact with the spiritual.

Thus one is able to constitute a metaphysical notion of being which has real content and amplitude. The spiritual creativity in ourselves allows us to also constitute a notion of causality which enables us to come to know *proper* names or attributes of God. To be sure, we do not experience "super or hyper being, life, and goodness" as they are in Divine Infinity, but our experience of them via spiritual creativity allows us to properly apply them in a positive way to ourselves and God. *To be*, for human kind, is to be free. And, to be free is to be able to create, both for God and man![10]

UNDENIABLE "COMMON SENSE" BELIEFS

Dugald Stewart was Reid's student, friend, and biographer. Stewart thought the term "common sense" too vague. He preferred to speak of the "fundamental laws of human belief" – as axioms governed mathematical reasoning, so these laws are governing presuppositions, some of them of all our thinking. It was because of Stewart's influence that Thomas Reid's work became popular in America.[11]

These "fundamental laws of human belief" are basic to all that we can know about ourselves and the world in which we live. Stewart listed the following as examples:

(1) *I exist.* To deny this is absurd because it involves one in the ultimate contradiction. You *must* exist in order to deny it. How can you meaningfully deny your own existence? Answer: you cannot! Yet, the philosophical skeptic says that you cannot know anything for sure. Why should you believe him/her

---

10. Miethe, *The Metaphysics of Leonard James Eslick*, pp. 146-156, 212.
11. Stewart and Thomas Jefferson were personally acquainted.

over your own knowledge and experience?

(2) *I am the same person now as I was yesterday.* There is a common sense knowledge of personal continuity which is undeniable. You cannot meaningfully deny either your own existence or the experience of that existence as a living part of a continuing reality. You could not function, or even act very long, if you deny this truth. So why should you accept another's statement about a supposed reality which contradicts the very basis of meaningful experience; an experience not only you share, but all others also share, (with the possible exception of the philosophical skeptic who is denying it.)

(3) *There is a real material world which exists outside of my mind.* Again, there is no meaningful way to deny this without involving oneself in a very real contradiction. We simply cannot live – function – if we try to act as if this premise is false. It is not only logically contradictory, it is practically impossible to live and deny this premise. You can assert that there is no real material world which exists outside of your mind all day long, all day long that is, until you decide to cross the street directly in front of a bus (which you assert is not there even though you see and hear it approaching, can even smell the exhaust, etc.). We predict that if you survive the "imaginary" bus you will certainly know that it was not imaginary!

(4) *The general laws of nature will operate the same in the future as they did in the past.* We not only experience personal continuity, but we experience a continuity of reality as a whole. Why do we experience reality as such? Answer: because it is undeniably the way things are. C.S. Lewis (1898-1963) quotes Sir Arthur Eddington as saying: "we sometimes have convictions which we cherish but cannot justify; we are influenced by some innate sense of the fitness of things."[12] Why does Sir Arthur say that we cannot justify such convictions? Perhaps, this "innate sense of the fitness of things" is justification enough. At least, certainly we are justified in accepting that which is fundamental to all of our experience. It is only this ridged, narrow "half" empiricism which can say that such universal experience is not justified.

Now, how can we trust these "laws of nature" to operate tomorrow as they have today? C.S. Lewis gives us the reason in saying that "the answer depends on the Metaphysics one holds,"[13] and in quoting Alfred North Whitehead:

---

12. C. S. Lewis, *Miracles: A Preliminary Study* (New York: Macmillian, 1947), p. 107.

13. *Ibid.*, pp. 108-109.

> The sciences logically require a metaphysic of this sort. Our greatest natural
> philosopher thinks it is also the metaphysic out of which they originally grew.
> Professor Whitehead points out that centuries of belief in a God who combined
> "the personal energy of Jehovah" with "the rationality of a Greek philosopher"
> first produced that firm expectation of systematic order which rendered possible
> the birth of modern science. Men became scientific because they expected Law
> in Nature, and they expected Law in Nature because they believed in a
> Legislator. In most modern scientists this belief has died: it will be interesting to
> see how long their confidence in uniformity survives it.[14]

If Lewis, and Whitehead, are correct, then perhaps an adequate examination
of experience itself will support not only the "fundamental laws of human
belief" of Stewart, but the existence of God as well.

(5) *Other intelligent beings exist besides myself.* Any philosopher who
denies this, or any of these "fundamental laws," must end up in complete
skepticism. These "fundamental laws of human belief" cannot be meaningfully denied, even though some speculative philosophy tries, because common
sense dictates their certainty.

Thomas Reid and the Common Sense School were fundamentally conservative in faith, and though not against a large degree of intellectual freedom,
they emphasized the need for clear thinking, especially in matters of religion.
For Scottish Common Sense, reason and conscience can be trusted and should
be obeyed. Perhaps they – reason and conscience (the informed intellect) –
should be trusted and obeyed by us as well.

AVOIDING SKEPTICISM & BELIEF IN GOD

As we have seen, complete philosophical skepticism is logically contradictory and practically unlivable. Even the statement: "We cannot know anything
for sure," begs the question[15] and turns out to be logically contradictory. Often
this statement is uttered during a discussion or argument to avoid the logical
conclusion indicated by the evidence presented. Yes, we should at times

---

14. See Alfred North Whitehead, *Science and the Modern World* (New York:
Macmillian, 1925), pp. 13-14. Whitehead actually makes a much stronger statement
in defense of Lewis' premise than Lewis indicates, see pages 98-99 of this book.

15. When one assumes as a premise for an argument, the very conclusion it is
intended to prove, this fallacy – "Begging the Question," [Petitio Principii] – is committed.

"reserve judgment." Certainly, on issues so very important as to be thought of as "truth about reality as such" or about "the existence of God," we should be very careful and think very clearly. But this does not relieve us from the responsibility of searching out the evidence, from making a decision, of taking a stand, or of being willing to constantly reexamine that stand.

Knowledge is certainly possible. The very question of its possibility presupposes, assumes, that knowledge is possible. Now the question becomes: "What can knowledge tell us about reality and/or God?" As we have seen, it can tell us all we need to know as long as we do not assume that we cannot know certain things or that some things do not exist *before* we examine the evidence. We must let fundamental experience be examined in regard to the claims to truth being made in the context of consistency and coherence within a world view. Truth claims made within the context of a world view must be examined according to the full range of experience itself. Sound reason (according to the laws of logic) and "common" experience must be used together to examine the truth claims.[16]

It is our contention that we can know truth about the reality we experience. There is basic truth which we do know and that cannot be meaningfully denied. What does this tell us about the existence of God? First, it tells us that we have a noncontradictory basis in experience for understanding truth claims. Second, it tells us that an examination of experience itself shows us the atheistic position that all reality is reducible to a mechanistic materialism is not logically or practically tenable. Third, it tells us if all of experience cannot be accounted for on the basis of matter alone, then we must look at the totality of experience carefully to see where it points, i.e., to the existence of an all powerful, eternal Being (God) who is necessary to explain the full range of actual experience *and* to account for the existence of finite, limited material existence (that is, us).[17]

---

16. See Norman L. Geisler, *Christian Apologetics*, chapter 8 "Formulating Adequate Tests for Truth," (Grand Rapids: Baker Book House, 1976), pp. 133-150.

17. See chapter 9 of this book, "The Nature of the Universe."

Chapter Five
GOD: A PSYCHOLOGICAL CRUTCH?

Introduction: Importance of the Question
Freud's Position & Critique
A Further Answer to Freud
The Need for God

INTRODUCTION: IMPORTANCE OF THE QUESTION

Who among us, in a discussion with a nonbeliever, has not heard the following: "So you believe in God. Well, I *don't* believe in your God. Don't you
know that your belief in God is nothing more than a 'wish fulfillment,' a psychological crutch. Men seem to have a psychological need for a giant father
image for security and comfort so they just project this need on to reality and
call it 'God,' when in fact there is no such thing." This is a very common
pseudo-argument. This idea is rooted in the thought of Sigmund Freud (1856-
1939).[1] Freud believed man's need for God and/or religion was purely psychological. It grows out of the illusory wish to have a Father-Protector.

Freud was not the only, nor the first, one to come up with such an idea. In
fact, Freud was heavily influenced by the thought of Ludwig Feuerbach
(1804-1872) in regard to Feuerbach's concept of projection and his theory of
man. In his *The Essence of Christianity* published in London in 1881 (but first
published in German as *Das Wesen des Christentums*, in 1841), Feuerbach
held that religion was only the imaginative projection of human needs and
hopes. "Man supposes, in his innocence, that he has immediate contact with

---

1. See Freud, *The Future of an Illusion*. Translated from the German and edited by
James Strachey (New York: W. W. Norton & Company, 1961).

superhuman Reality, but he is only communing with himself. What men worship as gods are nothing but *Wunschwesen*, "wish-beings." Gods are *personified wishes*.

This is a perfect example of the fact that ideas are very powerful and live on well after the person who espoused them. The "man on the street" who may not have even heard of Freud has certainly been affected by his thought whether he knows it or not. *Often times, as used popularly, such ideas become a sort of standard way of bypassing the importance of an issue* – in this case the evidence for the existence of God – *and pronouncing an "obvious fact."* These "obvious truths" are more often than not presented not so much as arguments, but as simple factual conclusions: "Stupid, didn't you know that because of 'x' your position is wrong, silly, etc."

The question of the *origin* of a person's beliefs is *logically* irrelevant to whether those beliefs are true or false. Any theory must be proved or disproved on its own merits, that is, on how the statements of argument fit the facts or evidence in the context of a consistent and coherent world view. That someone offers an alternative explanation – in this case for belief in God – does not prove or disprove any theory or idea. The appeal to the alleged origins of our beliefs as a substitute for arguments for or against the beliefs themselves is called in logic the *genetic fallacy* "because it attacks the source or genesis of the opposing position rather than that position itself."[2]

Yet, As Trueblood correctly says:

> The attack (from some forms of psychology) is difficult for the ordinary believer to answer because it tends to be condescendingly tolerant. [It] does not say that belief in God is false; it says that belief in God can be 'explained.' The critic thus poses as the wise man who can see more deeply than can others into the foibles and pathetic faith of other men. Instead of being crudely antagonistic . . . he may appear to be sympathetic, tender and helpful.[3]

So especially for those believers who have no training in apologetics, or in the ability to examine claims critically, the "friendly" atheist psychologist can be most dangerous.

---

2. See Irving M. Copi, *Informal Logic* (New York: Macmillan, 1986), pp. 112-114.

3. David Elton Trueblood, *Philosophy of Religion* (New York: Harper & Row, Publishers, 1957), p. 177.

FREUD'S POSITION & CRITIQUE

Freud's position is that all objective religious belief is groundless because it can be explained by psychological factors. Freud's serious convictions about religion are found in three important books: *Totem and Tabu, The Future of an Illusion*, and his last work, *Moses and Monotheism*. His most "philosophical" effort was *The Future of an Illusion* (a 56 page book) which proposes to deal with religious experience in general, including contemporary (to him) faith.

The best way of seeing Freud's position is to actually look at what he says. We can only wish Freud had done this with what Christianity actually teaches. Freud says his purpose is: "to take a glance in the other direction and to ask what further fate lies before it (civilization) and what transformations it is destined to undergo."[4] According to Freud there are three dangers in doing what he is about to do: (1) Only a few people can survey human activity in its full compass. It turns out, of course, Freud is one such person. (2) " . . . in a judgment of this kind the *subjective expectations of the individual play a part which it is difficult to assess; and these turn out to be dependent on purely personal factors in his own experience* [emphasis added], on the greater or lesser optimism of his attitude to life." And (3) "that in general people experience their present naively, as it were, without being able to form an estimate of its contents; . . . ."[5] This second danger is very telling with regard to Freud's own writings. Such a real danger applies to Freud as well. It is certainly clear what "subjective expectations" Freud had regarding religion.

Freud says: "I believe rather that when man personifies the forces of nature he is again following an infantile model."[6] This may be true, but can all "God talk" be explained as the "personification of the forces of nature?" We think not. Already, by page twenty-four of *The Future of an Illusion*, Freud says: "But it is not my intention to enquire any further into the development of the idea of God; what we are concerned with here is the finished body of religious ideas as it is transmitted by civilization to the individual." Yet Freud never does, in any of his works, systematically discuss the "idea of God" or the metaphysical reasons for belief. He is already guilty of begging the question. He has assumed that his explanation is either the only one, or at least the best one, to account for the concept of God.

---

4. Freud, *The Future of an Illusion*, p. 5.
5. *Ibid.*
6. *Ibid.*, p. 22.

Freud practiced a very rigid empiricist epistemology. He says: " . . . and no proposition can be a proof of itself."[7] Yet, his own empiricism can only be justified by its own method. This epistemology is inconsistent with his psychological relativism. Freud writes:

> Let us try to apply the same test to the teachings of religion. When we ask on what their claim to be believed is founded, we are met with three answers, which harmonize remarkably badly with one another. Firstly, these teachings deserve to be believed because they were already believed by our primal ancestors; secondly, we possess proofs which have been handed down to us from those same primeval times; and thirdly, it is forbidden to raise the question of their authentication at all.[8]

But these three "tests" are certainly not the basis for accepting, or for "faith," in the Christian context.[9]

About religious writings Freud says: "The proofs they have left us are set down in writings which themselves bear every mark of untrustworthiness."[10] Not in the case of the New Testament at least. One need only look at F.F. Bruce's *The New Testament Documents: Are They Reliable?* or John A. T. Robinson's *Can We Trust the New Testament?*[11] to see how inadequate is Freud's sweeping generalization. It is true that in the nineteenth century a number of unbelievers, equipped with considerable scholarship, went to great lengths to prove the Gospels were written in the middle of the second century A.D. when legend and imagination could have distorted the facts. But this attempt has failed! It was crushed under the weight of positive historical evidence.

Freud further says: "If all the evidence put forward for the authenticity of religious teachings originated in the past, it is natural to look around and see whether the present, about which it is easier to form judgements, may not also be able to furnish evidence of the sort."[12] There is no evidence that Freud

---

7. *Ibid.*, p. 27.

8. *Ibid.*, p. 26.

9. See Terry L. Miethe, *Living Your Faith.*

10. Freud, *The Future of an Illusion*, p. 27.

11. F.F. Bruce, *The New Testament Documents: Are They Reliable?* (Grand Rapids: Wm. B. Eerdmans Publishing Co., 1960), and John A.T. Robinson, *Can We Trust The New Testament?* (Grand Rapids: Wm. B. Eerdmans Publishing Co., 1977). Also see chapter 25 in this book: "The New Testament."

12. Freud, *The Future of an Illusion*, p. 27.

looked at either the evidence for the past or adequately judged his own present in regard to what was happening in religion. Samuel M. Thompson says it as well as it can be:

> Many of the things which Sigmund Freud has to say about religion were true enough. He has unusual insight into some of the *psychological uses of religious belief* [emphasis added], and he saw the frequent close relation of religious ideas with neurotic syndromes. But nowhere in Freud's principal writings is there the slightest indication that he ever dreamed of what religion at its best means to men and women whose religious faith feels itself completely at home and entirely secure in the company of their own highly developed critical intelligence.[13]

At the same time that Freud was writing such giant minds as those of Reinhold Niebuhr, William Temple, Karl Barth, Jacques Maritain, Albert Schweitzer and Martin Buber were vigorously at work, "but all that Freud could see was 'the forcible imposition of mental infantilism' and 'mass-delusion.' "[14] The point is not whether we accept all the above religious giants believed, but that they certainly represent a view of religion which transcended Freud's critique. As Trueblood so aptly says:

> There is a widespread belief that Freud's researches seriously undermined current religious belief, but the shocking truth is that he apparently never understood current religious belief and certainly never mentioned it. His attack seems serious until it is examined at first hand and then it is not formidable at all, because it is not scientifically sound. We must always listen to the hostile critic, providing he knows what it is whereof he speaks, but there is no reason to pay attention to one who has no real comprehension of his subject.[15]

Further, there is never in Freud any indication of familiarity with Augustine or Thomas Aquinas or any other intelligent metaphysical system. Freud's critique of religion is just that: a critique of "religion" in general at its worst. Most Christians would agree with much of this critique of "religion" in general.

"To assess the truth-value of religious doctrines does not lie within the scope of the present enquiry," writes Freud.[16] Yet this is exactly what he was doing! Many times Freud says that one cannot disprove the assertions of religion, and then goes on to act as if he had done just that. Further Freud makes an important admission:

---

13. Thompson, *A Modern Philosophy of Religion*, p. 135.
14. Trueblood, *Philosophy of Religion*, p. 184.
15. *Ibid.*
16. Freud, *The Future of an Illusion*, p. 33.

We shall tell ourselves that *it would be very nice if there were a God* [emphasis added] who created the world and was a benevolent Providence, and if there were a moral order in the universe and an after-life; but it is a very striking fact that all this is exactly as we are bound to wish it to be. And it would be more remarkable still if our wretched, ignorant and downtrodden ancestors had succeeded in solving all these difficult riddles of the universe.[17]

Reality is more than an object of wish-fulfillment. We could argue just as well (we think much better) that when we look critically at reality we see a basis for belief in God apart from wish-fulfillment. The fact that mankind has a universal (it seems) desire for God, as Freud admits, may be due to a truth about reality as well as a false projection.

The question then becomes: Who is interpreting reality correctly, Freud or believers? We cannot just dismiss the idea of God because we can see in history certain abuses as we look at "religion." But there is a further critique which must be made, in the next section of this chapter, on this idea that God can be dismissed because He is simply a projection of how we would wish it to be.

Freud constantly treats all religions in history as one. This is certainly a gross generalization and oversimplification.

Religion has clearly performed great services for human civilization. It has contributed much towards the taming of the asocial instincts. But not enough. It has ruled human society for many thousands of years and has had time to show what it can achieve. If it has succeeded in making the majority of mankind happy, in comforting them, in reconciling them to life and in making them into vehicles of civilization, no one would dream of attempting to alter the existing conditions. But what do we see instead? We see that an appallingly large number of people are dissatisfied with civilization and unhappy in it, ...[18]

Then, of course, when we start to look at the differences in individual religions and their teachings, it must certainly be asked if the "unhappy state" supposedly caused by the religion is due to the teachings of the faith, the condition of the people before or apart from the faith, or to the lack of real understanding and living of the faith by the people who claim to believe it.

Then Freud writes:

You will not find me inaccessible to your criticism. I know how difficult it is to avoid illusions; perhaps the hopes I have confessed to are of an illusory nature, too. . . . If experience should show – not to me, but to others after me, who think

---

17. *Ibid.*
18. *Ibid.*, p. 37.

as I do – that we have been mistaken, we will give up our expectations. Take my attempt for what it is.[19]

To which I answer: So be it!

A FURTHER ANSWER TO FREUD

There are many problems with Freud's assertions about God and religion. We have seen that: (1) A theory or belief must be judged on the evidence for it, not on its origin, psychological or otherwise. (2) Freud admitted there were real dangers in trying to do what he tried because one's analysis involves "subjective expectations" which "turn out to be dependent on purely personal factors in his own experience." (3) He *never* systematically discussed the "idea of God" or the metaphysical reasons for belief. (4) His rigid empiricist epistemology and his psychological relativism were in conflict. (5) There is no indication in Freud that he understood the great metaphysical systems or the thought of the religious "giants" of his own day. As Pascal said: "Let them at least learn what is the religion they attack, before attacking it."[20] (6) Freud's "lumping" of all faiths together as a universal "religion" was a gross generalization and oversimplification. Much more could be said, and should be said, but we have space for only a little more.[21]

What of this argument that religion must be false because it is nothing more than that which we would wish it to be? "Freud's greatest mistake, from the point of view of scientific objectivity, is his assumption that in all religious experience belief is in accord with wishes." Trueblood goes on to say:

> The blunt truth is that the upholders of the doctrine of *Wunschwesen* ("wish-beings"), from Feuerbach to Freud and beyond, do not know what they are talking about. They have spun a theory without bothering to check the evidence, most of which is never seen in clinics or laboratories. That there have been men whose alleged religious experience has been highly comforting, wholly in line with their desires, none doubts, but to assert that this has been the universal experience or even the characteristic one is to reveal gross ignorance.[22]

---

19. *Ibid.* p. 53.
20. Blaise Pascal, *Pensées*, (London: J.M. Dent and Sons, 1960), p. 187.
21. For further information see: Norman L. Geisler, *Philosophy of Religion* (Grand Rapids: Zondervan Publishing House, 1974), pp. 74-82; Richard L. Purtill's *Reason to Believe* (Grand Rapids: Wm. B. Eerdmans Publishing Co., 1974), pp. 31-37; and Trueblood, *Ibid.*, "The Challenge of Freud," pp.177-188.
22. Trueblood, *Philosophy of Religion*, pp. 186-188.

This certainly is not an adequate understanding of Christianity. There is much more to Christianity, and its teachings about God and an afterlife, than universal security and wish-fulfillment. The Christian teaching is that we are alienated from God by our sin. As Purtill says: "Man in relation to God is not only infinitely feeble and dependent, but is also condemned by his own sinfulness."[23]

Christianity does not teach universal security and a "pie in the sky" happiness for everyone. Yes, directly on the heels of our sinfulness, we find "the scheme of redemption,"[24] that God is merciful and has a plan for our salvation. But " . . . to be an object of mercy is hardly comforting to the ego." In Christian teaching, each individual is responsible, not only for his every action, but for accepting God's grace as well.[25]

> Now if there is one thing we all hate, it is responsibility. A good deal of our lives is spent in trying to evade one sort of responsibility or another. We can be bribed or flattered into accepting responsibility by being given power or admiration; but complete responsibility for our actions to a power infinitely superior to ourselves, without compensating power or admiration, is completely repugnant to us.[26]

Certainly, Christianity offers meaning and hope for this life – and the one to come. But the meaning and hope are related to responsibility for our actions before God, to acceptance of His grace, and to a life in response to a loving God. They – the meaning and hope – are not just based on "wishing" but on choosing and acting. They are demanding of real life, not just psychologically pleasing. So much for Christianity being simple wish-fullment.

There is in Freud *no* appreciation for or understanding of historic Christianity. Many have pointed out that Freud's science "demands a fair view of the available data," but we do not get this in Freud. As Trueblood writes:

> Freud's selection of religious data is almost as unfair as could be arranged. All of his major illustrations are of three related kinds, the pathological, the primitive and the infantile. The great religious tradition of the Western world, according to which men, acting under a sense of God's sovereignty, are able to stand

---

23. Purtill, *Reason to Believe*, p. 33.

24. The title of the great classic by Robert Milligan, *The Scheme of Redemption* (Nashville: Gospel Advocate Company), 582 pages.

25. See the two books Clark H. Pinnock edited: *Grace Unlimited* (Minneapolis: Bethany House, 1975) and *The Grace of God/The Will of Man* (Grand Rapids: Zondervan, 1989).

26. Purtill, *Reason to Believe*, p.33.

against the conventional morality, even unto death, is not so much as mentioned. One would never suspect, from reading Freud, that there ever were any Hebrew prophets or early Christians at all.[27]

It is quite clear that Freud should have taken the three dangers he mentioned more seriously in regard to his personal agenda.

THE NEED FOR GOD

The need for God is easy to establish.[28] Certainly, there is more than one theory about why there is such a need. It has been argued by Freud, and others, that this need is purely psychological. It seems Freud stopped short in his search for God because purely personal factors in his own experience led him to judge in advance that God was nothing more than a childish need. Stopping short in this all-important search "seems a bit abortive if not even cruel to the universally expressed need for the Transcendent." As Geisler goes on to say: "For if men, both believers and nonbelievers, have expressed such a deep-seated need for God, then surely one is cruelly unjust to himself to give up in despair before he has searched diligently for an answer."[29] There is little evidence that Freud did search diligently.

It can also be argued that this need was put in man by his Creator. We are never justified "to rule out in advance, *a priori*, the possibility of the existence of something. Logic is not the way to eliminate the possibility of the existence of unicorns. Looking, not logic, is the means to determine reality."[30] The question must be settled on the basis of the evidence. That evidence may, will, take many forms. It must be "factual," historical, scientific, theological, philosophical, psychological, experiential, etc. The "theory" that is judged to be the best in reference to a proper understanding about the nature of reality regarding the existence of God, must be judged true of reality as a whole, that it must be the one that fits all the factual evidence in the context of an understandable and defensible view of reality (a noncontradictory philosophical world view).

It is clear that "Freud's own theories can be discounted as easily as any

---

27. Trueblood, *Philosophy of Religion*, p. 184.
28. Freud admitted it. For further evidence of the need for a Transcendent see Geisler, *Philosophy of Religion* pp. 74-78.
29. *Ibid.*, p. 78.
30. *Ibid.*

other theory as a projection of our hopes and fears."[31] They are not exempt from their own criticism. In this case, the proverbial saying rings true, what is good for the goose is certainly good for the gander. As C. S. Lewis relates in *Pilgrim's Regress*:

> You must ask them whether any reasoning is valid or not. If they say no, then their own doctrines, being reached by reasoning, fall to the ground. If they say yes, then they will have to examine your arguments and refute them on their merits; for if some reasoning is valid, for all they know your bit of reasoning may be on of the valid bits.[32]

In short, as we have shown the issue of the existence of God and/or the need for God is not primarily a psychological one. It must finally be decided in the context of the evidence and a world view. We cannot just decide because some – or all – people seem to have a psychological need for God that God does not exist. We *must* examine the evidence, *all* the evidence, in *every* area!

---

31. Purtill, *Reason to Believe*, p. 34.

32. C. S. Lewis, *Pilgrim's Regress* (Grand Rapids: Wm. B. Eerdmans Publishing Co., 1958), pp. 71-74.

Chapter Six
THE IDEA OF GOD:
THE ONTOLOGICAL ARGUMENT

INTRODUCTION: IMPORTANCE OF THE QUESTION

If a case can be made, as many have done,[1] that there is a universal need for God in man (believer and non-believer have both admitted this), then it should be fairly easy to see man must have an idea of God.[2] It seems to us that "everyone who is at home in the English language understands the word 'God' in its common meaning. 'God' means 'the supreme and ultimate being.' "[3] The question then becomes: "Where does this idea of God come from?" But before we discuss this most important question, we need to say something here about what we mean by "God" since until now we have more or less taken what we mean for granted.

Everyone who uses the word "God" does not use the term to mean the same thing. By the term "God," Plato meant a being with soul and reason who is supremely good.

> So, being without jealousy, he desired that all things should come as near as possible to being like himself. . . . In virtue of this reasoning, when he framed the universe, he fashioned reason within soul and soul within body, to the end

---

1. Geisler, *Philosophy of Religion*, pp. 74-78.
2. Currently there is some discussion about whether man can or does have a valid concept of God. This is treated more fully in Terry L. Miethe and Antony G.N. Flew: *Does God Exist?* (San Francisco: Harper & Row, 1991).
3. Thompson, *A Modern Philosophy of Religion*, p. 212.

that the work he accomplished might be by nature as excellent and perfect as possible.[4]

For Plotinus (ca. 205-270) "god" was the "Good" or the "One." All things emanate directly from the "One." Yet, the "One" was beyond being, essence or knowledge.

In more modern times, for Sigmund Freud, as we have seen, "god" was nothing more than a psychological projection in the mind of man. For John Dewey (1859-1952), "god" means the relation between the ideal and the actual in relation to human and temporal existence. For Edgar Brightman (1884-1953), "God" is a Being who is perfectly good, yet limited in power because of uncreatedness within Himself.

For biblical theists, God is the supreme and ultimate Being who is infinite, perfect, and supreme in every conceivable way and who is revealed both in nature (general revelation) and in the Bible (special revelation). Most who use the word "God" would agree that it refers to a level of being which is ultimate (cannot be surpassed), not dependent on anything else for its own existence (totally independent Being), and is that on which all other things do depend for their existence (contingent beings depend on the necessary Being).

Within the past three decades or so there has been a gradual renewal of interest in metaphysics in general and the theistic arguments in particular. The first of the "grand old philosophical Arguments" to again raise its head in discussion and debate was the ontological argument for the existence of God.[5] The ontological argument (from the word *ontos*, being) is basically the argument that the very concept of an absolutely perfect Being or necessary Being demands that such exist. This is an *a priori* argument based on pure reason alone.

ANSELM'S ARGUMENT

Anselm (1033-1109) was born at Aosta in Italy. He was educated by the

---

4. Plato, *Timaeus* 29D-30C. Translated by F. M. Cornford in *Plato's Cosmology* (New York: The Humanities Press, 1948), pp. 33-34.

5. For a comprehensive bibliography on this argument, but now much dated, see T. L. Miethe, "The Ontological Argument: A Research Bibliography," *The Modern Schoolman*, Vol. LIV, No. 2 (January, 1977), 148-166. See also Alvin Plantinga, Editor, *The Ontological Argument: From St. Anselm to Contemporary Philosophers* (New York: Anchor Books, Doubleday & Co., Inc., 1965), 180 pages.

Benedictines and became one of them in 1060. In 1093 he was appointed Archbishop of Canterbury. His theory of truth and his general philosophy are thoroughly Augustinian. He is best known for his "ontological" argument to prove the existence of God.[6] Anselm was the first to formulate this argument. Most of those who have defended the argument have held it is rationally inescapable once the very idea of an absolutely perfect or necessary being is granted.

Anselm claimed to have thought of the argument while he was meditating on the concept of an absolutely perfect Being, i.e., the Christian God. Thus some have referred to it as a "proof from prayer." Above all Anselm believed that reason could demonstrate the existence of God. He agreed with the Augustinian formula in terms of the relation of faith and reason, i.e., faith seeking understanding. Anselm's ontological argument is found in his *Proslogium.*[7]

There are two versions of Anselm's ontological argument, one in chapter two, and a second in chapter three of the *Proslogium*. Thus, a second form of the ontological argument from the one for which Kant's criticism seemed telling was found in Anselm. If one grants the validity of Kant's criticism that "existence is not a predicate" (not everyone does) it affects only the first form of Anselm's argument based on predictability, not the second form based on the inconceivability of God's non-existence.

Anselm believed that it is better certainly to be than not to be at all, that existence is preferable to non-existence. Being is a perfection. That this kind of Being could exist in thought and not be objectively real is a contradiction, according to Anselm. After Kant, more recent philosophical speculation will say that there is a hidden premise in Anselm's first argument. From Kant on philosophers say that existence is not a predicate. This becomes one of the almost unchallenged dogmas of modern philosophy. What is meant by saying existence is not a predicate is that any proposition which predicates existence does so in terms of a synthesis of a subject and predicate. Existence attaches contingently, i.e., non-necessarily, to any subject of which it is said.

---

6. It was first called "ontological" by Kant who thought it had an ontological in-validity in it.

7. Anselm, *St. Anselm's Proslogium: With a Reply of Behalf of the Fool, by Gaunilo, and the Author's Reply to Gaunilo*, trans. by M. J. Charlesworth (New York: Oxford University Press, 1965).

Anselm's second argument can be paraphrased as follows:

1. God is by definition a being than which no greater can be conceived.

2. Existence without conceivable alternative of not existing is better than to exist with such alternative.

3. So that Greatness which is unsurpassable by others cannot not exist.

The difference between the arguments is that the chapter two argument is based on predictability of existence to an absolutely perfect Being and the chapter three argument is based on the inconceivability of the nonexistence of a necessary Being.

This is saying along with Gaunilo and others that existence as such is not a predicate, but the modalities (quality or attribute: FORM) of existence are. The very notion of an island does imply analytically contingent existence. Therefore the notion of a perfect island would be a contradiction. The very way in which islands must exist is always and exclusively contingent. But in terms of a most perfect Being the mode of existence which is analytically involved is necessary existence. To say that a Being who is defined as the most perfect conceivable Being, hence an absolutely necessary Being, is something which is possible not "to be" is a sheer self-contradiction. In this case, logical necessity (necessary in noncontradictory thought) and ontological (of the real world) necessity coincide. Such a Being is utterly unique. If one admits that we have the idea of a necessary Being which is entailed by being most perfect; but this still does not also involve extra mental existence, one is involved in a flagrant self-contradiction.

LATER FORMS OF THE ARGUMENT

Many later philosophers have argued for and against the ontological argument. Thomas Aquinas had three objections to the ontological argument: (1) Aquinas did not think everyone understood the term "God" to mean "that than which nothing greater can be conceived." (2) Even if this is the understanding of God, it does not prove that God exists actually but only mentally, says Aquinas. You are actually presupposing God's existence here to prove it. And (3), Aquinas thought that the proposition "God exists" was self-evident *in itself* but was not self-evident *to us*. "Because we cannot know God's essence (as a necessary Being) directly but only indirectly through His effects in creation."[8]

Thus for Aquinas, the only way we can arrive at the existence of God was through His creatures (*a posteriori*), not by a direct intuition of experience (*a priori*) by way of a pure conception of it. Geisler does admit that:

> Aquinas' objection grows out of the difference of his epistemological starting point (in experience) with that of Anselm's (in thought). In this respect Aquinas was more Aristotelian and Anselm was more Platonic. Other than this, it would seem that Aquinas does not appreciate the full force of the Anselmian argument. . . . Aquinas, too, had the concept of a necessary Being and yet he did not seem to appreciate that Anselm argued that this very concept (however one arrives at it) logically demands that one affirm that such a Being really exists.[9]

The argument was simplified by Descartes:

> In a second formulation Descartes held that the idea of God, who is infinite and perfect, could not be produced by any finite object and must, therefore, be caused by God Himself. Here is the same emphasis on the absolutely unique nature of one idea, with the principle of sufficient reason added.[10]

Trueblood goes on to make an important and telling statement that is worth quoting as a whole:

> The celebrated Kantian rejoinder that the real contains no more than is possible and that a hundred real dollars do not contain a cent more than a hundred possible dollars [in Kant's *Transcendental Dialectic*] really misses the point of the original argument in which reference is made not to any finite object, but only to the infinitely perfect being. *We may be sure that Anselm's argument is not so feeble as it appears superficially to be, but nevertheless it does not carry conviction today, largely because it represents a prescientific mentality* [emphasis added]. It seems irrelevant.[11]

It is certainly not valid to dismiss an argument "largely because it represents a prescientific mentality." That is scientism at its best, *and* worst! Scientism is the doctrine that *all knowledge* is scientific knowledge. It "insists that since science tells us something it must tell us everything. . . . The positive power of science comes from its method, and it is *by virtue of its own exclusion of any consideration of ultimates* that it can use the method it does [emphasis added]."[12]

---

8. Geisler, *Philosophy of Religion*, p. 138.

9. *Ibid.*

10. Trueblood, *Philosophy of Religion*, p. 91.

11. *Ibid.*, p. 91-92. It should be noted that Trueblood's book was published in 1957, several years before Hartshorne (1965) produced his work and before the revival of the ontological argument, though perhaps one can see in Trueblood's statement the anticipation of it happening.

12. Thompson, *A Modern Philosophy of Religion*, p. 174.

Many current philosophers feel that the ontological argument fails because it has a hidden cosmological premise, i.e., that something exists. "If one argues that 'something exists, therefore God exists,' he has left the purely a priori ontological approach and has moved into an a posteriori cosmological approach."[13] Thompson says: "The ontological argument fails, but this does not mean it is simply false. . . . If, however, we should discover a cogent proof of God's existence, then what the ontological argument says about God could have great significance."[14]

THE ARGUMENT TODAY

Anselm's second form of the argument has been rehabilitated by Charles Hartshorne (1897-1988) and others.[15] Many philosophers think the reformulation of Anselm's second argument by Charles Hartshorne is a logically valid (which would mean necessarily true of the actual world) ontological argument. Hartshorne's argument can be summarized as follows:

1. All thought must refer to something beyond itself which is at least possible, since –
   a. Wherever there is meaning, there must be something meant.
   b. The only thoughts that are less than possible are contradictory ones.
   c. Meaning must refer to something more than its own contents or inner consistency or else it is meaningless.
   d. The move from thought to reality is based on a prior reverse move from reality to thought.
   e. Total illusion is impossible; illusion presupposes a backdrop of reality.
   f. Confusion is possible about specific reality but not about reality in general.

2. The necessary existence of a necessary Being is "at least possible."
   a. There is nothing contradictory in the concept of a being that cannot *not* be.

---

13. Geisler, *Philosophy of Religion*, p. 161.

14. Thompson, *A Modern Philosophy of Religion*, pp. 278-280.

15. Charles Hartshorne, *Anselm's Discovery: A Re-examination of the Ontological Proof for God's Existence* (LaSalle, IL.: Open Court, 1965).

b. The only way to reject this is to plead a special meaning to the word "possible." (In the usual logical sense of the word "possible" there is no contradiction in the concept of a necessary Being).

3. With a necessary Being an "at-least-possible" existence is indistinguishable from a "possible and actual" existence. A necessary Being cannot have a "merely possible" existence (if a necessary Being *can* be, then it *must* be), for –
   a. God by definition is an independent Existence and, hence, cannot be produced by another as "merely possible" beings can be.
   b. God is everlasting and, so, He could not have come into being as "merely possible" beings can come into existence.

4. Therefore, a necessary Being necessarily has both a possible and an actual existence.[16]

If you are having trouble understanding the ontological argument, don't give up. Consider it a challenge, a most difficult challenge! The ontological argument is without question one of the hardest of all logical arguments. One of the most famous philosophers now alive argued it was not a valid argument for almost twenty years before he became convinced it does indeed prove the existence of God.

Where does the *idea* of God come from? Well, the popular implication of the ontological argument is that because we have the idea of God at all God must exist. The idea of God comes from God. He has "implanted" it in us, in both our minds and (later we will see) in the real world itself. Remember: "The ontological argument . . . is basically the argument that the very concept of an absolutely perfect Being or necessary Being demands that such exist." If everything were totally contingent (possible for it to be and not to be, finite, limited in every way that it exists) then how could we know either that fact, or have the idea of a necessary or infinite being. Some philosophers today believe the ontological argument of Anselm is one of the most living and vital contemporary issues in modern thought.[17]

---

16. Geisler, *Philosophy of Religion*, pp. 151-156.
17. Miethe, *The Metaphysics of Leonard James Eslick*, p. 80.

Chapter Seven
CAN SOMETHING
COME FROM NOTHING?

INTRODUCTION: IMPORTANCE OF THE QUESTION

Something exists, by way of example we do (at least when we wrote this we did); you do, the person reading this! This is actually undeniable. As mentioned in chapter one: "A few years back, we were asked . . . to debate . . . a philosopher on . . . the existence of God at a state university in the Washington, D.C. area." Regarding this premise, the atheist philosopher said:

> But let me address this argument. The argument says, "Hey, look, there's a world around you!" Okay, so let's look around. There's a world around you! You see it, you hear it, you feel it, you taste it. It is here – no question about that! Something exists. That premise is okay.

If something exists, then something has always existed.[1] There are only two possibilities: "Either the universe as we know it is eternal and therefore can account for itself." Or, "There is something beyond the physical, space/time universe which exists which is eternal and accounts for the existence of the universe, i.e., God exists." Thus the question is clear: "Is the universe as we know it eternal and therefore can account for itself?"[2]

But you say what about a third possibility? Something – the universe – came from nothing. The atheist debater went on to say:

---

1. We will argue this in the next chapter.
2. See chapter 3 of this book: "The Natural Versus The Supernatural."

Then we get a bunch of other premises which I don't need to go into because there's one question that all of that junk boils down to, and that's this: "Can you get something from nothing?" Right? That is what Miethe's whole big argument boils down to, "Can you get something from nothing?" Now if you can't, that means it had to come from something else. And that something else according to Miethe, is God. But I don't have to talk about that, because you *can* get something from nothing.

"The universe just happened." The answer from philosophy and science to this "possibility" is really very clear. Something cannot come from nothing! Historically, this has been a philosophical truth about reality (also a scientific truth) as universally accepted as any. "From nothing, nothing comes," is the old philosophical dictum – *ex nihilo nihil fit*.[3]

If it is so clear then why bring it up at all? Because today there is, so it seems, a great deal of misunderstanding about the "possibility" of something coming from nothing, even among philosophers and scientists. And, there are some related points, for example, the Christian doctrine of creation, which needs clarification for both believers and unbelievers alike.

The atheist philosopher in the debate – who rather unbelievably taught logic (among other things) – went on to say:

> So let us ask the question, "Can you get something from nothing?" The answer is "yes!" Physics says yes! He [Miethe] quotes going on and on about this and that you can't do it. You can do it! You can do it in a laboratory. It's been done! How come he doesn't know about it? He is a philosopher, and he is talking to you about philosophical ideas. He doesn't even know about what is going on in the physics lab! Because he is too busy studying some ancient, dusty, boring old text that doesn't even make a very good book![4] I don't even like the main character! The main character says – make no mistake about it – "I don't bring truth; I bring a sword." I wouldn't even bring the guy home for dinner! Okay? He's not my kind of guy!

---

3. Lucretius, the first-century Roman poet, wrote in *De Rerum Natura* of the creation of the world: *Nil posse creari de nilo*, "nothing can be created out of nothing," which is also rendered as *ex nihilo nihil fit*, suggesting that every effect must have a cause. Today the Latin phrase is applied rather broadly to suggest that a dull mind cannot be expected to produce great thoughts, anything worth doing requires hard work, you can't get blood from a stone, etc. All of which are quite true!

4. This is, of course, a logical fallacy known as an abusive "*argumentum ad hominem*," or "against the man" (sometimes said to be the "genetic fallacy") because it attacks the source of the opposition rather than that position itself. I am sure he knew what he was doing and was doing it intentionally.

The "ancient, dusty, boring old text" he thought I had been studying was the Bible. The "guy" he "wouldn't even bring home for dinner" was Jesus. Nevertheless we will look at his argument, that something can come from nothing in the physics lab, in the section "The Problem in Science," since he claims it is a *scientific* fact.

Believe it or not, this kind of attack is rather frequent these days in debates with atheists. They are often so convinced of their position (they really have been sold a "bill of goods!") that they really think no intelligent person can believe in God or Christianity today. They simply cannot conceive that such a person exists.[5]

THE PROBLEM IN PHILOSOPHY

As we have indicated, the idea that something can come from nothing has been totally rejected in the history of philosophy for it is clearly self-contradictory and irrational. "Nothing," by definition, does not exist. The dictionary says of "nothing:" "not any thing: no thing." It is absurd to assert that "something," a thing which exists can have as its cause no thing, i.e., that which does not exist. Even the famous skeptic, David Hume, said: "I never asserted so absurd a Proposition as *that anything might arise without a cause*: I only maintained, that our certainty of the falsehood of that proposition proceeded neither from intuition nor demonstration; but from another source."[6]

It has also been widely accepted in philosophy that when it comes to accounting for the present existence of something there are only three possibilities. Present existence refers to a thing's conservation in existence rather than its origination. A cause of present existence is a cause of *being*, not merely the cause of becoming. My Father and Mother were the cause of my becoming but they are not now the cause of my being.

The existence of something is either: (1) caused by itself, self-causation. In the history of philosophy, the idea of self-causation (*causa sui*) has been considered by most as existentially impossible. The argument goes: "For to cause existence one must exist. But to need one's existence caused, one would have

---

5. This shows clearly what kind of very sheltered "academic" world they have been living in.

6. David Hume, *The Letters of David Hume*, 2 volumes, ed. J.Y.T. Greig (Oxford: Clarendon Press, 1932), Vol. I, p. 187.

to not exist. Hence, to cause one's present existence one would have to both exist and not exist at the same time which is impossible."[7]

(2) Caused by another. The present existent is dependent on another for its actual existence. The "thing" is contingent in its act of existing, i.e., it is possible for it to exist or not to exist, in which case it needs a cause to account for its present existence.

Or (3), the present existent is uncaused, that is, it is independent, eternal existence. Again, there are only two possibilities: Either the universe is eternal, independent existence, or God is. The question is: "Does the evidence indicate that the universe is eternal?" We will examine this question more completely in the second part of this book.

THE PROBLEM IN SCIENCE

As we have indicated, the idea that something can come from nothing has been just as widely rejected in science as it has in philosophy. This is because the idea that something can come from nothing is both self-contradictory, as in philosophy, and also actual experience has shown it to be false. All of modern science, and its empirical method, is based on the universal validity of the relationship of cause and effect. Yet, as recently as 1964, G. G. Simpson was still rather naively stating the following claim: "Virtually all biochemists agree that life on earth arose spontaneously from nonliving matter and that it would almost inevitably arise on sufficiently similar young planets elsewhere."[8]

It is true that this idea (that from nothing, nothing comes) has to be constantly reaffirmed – and is – experimentally. This is not, however, because of any deficiency in the evidence, but because of the limits of science.[9] The modern scientific method cannot ever reach 100% absolute certainty, only high (perhaps very high) probability. Science is based on an inductive method, going from the particular to the general. You could never pronounce *absolute*

---

7. But in **process philosophy/theology**, the idea that self-causation is contradictory is denied. Charles Hartshorne has argued that it is possible. See Charles Hartshorne, "Whitehead on Process: A Reply to Professor Eslick," *Philosophy and Phenomenological Research*, Vol. 18, No., 4, pp. 514-522.

8. G. G. Simpson, *Science* (New York), p. 143, also 769.

9. See chapter 10 in this book.

certainty until every particular case had been examined. This is, of course, impossible because we are part of a process historically ongoing.

But what about this claim that something can come from nothing? It happens all the time – "in the physics lab." According to my atheist opponent: "So he [Miethe] is studying these old things. Why isn't he in the physics lab? Why don't Christians do that? Why don't they study science? If you want to know where everything comes from, why don't you turn to science? . . . Science has the answer!" The atheist philosopher goes on to say:

> There are two kinds of matter: positive and negative energy. All matter, as Einstein correctly pointed out, reduces to energy. $E = MC^2$ You've all heard of that, right? It means that a tiny little bit of matter, because "M" is the mass multiplied times the speed of light squared, it means that a little bit of mass means a great deal of energy. And there's a lot of mass energy in the universe. Where did it come from? Well, there are two kinds of energy: positive energy and negative energy. It's been done! In a physics lab, when you make a perfect vacuum. What happens is that two particles get created right there before the physicist's very eyes.

It turns out that you do not have to be a physicist at all to analyze this claim.[10] Yet, the physics does not support the claim either.

What is actually at issue here in the claim of the "vacuum generation of matter?"

> Electron-positron pairs are produced . . . in the laboratory by bremsstrahlung photons from particle accelerators. Other particle pairs, such as proton and antiproton, can be produced as well if the initiating photon has sufficient energy. Because the electron and positron have the smallest rest mass of known particles, the threshold energy of their production is the smallest. Experiment verifies the quantum picture of the pair production process . . . . Analysis of a bubble chamber photography reveals the creation of an electron-positron pair as *photons*[11] *pass through matter.* [emphasis added][12]

"As photons pass through matter" is an important phrase here. This is certainly not the same as saying "as nothing passes through nothing something comes into existence." One physicist I talked to regarding what the philosopher was claiming as "observed experimental fact" said: "This fellow is

---

10. But if you do want to read some of the physics of it see: *Quantum Physics*, by Eisberg and Resnick, pp. 48-53.

11. A "photon" is defined as: "The quantum of electromagnetic energy, generally regarded as a discrete particle having zero mass, no electric charge, and an indefinitely long lifetime."

12. Eisberg & Resnick, *Quantum Physics*, p. 49.

confused about the difference between a thought experiment and reality."[13]

Some very important facts are clear which are devastating to the atheist philosopher's claim that something can come from nothing: (1) A "photon" is not *nothing*. It is generally regarded as a particle of radiant energy. So assuming that the vacuum is a "perfect vacuum," as our atheist philosopher indicated, this still clearly is not something coming from nothing.

(2) If the atheist philosopher would have known physics as well as he claimed to, then he should have known of the Dirac theory, which: "According to this assumption, a vacuum consists of a sea of electrons in negative energy levels." And, " . . . Dirac's theory of a vacuum is [that it is] not completely vacuous because it predicts certain new properties which can be tested by experiment."[14] Light is required to remove the particle from the "vacuum." So much for something coming from nothing!

(3) What if you say that all matter – the physical universe – came from energy. You may call this "energy" "force" or "spirit." Does this help you? No! For either the "energy" or "force" is distinct from matter or it is not. (a) If it is distinct from matter you have something (not nothing), i.e., the "energy" creating matter. You do not have something coming from nothing. (b) If this "energy" is not distinct from matter, then you must show that the whole physical universe, made up of energy and matter, is somehow eternal.

This claim that the physical universe came from energy ("a" in the paragraph above) is really positing the immaterial in the role of creator. But let us analyze the claim more closely. (a) First, we must say that such a force or energy would have to be *self-existent*. If it were not self-existent it would not be the ultimate source. (b) It must be *eternal*. It had to have always been there or there was a time when it did not exist so something or someone would have had to bring it into existence. (c) It must be personal. For, if it were not *personal* how could it account for, have produced, persons? (d) When you have said all of this you have described much of what Christians call God. If it is not contradictory for the atheist to put the immaterial in the role of creator, why would it be contradictory for the Christian who says, after all, that God – who is immaterial – is the cause of all material things?

(4) Even on the very surface of this argument from the atheist philosopher, that something comes from nothing "everyday" in the physics lab, is prepos-

13. *Ibid.*, pp. 51-53.
14. *Ibid.*, pp. 52-53.

terous! How do you account for the very sophisticated scientific equipment, the lab, the scientist, etc. Did they come from nothing as well. You are right back at the old argument: "If they produced life in the test tube, wouldn't that prove there was no God." No! It would only *prove* that it took very intelligent men many many years of effort to *reproduce* (not really produce) what already existed! Technically, this would not "prove" anything, i.e., it would not prove that this was how life originally happened. But if it points to anything, then surely, it points to what Christians call creation, i.e., that it takes intelligence to create!

But isn't there a much more subtle claim in modern science that something can come from nothing? Yes, for that is really what "spontaneous generation" amounts to.[15] We mentioned this briefly in chapter 3, "The Natural Versus the Supernatural," under the section entitled, "The Existence of Life." We said, among other things, that life was "to some extent dependent on matter but not reducible to it." The science of chemistry has always acknowledged that there is a fundamental difference between living and nonliving things. We said that "it is pure conjecture that nonliving things gave rise to living things."[16] Of course, if living things come from nonliving things, then this is not something coming from nothing and we still have to either account for the "nonliving things," that is, matter, or prove that it is eternal.

One day when I was leaving my home to drive down to the university where I was teaching a summer course, I bent over in my driveway and picked up a rock. Arriving at my office, I promptly wrote on the rock with a black marker "test rock #1" and on the back I wrote the date – 12 July 1976. I took the rock to my class and put it on the desk and said: "Now today we are going to start an experiment. We are going to see how long it takes this rock to spontaneously generate, to come alive." Of course many students laughed. Some thought it was stupid. But was it really? I still have that rock. It has *not* generated life. But it has *only* been seventeen years now and as far as I know no lightning has struck it.

Did life arise from non-life? I think this would be tantamount to saying that something came from nothing. Why? Because spontaneous generation or

---

15. For a discussion of the history of spontaneous generation, see John Farley, "The Spontaneous Generation Controversy (1859-1880): British and German Reactions of the Problem of Abiogenesis," *Journal of the History of Biology*, Vol. 5, no. 2 (1972), pp. 285-319.
16. See the first part of chapter 3.

abiogenesis is impossible, at least it is certainly unproven.

> Spontaneous generation has never enjoyed security in prevailing scientific thought. The theory has been alternately embraced, abandoned, and accepted but ignored. The principal reason is that at various times in history two quite distinct concepts have been termed "spontaneous generation." These are (1) *abiogenesis*, the notion of life's first origin from inorganic matter, and (2) *heterogenesis*, . . . life's arising from dead organic matter . . . .[17]

Louis Pasteur (1822-1895), a French chemist, long ago proved that heterogenesis was impossible. He said: "Never will the doctrine of spontaneous generation recover from the mortal blow of this simple experiment."[18] And abiogenesis is an "even more difficult and remarkable form of spontaneous generation."[19] Yet, *materialists* must hold that it is not impossible. Why must they hold to its possibility? J.W.N. Sullivan says it well:

> It became an accepted doctrine that life never arises except from life. So far as actual evidence goes, this is still the only possible conclusion. But since it is a conclusion that seems to lead back to some supernatural creative act, it is a conclusion that scientific men find very difficult of acceptance.[20]

Perhaps we should add: It is a conclusion that *atheistic,* scientific men find very difficult to accept.

In 1981, Sir Fred Hoyle and N. C. Wickramasinghe, two scientists published their important book, *Evolution from Space.* In this book, they attack chemical evolution. They conclude that even if the whole universe were a kind of prebiotic soup the chances against life arising spontaneously would still be only 1 in $10^{40,000}$ (or 1 in 10 with 40,000 zeros written after). They compare this with the chances of a Boeing 747 resulting from a tornado raging through a junk yard, or about like the chances of finding one atom in the whole universe![21] Again, does it take more "faith" – I would prefer to call it

---

17. Charles B. Thaxton, Walter L. Bradley, and Roger L. Olsen, *The Mystery of Life's Origin: Reassessing Current Theories* (New York: Philosophical Library, 1984), p. 11. This is a very important, and highly acclaimed, book regarding a reassessment of current theories regarding the chemical origins of life.

18. R. Vallery-Radot, *The Life of Pasteur*, translated from the French by Mrs. R. L. Devonshire (New York: Doubleday, 1920), p. 109.

19. Thaxton, *et al.*, *op. cit.*, p. 12.

20. J.W.N. Sullivan, *The Limitation of Science* (New York: A Mentor Book, 1963), p. 94.

21. Sir Fred Hoyle and N.C. Wickramasinghe, *Evolution from Space* (London: Dent, 1981), pp. 24-26.

"irrationality" – to believe in a God who creates or the chance evolution of life?[22]

THE CHRISTIAN DOCTRINE OF CREATION

The Christian doctrine of creation is often referred to as *creatio ex nihilo*[23] and is also often misunderstood. Some atheists, for instance, will say to Christians: "Don't you Christians teach creation *ex nihilo*, creation out of nothing?" But creation "out of no *thing*" is not the same as "creation *from*" or, better perhaps, "*by* nothing." As we have already seen: "If it is not contradictory for the atheist to put the immaterial in the role of creator, why would it be contradictory for the Christian who says . . . that God – who is immaterial – is the cause of all material things?"

Christianity holds that the world is dependent, dependent on God for its very existence. It is not the idea that God created the world, in the distant past, and then "went off to play" as it were. The idea that the universe is only a machine God created, and wound up, and it runs totally on its own is not the Christian idea. The Christian idea is that without God's creative sustenance moment by moment, the world would not exist. He created the world and *He* holds it in existence.

By creation "out of nothing" Christians mean that there would have been *nothing* else unless God had made *something*. God did not make the world out of any *thing*! He brought it out of no *thing*, but not *from* – or *by* – nothing! "The doctrine of *ex nihilo* creation stresses the radical contingency of everything other than God. God alone is necessary Being. He is a Being that cannot *not* be. Everything else in the universe is contingent (something that *can* not be)."[24]

"Can something come from nothing?" As we have seen, this idea is philosophically self-contradictory and irrational, and as far as we know, the same is true scientifically. Certainly, there is no proof that something can come from nothing.

---

22. See Miethe, *Living Your Faith*.

23. From the Latin, literally meaning "creation out of nothing," the idea that God created without the use of previously existing materials.

24. Norman L. Geisler and Paul D. Feinberg, *Introduction to Philosophy: A Christian Perspective* (Grand Rapids: Baker Book House, 1980), p. 273.

Chapter Eight
FROM THE WORLD TO GOD:
THE COSMOLOGICAL ARGUMENT

Introduction: Importance of the Question
Thomas Aquinas' Argument
The Argument Today

INTRODUCTION: IMPORTANCE OF THE QUESTION

As we have said several times, the ultimate question in regard to the nature of the universe is: "Is the physical universe eternal?" "Can the physical universe as we know it account for itself?" The argument in philosophy which argues it *cannot* is known as the "cosmological argument for the existence of God."[1] Really, you do not have to grant that the physical universe as a whole is not eternal for the cosmological argument to prove its case. Thomas Aquinas held that reason could prove neither that the world is everlasting, nor that it has a beginning in time. Thomas accepted the temporal beginning of creation, not from rational necessity, but from revelation. The supporters of the argument say you only need to grant that some things, even "one blade of grass" is finite, contingent, limited for the argument to be valid.

The cosmological argument (from *cosmos*, world) usually begins with the existence of the finite world or "some condition within the cosmos, such as change," and argues "that there must be a behind-the-world Cause . . . to explain the existence of this kind of world." "It" is really a family of arguments. There are basically three "kinds" of cosmological argument: (1) The 12th and 13th-century form of the argument based on existential causality as in Thomas

---

1. See Miethe, "The Cosmological Argument: A Research Bibliography," *The New Scholasticism* 52 (1978), pp. 285-305.

Aquinas,[2] (2) the 17th and 18th-century form based on the principle of sufficient reason as discussed in Gottfried Wilhelm von Leibniz (1646-1716) and Samuel Clarke (1675-1729)[3], and (3) what is called the kalam (from the word *kalam*, which refers to Arabic philosophy or theology) cosmological argument which was popular among Arabic philosophers in the late Middle Ages.

Historically, the kalam argument was rejected by most Christian philosophers. Thomas Aquinas, who followed Aristotle, rejected it, though Saint Bonaventure (1221-1274), a contemporary and colleague of Aquinas, argued the kalam argument was valid.[4] Just recently a very small group of philosophers,[5] and even some Evangelical philosophers and theologians,[6] have defended this argument.

Many current philosophers have come to believe that one or more of Aquinas' forms of the argument can be reformulated to overcome the weaknesses originally found in it. Bruce Reichenbach says:

> The time has arrived for a reassessment of both the truth and validity of what is to me the most interesting and exciting of the theistic arguments. . . . The era is past when all metaphysical statements or arguments can simply be dismissed as silly or senseless, since they do not meet a preestablished criterion of verifiability.[7]

---

2. See Thomas Aquinas, *Summa Theologica*. Translated by the Fathers of the English Dominican Province (London: Burks, Oates and Washburne, 1920); specifically: Part I, question 14, answer 13; and Part I, question 2, answer 2, reply to objection 2; Norman L. Geisler, *Philosophy of Religion* (Grand Rapids: Zondervan, 1974), pp. 190-226.

3. Richard Taylor, *Metaphysics* (Englewood Cliffs, N.J.: Prentice-Hall, 1974); and William L. Rowe, "The Cosmological Argument," *Nous* 5 (1971), pp. 49-61, and *The Cosmological Argument* (Princeton: Princeton University Press), 1975; and Bruce R. Reichenbach, *The Cosmological Argument: A Reassessment* (Springfield, IL.: Charles C. Thomas Publishers, 1972).

4. Bernardino M. Bonansea, "The Impossibility of Creation from Eternity According to St. Bonaventure," *Proceedings of the American Catholic Philosophical Association* 48 (1974), pp. 121-135.

5. E. L. Miller, *Questions That Matter: An Introduction to Philosophy* (New York: McGraw-Hill, 1984), pp. 254-263.

6. Among Evangelicals, William Lane Craig is unquestionably the greatest supporter of the *kalam* argument. See Craig's works: *The Cosmological Argument:" from Plato to Leibniz* (New York: Barnes and Noble, 1980); *The Existence of God and the Beginnings of the Universe* (San Bernardino, CA.: Here's Life, 1979); *Apologetics: An Introduction* (Chicago: Moody, 1984); "Philosophical and Scientific Pointers to Creation ex Nihilo," *Journal of the American Scientific Affiliation* 32 (1980), pp. 5-13; and "Professor Mackie and the *Kalam* Cosmological Argument," *Religious Studies* 20 (1985), pp. 367-375.

7. Reichenbach, *The Cosmological Argument: A Reassessment*, pp. viii-ix.

In this chapter we will look at only two forms of the cosmological argument which are historically found in Thomas Aquinas.

THOMAS AQUINAS' ARGUMENT

Thomas "considered himself to be a faithful follower of Augustine." Many philosophers say the basic difference between them is that Augustine used the terminology and (epistemological) frame of Plato, while Aquinas put Christian truth in the terminology and frame of Aristotle. Thomas certainly thought that reason could prove the existence of God.[8] Earlier, in chapter 2, I gave a very short summary of Thomas' Five Ways.[9] Here we will look, in a *little* more depth, at the Second Way and the Third Way of Aquinas.

It is important to realize that Thomas is not arguing on the basis of "physical causality" which must be temporal and subject to an infinite regress.[10] Contemporary physics, especially in relativity theory and quantum physics seems to require that there be a time lag between cause and effect. This seems to destroy the possibility of an essentially subordinated causal series in which agent and patient exist, act, and are acted upon simultaneously.

The Second Way of Thomas, the argument from efficient causality, can be put thus:

1. There are efficient causes in the world (i.e., producing causes).
2. Nothing can be the efficient cause of itself (for it would have to be prior to itself in order to cause itself).
3. There cannot be an infinite regress of (essentially related) efficient causes, for unless there is a first cause of the series there would be no causality in the series.
4. Therefore, there must be a first uncaused efficient Cause of all efficient causality in the world.
5. Everyone gives to this the name of God.[11]

---

8. See pages 29-31 of this book for more on Thomas Aquinas.

9. See page 30.

10. See Patterson Brown, "Infinite Causal Regression" *The Philosophical Review* 35 (1966), pp. 510-525, and later published in *Aquinas: A Collection of Critical Essays,* ed. Anthony Kenny (Notre Dame, IN.: University of Notre Dame Press, 1976), pp. 214-36.

11. Geisler, *Philosophy of Religion*, p. 174. See Thomas Aquinas, *Summa Theologica*, I, q. 14, a. 13, "Whether the Knowledge of God is of Future Contingent Things."

In the Second Way, Thomas is talking about God in terms of a utterly unique kind of causation, i.e., a causation of existence itself. If there is a cause of that sort it cannot be involved in any kind of subordinated series. It would have to be immediate and direct. This would be "efficient causality" of existence itself, i.e., a cause of being, not a cause of becoming in the physical sense. We believe that Thomas employs efficient causality itself in every one of the "Five Ways," but it is explicit only in the Second Way. The sculptor who makes a statue is the efficient cause of the statue.

It is radically impossible, according to Thomas Aquinas, that anything should be the cause of itself (*causa sui*).[12] To cause itself it would have to pre-exist itself which is an impossibility. Without a first cause there would be no terminal effect, intermediate causes, or any efficient cause anywhere. Here, Thomas appeals to a type of causality unknown to Aristotle where existence itself is the effect, a type of causality where the effect is a finite efficient cause. This would be a metaphysical kind of causality rather than a physical one.

Of the Second Way, Leonard Eslick says in his Wade Memorial Lecture:

> The necessity engendered by an essentially subordinated causal series, without which the first two Ways could not work, not only requires causal simultaneity, *which is seemingly shattered fatally by relativity theory* [emphasis added], but also eliminates from the divine effects any real contingency and freedom, any creaturely share (however modest) in divine creativity.[13]

But as just stated in the above paragraph the causality talked about in the Second Way is a metaphysical one rather than a physical one.

Samuel Thompson says:

> When we are told that there is no scientific evidence which supports the view that there are causes operative in nature, we must reply that the question of whether or not there are causes is not a scientific problem. The causal principle can be neither established nor shown to be false by any special science. The findings of the special sciences may support or refute the belief that this or that cause

---

12. Some Christian philosophers now think that Charles Hartshorne is correct that there can be *causa sui*. See Leonard J. Eslick, "Substance, Change, and Causality in Whitehead," *Philosophy and Phenomenological Research* 18 (1958), pp. 503-513; and Charles Hartshorne's reply, "Whitehead on Process: A Reply to Professor Eslick," *Philosophy and Phenomenological Research* 18 (1958), pp. 514-22. For Thomas, unlike Spinoza, not even God can be *causa sui*.

13. Leonard J. Eslick, "From the World to God: The Cosmological Argument" *The Modern Schoolman* 60 (1983), p. 153.

is operative in a given situation, but the question of whether there are causes or not is beyond their reach. This is not in question; it is presupposed by the sciences. We do not expect the sciences to establish the existence of the things they investigate; they assume the existence of those things, and their investigations could not get under way unless they did make such assumptions.[14]

And as Eric L. Mascall further says:

. . . the method of investigation of the world which physical science adopts – observation of measurable phenomena and their correlation and prediction by general statements – is such as to exclude efficient causality from its purview, and hence renders it quite incompetent to decide whether there is efficient causality or not. Efficient causality is not a physical concept but a metaphysical one, and it is only because the physical scientists of the eighteenth and nineteenth centuries insisted on illicitly talking physics in terms of efficient causality that their successors, having discovered that efficient causality is not what physics is as a matter of fact concerned with, have only too often assumed that it is nonexistent.[15]

Eslick even admits,

It would be *meta*-physical precisely in the sense of transcending the physical and its material conditions. The latter may turn out to be historical and contingent, as relativity theory and quantum physics suggest, but the former, the causality of existence itself, as distinct from qualified existence, could be the work of a divine creative agent. It may even be suggested that this is the meaning of so-called creation *ex nihilo*, so significantly absent from the Greeks, and even from Genesis.[16]

But if what Eslick says about the Second Way eliminating "from the divine effects any real contingency and freedom" then there is in it a much more serious problem.

The Third Way of Thomas, the argument from possibility and necessity, can be put thus:

1. There are beings that begin to exist and cease to exist (i.e., possible beings).
2. But not all beings can be possible beings, because what comes to exist does so only through what already exists (nothing cannot cause something).
3. Therefore, there must be a Being whose existence is necessary (i.e., one that never came into being and will never cease to be).
4. There cannot be an infinite regress of necessary beings each of which has its necessity dependent on another because:

14. Thompson, *A Modern Philosophy of Religion*, pp. 332-333.
15. E. L. Mascall, *He Who Is* (New York: Longmans, Green and Company, Inc., 1948), p. 45.
16. Eslick, "From the World to God," pp. 156-157.

(a) An infinite regress of dependent causes is impossible.
(b) A necessary Being cannot be a dependent being.
5. Therefore, there must be a first Being which is necessary in itself (and not dependent on another for its existence).[17]

According to many Christian philosophers, the Third Way of Thomas is the most impressive of the five. It is more fully developed. In the Third Way the nominal definition which is the function of the middle term in the argument becomes God as the uncaused necessary Being who causes contingent beings and caused necessary being.[18] The fact from the world of our experience that one starts with in this argument is the existence of contingent beings, i.e., ourselves.

Contingent beings are defined as those which are possible to be and not to be. Eslick thinks this is a remarkable starting point.[19] A contingent being comes into being by generation and passes out of being by perishing. Such beings cannot have the reason for their existence in themselves. They must be caused to be by another. They do not exist by their very essence. That which exists by its very essence is necessary.

The question is whether there must be some necessary being or beings. Thomas tries to show that the assumption that there are no necessary beings whatever involves self-contradiction. To be contingent is to have the possibility of nonexistence. Thomas says that if universal nonexistence were possible it would still be the case. Even now nothing would exist whatever. This is counter-factual to the admission that there are existing things. It might be objected to this argument that all things indeed are possible to be and not to be but they exercise their existence successively without any radical beginning or end of existence. Out of nothing, nothing comes. If everything were simultaneously nonexistent there would indeed be nothing in existence now. This contradicts fact.

Eslick correctly says:

> The argument has two movements, the first seeking to establish that *some* necessary being must exist as a cause of the evident existence of contingent things *here* and *now*, and the second that an infinite causal regress of *caused* necessary beings is impossible.[20]

---

17. Geisler, *Philosophy of Religion*, pp. 174-175. See Thomas Aquinas, *Summa Theological*, I, q. 2, a. 2, reply to obj. 2.
18. Angels are for Thomas Aquinas examples of caused necessary beings.
19. Eslick, "From the World to God," p. 156.
20. *Ibid.*

The first movement of the Third Way is in the logical form of a *reductio ad absurdum* type of argument. Given the relations of contradictories on the square of opposition, if one is true the other is false, *and* if one is false the other must be true. "To say that all things without exception are possible to be and not to be is to say that *all* things 'at some time' are non-existent, which implies the counter-factual conclusion that *right now* nothing exists."[21]

Eslick sums it up well:

This is, I think, the point of absurdity and contradiction. Universal contingency can admit of no exception, and certainly not of the universe itself, whose possible non-existence, to be meaningful, must be actualized. It must, therefore, have come into existence from antecedent nothingness, but this is impossible, for *right now* nothing would exist.

Thus,

The Third Way is a *tour de force* which struggles to move from the contingent features of the world to the necessary existence of God, not directly but indirectly. I think the struggle succeeds. But it could have been achieved more expeditiously by the ontological argument of St. Anselm, at least as rehabilitated and reformed in our own day by Charles Hartshorne.[22] I think the absurdity of universal contingency is not merely counter-factual (and in this sense the argument is empirical and cosmological), but a *priori*.[23]

THE ARGUMENT TODAY

Two prominent Evangelical philosophers have reformulated the argument to present what they believe is a true and valid cosmological argument. First, Bruce Reichenbach in his *The Cosmological Argument: A Reassessment*[24] states the argument as follows:

(S1)   A contingent being exists.
   a.   This contingent being is caused either (1) by itself, or (2) by another.
   b.   If it were caused by itself, it would have to precede itself in existence, which is impossible.

21. *Ibid.*, p. 157
22. See Hartshorne, *Anselm's Discovery, Ibid.*
23. Eslick, "From the World to God," pp. 157-158.
24. Published by Charles C. Thomas, Springfield, Illinois in 3 parts: the first establishes what appears to be a true and valid cosmological argument; the second addresses the question of the nature of causation and the causal principle; and the third treats objections, both traditionally and more recently, are considered and evaluated.

(S2) Therefore, this contingent being (2) is caused by another, i.e., depends on something else for its existence.

(S3) That which causes (provides the sufficient reason for) the existence of any contingent being must be either (3) another contingent being, or (4) a non-contingent (necessary) being.

    c. If 3, then this contingent cause must itself be caused by another, and so on to infinity.

(S4) Therefore, that which causes (provides the sufficient reason for) the existence of any contingent being must be either (5) an infinite series of contingent beings, or (4) a necessary being.

(S5) An infinite series of contingent beings (5) is incapable of yielding a sufficient reason for the existence of any being.

(S6) Therefore, a necessary being (4) exists.

Reichenbach's argument is an important one which is based on the relationship of causality and *sufficient reason*.[25] His book is well worth reading.

Evangelicals have restated the cosmological argument thus:

1. Some limited, changing beings(s) exist.
2. The present existence of every limited, changing being is caused by another.
3. There cannot be an infinite regress of causes of being.
4. Therefore, there is a first Cause of the present existence of these beings.
5. This first Cause must be infinite, necessary, eternal, simple, unchangeable and one.
6. This first uncaused Cause is identical with the God of the Judeo-Christian tradition.[26]

Geisler's argument is *not* based on the principle of sufficient reason but on the principle of existential causality. "The former calls only for an explanation in the realm of reason; the latter demands a ground in reality." Geisler bases his argument on existential undeniability.

For the sake of space, we will briefly summarize only the argument based on existential undeniability.

(1) Some limited, changing beings(s) exist. This premise is *undeniably* true of experience. "The necessity of this affirmation is not logical but existential. That is, the nonexistence of everything is not inconceivable." Yet, the fact of the matter is that I do (or in the case of the reader, you do) exist. It is

25. Reichenbach, *The Cosmological Argument: A Reassessment*, pp. 19-20.
26. Geisler, *Philosophy of Religion*, pp. 190-226.

quite clear that I am limited in every way I exist. It is possible for me to be or not to be. I am limited to a spatio-temporal continuum. It is also very clear that we experience the world as limited and changing.

But you say, "I may be deluded. Reality may be an illusion." "The fact of illusion *in* the world demonstrates that we have no total illusion *of* the world." Total illusion is impossible. Even the concept presupposes a "backdrop of reality." If this were not true we would not, could not, know anything of "illusion." To deny this first premise involves one in an *actual*, i.e., about physical reality, contradiction.

(2) The present existence of every limited, changing being is caused by another. (a) Every limited changing being is composed of both an actuality (its existence) and a potentiality (its essence). (b) But no potentiality can actualize itself. (c) Therefore, there must be some actuality outside of every composed being to account for the fact that it actually exists, as opposed to its not existing but merely having the potential for existence.

(3) There cannot be an infinite regress of causes of being. We are not here talking about a linear series of historical causes of becoming, but a vertical series of causes of *being*, for existence itself. This argument is talking about a cause for the very being of a thing, not its coming into existence (its becoming) or the changes it may undergo. It is impossible to have an infinite regress (go backwards to infinity, has no first or beginning cause) of *existent-dependent* causes. An infinite regress of finite beings would not *cause* the existence of anything. At best, this is only sidestepping the issue of causality. Yet, it is impossible to deny that there is causality within the series. When you simply add another dependent being to a chain of such beings it does not *ground* the existence of the chain. "To say that it does is like saying one could get an orange by adding an infinite number of apples to a basket of apples. Adding apples to apples does not yield an orange;"[27] adding dependent beings to other such beings does not yield a cause, or ground for their *dependent* existence.[28]

(4) Therefore, there is a first Cause of the present existence of these beings. "This conclusion follows logically from the first three premises . . . . Indeed, if the last argument against an infinite regress is correct, then this first Cause must be the very first Cause beyond the changing beings, with no intermediary causes in between."[28]

---

27. J.P. Moreland, *Scaling the Secular City: A Defense of Christianity* (Grand Rapids: Baker Book House, 1987) p.17.
28. Geisler, *Philosophy of Religion*, p. 201.

(5) This first Cause must be infinite, necessary, eternal, simple, unchangeable, and one. Again, this follows logically. If this Cause is the first cause of all dependent, caused being, then it must itself be *unlimited* in every way it exists (be infinite), it *must* be (it is necessary), if it must be then it has always been (it is eternal), etc. There can be only one such Being. First, an uncaused being is pure actuality and it follows that there cannot be two such beings. Second, this uncaused Being is by its very nature unlimited. "Many things may *have* existence, but only one thing can *be* existence." Third, pure actuality cannot be divided or multiplied *in Being*. But the force of the argument is that such a Being cannot *not* exist for finite, limited beings exist.

(6) This first uncaused Cause is identical with the God of the Judeo-Christian tradition. It has often been said: "All right, you have proven the necessity of a first uncaused Cause of all that exists, but how do you know this God is the Christian God?" If you understand the argument, this conclusion is rather simple. First, as seen above there can only be one such Being. Second, when you have described the attributes of this Being, you have precisely defined what the Bible and Christians call God. He is creator (Gen 1:1; Heb 11:3), sustainer of all things (Ps 36:6; Col 1:17), one and supreme (Deut 6:4; Exod 20:3), infinite and eternal (Ps 147:5; 41:13), changeless in nature (Ps 102:27; Mal 3:16; Jas 1:17), absolutely perfect and loving (Matt 5:48; 1 John 4:16), etc.

Also, what is sometimes missed is that God must be able to account for all the positive attributes He is in fact responsible for in His creation. He must be personal, or He could not have produced persons. He must be intelligent, creative, loving, etc. "Pure actuality possesses all the perfections or characteristics of being in the highest and most eminent way possible (viz., infinitely)."

> There are not different Gods but only two different approaches: divine declaration and philosophical inference. It should not seem strange to those who believe (via divine revelation) in God's manifestation in His creation (Romans 1:19, 20; Ps. 19:1) that it is possible to arrive at a knowledge of God by inference through these manifestations.[29]

Thomas Aquinas was correct in positing that contingent physical existence cannot account for itself. We know too much about matter to be materialists. Physically existing things are clearly limited, changing, finite. The idea of

---

29. *Ibid.*, p. 208.

universal contingency is not merely counter-factual but ultimately absurd. Contingent existence cannot account for itself. Clearly, that which is itself an effect cannot be the cause of all things.

Chapter Nine
SUMMARIES AND CONCLUSIONS

PART ONE
Chapter 1: "God's Existence: The Importance of the Question"

In this chapter, we have laid – as it were – the foundation for the claim that the importance of the question of the existence of God is foundational to the most important queries of the human mind and heart. It is impossible to be even remotely aware of the history of philosophical thought and not realize the centrality of the question of God's existence to the enterprise of philosophy as a whole. Yet, the philosophical implications of the question are really motivated by, originated in the practical importance of the existence of God.

"Experience" though important to the discussion, cannot be viewed in the vacuum of only one individual. An individual's experience cannot be judged as reliable on its own. It be must "tested" against other experience and the claims and counterclaims in the context of a world view. It must be put into a context, an intellectual framework that makes sense of it in relation to the implications of the "experience" to the nature of reality of which it is supposed to inform. A view of experience – or "faith" – which is totally subjective is an inadequate basis – and, in fact, a very dangerous basis – for life for either the atheist or the believer![1]

---

1. A couple of examples may be important here: "Skip," whom I counseled for over two years, seemed to be fairly intelligent and articulate. In fact, enough so that he occasionally traveled in the circle of politicians, government officials, and their group in the state of California. He seemed to be in touch with reality in every way – but one, that is. For Skip believed God communicated with him in a personal way directly. Further, Skip believed God had chosen him to "save America" and had given him a "license to kill!" The truly amazing thing was that when he talked about anything,

The Bible is certainly not opposed to giving reasons for belief in God. In fact, we may say that the text of scripture clearly supports such activity in several ways. Certainly, anyone who claims a particular text to be true – and truth is always the opposite of error – could not consistently oppose an examination of its claims and the foundations on which its claims rest (in this case, the assertion that God exists).

The assertion "God exists" has, at one and the same time, the most astute theoretical as well as the most intensely practical importance of any claim. This claim must be answered "very thoughtfully and carefully" because of the clear personal implications of the answer – in either direction. If there is one fact in all the world we can be clear about, it is that "who cares?" can *never* be an honest option historically, intellectually, or practically to the question: "Does God exist?"

Chapter 2: "God's Existence: Historical Importance"

There have been a great many important historical contributions to the discussion of the question of the existence of God – far too numerous to treat adequately in one book.[2] These historical contributions have had, and do

---

but his "special" revelations from God, he seemed quite sensible. It was only when we talked about his "mission from God" that he seemed bazaar and dangerous – even frightening. After two years of trying to get to the heart of Skip's "problem" and of patiently trying to get Skip to "test" his wild claims about what God had told him, chosen him to do, against all possible rational claims to knowledge and by what the Scriptures said; one day as we were sitting in my home – rather out of the blue as it were – he turned to me and pronounced God's judgment on me and left. I must admit I was a little worried for my safety and the safety of my family for the next few days and weeks.

It turns out, in my experience in local ministry, that there are an alarming number of people out there "functioning" on the fringe of "sanity." These are people who make *their* experience the test, the only test, for reality. They are very dangerous people. About the same time I was counseling Skip, I remember the news reports of a woman in another state who claimed to be given a direct word from God to throw – to their deaths – each of her seven children in turn and finally herself off the balcony of a hotel. An individual's experience *must* be examined in the context of the whole of the reality of which it claims to be informative.

   2. Certainly, one should look as well at: Plato, Aristotle, Anselm, Descartes, Nietzsche, Bergson, Whitehead, etc.

have, practical importance for today. Here we have looked – however briefly at four such historical contributions; two that were deemed essentially negative, Plotinus and Kant; and two, Augustine and Aquinas, in which the historical contributions are essentially positive.

We have laid at the feet of Plotinus – as it were – many of the misunderstandings in philosophy which were rather uncritically adopted and adapted by the western world resulting in several important problems in Christian theology, for example: the idea that God is utterly transcendent, that He is totally "static," the problem of having a "Trinity," or an Incarnation, or any kind of communication with God or "prayer," or even the problem of humans having "fellowship" with God.

On the other hand, and partly *because* he lived in such an interesting and turbulent time, we see in Augustine foundations – still applicable – for answers to many of the problems. Augustine correctly saw God as the source of all order and happiness in this world. It was Augustine who really first put the philosophical resources of the mind of understanding, interpreting, and applying the truth of Christianity – a systematic understanding of it to the world. Augustine, quite correctly, believed that all of the resources of reason and philosophy should go into the task of understanding what is believed.

In many ways, it is in Aquinas that we first see stressed a need for a systematic understanding in Christianity of the importance of an empirical basis for what is believed about God and His relation to reality. One of Aquinas' greatest insights was the realization that the essence of existence, "to be (to exist) cannot be the same as to be (or exist) in only a material way." In Thomas, we see that the very reality of a "material (or physical) world," must show the existence of a non-material reality as well. That "contingent being" means, of necessity, that non-contingent Being must exist!

Though Kant thought he was doing a service to Christianity, it is in his thought that we see what was used later to support the very destruction of even the possibility of knowledge of God (and, therefore, His existence) – knowledge of that which was not "purely" physical. In a real sense, Kant is responsible for bringing to wide acceptance the division Plotinus had espoused. For Kant, "experience" can never disclose ultimate reality. Because the only knowledge we have is from the senses, there is no way reason can prove God exists.

Kant is a *very important* watershed in the history of philosophy and Christian thought. It is extremely hard for the person who has no background in philosophy to realize just how profound was Kant's effect. After Kant, what had for hundreds of years been proven/accepted views about the nature of reality – and of the relationship of thought to reality – were almost totally discarded by most philosophers.

Chapter 3: "The Natural Versus The Supernatural"

Though it is certainly not simplistic, nevertheless when discussing the natural *versus* the supernatural the choices are few. Either the universe is eternal or it had a beginning. In which case, there must be a cause – necessary and sufficient – to account for all that the universe holds, the existence of life, intelligent life, and creativity, etc. If one does not rule out of court the very possibility of the nonphysical before the evidence is closely examined, then it, again, seems fairly clear that there is abundant existence of the supernatural in the "natural" order. Clearly, the naturalists (mechanists, evolutionists) arbitrarily (define out of existence) reject the supernatural where there is clear evidence for its existence.

Chapter 4: "Fundamental Laws of Human Belief"

The mosaic constructed over the centuries, as one looks at the history of philosophy, of the possibility of absolutes, reliable knowledge of the world we experience, and evidence of the relation of logic to thought is not nearly as bleak, nor as silly as modern philosophers seem to think. Certainly, part of the problem has been a philosophical world view – and the philosophers who hold it – which rejects certain "common sense" beliefs that are basic to all that we can know about ourselves and the world in which we live. These "fundamental laws of human belief" are very important – essential really – to formulating an adequate view of the world that can meaningfully speak about God's existence and thus avoid philosophical, religious, and personal skepticism.

It is quite clear that what is needed is a more rigorous empiricism! It is also abundantly clear that when we engage in an empiricism that looks more critically at reality itself, and does not define out of existence broad ranges of reality, that naturalism (or mechanism, or materialism) cannot account for all that we experience. Far, far too long we have accepted uncritically the atheistic theory that experience is purely physical. It is not! This narrow empiricism cannot account for a vast range of what we do experience in life and in the real world.

Chapter 5: "God: A Psychological Crutch?"

Belief in the existence of God on the part of the Christian is certainly not "wish fulfillment." Just the opposite is true. It is the atheist, in believing that God does not exist, who is experiencing "wish fulfillment," – one that does not stand up to the evidence – and one which will prove personally dangerous and eternally fatal. It is the atheist who walks with the huge "psychological crutch" which helps prop him or her up against the wooing of a loving God. Hell *is* the only place where the atheist will be truly, finally, *free* from the love of God.

It is more than sad, much more – tragic really – that a system of thought – that of Sigmund Freud – based on such false assumptions, bad research, which was so obviously faulty in its methodology and conclusions, has been allowed to exert such an incredible influence on the world! To not examine one's own presuppositions, make such gross generalizations, treat all religions as one, and to show no indication of having examined the evidence of that which you are railing against is not only the "unforgivable sin" for the scholar; but, ultimately we have to ask about the personal integrity of the person so disposed.[3]

The need for God is not there because of "wish-fulfillment." On the contrary, it exists because of the nature of man as created by God. We are convinced that if anyone will spend the time and effort needed to examine the evidence – all the evidence, from every discipline, in the context of a world view – this is the only logical conclusion which can be reached. As we saw, Purtill writes: "Freud's own theories can be discounted as easily as any other theory as a projection of our hopes and fears." In fact, given the state of Freud's scholarship, a much stronger statement is in order: Freud's own theories must be discounted as a projection of his hopes and fears.

---

3. I was truly amazed that Christian scholars I studied under while working on my second Ph.D. at the University of Southern California did not seem to be aware of the totally unacceptable job of scholarship on Freud's part.

Chapter 6: "The Idea of God: The Ontological Argument"

The Ontological Argument for God's existence is really one of those subjects mentioned in the "Preface" which is impossible to treat in a way that is, at the same time, both simple and really responsible to its complexity. But, we have given it a shot. Most who have defended the argument have held that it is rationally inescapable once the very idea of an absolutely perfect or necessary being is granted. It is the second form of the argument – based on the inconceivability of the nonexistence of a necessary Being – which is believed to be the strongest. This is the form which has gained favor among several philosophers today. As we said in the chapter: "If you are having trouble understanding the ontological argument, don't give up. Consider it a challenge, a most difficult challenge!"

Chapter 7: "Can Something Come from Nothing?"

"Can something come from nothing?" Perhaps no question in the history of philosophy has engendered such a universally agreed upon negative answer – until fairly recently, that is. Even the famous skeptic, David Hume, did not go that far! Today there is a great deal of misunderstanding about this issue. Yet, there is still an important lack of evidence, philosophical and scientific, for the possibility of spontaneous generation. The only reason it is considered a serious alternative to belief in God is that the atheist really has no other alternative given the scientific evidence that the universe is not eternal.

Historically, the idea that something can come from nothing has been just as widely rejected in science as it has in philosophy. In spite of the young atheist philosopher's claim, actual experience has shown it to be false and continues to show it as false. Something still does not come from nothing. As we mentioned, there are theories which say that a vacuum is not completely vacuous.

In fact, as recently as 18 January 1993, an article entitled "The Dark Side of the Cosmos" in *Time* (pages 34-35) says "astronomers struggle with dark matter." The subtitle of the article reads: "As astronomers struggle to illuminate the nature of dark matter, a new report hints that as much as 97% of the universe could be made of the mystery stuff." We used to think of deep, dark space as a vacuum, but is it really? The article actually starts by saying:

When Charles Alcock peers up at the nighttime sky, he wonders not at the luminous stars but at the blackness that enfolds them. The Milky Way, Alcock knows, is like a sprinkling of bright sequins on an invisible cloak spread across the vastness of space. This cloak is woven out of mysterious stuff called dark matter . . .

In a brightly colored centerfold, the article goes on to proclaim that perhaps this "dark matter" is made up of Neutrinos, WIMPS, MACHOS, Black holes, or Bowling balls. Now, "Bowling balls" are defined – we kid you not – as: "Spherical objects used to knock down pins (astronomer's shorthand for ordinary matter in some hard-to-detect form)." Over the color centerfold is the caption: "What is most of the universe made of? Dark matter could be composed of any, some or none of these possibilities." A rather interesting way of saying we really have no idea. It then quotes Alcock, head of astrophysics at Lawrence National Laboratory in California as sighing when saying: "After all this time and all this effort we still don't know what most of the universe is made of." Quite interesting, don't you think! Especially so in light of the atheist philosopher's claim that when "you make a perfect vacuum" something is created from nothing. It happens all the time "in the physics lab."

Chapter 8: "From the World to God: The Cosmological Argument"

The cosmological argument claims – if true – to prove that contingent, limited, or finite existents in the physical universe show that there must be a God. It is an argument from efficient causality of "existential causality" which demands a ground in reality. Thomas Aquinas, correctly, tries to show – as we do – the assumption that there are no necessary beings whatever involves self-contradiction.

It is a mistake to say that the cosmological argument, if it proves anything, only proves the "god of the philosophers." The argument proves that "there can be only one such being" and once the "God of the argument" is understood and described, it becomes clear we are talking about the same attributes for this Being as stated in the Bible as describing the Christian God. It is also important to realize that the God of the argument must be able to account for all the positive attributes *in* the actual universe, e.g., personality, intelligence, creativity, love, etc., or else He is not, He cannot be the ultimate first, uncaused Cause of all that exists.

Further, we argue – throughout the first and second parts of this book – that an examination of the "here and now" physical universe shows it is not eternal. If this is true, then there must be a God not only to create it, but to (sustain) support it. We claim this presently existing universe actually tells us some very important facts about God's nature.

PART TWO

Evidence
from Science

Chapter Ten
THE LIMITS OF SCIENCE

Introduction: Importance of the Question
The Nature and Definition of Science
A Call for Constructive Dialogue

INTRODUCTION: IMPORTANCE OF THE QUESTION

If you will permit us a "small" tautology (after all, the world allowed Darwin a tautology – in the form of his theory of the survival of the fittest[1] – for over one hundred years), we will say that the place to begin this chapter is in the beginning. The beginning for this chapter involves two disclaimers as: (1) we are not, by way of academic training, *scientists*, nor are we (2) strictly speaking *philosophers of science*.[2]

Yet, we want to discuss "The Limits of Science." Now perhaps our two dis-

---

1. A "tautology" is a term used in logic which refers to needless repetition of an idea in a different word, phrase, or sentence; redundancy. To say "the world allowed Darwin a tautology" is to mean that really he did not come up with the idea of evolution. He certainly did not come up with it from experimentation, but from what he already thought was true. Then he simply "fashioned" a theory – the survival of the fittest – to explain what he already believed to be true. But how do we know that something is the "fittest," because it survives. And how do we know it will survive, because it is "fittest." Thus it is a tautology, i.e., just restating what you have already said in the subject of the sentence in the predicate only in different words. See chapter 17, "The Case of Darwinism."

2. The second is true because our three Ph.D.'s are not in the philosophy of science. At most American universities to be admitted into a Ph.D. program in philosophy of science one has to hold at least a bachelor's degree in a field of science, e.g., biology, chemistry, physics. Needless to say it would be helpful if *others* would make such appropriate disclaimers *in print* before they started "pontificating" on a subject.

claimers are *not* so condemning that you should close this book, arise from your seat and go out to "play ball" or something. For it turns out that the issues we are about to address are *very* important to the "average" Christian and that the issues also are not strictly speaking, in the modern sense, "science," nor have they ever been. Scientist Robert Gange, in his excellent book *Origins and Destiny*, writes: "Early in my scientific career I became impressed with the way differing world views influence how data is interpreted. I soon realized that *all conclusions require assumptions that are colored by philosophy*" [emphasis added]. Gange goes on to say:

> The problem we face in questions of origins and destiny is that our inquiry essentially involves one-time events that cannot be reproduced for our examination. We are free to design experiments whose data may be repeatedly examined, but it is an entirely different matter to realistically impute the results of those experiments to circumstances billions of years removed in time. Thus, as a practical matter, when something happens only once it becomes a matter for legal [I add, philosophical] rather than scientific inquiry. We can guess at what happened and use science to gather evidence to support one or another hypothesis. But science has no proper jurisdiction in matters of origin or destiny.[3]

This means that science as a modern methodology will not – cannot – solve the problems, answer the questions, inherent within this discussion.

It also needs to be clear from the beginning that we are not condemning science nor throwing out the proverbial baby with the bathwater. In this case the "baby" is science and the "bathwater" is the incorrect thinking and faulty conclusions of some scientists. There is much that could be said, and needs to be said, in a chapter like this which we will not have time to say. For instance, in the next chapter we will briefly outline the development of modern science (what we call "the new science" – what others call "the modern mind").

One could introduce evolution in terms of a historical perspective on the evolution of evolutionary ideas. A scholar's task, indeed any educated person's, is to contribute more light than heat to a discussion. We like what Woodrow Wilson said about the object of education:

> The object of a liberal training is not learning, but discipline and the enlightenment of the mind. The educated man is to be discovered by his point of view, by the temper of his mind, by his attitude towards life and his fair way of thinking. He is more apt to contribute light than heat to a discussion, and will oftener than another show the power of uniting the elements of a difficult subject in a whole

---

3. Robert Gange, *Origins and Destiny* (Waco, TX.: Word Books, 1986), pp. xiii, xv.

view; he has the knowledge of the world which no one can have who knows only his own generation or only his own task.[4]

We hope within the limitations of this section to accomplish this. We hope to make some clear statements of the real issues at hand in the seemingly never ending debate between science and religion.

THE NATURE AND DEFINITION OF SCIENCE

In large part what is at issue here is the very definition of "science." "The modern mind," or as we call it "the new science" defines what constitutes "science" in terms of a very restrictive methodology. "Science" is synonymous with the method of observing repeatable phenomena in a laboratory, i.e., the empirical method. Thus according to the *Oxford Dictionary*, Science "must involve proof and certainty, must not depart from what can be generated rigorously from immediate observation, and *must not speculate beyond presently observable processes*" [emphasis added].

Certainly, in the modern technical sense there is nothing wrong with these methodological limits. Our point is if science can, and should, only deal with repeatable phenomena via the empirical method; that is, their operational method has been justifiably limited; then scientists should not make absolute statements about truth (or say origins) in areas *outside* their very field of investigation, i.e., in history, religion, psychology, etc. Yet, it is true that historically, this is a woefully inadequate construal of science, and does indeed stick one with a methodic – if not a positively positivist – conception. This is especially true if scientists are going to make claims regarding the truth of something, or statements ruling out possibilities that are themselves outside the realm of their method. We are not saying here that there are not many important benefits from seeing science in the context of the modern laboratory method. It is, however, to say that to then allow "science" or scientists to make absolute statements about what absolutely did nor did not happen in prehistory is *not* in the province of its own methodology and definitional restrictions. Modern "Science" can no more rule the spiritual out of the natural than it can tell us what caused the world!

4. See Woodrow Wilson's *The Spirit of Learning* (1909) which is quoted in part in the *Phi Beta Kappa Handbook for New Members*, p. 4.

In the history of the Western world, science was defined as the search for truth about reality, all reality! This included not only the physical, but the metaphysical. It is also undeniably true that historically, modern science as we know it was born out of a Christian Metaphysic or world view. C. S. Lewis talking about the Uniformity of Nature, our belief that nature acts and will always act in the same way which is the basis for all science, says:

> This faith – the preference [in the Uniformity of Nature] – is it a thing we can trust? Or is it only the way our minds happen to work? . . . The answer depends on the Metaphysic one holds. If all that exists is Nature, the great mindless interlocking event . . . then clearly there is not the slightest ground for supposing that our sense of fitness and our consequent faith in uniformity tell us anything about a reality external to ourselves. . . . It can be trusted only if quite a different Metaphysic is true. If the deepest thing in reality, the Fact which is the source of all other facthood, is a thing in some degree like ourselves – if it is a Rational Spirit and we derive our rational spirituality from It – then indeed our conviction can be trusted.

Lewis goes on to say:

> The sciences logically require a metaphysic of this sort. Our greatest natural philosopher thinks it is also the metaphysic out of which they originally grew. Professor Whitehead points out that centuries of belief in a God who combined "the personal energy of Jehovah" with "the rationality of a Greek philosopher" first produced that firm expectation of systematic order which rendered possible the birth of modern science. Men became scientific because they expected Law in Nature because they believed in a Legislator. In most modern scientists this belief has died: it will be interesting to see how long their confidence in uniformity survives it.[5]

It is interesting to see the actual context of the quote that Lewis takes from Whitehead. In *Science and the Modern World*, Whitehead says:

> But for science something more is wanted than a general sense of the order in things . . . I do not think, however, that I have even yet brought out the *greatest contribution of medievalism to the formation of the scientific movement.* [emphasis added] How has this conviction been so vividly implanted on the European mind?
> When we compare this tone of thought in Europe with the attitude of other civilizations when left to themselves, there seems but one source for its origin. It must come from the medieval insistence on the rationality of God, conceived as with the personal energy of Jehovah and with the rationality of a Greek

---

5. C. S. Lewis, *Miracles: A Preliminary Study* (New York: Macmillian, 1947), pp. 108-109.

philosopher. Every detail was supervised and ordered: the search into nature could only result in the vindication of the faith in rationality. Remember that I am not talking of the explicit belief of a few individuals. What I mean is the impress on the European mind arising from the unquestioned faith of centuries. . . . My only point is to understand how it arose. My explanation is that the faith in the possibility of science, generated antecedently to the development of modern scientific theory, is an unconscious derivative from medieval theology.[6]

Whitehead actually makes the stronger statement / claim.

It is really when one defines the goal of "science" to be the discovery of explanatory truth*s* (not truth as it ought to be stated; by using the nonexistent plural for truth, one has already put oneself in a camp which is totally against the historic position of Western thought via even the possibility of a unified field of knowledge) about the *appropriate domain of reality* that we get into trouble. After all, who decides (and by what method) what constitutes "the appropriate domain of reality." Of course, if one accepts the positivistic definition then one is forced to limit science to the merely repeatable and observable physical world.

Thus part of the problem is a conception of science which confines "science" by its methodology. According to this view what constitutes "science" must be pursued under a variety of methodological constraints. Truth which does not pass the required methodological criteria is not a proper part of science; and therefore, by definition, is not true. Also topics for which the stipulated methodology is inappropriate (examples are history, psychology, religion, metaphysics, and anything which cannot be duplicated in a laboratory) are not scientific concerns. Except, of course, when a "scientist" wants to make a pronouncement in one of these above mentioned areas and then he or she is oftentimes considered an acknowledged expert. This view of science as defined *only* by its method has fallen into disfavor with many philosophers of science today.

Yet, the real problem even here is that some scientists themselves go beyond their own method to make claims to truth that their own methodological constraints do not allow. Creationists would have fewer grounds for quarrel with their "foes" (in alternatives, say, to flood geology) if they did not make "claims" about what mechanisms had *really* accounted for various observables, or what the age of the earth *really* was, or whether species had

---

6. Alfred North Whitehead, *Science and the Modern World* (New York: Mentor Books, The New American Library of World Literature, Inc., 1925), pp. 13-14.

really evolved out of ancestor species. In other words, if the method was in fact allowed to remain neutral as a method! It should be added here that Creationists must also allow the same neutrality of method, if the method is to be defined so narrowly.

But assume for argument sake that "the new science" or the empirical laboratory method of "the modern mind" is the only valid method of science. What does this tell us about origins? Answer: *nothing*! Donald M. MacKay, the well-known British scientist, in his *Science and the Quest for Meaning*, asks the question: Can science and technology provide an answer to the quest for meaning?

> My answer, as you can see, is ultimately "no." I don't, on the other hand, think they do anything to destroy the meaning of the mystery of our world when properly understood; and they do, I suggest, enlarge our understanding. . . . On ultimate questions of the meaning of the whole show, however, they are systematically silent, *because these are not scientific questions* [emphasis added]. But – and this is the point – the fact that they are not scientific questions doesn't mean that they are improper questions for the scientist or anyone else to ask as a human being. It means only that if they are to be answered, the answers will have to come from outside the system within which the game of science is defined. It's like chess-playing. If someone says, "Let's play chess," and someone else asks, "Why?" a question has arisen that the rules of chess are not framed to answer.
>
> What I've tried to show, in particular, is that Christian theism is far from being an enemy of science: it actually offers the most rational basis for the practice of science as but one aspect of the obedience that the creator requires of us and our world. There is no question of having to isolate Christianity from science in order to maintain peace between them. Rather, I suggest, they belong together as naturally as root and fruit: there is in principle an organic unity between biblical Christian faith and natural science.[7]

Once the scientist, so limited by his or her own method, stops doing repeatable laboratory experiments and recording results and starts talking about what these results mean in the context of the world he or she has taken off the "hat" of scientist and has in fact put on the "hat" of the "philosopher of science." And, once the scientist starts relating these experiments and findings to the question of origins he/she puts on the "hat" of "philosopher" or "theologian" with the same – or different – (but) metaphysical presuppositions nevertheless.

Given the nature of the scientific method, scientific theories about origin events,

---

7. Donald M. MacKay, *Science and the Quest for Meaning* (Grand Rapids: Eerdmans, 1982), pp. 30-31.

whether they come from creationist or evolutionist perspectives, are "more metaphysical than methodological." Hypotheses here are "often colored by one's outlook on life." There is a tendency to fit the facts to the theory – theories that are not subject to the kind of "seeing is believing" test of truth characteristic of operational science.[8]

That is to say the question of origins, whether one accepts "the new science" or not cannot strictly be a "scientific" question, but must of necessity be a metaphysical, historical, philosophical and theological question.

We should point out here that some "creation scientists" have perhaps themselves been too quick to accept the very limited methodological constraints of "the new science" or "the modern mind" as *the* only valid methodology of science, really for knowing truth. These creationists take their definition of science directly from the aforementioned one in the *Oxford Dictionary*. This, I believe, has gotten them into all sorts of trouble.[9]

Of course, the question remains: "Why insist that one should ignore certain sources of knowledge simply because they do not fall within some conventional boundaries of scientific methodology – especially when (so it is currently argued) those boundaries have been to great extent humanly and historically shaped?" Certainly if the real object of science is to get at the truth then *a priori* limitations, based on the method of acquiring information about the nature and history of the world, are a bit hard to understand.

But we must be clear: we are not condemning the empirical method as necessary for experimentation in the physical sciences. We certainly agree with biologist Pattle Pun here when he said that Operational or empirical science is a precise, though limited, method of understanding the natural world.[10] But we are saying that to say we can *only* have reliable knowledge, and therefore know truth, when a claim can be examined by way of the empirical method is to rule out of court vast ranges of reality as "unknowable" or as "untrue." A *priori* limitations on science – even by scientists as we will see in the case of Darwin himself – have often been misguided and counterproductive to real "science" and its search for truth.

---

8. Bill Durbin, Jr., "How It All Began: Why can't evangelical scientists agree?" *Christianity Today* (August 12, 1988), p. 36.

9. It has caused their positions to be tagged as thinly disguised religion (Kitcher and the Overton decision), as dishonest (by most critics) and as scientifically indefensible (by all but a very few critics), because it looks as though they simply have not produced what holding their present position would demand of them.

10. Bill Durbin, Jr., "How It All Began," p. 35.

A CALL FOR CONSTRUCTIVE DIALOGUE

We need to be "crystal clear." Atheist and theist alike, must realize once and for all that the issues involved in deciding the creation of the world and the Creator behind it; the existence of an all powerful, supremely loving God; are not issues which will or can be decided by the methods of modern science. These issues must be decided in other arenas, for example the claims of the Bible and the historicity of the text, a philosophical analysis of the evidence for God in the context of a world view, and the validity of religious experience also in the context of a world view, etc.

Why then do atheists and theists "fight" so on these issues, especially the scientists on both sides? Because these are very important issues that involve not just theoretical questions, but answers that will – must – have practical implications as to how we live. Because these issues and the answers are *so important* it is hard to divorce them from the emotionalism which often accompanies them. Because "emotional" issues are argued heatedly by those involved on either side. Because often we allow the emotional nature of the issue to effect our personalities and instead of expressing mutual respect, common sense, and a sincere desire to find truth within the limits of our present method or understanding, we start calling names, etc. Whatever the final answer to the question of the existence of God, it will *never* be arrived at in that way!

We must issue a clear call to reason; to dialogue; even to disagree, but agreeably; and perhaps most of all to respect each other and continue the dialogue at all costs! The importance of the question demands such action. Almost everyone with integrity realizes this and most will admit it if not forced to do so as if they were "revealing some great lack or sin in their lives."

I will always remember a very kind man, Wendy Lewis, the owner of a men's clothing store ("Spruce Up" in Lincoln, Illinois), whom I worked for in undergraduate school. He smoked! There was a "Bible college" in the town, an "angel factory" as it was often referred to by non-Christians in the community. Often one of the Bible college students would come into the store to buy clothes and started lecturing my boss about how bad smoking was for his health. He bristled and argued back as if his life depended on it, all the time with cigarette in hand. After the belligerent (all too often self-righteous student) would leave and my boss was not under attack, we would begin talking in a much more reasonable manner. He readily admitted that "smoking was bad for your health" and that I (also a student at the same Bible college) was wise in not taking up, or becoming "hooked," on the "filthy habit" as he called it. In my experience, very often the response we get is directly dependent on our approach, not necessarily on the content, or truth, of our argument. We must remember this![11]

---

11. See Appendix B in this book: "The Christian and Debate."

Chapter Eleven
GOD AND THE "NEW SCIENCE"

INTRODUCTION: IMPORTANCE OF THE QUESTION

As we saw in the last chapter, science certainly has its limits. Yet, some people believe that God has outlived His usefulness. It's an old, old story, but just as current as today's "new science." Carl Sagan, science popularizer and Professor of Astronomy at Cornell University, believes exactly that. He is on record over and over again, saying things like: "As we learn more and more about the universe there seems to be less and less for God to do."[1] But Professor Sagan is telling us *nothing new*. All he is relating is an old "philosophical" prejudice rather than "fact" which can be, or is, supported by science.

A seminary professor tells the story of being on a plane in 1969, just weeks before man's first landing on the moon. He was seated by a graduate student from Berkeley. When the Berkeley student found out the man next to him was a teacher in a theological seminary he flatly asserted: "I can't think of a more outdated field to be in than theology. With the prospects of man on the moon and the frontiers of knowledge being shoved back more and more by scientific discoveries, the idea of God becomes less and less valuable as a means of explaining the unexplainable."[2] This old ruse is actually centuries old! It was not original in 1969, nor is it in 1993.

---

1. See, for example, Carl Sagan, *Broca's Brain* (New York: Random House).
2. This story is recounted by Edward L. Hayes in *The Mount Hermon Log* (November/December 1988), p. 2

In fact, the opposite may be true for there is a whole new generation of scientists, and scientific facts, which seem to point to the grandeur of the Creator God more than ever before. What is accepted as scientific truth is constantly being refined and going through changes – as it should be. In our time, the recent period when science and scientists were "revered" almost as God or gods is (hopefully) over. It is time scientists stopped pontificating on behalf of their disciplines, as should we all! We are not "fighting" with science, but the scientist who insists on telling the world that there is no God because God cannot be studied in a test tube. On the other hand, the Christian scientists and the Christian community ought to respect the good, honest job that is being done by many many natural scientists.

We have great "faith" in science, and scientists (when they are educated beyond the narrow constraints of their particular branch of science) to help us discover truth about the physical world in which we live, and even to be fellow searchers after truth in the broader sense. Mistakes will be made, but that is part of the refining process. To refer, again, to biologist Pattle Pun, when empirical science is "practiced by the 'moral scientist' this approach to knowledge 'is self-corrective,' judging its conclusions by its own criteria."[3] We believe eventually this will broaden our understanding and lead us all closer to the Truth.

To do a thorough job of discussing the New Science one would have to start by analyzing the historical development of the revolution in Western thought and educational assumptions of the modern world from the *Graeco-Roman* or Classical *weltänschauung* which flourished until the fourth century A.D. through the triumph of the Christian world view which dominated Western civilization until the seventeenth century when the rise of modern science inaugurated a third way – "The Modern Mind." This we will have to leave up to the historians of the philosophy of science.[4]

Particular areas of scientific research, for example genetic science, have become so complicated *and* so potentially dangerous to us or our environment that many times the scientists themselves are turning to philosophers, ethicists, and theologians, to discuss and better understand their moral responsi-

---

3. Bill Durbin, Jr., "How It All Began," p. 36.
4. For a good, brief treatment see L.L. Woodruff, Editor. *The Development of the Sciences* (New Haven: Yale University Press, 1923; and also the philosophical classic by E. A. Burtt, *The Metaphysical Foundations of Modern Physical Science* (London: Routledge and Kegan Paul Limited, 1932).

bilities with regard to the research and application of such advanced technology. This is undoubtedly very positive! But we must still be very careful that we do not have foisted off on us what is really an "old prejudice" and not a "new science" at all.

THREE "SCIENTIFIC" WORLD VIEWS IN HISTORY[5]

Perhaps the best way to see the fact that the boundaries of science are culturally and historically shaped is to *very briefly* outline the metaphysical and "scientific" assumptions of the three world images that have controlled the Western world, i.e., Aristotle, Newton, and Einstein's world views. Every person has some sort of world image or over-all vision of the cosmos which serves as a framework within which individual day-to-day events take place. The primitive with his animistic view and the modern scientist with his mathematical view both conceive of some matrix and the processes by which events occur within the matrix in order to explain the phenomena which they observe. The image will be a product of the particular culture of each and will change and develop with advance of disciplined thinking within that culture. This development can be seen by comparing the cosmological images of Aristotle, Newton, and Einstein which evolved in our European culture.

Aristotle's World: This image with the Ptolemaic modification of astronomy was valid from the time of Aristotle until the time of Galileo.

1. There is a world. The scientist has confidence in empirical perception.
2. The world is made up of substantial, subsistent bodies, so distributed that the stable, opaque earth is the center of a system of concentric, transparent spheres on which the heavenly bodies are attached. The spheres move as spheres, thus moving the heavenly bodies.
3. Bodies are known intellectually through abstraction of their forms and species.
4. For every body there is a natural place which geometrically could be located by Euclidean geometry, thus supposing an absolute space.
5. Time is also absolute.
6. There is no empty space. Nature abhors a vacuum.
7. Bodies change in space and in quality.
8. Bodies are at rest by nature, and if moved, they are moved by another.

---

5. Miethe, *Living Your Faith*, pp. 101-105.

9. If a body is moved from its place, it returns to its place by the inherent qualities of lightness or heaviness, or at least seeks to do so.
10. Light (color), heat, and sound are immobile qualities of bodies. Through immediate or mediate contact with a perceiver the bodies communicate the qualities or forms. There is no action at a distance, i.e., action without contact of bodies. Force is resident in the bodies, which must be active by the fact that they *are*. Not all change is spatial. Bodies fall into four ultimate genera – fire, air, water, and earth.

Newton's World: This image, the outgrowth of the new scientific discipline of the Renaissance, was presented by Newton at the close of the 17th century.

1. There is a world. The scientist has confidence in empirical perception.
2. The world is made up of bodies in a Euclidean absolute space with much empty space.
3. Bodies are known empirically and in terms of their motion. They are not known by intellectual abstraction. (The image is thoroughly empirical and is not the half-hearted empiricism of Aristotle.)
4. Body is matter and matter is measurable in terms of a determined standard. This measurement is called the mass of the body.
5. Mass is inert. It is defined as the physical measure of a body's resistance to change of motion. It persists in a state of rest or of uniform motion unless a change is produced by an impressed force. Force is defined in terms of mass. Force is mass multiplied by acceleration, or mass resisting change of motion.
6. The average rate of motion of a body is measured by the distance divided by the time involved in the motion.
7. Space is Euclidean and absolute.
8. Time is absolute.
9. There is cosmic force, described as gravitational attraction, at work everywhere. Every particle in the universe attracts every other particle with a force which is directly proportional to the product of their masses and inversely proportional to the square of the distance between them.

$$F = \frac{k\,Mn}{d^2}$$

10. Heat, light, and electricity are corpuscular. The axiom of action at a distance is practically discarded, although the ether (Ether in physics is an invisible substance postulated as pervading space and serving as a medium for transmission of light waves and other radiant energy) would explain contact. The axiom that nature abhors a vacuum is definitely discarded.

This image was slightly modified by introducing the concept of energy, the source of force. Energy is the correlative of mass but not identical with it. The ether was also introduced into the space of the universe. The whole thing was utterly mechanical – matter and spatial motion explained all phenomena.

Einstein's World: This image is the current one and begins about 1915.

1. There is a world. The scientist has confidence in empirical perception.
2. The world is made up of a basic matrix in which events take place. Bodies are only observational events without or with a conscious observer.
3. There is no Euclidean absolute space. Space is three-dimensional (at least) and relative to an observer.
4. There is no absolute time. Time is the fourth dimension of events, necessitating a Riemannian multidimensional universe rather than the three-dimensional Euclidean universe, though Euclid is valid enough for events on our human plane.
5. The gravitation of Newton is not an attraction but acceleration caused by the only movement possible in the universe, curved movement. But the equation still remains $F = Kmn/d^2$ to a close approximation.
6. No body is at rest. All are in motion.
7. Energy is proportional to mass and mass is proportional to energy. According to the Newtonian image, a body in motion possessed an amount of energy equal to one-half the mass of the body multiplied by the square of its velocity. In the Einstein image, even a body at rest possesses energy, called rest energy, which is given by the formula $E = mc^2$, where "c" is the velocity of light. The speed of light is the observational absolute. Also, $m = E/c^2$. Of course, we all know that the new physics has not called into question Einstein's absolute, the speed of light.
8. Movement is not merely spatial. Mechanism cannot explain the universe as as whole.
9. The matrix of the universe is a field, quite real, though "immaterial." It is a continuum, knowable by four inter-dependent dimensions of time and space, finite and unbounded, studded by movement, and where two world lines of movement intersect, a material even is achieved to be recognized by an observer as mass or energy.
10. The absolutes in the system are: empirically, the speed of light; approximately 300,000 kilometers per second (186,000 miles per second); philosophically the space-time continuum which is the condition and limit of events. The system is wrongly called "relativity," because it is in reality a search for absolutes. (The absolute of light, as I have mentioned, has been challenged at the Princeton Institute of Advanced Studies and the Space Research Center.)

Thus, science is, to some extent, historically and culturally conditioned. Science and world views are continually in flux, as they should be. Let not the

Church make the mistake it made in the time of the Renaissance!

> Traditional theology had become almost inextricably intertwined with Aristotelian philosophy [and science we might add] and the earth-centered universe. Besides, the earth must be the centre, ran the argument, because it was the scene of Christ's coming. The sun must move because, according to the psalmist, "he rejoices to run his course." . . . The story is told that once a certain Father Scheiner mentioned to his superior that he had seen spots on the sun, to which he received the following reply: "You are mistaken, my son. I have studied Aristotle and he nowhere mentions spots. Try changing your spectacles." (quoted in A. E. E. McKenzie, *The Major Achievements of Science.* Cambridge University Press) So great was the authority of ["scientific"] tradition, that it could decide in advance what men might see.[6]

Likewise, we must not make the mistake of assuming that modern science has achieved an absolute definitive understanding of the universe, physical or metaphysical, therefore allowing it to tell us what could or could not have happened in the distant past or what method is the only valid one by which to discover truth.

THE CURRENT SITUATION

Many non-Christian scientists are beginning to see the implications of the limitations of their own methodology and also to be much more open to a view which not only allows, but seems to point to, the idea of a Creative Intelligence. This openness has been brought about *by* the directions in which the best of current scientific research seem to clearly point, that is away from a closed, entirely independent and self-supporting, mechanical system.

As with most – if not all – of the great "battles" in church history in the "theological arena," much of the problem in the "scientific arena" is with differences in personalities more than with the actual issues being fought over.[7] If each side could and would avoid "name calling," then much more constructive dialogue could happen as well as scientific advance, and perhaps even agreement regarding scientific truth. Thus, there is today, a great need for non-

---

6. T. M. Kitwood, *What is Human?* (Downers Grove: InterVarsity Press, 1970), p. 17.

7. This is not to say the issues are not important and that they do not play an important role, because certainly they do. But often the "heat" which results from how they are approached or "discussed" comes from personality differences between the opponents and not the issues in themselves.

Christian and Christian scientists to come together – even to the extent of establishing teams to do joint research, with the professional integrity each should – *must*– possess in dialogue as *each* is committed to "scientific" truth.

Yet, there certainly are atheist scientists who strongly push their "atheistic scientific religion." "The camera moves gracefully through a brilliant cloud of stars. Classical music swells, providing a majestic audio carpet for the journey. The voice of the astronomer purrs reverently, 'The Cosmos is all that is or ever was or ever will be.'" Many thousands of people have seen Carl Sagan's television programs on the universe. "Carl Sagan's vision of an eternal material universe wins a large audience, but does not correspond to the current scientific picture of a universe that began, will end, and likely not recur. Sagan's is a vision more religious than scientific."[8] This is exactly the point! Sagan's view turns out not to be a "new science," but an old prejudice!

When an atheist scientist starts pontificating, making "absolute statements," about questions that properly lie outside the parameters of his own science, then he has to base his conclusions on "evidence" other than his science, e.g., an "inspired text," theology, philosophy, and/or his own prejudice or presuppositions. These may be correct or incorrect. They would have to be examined, and a decision made, within the frame of the particular discipline to which he is ultimately appealing or within the frame of a larger world view and the criticisms of it. It must also be pointed out that this is equally true of the Christian scientist, or theistic scientist. Their claims must be verified in the content of where the best of modern science "points" in regard to issues that cannot be settled once and for all in a laboratory, the best evidence for and exegesis of the Bible, and the Christian world view.

Is there room for God in the scientific enterprise? The answer must be: *Of course there is*! In fact, as we have already said "Science," as science has *no right* to either (a) rule out of court the existence of the supernatural just because the natural cannot quantify it, or to (b) make absolute statements about the existence of something outside of its own defined methodology.

Again, as we have already shown by way of C.S. Lewis and Alfred North Whitehead, Christians can account for our belief in an orderly universe. Thus, "orderliness" in the universe is no argument for atheism. As we will see the clear indication of the best of modern science is that the space/time universe as we know it, as it is known to modern science is *not* eternal. All of the

---

8. Bill, Durbin, Jr., "How It All Began," pp. 31-41.

scientific evidence points to a beginning of the universe – the *Big Bang* theory.

Professor Robert Jastrow has done more than perhaps any other astronomer (Carl Sagan is also an astronomer, but an atheist) to announce the implausibility of the eternality of the material universe. Jastrow said: "Now three lines of evidence – the motion of the galaxies, the laws of thermodynamics, and the life story of the stars – pointed to one conclusion; all indicated that the Universe had a beginning."[9] The second law of thermodynamics says that the amount of available energy in the universe is decreasing. The fact that the universe is "running down" means it could not be eternal. We will look at the second law of thermodynamics in Chapter 13.

Jastrow's point is really that twentieth-century science has shaken faith in the universe as an eternal, independently operating mechanism. "The religious faith of the scientist is violated by the discovery that the world had a beginning in which known laws of physics are not valid, and as a product of forces or circumstances we cannot discover."[10] Again, it is very important to realize that the atheist scientist also has a "faith." The ultimate question is who's "faith" is "blind," the atheist or theist?

Science cannot give ultimate answers to question of the creation of the universe because this question goes beyond the empirical. As Jastrow writes:

> . . . the cause of the Universe cannot be investigated by the study of cause and effect *within* the Universe; or, quoting my friend Steven Katz, Professor of Religion at Dartmouth College, "The radicalism of modern science resides in its denial of teleological causation; but we must, however, recognize that teleology is a metaphysical concept, *whose ultimate reality cannot be affirmed or denied on the basis of empirical or scientific evidence.*[11]

Thus, modern science, as science, cannot decide questions of ultimate origins.

About the big bang, Professor Allan Sandage says: "Here is evidence for what can only be described as a supernatural event. There is no way to predict this in physics as we know it."[12] British theorist E. A. Milne, in his book on

---

9. Robert Jastrow, *God and the Astronomers* (New York: W.W. Norton, 1978), p. 111. See also Robert Jastrow, "The Astronomer and God," in the important book *The Intellectuals Speak Out About God*, edited by Roy Abraham Varghese (Chicago: Regnery Gateway, Inc., 1984), pp. 15-22.

10. Jastrow, *God and the Astronomers*, pp. 113-114.

11. Jastrow in "The Astronomer and God," p. 18.

12. Quoted from Allan Sandage's presentation during the conference entitled:

relativity, writes: " . . . as for the first cause of the universe that is left for the reader to insert, but our picture is incomplete without Him."[13] Physicist Paul Davies says: "The present arrangement of matter indicates a very special choice of initial conditions."[14] In other words, there seems to be a definite scheme, or great planning, even in regard to initial conditions. Stephen Hawking, a leading theoretical physicist, says: "If one considers the possible constants and laws that could have emerged, the odds against a universe that has produced life like ours are immense."[15] And on and on. In fact, for reasons we will address in the following chapters, even some recent scientists who are not avowed theists seem to be open to the possibility of Creative Intelligence.

Christianity Challenges the University, February, 1985. See also his short article: "A Scientist Reflects on Religious Belief," in *Truth,* Volume I, pp. 53-54.

13. Jastrow, *God and the Astronomers,* p. 112.

14. See Paul Davies, *God and the New Physics* (New York: Simon and Schuster, 1983).

15. Durbin, "How It All Began," p. 32.

Chapter Twelve
ORDER IN THE UNIVERSE:
THE TELEOLOGICAL ARGUMENT

INTRODUCTION: IMPORTANCE OF THE QUESTION

For many centuries, philosophers and scientists alike have argued for the existence of the theistic God on the basis of the great – truly wonderful – order we find in the universe. When we look at the physical universe we see an almost unbelievable orderliness and complexity there. In fact, modern science is now beginning to realize *just how complex* our universe really is. Though this argument is one of the traditional philosophical arguments for the existence of God, this chapter is placed here in the section on science: (a) because, more than any other argument, it has to do with the actual functioning of the physical universe and (b) because some major scientists have been converted to Christianity of late as a result, in part, of a renewed interest in, and analysis of, the order in the physical universe.

In 1985, we went to Dallas to participate in a series of panel discussions[1] entitled "Christianity Challenges the University: An International Conference of Theists and Atheists."[2] After the panel discussion in the natural sciences, we asked some of the Christian scientists who were relatively recent converts

---

1. This conference, and the four day series of panel discussions in philosophy, the natural sciences, the social sciences, the historical foundations of Christianity, culture, morality and education, were sponsored, in part, by The Institute for Research in Christianity and Contemporary Thought.

2. In fact, it was at this very conference in Dallas, Texas that I got the idea of challenging Antony G. N. Flew, perhaps the most famous living atheist philosopher

to Christianity what had played an important place in their conversion. The reply was the incredible design or order in the universe was overwhelming evidence for a divine plan and the existence of a Divine Planner. We then asked why this lead them to Christianity rather than a religion which accounted for the existence of the universe on the basis of an impersonal god. The answer: Because the amazing complexity of the physical universe was so intricate as to indicate a Divine Mind, a Divine Personality, behind the universe, not just a simple orderliness.

The word "teleology" comes from the Greek *telos*, "end," "purpose," and *logia*, "the study of" meaning the study of evidences of design in nature, of apparent order or purpose in the universe. Thus, the teleological argument is an argument for God's existence based on the premise that an undeniable relationship exists between the order and regularity of the universe and an intelligent Architect, a Designer of the world. In summary, it states that it is hard to deny that the universe seems intricately designed in ways necessary to support intelligent life. This purposeful order exists either by the intent of a designer or by a chance process, such as evolution. The universe, in other words, is either a plan or an accident. Since it cannot be an accident, it must be planned.[3] Our world is so ordered – means adapted to ends – that one must opt for the existence of God to explain it. This old argument, the design argument, is stronger today than ever.

WILLIAM PALEY'S TELEOLOGICAL ARGUMENT

William Paley (1743-1805), archdeacon of Carlisle, framed the most popular form of the argument.[4] He thought if he found a watch in an empty field, he would rightly conclude from its obvious design that there was a watchmaker. Similarly, when we look at the exceedingly more complex design of the world, we cannot help but conclude a great Designer is behind it. Paley's

---

who was one of the participants in the philosophy debate, to engage Gary R. Habermas on the question of the resurrection of Jesus. This debate was later published, see Terry L. Miethe, Editor, Gary R. Habermas, and Antony G. N. Flew, *Did Jesus Rise From The Dead? The Resurrection Debate*. San Francisco: Harper & Row, 1987, 190 pages.

3. Terry L. Miethe, *The Compact Dictionary of Doctrinal Words*, p. 202.

4. William Paley, *Natural Theology* (1802), abridged ed. by F. Ferré (Indianapolis: Bobbs-Merrill, 1963).

argument can be summarized thus:

1. A watch shows that it was put together for an intelligent purpose (to keep time).
   a. It has a spring to give it motion.
   b. It has a series of wheels to transmit this motion.
   c. The wheels are made of brass so that they do not rust.
   d. The spring is made of steel because of the resilience of that metal.
   e. The front cover is of glass so that one can see through it.

2. The world shows an even greater evidence of design than a watch.
   a. The world is a greater work of art than a watch.
   b. The world has more subtle and complex design than a watch.
   c. The world has an endless variety of means adapted to ends.

3. Therefore, if a watch calls for a watchmaker, then the world demands an even greater intelligent Designer (viz., God).[5]

In general, most philosophers have objected to Paley's argument. There have been several standard criticisms of the argument as we will see. Yet, Hume and Kant seem to have granted some weight to the teleological argument.[6]

OTHER FORMS OF THE ARGUMENT

The teleological argument for God's existence is an ancient argument. As an argument, it can be traced back to the ancient Greeks. Very early forms of the argument are found in Socrates (see Xenophan's *Memorabilia*, I, IV, 4ff.), Plato (*Phaedo*), Philo (*Works of Philo*, III, 182, 183, Sect. 33), and Thomas Aquinas (*Summa Theologica*, 1,2, 3) "fifth way."

In David Hume's *Dialogues Concerning Natural Religion*, the theist Cleanthes offers a form of the teleological argument.[7] Cleanthes' argument can be summarized as follows:

1. All design implies a designer.
2. Great design implies a great designer.

---

5. See Donald Burrill, *The Cosmological Argument* (New York: Doubleday & Co., 1967), pp. 165-170; Geisler, *Philosophy of Religion*, pp. 104-105.

6. Burrill, *Ibid.* p. 189.

7. *Ibid.*, pp. 171-176; Geisler, *Philosophy of Religion*, p. 105.

3. There is a great design in the world (like that of a great machine).
4. Therefore, there must be a great Designer of the world.

Cleanthes' argument goes beyond Paley's argument in several ways, for example: (a) He uses illustrations of design such as the human eye, male-female relation, a book, and a voice from heaven. (b) He makes it clear that the argument is an argument from analogy because like effects must have like causes. (c) He insists that irregularities in nature are exceptions to the rule and therefore do not affect the argument.

A. E. Taylor gave a much more involved form of the argument which he hoped would handle both the evolutionary and chance alternatives.[8] It can be summarized as follows:

1. Nature reveals an anticipatory order, i.e., it plans for its own preservation.
   a. Bodily need for oxygen is anticipated by membranes which exist to provide it.
   b. Many insects deposit eggs where food is available so their babies will have it to eat.
   c. A cat's movements are prospectively adapted to capture its prey.

2. Nature's advanced planning cannot be accounted for by physical laws alone, for there are countless ways electrons *could* run, but they *do* move in accord with the advanced planning of preserving the organism.
   a. This is true in both healthy and unhealthy organisms (cf. antibodies).
   b. On the basis of physical laws alone, misadaptations would be as probable as adaptations.
   c. Unless we retreat to the absurd, there must be something more than physical laws to account for the indefinitely high improbabilities involved.

3. Mind or intelligence is the only known condition (or agent) that can remove these improbabilities against life emerging despite these improbabilities.
   a. The human mind is direct evidence of anticipatory adaptation.
      1) Men plan ahead. (Even aged people [one might say especially aged people] make wills.)
      2) No jury considers a man guilty of first-degree murder unless he anticipated (planned) the result of his actions.
   b. Even scientists who reduce anticipation to complicated reflex action do not (cannot) live that way themselves. For example:
      1) They write books in hope that others will read them.
      2) They vote for a better future.

---

8. A. E. Taylor, *Does God Exist?* (London and New York: Macmillan, 1945).

4. The mind or intelligence that explains anticipatory adaptations cannot be explained as a result of evolution, for
   a. Mind is not a life-force that resulted from evolution and then took over and captured lifeless matter (since the advanced planning which gave rise to mind can only be explained as a result of Mind).
      1) We use tools which other minds make, but some mind had to make the tool to begin with.
      2) Likewise, the fact that mind can use nature as a tool assumes that the process of nature that produced mind is itself intelligently directed.
   b. The very appearance and persistence of species is impossible without preparatory adoption of the environment.
      1) With different chemicals, life would not have been possible.
      2) With the right chemicals and different conditions, life would not be possible.
   c. Therefore, either prospective adoption is meaningless or else there is a Mind beyond man that is guiding the whole process.

5. Darwinian natural selection cannot explain the advance planning evident in nature, for
   a. The fittest are not necessarily the best; the most stupid sometimes survive (e.g., a drunk in an accident).
   b. Even mutations imply design, since to make evolution work, mutations,
      1) must not be random and impartial but in trends, implying design;
      2) must be not small and gradual but large and sudden, indicating design.
   c. Darwinism does not explain, but merely presupposes, life with a preparatory environment.
   d. The human mind cannot be explained by survival of the fit or adoption to its environment, for
      1) there is no reason these adjustments should produce foresight in man;
      2) the human mind does not adapt to the environment but transforms it.
   e. Therefore, if mind was not totally produced by nature, then it must have been active in the producing of nature (since nature indicates advanced planning explainable only by intelligence).[9]

R. E. D. Clark, in his *The Universe: Plan or Accident?*, used the second law of thermodynamics[10] in another attempt to formulate a teleological argument as follows:

1. Whatever had a beginning had a Beginner.

---

9. *Ibid.*, pp. 209-232; Geisler, *Philosophy of Religion*, pp. 109-110.
10. Robert E. D. Clark, *The Universe: Plan or Accident?* (Philadelphia: Muhlenberg Press, and London: Paternoster Press, 1961); Geisler, *Ibid.*, p. 111.

2. The universe had a beginning (as evidenced by the second law of thermody-
    namics).
    a. The universe is "running down" and, hence, cannot be eternal.
    b. The second law applies to the whole universe so far as we know (this is
        still true in 1993).
    c. A "rewinding" of the universe on its own is not probable (for there is no
        scientific way to explain this).
3. Therefore, the universe had a Beginner.
4. This Beginner must be:
    a. intelligent, since He engaged in advanced planning, and
    b. moral, because He obviously valued creation.

The obvious fact of the argument is that since intelligence and morality are
essential to personality, the Designer of the universe must be personal.

Philosophers have generally considered this the weakest of all philosophical arguments for God's existence, thought it was the favorite argument of
Immanuel Kant. Kant, however, did not believe God could be proven rationally. Philosophers maintain that if the teleological argument proves anything, it
is only a cause big enough to explain the physical universe, not an eternal,
uncaused Cause of all that exists.

The general objections made against the teleological argument are as follows: (a) The argument makes it probable but not absolutely certain that there
is some kind of intelligence behind the design in the world. Chance is possible
though not probable. (b) The argument does not demand that the Designer be
absolutely perfect as must be the case with the Christian God. (c) The argument does not explain the existence of disorder, or evil, in the world. (d) It is
based on the cosmological argument because it claims that there must be a
cause for the design in the universe. (e) At best, it proves only a designer, not
the Designer.

THE ARGUMENT TODAY

As we said, several scientists who are recent converts to Christianity relate
that the teleological argument played an important role in the process. But
what gives this old argument such popularity today? They argue that the
complexity of the universe is so overwhelming today as to preclude any other
possibility than that a Divine Mind is behind it. The only possible explanation
of this, they go on to say, is what the Christians have always called God.
Some of the recent evidence of this very great complexity (and therefore real-

ly a continuation of teleology) will be discussed in chapter 15, "Information Theory and the Gene Code."

The case against chance-origins (and therefore in support of design) goes far beyond the loose analogies Christian apologists have often used, e.g., "of monkeys producing a line of Shakespeare by random typing, of the wind blowing a pile of letters into a sentence, or of a heap of metal molecules being shaken into a Volkswagen . . . ."[11] M. Golay calculates the chance production of the simplest living system at only one in 10^{450}. This means a number so large as to be one in ten with 450 zeros after it! Henry Morris figures the chance origin of life anywhere anytime in the universe is one in 10^{283}.[12] For all practical purposes this means a zero chance. When you take the longest (oldest) estimates of the age of the universe, there simply is not enough time for a chance origin in a world whose available energy is both limited and running out.[13]

Of course, some try to get around these unbelievable numbers by suggesting "luck." Some scientists have acted as if a lucky event or two could somehow account for all of the life that exists today.[14] But this seems to deify chance itself, calling for conclusions which are certainly not proven by the scientific data. This kind of "reasoning" is not only not scientific, but goes against everything which the atheist scientist holds in the strongest possible way, i.e., cause and effect and no chance whatever given such astronomical probabilities, in every other case but the supposed "chance" creation of the universe. Some atheists have been so naive as to argue: "Improbable as it might be on paper – well . . . here it [the universe] is, so it must have happened that way!" But that's simply begging the question.

Biologist Dean Kenyon once believed that molecules had some "built-in" tendency to form the special complexity of life. Now, he is convinced that life originated from "an intelligence capable of generating an enormous amount of complex information rather quickly."[15] But this great claim of a Super

---

11. William F. Luck, "How Probable is Chance?" in *The LodeStar Review* (October, 1987), p. 5.

12. Henry Morris and Gary E. Parker, *What is Creation Science?* (San Diego: Creation-Life, 1982), pp. 235ff.

13. See chapter 13: "A Finite Universe and the Second Law."

14. J. Huxley, *Evolution in Action*, p. 46.

15. In an interview with Kenyon by Bill Durbin, Jr. for *The 700 Club*, January, 1985.

Intelligence behind the physical universe is not limited to scientists who are recent converts to Christianity. Scientists Sir Fred Hoyle and Chandra Wickramasinghe, have been called two of Britain's most eminent scientists. They startled the scientific community with the announcement that their research showed that "there must be a God."[16] Hoyle once postulated a "Steady State" or continuous creation model for the physical universe in an attempt to avoid the implications of a beginning to the universe. Hoyle now says: "A common sense interpretation of the facts suggests that a superintellect has monkeyed with physics, as well as with chemistry and biology, and that there are no blind forces worth speaking about in nature."[17]

When it comes to intelligence, neuro-biologist and Nobel laureate Sir John Eccles (author of several noted books on the body-mind problem as well as over 500 scientific papers) sees the "interaction" between mind and brain as leading "to the extraordinary doctrine that this world of matter-energy is not completely sealed, which is a fundamental tenet of physics, but that there are small 'apertures' in what is otherwise a completely closed world."[18] Regarding conflict between science and religion, Sir John says:

> Science and religion are very much alike. Both are imaginative and creative aspects of the human mind. The appearance of conflict is a result of ignorance. We come to exist through a divine act. That divine guidance is a theme throughout our life; at our death the brain goes, but that divine guidance and love continues. Each of us is a unique, conscious being, a divine creation. It is the religious view. It is the only view consistent with all the evidence.[19]

Carl Sagan's "vision" of a self-contained material cosmos blurs as science begins to fine-tune a new image. The universe as we experience it is definitely not completely necessary and certainly does not seem to be self-explanatory. Today, it is very hard to believe the universe just happened by accident. "The

---

16. See "Science and the Divine Origin of Life," in *The Intellectuals Speak Out About God*, pp. 23-38.

17. Fred Hoyle, "The Universe: Past and Present Reflections," *Engineering and Science* (November 1981), pp. 8-12.

18. John Eccles in a paper delivered at a conference entitled: "Artificial Intelligence and the Human Mind," at Yale University, March 1-3, 1986. See also Bill Durbin, Jr.'s article on this conference in *Christianity Today* (April 4, 1986), pp. 48-49.

19. See "Modern Biology and the Turn to Belief in God," a discussion with Sir John Eccles in *The Intellectuals Speak Out About God*, pp. 47-50.

special design of its internal structures – from vast galaxies to microscopic proteins – indicates a 'createdness,' to use historian of science Stanley Jaki's word. Our world appears dependent upon a context beyond itself"[20] to account for its existence.[21]

20. Bill Durbin, Jr., "How It All Began," p. 32. Jaki's 1978 book, *The Road of Science and the Ways to God*, was called "the publishing event of the year."

21. Stanley Jaki has many writings on the topic of "createdness" and theology and science in general. See Stanley L. Jaki, *Cosmos and Creator* (Edinburgh: Scottish Academic Press, 1981; Chicago: Regnery Gateway, 1982) and *Angels, Apes and Men* (La Salle, IL.: Sherwood Sugden and Company, 1983). See also Jaki, "From Scientific Cosmology to a Created Universe," in *The Intellectuals Speak Out About God*, pp. 61-78, reprinted from *The Irish Astronomical Journal* 15 (March 1982), pp. 253-262. Jaki's comprehensive account is *The Road of Science and the Ways to God* which comprised his Gifford Lectures of 1975-1976.

Chapter Thirteen
A FINITE UNIVERSE
AND THE SECOND LAW

Introduction: Importance of the Question
The Importance of the Second Law of Thermodynamics

INTRODUCTION: IMPORTANCE OF THE QUESTION

There are several "basic laws" of science, i.e., principles which are observed to be universal (apply everywhere) in the universe. To be accurate here, we should add that these laws are said to be universally applicable in the known or observed universe. In fact, this is how some try to get around the implications of the second law of thermodynamics, i.e., by saying that: "Yes, it applies in the whole of the known universe, but it may not apply – or work – in the part, or part of the part, of the universe we do not know, or have not observed. But this is bad logic and bad science. (1) In logic this is called arguing from silence. It is a logical fallacy because you can never argue to the positive truth of anything from nothing, from silence. (2) It is a scientific "cop-out" because there is absolutely no evidence in the known universe (and, importantly, we add in our constantly expanding knowledge of the universe) that this law doesn't apply universally. All our present physical science, and the implications of it, are based on the premise that the law is universal.

There are actually *two* laws of thermodynamics, the first and the second. The first law of thermodynamics involves laws of energy and mass conservation.

The law of energy conservation states that in a closed system [which the Atheist *must* maintain and seek to support], in any transformation of energy from one form of energy into another (and everything that happens involved such energy transformations), the total amount of energy in the system remains unchanged. No energy is either created or destroyed. A similar law is the law of mass conservation, which states that although matter may be changed in state, density, or form, its total mass is unchanged. In other words, these basic laws teach that no creation or destruction of matter or energy is now being accomplished anywhere in the physical universe. Since matter and energy are themselves interchangeable under certain conditions, the two laws can be combined into the principle that the total of mass-plus-energy is conserved.

This, first law of thermodynamics, is "generally recognized as the most important and basic law of science."[1]

The second law of thermodynamics deals with the corollary principle of mass and energy deterioration. In any energy conversion, although the total amount of energy remains unchanged, the amount of usefulness and availability that the energy possesses is always decreased. This is also called the law of entropy. "Thus, in any isolated system (that is, a system from which all external sources of energy are shut off), the energy of the system is conserved in quantity but is continually being degraded in quality as long as any energy change is taking place in the system." This is because some available energy is constantly being dissipated as nonrecoverable friction. Every activity in nature, including biological ones, has this resultant loss of heat energy. Thus, "there is an ever-decreasing supply of usable energy for maintaining all natural processes in the universe as a whole."[2]

This is, of course, why we cannot construct any machine with 100 percent efficiency. For example most internal combustion engines have only about a 23 percent or less efficiency. Because of this law of entropy, that is the fact that the sun's energy is dissipating in space in the form of unrecoverable heat energy, scientists theorize that eventually the sun will grow cold, or "burn itself out." Not to worry; this will not happen for many hundreds of millions of years. As we have said, this law applies everywhere in the universe and is therefore true of all stars.

THE IMPORTANCE OF THE
SECOND LAW OF THERMODYNAMICS

Now we need to examine, however briefly, the implications of just one of the lines of evidence Professor Jastrow mentioned – the second law of

---

1. Henry M. Morris, *Science and the Bible*. Revised and Expanded. (Chicago: Moody Press, 1986), p. 17.

2. *Ibid.*, p. 18.

thermodynamics.[3] According to the second law of thermodynamics, in a closed system the amount of usable energy is constantly decreasing. This is exactly the type of system the materialist must conceive the whole universe to be. That is, there is a heat loss. This process is going on throughout the whole universe as nuclear fission occurs.

But if the universe is "running down" then it must have had a beginning. "If it is growing old, it must once have been young; if it is wearing out, it must first have been new; if it is running down, it must originally have been 'wound up.' "[4] In Professor Jastrow's words:

> Now we see how the astronomical evidence leads to a biblical view of the origin of the world. The details differ, but the essential elements of Genesis are the same: the chain of events leading to man commenced suddenly and sharply at a definite moment in time, in a flash of light and energy.[5]

The implications of the second law of thermodynamics apply just as well to the biological realm. "In biology, an important example is found in the agencies supposed to bring about evolution; that is, gene mutation." Much recent evidence indicates that gene mutations may not only be neutral to evolutionary change, but many times are actually harmful. This is true because mutations "represent a breaking down of the highly structured arrangement of the genes in the germ cell."

> Evolutionists still may insist that the law of increasing entropy does not preclude evolution since biological systems are "open" systems and can draw enough energy from the sun to support an upward evolution. That is nonsense, however, since the equations of thermodynamics clearly show that an influx of raw heat energy (as from the sun) into any open system (say, like the earth) will increase the entropy (or decay) of that system more rapidly than if it were an isolated system.[6]

Certainly, we find birth and growth in the biological world. But clearly within what may appear as ever "building up" is ultimate decay and death. Being over forty, we simply cannot do some of the things we could do at twenty as well or as quickly – however much we tell ourselves we can! Yes, the human body can be maintained, and even improved for a while; for example, at thirty-five one of us could run thirteen miles without stopping and

---

3. See page 122 of this book.
4. Morris, *Science and the Bible.*, p. 19.
5. Jastrow, *God and the Astronomers*, p. 14.
6. Morris, *Science and the Bible,* p. 60.

certainly could not do this at eighteen or twenty. But as much as I try to condition my body eventually the constant decay will be visible and *permanent*. It is said that Descartes thought if he could live long enough, he could find the cures for all diseases and could thereby maintain his life indefinitely. Unfortunately, he caught cold and died! I will die someday as well, and so will you.

Some scientists had hoped to find a source for fresh hydrogen atoms coming into the universe which would maintain it in a steady state.[7] But no observational evidence for the coming into existence of such atoms has been found. In fact, scientists have recently discovered what is called "the radiation echo" (see chapter 14) of the original blast at the beginning of the universe. A Nobel Prize has been awarded for this discovery in 1978.[8] But even if a source for fresh hydrogen atoms were found, the source would have to be examined for these created "fresh hydrogen atoms." If anything, this would seem to indicate some creative Force beyond the universe, not the naturalistic, mechanistic universe of the atheist.

Some have postulated that black holes are sucking up the energy and returning it as quasars.[9] This is purely speculative. There are many conflicting theories in regard to exactly what a "quasar" is and where they are located. Even if this were true you would not have the totally recoverable system that one would need to invalidate the second law of thermodynamics. The fact is that the second law applies in all the known universe. But if the universe will eventually collapse then the cornerstone of atheism will also collapse with it. For if the universe is not eternal, then traditional atheism faces an utter lack of rational explanation.

This dilemma was put well by the British scholar, Anthony Kenny, when he wrote: "According to the big bang theory, the whole matter of the universe began to exist at a particular time in the remote past. A proponent of such a theory, at least if he is an atheist, must believe that the matter of the universe

---

7. This, as was mentioned on page 132, was Sir Fred Hoyle's former view.

8. A Nobel Prize in physics to Robert W. Wilson and Arno A. Penzias, Bell Laboratory scientists, in 1978.

9. See Rick Gore, "The Once and Future Universe," *National Geographic* 163(June 1983), pp. 704-749; Stephen P. Maran, "What Makes Quasars Shine?," *Natural History* (December 1983), pp. 76-79; "The Quasar Debate," *Astronomy* (June 1983), p. 62; "What is a Quasar?," *Science Digest* (January 1983), p. 95.

came from nothing and by nothing."[10] But, as we have seen[11], this is philosophically contradictory and scientifically ridiculous.

The embarrassing situation the atheist finds himself in has been stated very well by Professor Jastrow:

> For the scientist who has lived by his faith in the power of reason, the story ends like a bad dream. He has scaled the mountain of ignorance; he is about to conquer the highest peak; as he pulls himself over the final rock, he is greeted by a band of theologians who have been sitting there for centuries.[12]

While our "faith" is not vested in the power of reason (for the Christian, our hope rests in nothing less than Jesus and His righteousness), yet certainly, we all must live within the limits of the power of reason. But the eternal question is: "What does reason tell us?" One thing is certain, that is the view maintained on the basis of the religion of scientific naturalism which casts out, or denies, the possibility of the supernatural or the existence of God is not being honest in terms of living within the power of reason. There is much evidence to point away from naturalism and to theism!

---

10. Anthony Kenny, *The Five Ways: St. Thomas Aquinas' Proofs of God's Existence* (New York: Schocken Books, 1969), p. 66.
11. See chapter 7: "Can Something Come from Nothing?"
12. Robert Jastrow, *God and the Astronomers*, p. 15.

Chapter Fourteen
THE RADIATION ECHO:
"NOISE" OF THE BIG BANG

Introduction: Importance of the Question
What Happened After the Big Bang
Problems in the Big Bang for Atheists
The Anthropic Principle

INTRODUCTION: IMPORTANCE OF THE QUESTION

In 1978 a Nobel Prize in physics was awarded to Robert W. Wilson and Arno A. Penzias. They discovered an "extra noise" in the universe. But this was no ordinary noise. Wilson and Penzias, working for Bell Laboratories, were using a large, horn-shaped device to identify all the radio sources outside our own galaxy. However, after they had identified all the noises they could, there was one left over. Eventually they came to realize that they were not picking up a noise, but rather, the 3° Kelvin radiation that is a necessary part of the Big Bang Theory. It was for discovering this event and, in the eyes of some, validating the Big Bang Theory, that they shared a Nobel Prize. According to Soviet physicist Jacob Zel'dovich: "We can regard the Big Bang model to be as well established as celestial mechanics."[1]

Though – as we acknowledge throughout this section of the book on science – "It never pays to base a philosophical position on what scientists do not know,"[2] we can see where the best of modern science seems to point. This statement is simply to remind us that ultimately questions of origin are philo-

---

1. David M. Schramm, "The Early Universe and High Energy Physics," in *Physics Today*, 36 (April 1983), p. 28.
2. James S. Trefil, *The Moment of Creation* (New York: Charles Scribner's Sons, 1983), p. 178.

sophical (metaphysical) and theological questions, not scientific ones *per se.*

According to most Big Bang Cosmologists, the universe is approximately sixteen billion years old,[3] although some will cite as great a range of flexibility as eight to nineteen billion years. Most cosmologists do not consider this uncertainty very important, though.[4] The big question, of course, is whenever it occurred, what caused the Big Bang? How did the universe spring from nothing?

The first part of the answer could lie in the physicists idea of a vacuum. According to the modern quantum theory a vacuum is not really empty but is actually teeming with subatomic particles fluctuating between being and non-being. The particles come into existence for a fraction of a second by borrowing on the energy base of a field.[5] These particles almost immediately "blink" out of existence, leaving nothing behind. In this way, what appears to be a placid vacuum is actually swarming with subatomic particles.[6] Of course, the atheist scientist still has the problem of accounting for the "energy base," the "field" and the "subatomic particles."

One possible way the universe may have "banged" into being would be if gravity could somehow intensify a particle-wave[7] until it became the fireball from which the universe came.[8] Many physicists do not buy into this theory for one probable reason. The event described must take place in space, and most cosmologists believe space came into being at the Big Bang. However, other physicists say that gravity and space-time are subject to the quantum factor. Thus if particles can spontaneously appear, so could space-time and gravity.[9] But too much weight must not be placed on the accuracies of such theories. A brief amount of study in the Big Bang Theory will reveal that the farther back one gets – the closer to the actual Bang – the less accurate the theory becomes. Even the author who lists such theories says they could be called "guesses."

---

3. M. Mitchell Waldrop, "Going With the Flow," *Science* (8 Feb. 1985), p. 622.

4. Trefil, *The Moment of Creation*, p. 12.

5. Paul Davies, "Birth of the Cosmos," in *Current* (May 1983), p. 7.

6. Heinz R. Pagels, "Before the Big Bang," in *Natural History* (April 1983), p. 26.

7. In quantum physics particles have both wave and traditional particle characteristics. Paul Davies, *God and the New Physics*, p. 161.

8. Pagels, "Before the Big Bang," p. 26.

9. Trefil, *The Moment of Creation*, p. 34.

WHAT HAPPENED AFTER THE BIG BANG

At this point it would probably be best to give a rundown of the general chronological events immediately following the Big Bang before a closer look is taken at any of the stages or problems within the stages. As will soon become apparent, the very early stages of the Big Bang replaced each other with great rapidity. All of the times given are extremely arbitrary and ill-defined.

The first major state after the Big Bang is when, according to the Grand Unification Theory (GUT), energy and matter separate. Prior to this separation the "bosons," which will make up the energy particles, and the "quarks," which will make up the matter particles, are interchangeable. At present no time has been given to the end of this stage.[10]

The second stage ends at 10^{-43} second after the Big Bang. In this stage gravity breaks off from the still unified other three energies – electromagnetic, strong, and weak (strong and weak operate at the sub-atomic level only).[11] By 10^{-35} second the "electroweak" force and the strong force have separated. By the 10^{-10} second stage the electromagnetic and the weak force have separated. Between the end of this stage and .001 second particles form the quarks. Between .001 second and three minutes nuclei form. Nuclei are made up of the combination of protons and neutrons. It is the nuclei which provide the primary mass component of atoms.[12]

The next stage, known as the plasma and nuclei stage, takes a whopping 500,000 years. This stage, as all the others, is marked by a cooling of the universe. At the beginning of this stage the temperature of the universe is so high that electrons cannot stay attached to nuclei. Because of this, atoms cannot form and there is thus no way for matter as we know it to form. This chaotic pre-substance is known as plasma. This substance can be made in a laboratory and is found at the centers of stars. As the plasma and nuclei stage wear on, the temperature of the universe cools to the point where substantial matter can be formed. This is the beginning of the present era.[13]

---

10. *Ibid.*
11. For a discussion of these forces see *Ibid.*, Chapter 5.
12. Trefil, *Ibid.*, p. 34.
13. *Ibid.*

PROBLEMS IN THE BIG BANG FOR ATHEISTS

The Big Bang theory, like all other theories, is not without problems. One of the more immediate problems which needs to be dealt with is the matter/anti-matter problem. In theory and experimentation whenever energy is converted into matter at least two particles are formed, a particle of matter and its corresponding antimatter counterpart. In this scenario, when energy is concentrated and converted into an electron, another particle is always formed. This corresponding particle is called a positron and has the same mass as an electron, but has a positive electrical charge instead of the electron's negative charge.

Immediately after formation, the two corresponding particles "fly off" in approximately opposite directions. Should the two ever "bump" into each other, or any particle like their opposite, immediate annihilation occurs; their mass is converted into energy. This occurs whenever any form of matter particle (protons, electrons, etc.) meet their antimatter counterpart (antiprotons, positrons, etc.). The problem is this, if energy was the primary cause of the creation of matter in the universe, as is presumed, then there should be just as much matter as antimatter. And if matter and antimatter were created in equal amount, why did they not just "bump" into their many counterparts and be turned back into energy?

Early in theorizing about the Big Bang it was thought that maybe a matter/antimatter repulsive force was acting to keep the two apart and drive them to opposite ends of the universe. There are two problems with this theory. The first problem is that there is no evidence that matter and antimatter could ever repel each other, and in fact, just the opposite occurs; opposites attract. If such a force is said to have existed at the Big Bang, two more explanations need to be thought up: Where did it come from? And, where did it go?

Before answers to these questions could be thought of an inescapable problem was encountered; the universe is blatantly anti-antimaterial.[14] It is not just our part of the galaxy that is materially inclined. (If it were not, we would be quite aware of the fact due to the explosions which would be constantly going on around us.) It seems that the entire universe is made up primarily of matter. This is made apparent by the constant radiation which bombards our atmosphere from all over the universe. Of the rare antiprotons which hit our atmo-

---

14. Michael Guillen, "The Paradox of Antimatter," *Science Digest* (February, 1985), p. 35.

sphere it is believed almost all were created en route from the high energy collisions with other particles throughout space.[15]

The material bias is also apparent from the lack of a "Leidenfrost layer." A Leidenfrost layer is formed, for example, when drops of water dance across a hot skillet. The evaporation of water on the drop's underside creates a steam layer, the Leidenfrost layer, which insulates the rest of the drop from the heat of the pan and keeps the droplet around much longer than should be expected. In the same way, it is assumed that if large territories of matter and antimatter were to cross paths, a different type of Leidenforst layer would form.

In this case, a layer of gamma and X-rays would form between the two territories, acting as the "steam" and delaying the annihilation. However, rocket and satellite X-ray astronomy has been unable to locate a single extended source of X-rays which could be a Leidenfrost layer. This makes the repulsive theory highly unlikely.[16]

The only solution remaining to the matter/antimatter problem is that there has always been more matter than antimatter. Currently there is a complex theory, with some evidence in support of it, that there has always been such an imbalance. According to this theory, which is too complicated to be dealt with here, for every one-billion antiparticles created by the Big Bang, one-billion-and-one particles were created. This is enough of an imbalance to cause the particle imbalance and predominance we now see.[17] Of course, this still does not explain the imbalance which is so very important to supporting and sustaining the existence of matter.

There are a number of other problems which seem to have a common solution. The first of these is the *uniform explosion* problem. If a telescope is aimed at any region of space, the viewer will discover an almost disconcerting sameness. Galaxies seem to populate space with a remarkably constant density. The expansion rate of the universe does not seem to vary whether one looks at the "local" region or to the visible edge of the universe. And the universe as a whole is bathed in a thermal radiation left over from the Big Bang, i.e., the radiation echo.

No matter which direction is observed, the radiation coming from that region is "astonishingly uniform." The problem is this: Why was the Big Bang so uniform? Why was it not turbulent and chaotic like an ordinary

---

15. *Ibid.*, pp. 35-36.
16. Trefil, *The Moment of Creation*, pp. 39-40.
17. See Trefil, *Ibid.*, pp. 171-175 for details of this theory.

explosion? If a large chunk of gunpowder blew up the odds would be infinitesimal against it scattering debris evenly in all directions, with each piece of debris moving at the same rate and the surrounding area being heated evenly. Why was the Big Bang different?[18]

The second problem is called *flatness*. This is represented by the Greek capital letter omega, Ω, which represents the ratio of the total gravitational pull of all the mass in the universe compared to the initial force exerted by the Big Bang. Had the gravitational pull been too much greater the universe would have collapsed on itself. If the gravitational force is too great the universe is considered closed. But if the Big Bang has been too forceful, the matter would have dispersed too quickly and galaxies could never have formed. Then the universe would be considered open.

The problem is this: Omega is so close to one that fifteen billion years later we still do not know if the universe is open or closed. Scientists still do not know if the universe will continue expanding forever, or if it will eventually begin to collapse back toward itself. Omega is now figured to be within 50 decimal places (10^{-50}) of one.[19]

The third problem is known as the *monopole* problem. It is named after one of the spatial disturbances which should have accompanied the Big Bang's cooling process. Although this problem is too complicated to be dealt with in this short chapter, suffice it to say that the slower the rate of expansion, the more monopoles which should have been formed; and it is questionable if a monopole has ever been found.[20]

A number of theories with the same basic idea have been proposed to explain these problems. The solutions are known as inflationary theories. According to the inflationary theories the universe underwent a phase of "immense expansion" very early in its life when its temperature was still about 10^{15} degrees Kelvin. If the entire universe was in close contact one moment and extremely far apart the next, the constant temperature of the universe is explained. The inflation theories also explain the other properties of the universe's sameness, as well as its flatness but the solutions are too involved to be treated here.[21] Another possible solution to the flatness prob-

---

18. Davies, "Birth of the Cosmos," pp. 4-5.

19. Davies, *Ibid.*, p. 5; Schramm, "The Early Universe and High Energy Physics," p. 7.

20. For a detailed explanation of the monopole problem, see Paul Davies, "Relics of Creation," *Sky and Telescope* (February 1985), pp. 112-115.

21. See Trefil, *The Moment of Creation*, pp. 178-181 for details.

lem, along with many other concerns, will be presented later in this chapter dealing with the anthropic principle.

The inflation theory has its greatest success in answering the monopole problem, since monopole is a result of slow cooling. The answer lies in the fact that as the universe expands it necessarily cools. The faster the expansion, the faster the cooling. The faster the cooling, the fewer the monopoles.

THE ANTHROPIC PRINCIPLE

As mentioned, there is another theory which has been suggested to solve the problems listed previously. In addition it accounts for a number of other nice "coincidences." This theory is known as the "anthropic" (from the Greek *anthropos*, meaning man) principle. Among the coincidences mentioned in regard to the anthropic principle is the structure of the atomic nuclei. The nuclei are held together by a highly balanced force. If the force were reduced by only a few percentage points, it would cause the simplest composite nucleus, that of *deutrium* which contains one proton and one neutron, to fly apart. If this happened all the stars, including our sun, would be in "severe difficulties" since they use deutrium in their fuel chain. But if the nuclear force were very slightly stronger an even worse event would occur; two protons could possibly stick together (the force is not actually strong enough for this to occur). If this were possible, at the Big Bang all the free protons would have matched up. There would have been no single protons left to make hydrogen, the building block for stars.

Another delicate balance is between electromagnetism and gravity. Electromagnetism provides the support which keeps the star from collapsing on itself from its own gravity. A minute shift in the balance would cause all stars to become either blue giants or red dwarfs. The point the anthropic principle makes is that the universe is full of these very important "coincidences." This leads to the anthropic principle; the idea that life will arise only in those universes in which conditions are suitable and it is only in these universes that anything can be contemplated.

But the contemplations will be limited by the fact that the existence of the contemplators places constraints on what sort of world they can perceive. This "observer-oriented" approach to the basic cosmological questions is quite different from the traditional scientific approach. Traditionally the observer plays no part, but in today's new physics man plays "an essential role in determining the nature of the world he observes with increasing amazement."[22] It is this increasing amazement which has led many astronomers and physicists to change the anthropic principle somewhat, and announce with Sir Fred Hoyle that "there must be a God."[23]

It has only been in the last hundred years – really less – that scientists have been talking about scientific cosmology.[24] Of recent developments, Stanley Jaki writes:

> Is it reasonable to assume that an Intelligence which produced a universe, a totality of consistently interacting things, is not consistent to the point of acting for a purpose? To speak of purpose may seem, since Darwin, the most reprehensible procedure before the tribunal of science. *Bafflingly enough, it is science in its most advanced and comprehensive form – scientific cosmology – which reinstates today references to purpose into scientific discourse* [emphasis added]. Shortly after the discovery of the 2.7° K radiation cosmologists began to wonder at the extremely narrow margin allowed for cosmic evolution. The universe began to appear to them more and more as if placed on an extremely narrow track, a track laid down so that ultimately man may appear on the scene.[25]

Thus it is "no wonder that in view of this quite a few cosmologists, who are unwilling to sacrifice forever at the altar of blind chance, began to speak of the anthropic principle." They seemingly were forced by their own findings to formulate this "principle of man." This is because it seems more and more like the universe "may have after all been specifically tailored for the sake of man."[26] In reality, this is a very old philosophical view. In fact, a central tenet of Thomas Aquinas' philosophy is that the universe was created for the sake of man.[27] But as Jaki reminds us: "It must not however be forgotten that such a tenet, or the anthropic principle, can never be a part of scientific cosmology. Science is about quantitative correlations, not about purpose."[28]

---

22. Paul Davies, "The Anthropic Principle," *Science Digest* (October 1983), p. 24.

23. Roy Abraham Varghese, *The Intellectuals Speak Out About God*, pp. viii, 23-37.

24. There are several forms of the anthropic principle. A "weaker" version is sometimes employed which does not require God's existence. 52
See "From Scientific Cosmology to a Created Universe," by Stanley L. Jaki in *The Intellectuals Speak Out About God* edited by Roy Abraham Varghese (Chicago: Regnery Gateway, Inc., 1984), pp. 61-78.

25. *Ibid.*, p. 71.

26. Jaki, *The Intellectuals Speak Out*, p. 72.

27. See "Thomism," in Miethe's *The Compact Dictionary of Doctrinal Words*, pp. 206-207.

28. Jaki, *The Intellectuals Speak Out,* p. 72.

Chapter Fifteen
INFORMATION THEORY AND
THE GENE CODE

Introduction: Importance of the Question
What is "Information Theory?"
What Does Information Theory Tell Us?
Where Do We Go From Here?

INTRODUCTION: IMPORTANCE OF THE QUESTION

By this late date in the twentieth century, we hope most of us are well aware (though unfortunately we have reason to doubt this) that evolutionary theory has "retreated" over and again in an attempt to explain the most complex of living things by chance evolution or by an evolution which is "self-ordering." Finally, evolutionists came to the idea that life comes from nonlife and this can be seen on the smallest level, that is spontaneous generation of life on the scale of the protein molecule. As Scientist Robert Gange writes:

> Then came the twentieth century and we were told science had the answer. And many believed the new story: "Life was created by a chance combination of chemicals." But was it true? Had we finally found the level at which non-life spontaneously generated into life? As long as this level remained unseen, people could believe the answer was yes. But, with the advent of electron microscopes and information theory, the *answer changed to no.*[1] [emphasis added]

The calculation necessary to learn whether life could have come about by accident was not possible until rather recently because we needed both "insight from information theory and the data from electron microscopy."

---

1. Robert Gange, *Origins and Destiny* (Waco, TX.: Word Books, 1986), pp. 69-70.

Gange writes:

> Although the mathematical tools necessary to interpret the data from electron microscopy had been discovered a decade earlier, as a practical matter realistic knowledge of the microstructure of cellular systems wasn't available until the early sixties. Thus if we believed life was an accident, before 1960 no one could prove us wrong. Today that's changed. For the first time in history we can *calculate* the "next unseen, smaller level." The result is this: *To get life, you need life. Nothing less will do. Anything else is wishful thinking.*[2] [emphasis added]

This is so incredibly important because this view of the evolution of life from nonlife is not only the most recent but by far the most sophisticated to date. If evolution reaches a "dead-end" scientifically, where do we go from here? Perhaps in the direction that atheists resist, it seems, at all costs.

WHAT IS "INFORMATION THEORY?"

There are still many, more important recent scientific advances which show materialism to be causally bankrupt. Information theory is but one of them.[3] "Since about 1950, scientists have been able to evaluate material structures in the physical world, using a mathematical tool called information theory. . . . In information theory, the unit used "to measure these systems isn't inches or pounds or seconds, but rather *bits of information.*" As Gange says so very well: " . . . information is something that ordinarily comes from intelligence, not natural processes, and the truly astonishing thing is that the latest discoveries show that the structures that make life what it is are just jammed full of this 'stuff' called information."[24]

Thus, one needs to treat seriously the most recent discovery in the area of biogenesis, that is the connection between linguistic information theory and the information code in living systems. Hubert P. Yockey in a most important

---

2. *Ibid.*, p. 74.

3. Information theory was first described by Claude E. Shannon of Bell Laboratory in "Mathematical Theory of Communication" (July and October, 1948) *Bell Systems Technical Journal.* See also C. Shannon and W. Weaver, *The Mathematical Theory of Communication* (Urbana: University of Illinois Press, 1949); and H. Yockey, Editor, *Symposium On Information Theory in Biology Gatlinburg, TN Oct. 29-31* (New York: Pergamon, 1956).

4. Gange, *Origins and Destiny*, pp. 70-71.

article, "Self Organization Origin of Life Scenarios and Information Theory,"[5] details his discovery regarding the connection between linguistic information theory and the information code in living things. This "theory" provides a mathematical basis for specifying the theoretical information carrying capacity of any communication channel. For example, using this method the information patterns of a written language are mathematically expressible. That a certain mathematically expressible pattern in the chemical structure of living things exists is a fact of genetics. Information theory can thus compare the information in a language and the information in a living organism.

Yockey states:

> The statistical structure of any printed language ranges through letter frequencies, diagrams, trigrams, word frequencies, etc., spelling rules, grammar and so forth and therefore can be represented by a Markov process given the states of the system, the pi and the p(j/bi) probabilities. . . . The entropy of the Markov process is a measure of the amount of chance, that is, uncertainty reflected in the statistical structure.

Yockey found the mathematical pattern represented by the letter frequency, etc., of a written language when compared to that known to exist in living systems to be exactly the same. Yockey says: "It is important to understand that we are not reasoning by analogy. The sequence hypothesis applies directly to the protein and the genetic text as well as to written language and therefore the treatment is mathematically identical."[6]

Thus, if the mathematic relation between information in a DNA and information in a written language are identical, then we can conclude that what we observe to be the cause for information in a language will have to be posited for the source of information in the DNA too. Intelligence is always the cause for information. Thus it is scientifically necessary to posit intelligence as the cause of the first living cell. If it takes intelligence to produce the information in a single sentence, then it also takes intelligence to create the first simple form of life, to say nothing of the infinitely more complex human brain. Many scholars feel that with the discovery of the relation between information theory and DNA, we are witnessing the scientific collapse of atheistic explanations of origin.

---

5. Hubert P. Yockey, "Self Organization Origin of Life Scenarios and Information Theory," in *Journal of Theoretical Biology* 91 (1981), pp. 13-31.

6. *Ibid.*, p. 16.

The DNA code, in even the simplest organisms has been clearly shown, by NASA computers among other sources, to represent not just a high level of complexity but a language which could only have its origin in intelligent being! Thus the scientific evidence is clearly, and decisively against materialism.

WHAT DOES INFORMATION THEORY TELL US?

"A popular explanation for life's origin is that a fortuitous chemical accident brought it into being. But although this miraculous accident idea is fashionable, it is out of step with the actual data of science." This is *what* Information Theory tells us! Scientist Gange goes on to write:

> Calculations on the idea have been done by a number of investigators [see Thaxton, Hoyle & Wickramasinghe for example[7]], and their conclusion is unanimous: It is simply too unlikely to be credible. Prior to the practical development of the electron microscope the true extent of the complexity of livng cells was unknown. However, when facts began to accumulate and data analyzed, the results suggested that believing in the Great Pumpkin might be more credible than the "miraculous accident" idea. Although this might sound silly it really isn't. The calculations show that the belief that life arose accidently is statistically impossible and intellectually outrageous.[8]

Two examples which Dr. Gange relates of this complexity of information in the most basic elements of living things will be sufficient here. The first gives what Gange calls "a good picture" of the complexity of hemoglobin. Hemoglobin is important because it is a protein in our blood that carries oxygen throughout the body. "Iron is located within hemoglobin in a special way that allows the molecule to carry oxygen more efficiently than anything else known. Were it not for hemoglobin, our heart would need to pump fifty thousand gallons a day just to keep us alive." And our blood pressure "would be almost seventy pounds per square inch, or about five times the pressure of the atmosphere."[9]

According to Gange, "a rough idea of what protein looks like under an

---

7. See Charles B. Thaxton, Walter L. Bradley, and Roger L. Olsen; *The Mystery of Life's Origin: Reassessing Current Theories* (New York: Philosophical Library, 1984); F. Hoyle and C. Wickramasinghe, *Evolution from Space* (Hillside, N.J.: Enslow Publishing, 1982)

8. Gange, *Origins and Destiny*, p. 72.

9. *Ibid.*, pp. 72-73.

electron microscope" would be to think of it as "a string of 'chemical railroad cars' called amino acids." We would have to picture two kinds of trains with 574 cars in all for hemoglobin. The information needed "to assemble a 'hemoglobin train'" is very hard to believe because it is so extremely complex. Each "railroad car" is an amino acid. "There are twenty different kinds of useful amino acids in our body. If we are to simulate protein, then in designating the first car we can select from among twenty different kinds," and so on with the second and also with the third and eventually with all 574 cars on the two trains.

> We can assemble the first and second cars in four hundred ways (combinations). If we were to make a train with three cars, we would choose from eight thousand combinations. . . . The number of ways we can assemble these hemoglobin trains is so vast that it is a trillion, trillion, trillion (repeat twenty times more) *times the entire number of stars in the universe.* Yet despite this, *only one combination known to man carries oxgyen most efficiently in your blood.* . . . Consider this: 270 million of these hemoglobin protein molecules of just the right combination reside in *each* of the 30 trillion red blood cells in your body. Did this just happen by chance? Some people have enough faith to believe that it did. Faith can be good if it's based on evidence. But where is the evidence that this system came into being by chance? There is none!

Gange goes on to say that we cannot calculate the certainty (inverse probability) that hemoglobin could have happened by chance because it is "so complicated that we can't fully describe it."[10]

Thus, says Gange, we will need to settle for calculating something much simpler in this regard. "The argument then is that if a simpler thing couldn't have happened by chance, then neither could the more complicated structure of hemoglobin." So he looks at a smaller protein "which scientists have extensively studied . . . called 'cytochrome C.' It's a much shorter protein than hemoglobin in that the length of its 'train' is only 101 railroad cars." This smaller protein "is also of interest because it is basic to all of life. Among other things, it controls both the respiration and energy transfer in the living cells of a broad spectrum of life."

"When scientists calculate probablities showing that cytochrome C could not have been produced by an accident, it's a little more complicated than just asking the question, How many ways can we assemble a train?" Gange goes on to say:

---

10. *Ibid.*, p. 73.

Of course, many technical details must be carefully taken into account . . . including the fact that not all 'railroad cars' are equally available (residue probability) or significant (codon degeneracy). Likewise, when selecting the "railroad cars," it is necessary to distinguish among those choices that are selected from comparable locations (homologous protein lineage) and the extent to which they may be similar (synonymous amino acid residues).[11]

But all this has been carefully done and the resulting calculations published in the scientific literature.[12]

According to Gange, "The result is staggering . . . . The certainty that we know chance did not produce cytochrome C is so vast that to communicate it in simple terms isn't easy."

Picture an 8 ½ x 11-inch sheet of paper with letters printed on both sides. Let's allow eighty columns by sixty-six lines of letters, giving us just under 5,300 letters on each side of the paper, or 10,600 letters per sheet. Putting the sheets into piles, we can stack about 320 sheets per inch, giving us just over thirty-six thousand letters in a cube one inch on a side. Now what volume of space do we need to store enough sheets whose total number of letters equals the certainty that chance did not produce cytochrome C? When I first did the calculation the answer astounded me. *We need the space of almost forty thousand universes, each 30 billion light-years wide!*[13]

Scientists believe that *our* universe is about 30 billion light-years wide out to the visible horizon. Gange observes:

Consider this. You and I are both aware that we exist. Yet we're told that all of life, including you and me, bounced itself into existence eons ago by a fortunate accident involving cosmic dust. But if we honestly face what we've uncovered in the past thirty years or so, we find ourselves up against the following question: When we believe, in the light of modern knowledge, that lifeless particles eventually endowed themselves with a living awareness of their own existence, do we not engage in the secret and irrational worship of interstellar dust under the guise of atheism? In short, do not the scientific calculations outlined above point to a God . . . as the source of our life?[14]

Gange goes on to show that the certainty that cytochrome C was not produced by accident is far greater than our belief that "the inverse square law of gravity is true." And, after about three hundred years of experiments have

11. *Ibid.*, p. 74.

12. Hubert Yockey, "A Calculation of the Probability of Spontaneous Biogenesis by Information Theory," *Journal of Theoretical Biology* 67 (1977), pp. 377-398.

13. Gange, *Origins and Destiny*, pp. 74-75.

14. *Ibid.*, p. 75.

confirmed its validity, almost everyone would agree that this law of gravity is true! "To compare the two, we'll again fill both sides of our paper with letters and ask: What volume of space do we need to store all the letters whose total equals the certainty that the inverse square law is true? The answer is surprising. It's a cube less than two miles on a side." When we compare this with the numbers for the certainty that chance cannot produce cytochrome C (simple protein) above Gange concludes that: "*It is nonsensical to believe that an accident created life.*"

> To compare a cube under two miles with forty thousand universes is to liken the finite with the infinite. The groundless belief that life spontaneously arose from nonliving physical matter was rationally defended for centuries because no one had any information to the contrary. Now that is over, and we know better. Today, we can see inside living cells and study the resplendent majesty of a structure so awesome that it reeks of divine fingerprints. It's one thing to defend wrong beliefs out of ignorance, but it's quite another to perpetuate the folly when the light of day shows a more truthful way.[15]

WHERE DO WE GO FROM HERE?

Many modern scientists, like Robert Gange, say that the evidence is so strong that the direction of our conclusions is quite clear:

> Since the universe is simply too young and too small, to account for its appearance, (even at 13 billion years and 30 billion light-years across) we are forced to ask, "From where did it come?" The logical answer is that it came from a Supreme Intelligence! Not only is this logical, but it's also the *simple*st answer. If this implies religion, then this is something the individual will have to grapple with. But the irrefutable fact is that information theory and the data from electron microscopy, when applied to living cells, force the conclusion that they have been *designed*. Why do they force this conclusion? Because they are jampacked with information that cannot be logically explained as the issue of natural processes within this universe."[16]

Many scientists who understand information theory, say the universe is simply too young and too small to have produced the information found in even a simple bacterium. Gange says: "Furthermore, the accidental story of life is believed, not because the facts of science have shown it to be true, but rather because no other alternative is plausible without recourse to "God."

---

15. *Ibid.*, pp. 76-77.
16. *Ibid.*, p. 71.

The concept of "God" as an explanation is offensive to some people for two reasons. First, "God" is equated with religion, which many believe has no place in science. And second, "God" implies an authority under whom one must arrange his or her life. But while this latter concern is something we all may wrestle with at one time or another, the notion of "God" does not have to equate to religion. Instead, *the concept is more properly identified with intelligence.*"[17] [emphasis added]

In much of this chapter, we have let science and the scientists speak and draw (what we are sure to some will be) rather startling conclusions. And though we must be quite careful, even in this case, not to make scientific findings absolute (as Dr. Gange also admits), many scientists think the evidence from information theory is so clear, so overwhelming that there can be no other choice than that life begets life, that intelligence begets intelligence!

---

17. *Ibid.*, p. 70.

Chapter Sixteen
THE CASE OF DARWINISM

Introduction: Importance of the Question
Some Clear Statements About the Issues
Where Do We Go From Here?

INTRODUCTION: IMPORTANCE OF THE QUESTION

The term "evolution" and its implications has generated more hostility, at least among Western Christian thinkers, than any other concept in the modern period. The English noun "evolution" (See *Oxford Dictionary of the English Language* for a history of the use of the word in English) comes from a Latin verb, *evolvere* – to unroll; "*e*" out and "*volvere*", to roll – and signifies the act or process of unfolding or developing. The crucial problems for the Christian can be reduced to three areas – the origin of the universe, the origin of life, and the origin of man and his sociological institutions.

Contrary to popular opinion (and popular teaching), there is no single theory of evolution – there are many theories and they all have the problem of causation (the actual necessary and sufficient cause to account for why we have lions and tigers and such) as a common factor. Change is undeniable – the question is how and why does it take place? The Christian immediately perceives that the necessity to affirm "absoluteness" (Incarnation, Atonement, Revelation, etc.) concerning the core of the Christian faith places as great responsibility upon the Christian apologete (defender of the faith[1]) in our "scientific" age. Many of the specialized sciences had arisen (as understood by the contemporary mind) – Chemistry, Physics, Geology, Psychology,

---

1. In Latin: *Fidei Defensor*, abbreviated F.D., is one of the many titles of British monarchs. Henry VIII was the first to have this one.

Astronomy, and Biology, etc., before Darwin.[2] These were preliminary for Darwin's work. Evolution as an interpretative principle spread into literature, history, ethics, religion, and on. No field made any claim to exemption from this principle or orientation. Spencer had already produced his system of evolution and it became overt in his *First Principles* before Darwin's *Origin of Species* in 1859.

Evolution as an explanatory principle was proposed by a number of learned men before Charles Darwin, among them Jean Baptiste Lamarck and Erasmus Darwin (Charles' grandfather). Reinhold Treviranus introduced the word *biology* into the nomenclature in his *Biologies oder Philosophies der Lebenden Natur* in 1802. It was Charles Darwin who proposed the machinery of evolution, and claimed that it existed in nature; natural selection, he called it. Thus Darwin's "greatness" was that he provided a causal explanation for genetic change. His idea was accepted very quickly! Once stated it seemed only too obvious. Some types are fitter than others. Given the competition, i.e., the struggle for existence, the fitter ones will survive to pass on their traits in their kind. Thus all life (animals, plants, *all life*) will tend to get better and better. This was an inevitable process of nature because Nature itself had evolving machinery built into it.

> That was a little over 100 year ago. By the time of the Darwin Centennial Celebrations at the University of Chicago in 1959, Darwinism was triumphant. At a panel discussion Sir Julian Huxley (grandson to Thomas Henry) affirmed that "the evolution of life is no longer a theory; it is a fact." He added sternly: "we do not intend to get bogged down in semantics and definitions." At about the same time, Sir Gavin de Beer of the British Museum remarked that if a layman sought to "impugn" Darwin's conclusions, it must be the result of "ignorance or effrontery."[3]

Yet all during the preceding hundred years, there had been a great debate going on within biology itself about the "facts" of evolutionary theory of which the general public was unaware.

> What was it, then, that Darwin discovered? What was this mechanism of natural selection? Here it comes as a slight shock to learn that Darwin really didn't "discover" anything at all, certainly not in the same way that Kepler, for example, discovered the laws of planetary motion. *The Origin of Species* was not a

---

2. For good, brief chapters on the rise of the sciences besides the larger histories of science see L. Woodruff, Editor, *The Development of the Sciences* (New Haven, CT.: Yale University Press, 1923).

3. Tom Bethell, "Darwin's Mistake," *Harper's Magazine* (February, 1976), p. 70.

demonstration but an argument – "one long argument," Darwin himself said at the end of the book – and natural selection was an idea, not a discovery. It was an idea that occurred to him in London in the late 1830's . . . .

While in his country retreat Darwin spent a good deal of time with pigeon fanciers and animal breeders. He even bred pigeons himself. Of particular relevance to him was that breeders bred for certain characteristics (length of feather, length of wool, coloring), and that the offspring of the selected mates often tended to have the desired characteristic more abundantly, or more noticeably, than its parents.[4]

Thus, Darwin got his great idea of Natural Selection not really from "nature" and certainly not from scientific observation of nature, but from men. If it proved anything – which it did not – it proved that it took intelligent men great effort to make changes. It certainly did not justify making nature into *Nature* and, thus, a causal force.

For quite some time Darwin's mechanism was not seriously examined. Finally, T. H. Morgan, renowned geneticist and winner of the Nobel Prize for his work in mapping the chromosomes of fruit flies, suggested that natural selection "looked suspiciously like a tautology."

"For, it may appear more than a truism," he wrote, "to state that the individuals that are the best adapted to survive have a better chance of surviving than those not so well adapted to survive." . . . The philosophical debate of the past ten to fifteen years has focused on precisely this point. The survival of the fittest? Any way of identifying the fittest other than by looking at the survivors? . . . Any way of identifying them other than by looking at the preserved ones? If not, then Darwin's theory is reduced from the status of scientific theory to that of tautology.[5]

Very quietly the Darwinians lost the debate and the theory of natural selection changed. "The admission that Darwin's theory of natural selection was tautological did not greatly bother the evolutionary theorists, however, because they had already taken the precaution of redefining natural selection to mean something quite different from what Darwin had in mind."[6] But, again, the general public was not told of the change – as far as they were told Darwinian theory remains a "fact"!

British statistician and geneticist R. A. Fisher did the redefining of natural selection in his widely heralded book, *The Genetical Theory of Natural*

---

4. *Ibid.*, p. 72.
5. *Ibid.*
6. *Ibid.*, p. 74.

Selection. Fisher made certain assumptions about birth and death rates and by combining them with Mendelian genetics he was able to qualify the resulting rates at which population ratios changed. In 1976 C. H. Waddington, a prominent geneticist (who also spoke at the aforementioned Darwin Centennial in Chicago) said of Fisher's redefinition:

> The theory of neo-Darwinism is a theory of the evolution of the population in respect to leaving offspring and not in respect to anything. . . . Everybody has it in the back of his mind that the animals that leave the largest number of offspring are going to be those best adapted also for eating peculiar vegetation, or something of this sort, but this is not explicit in the theory. . . . There you do come to what is, in effect, a vacuous statement: Natural selection is that some things leave more offspring than others; and, you ask, which leave more offspring than others; and it is those that leave more offspring, and there is nothing more to it than that. *The whole real guts of evolution – which is how do you come to have horses and tigers and things – is outside the mathematical theory* [Bethell's emphasis].[7]

Darwin's theory was supposed to answer the question of how we got "horses and tigers and such." Yet, after several rather "secret" serious changes in the theory we are no closer to an answer (apart from God) than we were over 100 years ago!

Well, as interesting as this discussion is, space does not allow much more. We think you can see the point: Darwinism has *not* stood the test of time. There is a great deal of evidence for speciation – change within species – but none for the general theory of evolution – amoeba to man. Yet, the debate goes on. A recent edition of *Harper's Magazine* (February 1985) had an excellent article by Tom Bethell entitled: "Agnostic Evolutionists: The Taxonomic Case Against Darwin," which we recommend to you. Bethell related that there are a growing number of agnostic scientists (which here means *not* Christian scientists pushing creationism) who would be very happy if the theory of evolution just went away because it does not help explain anything.

Colin Patterson, an eminent scientist who published a pro-evolution book in 1978 entitled *Evolution*, published by the British Museum, now says, in reply to a creationist-activist:

> You say I should at least "show a photo of the fossil from which each type of organism was derived." I will lay it on the line – there is not one such fossil for

---

7. *Ibid.*

which one could make a watertight argument. The reason is that statements about ancestry and descent are not applicable in the fossil record. Is *Archaeopteryx* the ancestor of all birds? Perhaps yes, perhaps no: there is no way of answering the question. It is easy enough to make up stories of how one form gave rise to another, and to find reasons why the stages should be favored by natural selection. *But such stories are not part of science, for there is no way of putting them to the test.*[8]

Allow me one last quote from this article of Bethell's in the February *Harper's* which we highly recommend.

Our belief, or "faith," that, as Patterson says, "all organisms have parents" ultimately derives from our acceptance of the philosophy of materialism. It is hard for us to understand (so long has materialism been the natural habitat of western thought) that this philosophy was not always accepted. In one of his essays on natural history reprinted in *Ever Since Darwin*, Steven Jay Gould suggests that Darwin delayed publishing his theory of evolution by natural selection because he was, perhaps unconsciously, waiting for the climate of materialism to become more firmly established. In his 1838 *M Notebook* Darwin wrote: "To avoid stating how far, I believe, in Materialism, say only that emotions, instincts, degrees of talent, which are hereditary are so because the brain of the child resembles parent stock." Darwin realized that the climate *had* changed – that evolution was "in the air" – in 1858 when he was jolted by Alfred Russell Wallace's paper outlining a theory of the mechanism of evolution very similar to his own.[9]

SOME CLEAR STATEMENTS ABOUT THE ISSUES

1. There is a real – an important – epistemological[10] question as we have discussed in the section "The Nature and Definition of Science" as to what, in fact, constitutes "science." We seem to operate under the assumption that there are only two issues in the debate between science and religion, that is, what has the status of "hypothesis" and what the status of "fact." But there is as third issue more foundational than either of these – what is the philosophical framework of the discussion. It is clear that the scientist *qua* (as) scientist has nothing to contribute to answering the ultimate question of origins. We have referred to many scientists who admit this in this book.

---

8. Tom Bethell, "Agnostic Evolutionists: The Taxonomic Case Against Darwin," *Harper's Magazine* (February, 1985), p. 49.

9. *Ibid.*, p. 61.

10. That area of philosophy which deals not with *what* we know, but how we know, i.e., "How we know what we know."

2. The scientist can show that certain mechanisms do work or do not, in fact, work (for instance that the Lamarckian theory of genetic choice that Darwin used is wrong) but he cannot, as scientist, answer the historical question in regard to origins – what actually *caused* in prehistory this or that to originate, what was the "necessary and sufficient condition" for its coming into being. Suppose Lamarck was right that one of these mechanisms for evolution does, in fact, work. What would it prove? That evolution was true? Certainly not! It would only prove that certain mechanisms work. Nothing else! It certainly would not answer the question of origins, nor prove it happened by that – or any other – particular mechanism historically. The scientist *qua* scientist can tell us what does work now – given the current state of things.

3. Remember: What if a scientist, or much more likely, many scientists succeeded in creating life in a test tube? Again, the old question! What would it prove about the question of origins? Answer *Nothing*! If anything it would *indicate* that it took extremely intelligent beings involved with very deliberate controlled conditions to *create* life. It certainly would not be in anyway positive to the theory of the chance coming into being of life as some seem to think.

4. In this chapter, we mentioned the danger to Christian scientists of assuming the definitive truth of modern science, either via definition or methodology and reading an interpretation of modern science back into Scripture. But another *real* danger exists – that of a Christian scientist totally bifurcating his/her science from his/her "faith" stance. Science and Scripture must relate, as MacKay says. Truth is truth. Fact is fact. (Here we go with the tautologies again!) We must, as Christians, accept the challenge of John 8:32, for we must know the truth and the truth will set us free.

5. There are two very important questions in this discussion with regard to the theological nature of the issue which need to be addressed: First is the proper exegesis of Genesis 1-11. Allow me to say that we must not be so quick to "pontificate" on the meaning of Genesis 1-11 *without detailed exegesis*. It should be obvious that well educated Christians committed to the fundamentals of the faith and biblical inerrancy differ on the implications of such exegesis. Second, whatever one's conclusions about what Genesis 1-11 teaches in regard to origins, we must realize that the question only really has interest – and merit – in the context of the question of the inspiration and authority of Scripture and biblical inerrancy.

6. Again, clearly what is at stake here is philosophical materialism, not the scientific data. What we need besides Christian scientists – and we *do need* Christian scientists – is Christian philosophers and Christian philosophers of science. We issue a call for some of you to consider meeting such a challenge. For you must see that Christian scientists alone will not, cannot, answer the questions of origins. That will take Christian philosophers who are willing to pay the high academic price to be able to carry on credible world view construction and criticism.

Darwin's natural selection is no longer a metaphor or an analogy but is mistaken for the reality it only represents. According to some scientists, the process of evolution has come to be regarded as a creative agency like unto divine creativity. Evolution, the "neutral theology," takes on the qualities of a belief system that defines its own reality and gives meaning to life – in this case, the meaninglessness of survival of whatever happens to survive. Here we are at Darwin's tautology again. "The world view of evolutionary naturalism replaces the God of creation with the god of happenstance, just as Darwin sought to replace special creation with a theory of organic evolution."[11]

WHERE DO WE GO FROM HERE?

From [Biologist] Pun's viewpoint, the prevailing neo-Darwinian evolutionary scenario requires "a leap of faith." Similarities between the anatomy of a chimpanzee and a human being, or between the DNA of a bacterium and an amoeba, offer only "circumstantial evidence" that macroevolutionary transitions occurred. [Pun goes on to note that there is no experiment] that can verify or falsity the macroevolutionary scenario.[12]

If this is true, then not only is the over one hundred year old theory of Darwin inadequate, but so are the *current neo-Darwinian* evolutionary theories. " 'The fact is that the evolution of life,' Pun concludes, 'from a single origin, an assertion adamantly maintained by most evolutionists, *is more an a priori assumption than an empirically falsifiable theory*.' " Pun then makes a statement that is truly remarkable, if true: "The stage may be set for a paradigm shift in future biological thinking."[13]

Where does this leave the Christian and the present or future Christian scientist? Right where they have always been! In need of paying the price to

---

11. Bill Durbin, Jr.,, "How It All Began," p. 34.
12. *Ibid.*, p. 36.
13. *Ibid.*

get the "credentials" and "do their homework." I have realized this need and felt the desire to do such in my one life, and areas of academic interest, for many years now. In fact, wc were in Dallas for "Christianity Challenges the University: An International Conference of Theists and Atheists" in 1985; I wrote this on the front of my program:

> If you don't want to, or refuse to, gain the kind of credentials necessary so that people will listen to you (even though you may not have anything to say – as *many* of those I heard really did seem to have nothing to say) then *at least* be willing to spend two years learning a "scholarly" accent [project an "air" with "appropriate" accompanying jargon]!

Of course, we were "joking" about just "learning a 'scholarly' accent," for the Christian *must* be willing to "pay the price" of excellence in service for Christ. Whatever the price! As Christians we simply cannot effort the luxury of ignorance. It will *never* (as we have heard some Christian "scientists") do to complain about the prejudice of the "secular" scientists and their professional scientific journals when *you* – the Christian – don't have the credentials and have not engaged in the level of research necessary to get your material published![14]

If Professor Pun is correct and the stage is being set for a paradigm shift in future biological thinking, then just possibly an unprecedented opportunity – and challenge – awaits any young Christian serious enough about their faith, and the world of science, to engage in the highest level of preparation and scientific experimentation. This challenge must be faced so Christians can lead the shift into a new paradigm which honors all truth and harmonizes the Christian world view and the world view of the physical sciences once again!

What an incredible opportunity and incredible challenge! We are convinced that Professor Pun is correct in saying that this will not happen if all we do is "fight" the "secular" scientists and their research. Again, the challenge is clear and the challenge is before us. It is to honor our Lord, and His Truth (including looking questions squarely in the face – yes, Christians have an obligation to be that honest, 1 Corinthians 15:13-19, read also 20) and be willing to obtain the training to be scientists *par excellence*!

---

14. We are am not saying that there isn't any "prejudice" out there toward Christian scientists. But, as we said, we have known personally Christian "scientists" who cried about the fact that they couldn't get their articles published in reputable journals when we knew for a fact that they did not have the credentials, had not done the research, nor had they written it up adequately to get it published in the first place.

Chapter Seventeen
SUMMARIES AND CONCLUSIONS

PART TWO
Chapter 9: "The Limits of Science"

It is most important to realize that: (1) There have been differing views of "science" over the centuries. Scientific methods, as well as conclusions, have changed and will again. (2) All physical science is based on – and all scientists have – metaphysical presuppositions which are informed by a particular world view. Differing world views influence how data is interpreted. Such presuppositions cannot be tested by the scientific method. (3) "One-time events" cannot be reproduced for examination so questions regarding such events are not in the realm of modern science. As Gange says: "We can guess at what happened and use science to gather evidence to support one or another hypothesis. But science has not proper jurisdiction in matters of origin or destiny." (4) Science, because of its empirical or inductive method cannot reach "absolute certainty" about anything. We are reminded of scientist Alcock's statement in regard to "dark matter," the mystery stuff which supposedly makes up 97% of the universe: "After all this time and all this effort," sighs Alcock . . . "we still don't know what most of the universe is made of." It could be Neutrions, WIMPS, MACHOs, black holes, or Bowling balls; or, "none of these possibilities."[1]

It is also important to realize that we are not condemning modern science, nor are we saying that modern scientific method should not be limited to strict empirical observation. But, we are saying that it is unfair to the scientist – and totally outside their function *as scientist* – to expect of them what their

---

1. *Time*, "The Dark Side of the Cosmos," 18 January 1993, pp. 34-35.

method cannot do; i.e., to make definitive statements about the truth of claims in religion, origins and destiny, etc., or anything which is strictly speaking outside the realm of their jurisdiction. Although mistakes have been made (and will be), we have confidence in scientists when empirical sincerity is practiced by someone dedicated to truth, for then this approach to knowledge is self-corrective, judging its conclusions by its own criteria. It is just that we must be clear about what "its own criteria" can and cannot do!

Chapter 10: "God and the 'New Science' "

Recently, a number of scientists have become Christians because much of the most current and most complicated scientific developments not only point to a power behind the universe, but a Personal Intelligence. As Professor Sandage says: "Here is evidence for what can only be described as a supernatural event." A growing amount of evidence, on many fronts, indicates that the universe did not happen by accident. This evidence will be introduced in the rest of this part of the book.

People like Carl Sagan – far from being "neutral" scientists – are really more like "priests" of atheism than objective presenters of where current scientific developments lead. These scientists are pushing their "atheistic scientific religion" more than "science." Their paintings do not correspond to the current scientific picture of a universe that began and will someday end.

To do a thorough job of discussing the New Science, one would have to start by looking at history and the development of modern science from the philosophical world views which informed it and the developments in science down through the centuries. It is important to be aware of the Aristotelian, Newtonian, and Einsteinian scientific world views and the metaphysical assumptions on which each was based. It is a great mistake to assume that modern science has achieved an absolute definitive understanding of the universe, physical or metaphysical.

Chapter 11: "Order in the Universe: The Teleological Argument"

As we continue to advance in our scientific knowledge, instead of our view getting simpler, or the universe being more easily understood, we are finding that it is even more complex than we could have imagined. It is not uncommon for the scientists themselves to say the universe is so ordered that one must opt for the existence of God to explain it. In some ways this "new" development is truly amazing!

This old "teleological" argument – the design argument – has long been one of the traditional philosophical arguments for the existence of God. But, now it seems stronger than ever and is being used not by "feebleminded" preachers, but by the scientists themselves. In fact, as has been mentioned before several scientists we are aware of have become Christians, in part, because the incredible design or order in the universe is, to them, overwhelming evidence for a divine plan and the existence of a Divine Planner.

The interesting fact of the matter is this: Instead of there being less need for God to explain the existence of the physical universe as our knowledge of its intricacies grows and grows (the old ruse, or decoy), just the opposite has happened. "Father" – "High Priest of the New Atheism" – Sagan's vision of a self-contained material cosmos blurs as science itself begins to fine-tune a new image. The more we learn, it seems at least according to many scientists, the more it looks as if the only way to explain the actual complexity is to look beyond the physical universe itself! Maybe old Archdeacon Paley wasn't so far off after all.

Chapter 12: "A Finite Universe and the Second Law"

The implications of this universally accepted scientific law, the Second Law of Thermodynamics, both to the theory of evolution and the existence of the Christian God have not gone unnoticed by philosophers and scientists alike. It seems to be just one of several "pointers" actually arising out of modern scientific knowledge which support the fact that the physical universe needs something beyond itself to make sense of what we actually experience in this "physical world." Thus, it is beginning to look, even scientifically, quite strongly like the universe as we experience it is not the closed mechanical system the strident unbeliever must have to maintain his or her atheism with intellectual integrity.

Chapter 13: "The Radiation Echo: 'Noise' of the Big Bang"

The implications of this new finding in science seems to be rather devastating for the naturalistic or materialistic view of the universe for, again, we seem to have a strong pointer to a theistic world view. The Big Bang theory, like all other theories, is not without problems. But at this time it certainly presents many more problems for the atheist than for the theist!

In addition, the anthropic principle also seems to answer many of the problems in the current theory. The range in the known universe is so small as to point rather forcefully toward it acting for a purpose. As Jaki has said: "Bafflingly enough, it is science in its most advanced and comprehensive form – scientific cosmology – which reinstates today references to purpose into scientific discourse."

Chapter 14: "Information Theory and the Gene Code"

Yes, without question, in the last decade or so evolutionary theory has "retreated" again and again in its attempt to explain the most complex of living things by chance evolution. The new evidence from information theory, again, seems to strongly suggest that the very most basic substance of life is so complex that it indicates a "language" structure – and language comes only from intelligence – not a chance coming into existence. Did we prove the workings of evolution once-and-for-all with evidence from the micro chemical level as the atheists said we would. Robert Gange answers with an emphatic no: "As long as this level remained unseen, people could believe the answer was yes. But, with the advent of electron microscopes and information theory, the answer changed to no."

The DNA code of even the simplest organisms has clearly been shown not just to be a high level of complexity, but a language which could only have its origin in Intelligent Being! Perhaps, no "scientific evidence" is more clearly or forcefully against materialism. We find no fortuitous – or "miraculous" chemical accident here! It may turn out that it is the atheist who must believe in the miraculous – *if* the "miraculous" is defined as a leap into the dark (as the atheists have chided theists with regard to miracles for such a long time[2]). Many modern scientists think the evidence against mechanism is so strong that the direction of our conclusions is quite clear.

---

2. But, of course, the theist claims that biblical miracles are of quite a different sort than the atheist's leap into the dark! Again, I would recommend the unbeliever to books in the bibliography on the Resurrection and miracles.

Chapter 15: "The Case of Darwinism"

Well, perhaps old Charles D. has more than had his day! We think so. Even biologists are beginning to recognize this. It's about time someone told the popular press, don't you think? In this chapter, we have tried to make some clear statements about the issues and where we must go from here. For *evident* in the *evidence* is a new direction for both the theist and the atheist!

Theists never could nor can they now afford the "luxury of ignorance" with regard either to their faith or knowledge of the modern world. All of us must pay the price of knowing not just *what* we believe (as important as this is), but of also knowing *why* we believe it. And, at least some of us must pay the high price of understanding the implications of the Christian faith in the context of the demands and challenges of the world in which we live – if we are to be faithful to the calling of Christ, to ministry and evangelism! Perhaps the biggest problem in the world is the apathy and laziness of Christians today!

To the atheist, let us be the first to admit that all the "evidence" – scientific or otherwise – is not yet in. Atheist or theist must constantly be willing to examine the evidence in the context of the adequacy of a world view. Yet, the realization that new evidence cannot be "ruled out of court" before it is discovered or assessed does not give the individual an excuse to refuse to accept the clear evidence for the Christian position in the context of a sound historic, philosophic, and scientific world view. To say that we do not yet know everything – that we will most probably never know "everything" in this life – does not excuse one from responsibility to the great treasure we do know. If it turns out in fact – as we believe the evidence clearly shows – that, far from it being the theist who is running away from reality, we would think any atheist with intellectual integrity would want to know it. The only way it can be known is if the evidence is pursued with the greatest of intellectual honesty and vigor.

We end this chapter and this part of the book with a quote from the philosopher and historian of science, Stanley Jaki:

Science, philosophically and historically, is an ally, not of the Academy of agnostics but of that Church which, unlike some of her theologians, knows all too well why her creed starts with the words: "I believe in God, the Father Almighty, Maker of Heaven and Earth." The effort which tries to resolve conflicts between Christianity and science by stating that religion is about persons and not about the universe of things, should seem a very poor half truth. For, God, at least the Christian God, is above all the Creator of the Universe. Thanks to science, that universe appears less and less mysterious, though at the same time more and more specific, and thereby an irrefragable pointer to God, the mysterious origin of all.[3]

---

3. Stanley L. Jaki, "Scientific Cosmology to a Created Universe," in *The Intellectuals Speak Out About God*, edited by Roy Abraham Varghese (Chicago: Regnery Gateway, Inc., 1984), pp. 77-78.

PART THREE

Evidence
from Morality

Chapter Eighteen
SO MUCH PAIN AND EVIL

INTRODUCTION: IMPORTANCE OF THE QUESTION

Now it is time to turn to an entirely new topic. Beyond the philosophical and scientific evidences for a theistic world view, what about the area of ethics? Isn't it true that here we have to face the hardest objection against the God of the Bible? All of us have witnessed the devastation that life appears to bring to countless numbers of human beings. It is true that philosophy and science present some exciting evidences for God. Yet somehow, our "real life" situations often overshadow our interest in more theoretical matters. The truth is that we *really do* suffer. But how could God allow such heartache and misery?

In this section, we will try to face the dilemma squarely. This chapter will describe the problem, along with a wide spectrum of commonly-suggested answers. The following chapter will ask why God allows so much anguish in the world. Next, we will even argue that atheism has worse problems with the issue of pain and evil than do theists! Then we will return to the overall theme of this book: what does ethics have to say about God's existence? Last, we think there is a special case in Scripture that might just unlock the deepest of all truths on the subject.

One important point should be mentioned at the outset. The problem of pain and evil is many-faceted and simply cannot be dealt with in this volume in all its complexity. Besides, many of the individual features extend beyond the interests of the average reader. While we will endeavor to discuss some of the outstanding issues, certain others will only be mentioned briefly, or not at all. Accordingly, the reader interested in pursuing additional aspects may find that other treatments are most helpful.[1]

OUR EXISTENTIAL SITUATION

We hurt! It sometimes appears that life itself causes pain! Maybe you've had this experience: you've read a good book or listened to a moving sermon, thinking you've grown in your ability to make sense of the world around you. You think that, finally, you have learned the key that will tie your life together and move you to the next step. Then boom! Something happens to make you question whether God even cares about you and your needs.

To make matters worse, we are all emotional beings, some to a greater extent than others. Our experiences – what seems to be the "raw data" of life – jump up and wage war with our heads. Unfortunately, what happens to us often weighs more heavily on our minds than do the more abstract truths that we learn. As a result, pain and evil upset our theological equilibrium – they slam head-on into our most cherished beliefs.

Suffering is so pervasive in our lives that it's even difficult to imagine someone saying they don't know what we mean. We've seen it in our lives and you've seen it in yours. It happens to our best friends. In fact, it appears to extend to everyone. No one is immune. As we observe these circumstances, we regularly experience the hope that whatever is "going around" doesn't affect our own families.

Then there is always the various media input we get daily. Newspaper

---

1. For texts which embody a wide variety of issues from differing theistic perspectives, and at different levels of difficulty, we recommend the following: John S. Feinberg, *Theologies and Evil* (Washington, D.C.: University Press of America, 1979); Norman L. Geisler, *The Roots of Evil* (Grand Rapids: Zondervan, 1978); John Hick, *Evil and the God of Love* (New York: Harper and Row, 1966); C.S. Lewis, The *Problem of Pain* (New York: Macmillan, 1962; George I. Mavrodes, *Belief in God: A Study in the Epistemology of Religion* (Washington, D.C.: University Press of America, 1970); Ronald H. Nash, *Faith and Reason: Searching for a Rational Faith* (Grand Rapids: Zondervan, 1988); Michael L. Peterson, *Evil and the Christian God* (Grand Rapids: Baker Book House, 1982); Alvin Plantinga, *God, Freedom, and Evil* (Grand Rapids: Eerdmans, 1974); Richard Swinburne, "Natural Evil," *American Philosophical Quarterly*, Volume 15 (1978).

articles describe in detail the different crimes and diseases in our society, many of them in our own backyards. The headlines scream their bad news at us. Television and radio provide the most recent updates on wars and hot spots around the globe. Reporters "on location" bring the anguish directly into our living rooms. We see parents weeping over the graves of their dead children killed in battle. Third-world famine rips our hearts out as small bodies are placed in common pits. Sometimes we are tempted to wonder if the chief purpose of the media is just to make us feel badly! "What has this world come to?" has long been a popular slogan.

And it's not just the pain itself that bothers us, it's the sheer *volume* of it – what philosophers often call gratuitous evil. There seems to be a purpose for some suffering – but *this much*? How do we account for the thousands of "innocent" lives that are sometimes lost in wars or nature's mishaps?

This introduces us to the famous problem of pain and evil. It is generally agreed that it constitutes the number one objection to belief in the God of the Bible. It is probably true that nothing in Christianity is questioned as much, not the nature of Scripture or the virgin birth; not the Deity of Jesus Christ or His resurrection. Sometimes the question is phrased the way of David Hume's fictional character Philo does it. Speaking of God and evil, Philo says: "Is he willing to prevent evil, but not able? then is he impotent. Is he able, but not willing? then is he malevolent. Is he both able and willing? whence then is evil?"[2]

One of the basic ideas in formulations such as these is that the biblical view of God is incompatible with what we all perceive in the world around us. Some even say that the classical position contradicts itself. To most people, evil undeniably exists. Some of those who believe in God think there is a dilemma here, while others just do not. How do scholars respond to this problem? Perhaps surprisingly, more than just Christians are interested, and even atheists struggle with the issues. Evil is simply a problem that affects us all.

PROPOSED SOLUTIONS

How have intellectuals sought to handle the quandary of pain and evil?[3] Actually, many approaches have been suggested. We will summarize a few of

---

2. David Hume, *Dialogues Concerning Natural Religion*, Section X.

3. We will distinguish different types of evil and provide definitions in the next chapter. Here we are only interested in a general approach.

the more prominent responses.[4] Eastern philosophies frequently teach that pain and evil are, in some sense, appearances or illusions caused by ignorance. Accordingly, changing the cause eliminates the condition. For instance, Buddhism says that the origin of suffering is craving and that "the utter and passionless cessation of this same craving" will cause pain and suffering to cease.[5]

Most philosophers oppose positions which argue or assume that evil is some sort of illusion. Doubtless, some suffering, perhaps even much of it, is due to our outlook and thinking patterns. But this is not a comprehensive explanation.) After all, those who hold that suffering doesn't objectively exist still face the same ills that others do – they hurt, too. Further, the data argue otherwise. Suffering is not just something in my mind that I can stop by suspending all craving, for example. Events in nature like earthquakes and hurricanes do not cease just because we change our thinking patterns. Another question concerns the source of pain. Even if it is due to ignorance or wrong thinking, how did this become the case? What is its true origin? As Geisler concludes rather graphically: "Illusionism is no more than a 'beautiful theory' that is ruined by a brutal gang of facts."[6]

On the other hand, many naturalists[7] argue that evil is quite real and that its presence in the world disproves God's existence. But there is disagreement over the degree of seriousness involved in this problem. Sometimes a harder line is taken – that the presence of evil actually contradicts classical theism. A somewhat softer position is that, while there is no formal contradiction, pain and evil still count as a significant objection to the views of orthodoxy. Either way, naturalists consider this problem to be their "trump card" against theistic world views. We will return to this distinction in chapter 20. For now, we will survey some representative positions.

Albert Camus retells the story of the horrible plague of rats that infected the city of Oran earlier this century. He surmised that the humanitarian thing to do

---

4. For some options not discussed here, along with theistic responses to them, see Norman L. Geisler, *Philosophy of Religion* (Grand Rapids: Zondervan, 1974), pp. 311-317. The latest edition of this work is co-authored by Winfried Corduan.

5. Majjhima-nikaya 3:248-252; Anguttara-nikaya 3:134. For these texts, see Sarvepalli Radhakrishnan and Charles A. Moore, Editors, *A Source Book in Indian Philosophy* (Princeton: Princeton University Press, 1957), pp. 274-278.

6. Geisler, *Philosophy of Religion*, p. 312.

7. Naturalism is a world view which believes that nature is all there is and that we therefore need no appeal to the supernatural. Knowledge is usually said to be gathered by the scientific method.

was to assist fellow human beings in their plight. Yet, to do so meant that one was not following the priest, who did nothing because helping the sick would constitute fighting against God, Whom he believed sent the epidemic in the first place. Similarly, we are also faced with the dilemma – be humanitarian or be religious. But one cannot choose both.[8]

H.J. McCloskey has argued somewhat similarly. He contends that theists cannot fight evil because, in so doing, they fight against the greater good that is supposedly achieved by the suffering. Therefore, the theist is morally bound not to attempt to exterminate evil or the resulting good will not be attained.[9] J.L. Mackie has joined McCloskey in the contention that theism's basic beliefs about God – that He is omnipotent and omnibenevolent – strongly oppose the belief that evil exists.[10]

From the first two sections of this book, one major response to naturalism should be obvious. If God exists, then the major tenet of atheism is gravely mistaken. But the naturalistic challenge regarding evil requires a more detailed discussion, and we will turn to such in the next three chapters.

Still, we need to make a brief comment about Christian theists doing humanitarian acts. Atheologians (scholars who are critical of classical theism) like Camus and McCloskey have totally "missed the boat." Christians have *every* reason to fight against pain and injustice. Even if greater goods proceed from every evil,[11] we still have numerous biblical examples from Jesus and others. The Jews in the Old Testament were commanded to make various provisions for the poor, Jesus healed assorted maladies and fed the hungry, while Paul took up offerings for poor believers. In fact, the Incarnation itself is the greatest biblical example of God fighting evil, especially at the Cross. So believers are *repeatedly* encouraged, even commanded,[12] to do humanitarian

---

8. Albert Camus, *The Plague*, translated by S. Gilbert (New York: Random House, Inc., 1948).

9. H.J. McCloskey, "God and Evil," *The Philosophical Quarterly* (April, 1960). The essay is also included in Nelson Pike, Editor, *God and Evil* (Englewood Cliffs: Prentice-Hall, Inc., 1964). For an evaluation of Camus and McCloskey, see Norman L. Geisler, *Philosophy of Religion*, Chapter 17.

10. J.L. Mackie, *The Miracle of Theism* (Oxford: The Clarendon Press, 1982).

11. We will deal with this subject when we evaluate gratuitous evil in the next chapter.

12. One very instructional example is provided by Paul: "Therefore, as we have opportunity, let us do good to all people, especially to those who belong to the family of believers" (Gal 6:10, NIV).

acts, whether or not good results from suffering.

A third response is that God exists, but the reality of evil indicates that He cannot solve the problem. In short, God is finite or limited in one or more of His attributes. Although Mackie does not take this view himself, he does comment that one way for the theists to avoid the problem of evil is to abandon one or more of the conflicting propositions regarding God's nature.

One might discontinue belief in God's omnipotence or His omnibenevolence, for examples.[13]

A number of philosophers have taken this option, such as some of the idealists[14] earlier this century. Peter Bertocci states that "the creative Intelligence does not, or cannot, succeed in all his undertakings."[15] Edgar Brightman holds that God's inability to completely control the evil in the world, especially unexplained, "surd" evil, indicates the presence of a nonrational element (termed "The Given") in the very nature of God.[16]

In more recent times, the best examples of those who hold that God is finite are probably the process philosophers,[17] who generally think that God has both classical and non-classical attributes. Schubert Ogden charges that the traditional notion of God cannot answer the problem of evil. In particular, "classical Christian theism . . . cannot both admit the reality of evil and still maintain that God is all-good as well as all-powerful . . . ." Rather, we must challenge the orthodox conception of God's attributes.[18]

Process scholars celebrate certain of the classical virtues of God, such as His love. On the other hand, the most challenged attributes of orthodox theism

---

13. J.L. Mackie, "Evil and Omnipotence," *Mind*, Volume XLIV, Number 254, 1955. This treatise is also found in Pike, *op. cit.*

14. Idealism is a world view with wide variations, but which generally holds that reality proceeds from the mind's ideas, not from material objects in the world.

15. Peter A. Bertocci, *An Introduction to the Philosophy of Religion* (New York: Prentice-Hall, Inc., 1951), p. 338.

16. Edgar S. Brightman, *A Philosophy of Religion* (New York: Prentice-Hall, Inc., 1940), pp. 336-338.

17. Process views emphasize change – the continual transformation of reality. Even God (who had both a transcendent and an immanent nature) is a part of this growth as he develops and learns.

18. Schubert M. Ogden, *Faith and Freedom: Toward a Theology of Liberation* (Nashville: Abingdon Press, 1979), pp. 75-82; Schubert M. Ogden, *The Reality of God and Other Essays* (New York: Harper and Row, 1964), Chapter I.

are the omnipotence, omniscience, and immutability of God.[19]

Interestingly, a number of prominent idealists disagree with the conclusions of some of their colleagues and oppose the notion that God is finite. Others have also offered multiple critiques against such a notion. For example, Brightman denied that God has a beginning or ending,[20] but how can finitists know exactly where God is limited? And if God needs a cause for His existence, then this position is seriously hobbled, as we saw in earlier chapters. Existence requires an eternal cause. Further, Christian theists might point out that Jesus' brand of theism has been validated by the God of the universe when He raised His Son from the dead (see next section), and Jesus' view gives no hint of finitism.

Additionally, scientific methodology often places unexplained phenomena which oppose one's world view on "hold" until a solution can be addressed. So in religion, we should be willing to admit our own lack of knowledge and search for additional information regarding unexplained evil.[21] We will examine the legitimacy of a related concept in Chapter 22.[22]

------

19. Many process writings clearly denote some of the lines of demarcation with classical theism, such as: Charles Hartshorne, *Omnipotence and Other Theological Mistakes* (Albany: State University of New York Press, 1984); Delwin Brown, Ralph E. James, and Gene Reeves, Editors, *Process Philosophy and Christian Thought* (Indianapolis: The Bobbs-Merrill Company, Inc., 1971). Part Two of the latter contains seven essays on God by a number of the most influential scholars in this school of thought, like Ogden, Hartshorne, John B. Cobb, Jr., Bernard Loomer, and Lewis S. Ford.

20. Brightman, *A Philosophy of Religion*, pp. 336-337.

21. L. Harold DeWolf, *The Religious Revolt Against Reason* (New York: Harper and Brothers, 1949), pp. 172-174; Albert C. Knudson, *The Doctrine of Redemption* (New York: Abingdon-Cokesbury Press, 1933), pp. 206-212. For a good discussion of the debate among the idealists as to whether or not God is finite, including many of these details, see Warren Young, *A Christian Approach to Philosophy* (Grand Rapids: Baker Books, 1957), pp. 166-173.

22. Other critiques of finitism often seem to miss the mark just a bit. While amounting to good questions for the philosophers who take this position, they might actually achieve some unwanted results. DeWolf and Knudson complain that finitistic concepts compromise God's character and are too anthropomorphic. Further, creation shows God's power. Lastly, a finite God could not guarantee classic beliefs such as salvation, answers to prayer, a final victory over evil, or even justify worship. (See Knudson, pp. 208-209; DeWolf, pp. 172-174; Geisler, *Philosophy of Religion*, p. 313). A more fruitful criticism might emerge from questioning Brightman's "Given" and the finitistic approach to evil (Knudson, pp. 184-185).

However, it would seem that the finitist might try to answer that, while he wished he didn't have to compromise God's nature, maybe we need to do so. And perhaps

Another approach to evil is deterministic in nature, and is frequently associated with some of the more extreme forms of Calvinism or Islam. It holds that God actually created good and evil, and that He is therefore the direct Cause of both.[23] We will also address this view in the next chapter.

Last, probably the most common theistic view is that, while God does not cause evil, He allows it in order to obtain greater goods, or to thwart some greater evils. Often, this good is associated with the free will of created persons. There are different slants on this view, and it is widely held by thinkers with quite different concepts of God.

We will support the last position in this volume, devoting the next chapter to specific details. Why does God allow evil at all? In particular, are there any reasons that could adequately explain the kind of suffering referred to above? What about the large amounts of gratuitous evil which do not seem to be directed to any purpose? It would seem that taking this view requires some good answers to tough situations.

CONCLUSION

Suffering really exists. Countless numbers of people experience it in immeasurable ways. It seems fruitless to deny the reality of evil, being satisfied to consign it to ignorance or illusion. We need to face it directly.

God cannot ultimately guarantee salvation, respond to prayer, or insure a complete victory over evil. Last, the finitist just might believe that it is more difficult to overcome evil than it is to create the world.

In other words, if we are not careful, we raise questions that are double-pronged. While they are certainly tough issues for finitists to deal with, they sometimes have the affect not of disproving the position, but of pushing them to more radical conclusions, more like the process philosophers. A more perceptive exposition and critique of the more extreme options is found in Norman L. Geisler, "Process Theology" in *Tensions in Contemporary Theology*, Second Edition, edited by Stanley N. Gundry and Alan F. Johnson (Grand Rapids: Baker Book House, 1976), pp. 237-284.

23. For an insightful critique of what the author determines "theological fatalism," see William Lane Craig, *The Only Wise God: The Compatibility of Divine Foreknowledge and Human Freedom* (Grand Rapids: Baker Book House, 1987), especially Chapters 3-5. For some comments on the Muslim view, see J.N.D. Anderson, *Christianity and World Religions* (Downers Grove: InterVarsity Press, 1984), pp. 130-131.

Therefore, we join the majority of philosophers and theologians who inquire concerning the nature and causes of pain and suffering. Does it help to differentiate types of evil? How might each be explained? We addressed some of the possible options here, and offered critiques of several. We favor the view that God allows evil in order to achieve a greater good, or to prevent a greater evil. We turn now to a discussion of this subject.

Chapter Nineteen
WHY DOES GOD ALLOW SUFFERING?

INTRODUCTION: IMPORTANCE OF THE QUESTION

We have said that pain and evil really exist. Most people concur wholeheartedly – often due to personal experience. When suffering of some sort befalls us, it is normal for believers and unbelievers alike to ask, "Why?" We assume that there is some purpose behind our troubles and theists seem to be most interested in God's reasons for allowing them. In fact, it is rather difficult to imagine the position that denies the objective reality of suffering.

Scholars have responded differently to these predicaments. We looked at some of the major options in the last chapter, providing critiques of several of them. Even though God's existence alone disproves atheism, we need to look in detail at some of the intricacies posed by this perspective. In this chapter, we will define two sorts of evil, concentrating on some of the reasons for each. We think God allows evil, but this raises the question of His purposes in so doing.

MORAL EVIL

Two kinds of evil are usually distinguished – moral evil and natural (or physical) evil.[1] Moral evil arises due to the free choices of created beings. We might

---

1. Some philosophers, like Geisler, add a third: metaphysical evil. See his *Philosophy of Religion*, Chapter 15.

say that it is characterized in one sense as the sort of suffering that results from persons versus persons. It includes such atrocities as war and crime. Natural evil might be identified as the result of nature versus persons, and encompasses disasters such as earthquakes, volcanoes, hurricanes, and floods.

While such a general distinction is certainly helpful, it by no means guarantees that it will always be easy to untangle one sort of evil from another. For instance, while birth defects may at first seem to be of natural origin, medical science has discovered in recent years that non-prescription drugs willingly taken by a pregnant mother can cause untold problems for the unborn. Similarly, a famine may create havoc in a certain land, but people may refuse or neglect to help their fellow human beings afterwards, making it a moral issue, as well.

Moral evil results from the free actions of persons who use their freedom to oppose others. On the one hand, to be a human being generally entails some measure of freedom of choice. But on the other, creatures are not truly free unless they have the possibility to perform evil actions as well as good ones. Such choices are the source of moral evil.

The atheistic response is often to ask whether God had to create persons in this way. Were other options available? Could God have created worlds with conditions significantly different from the one we now inhabit? A few alternative possibilities have been suggested,[2] but one of them gets far more attention than the others. Mackie suggests that it is logically possible for God to create free moral creatures who nevertheless always make the proper choices, thereby never "sinning" or otherwise harming others. Since God could do so without contradiction, but didn't, he failed to act consistently with his omnipotence and benevolence.[3]

In response to Mackie, Alvin Plantinga questions the premise that God can do whatever is logically possible; in fact, He may not be able to actualize certain of these possible scenarios. For instance, if God created morally free creatures that couldn't choose evil, are they truly free? If they are, could He guarantee that they would not act wrongly? If they are not free, then this is a lesser creative option.[4]

Some theists tend to state the issue even more strongly: Mackie's scenario

---

2. See *Ibid.*, Chapter 16, for an investigation of several of these other schemes.
3. J.L. Mackie in Pike, *God and Evil*.
4. Plantinga *God, Freedom, and Evil*, pp. 48-49.

is not an option because it is *not* logically possible for God to act in this manner. To create free creatures who cannot choose evil is to deny the very freedom we claim they possess; hence, we are faced with a contradiction. Or, to say it another way, such a creative act places God's freedom over against that of the persons whom He creates. Although Nash applauds Plantinga's position, he appears to approach the harder view when he says: "In other words, God cannot guarantee that significantly free creatures will always do what is good without depriving them of their freedom."[5]

Therefore, in order to guarantee the freedom of creaturely choices, God clearly allowed persons to engage in evil acts, including causing pain to others. While many question whether God should have allowed this suffering, presumably few would give up their freedom in order to get rid of it. It seems that we value the latter even more!

But others charge that God is responsible even for what He allows – so evil still ought to be laid at His doorstep. But it is critical that we understand the difference between an infinite God *causing* evil and His *allowing* it. Perhaps an analogy will help, although such is an imperfect one, if only because we lose something when we compare human beings to God. At any rate, how would we respond to the convicted mass murderer who charges that U.S. Supreme Court justices are actually responsible for his crimes on the grounds that, by defining and defending the law, they also allowed him to break it? As a result, he should be freed.

As we said, God is far different than a human judge. But is He any more able to step in and prevent the lawbreaker? Christian theists have long argued that God does just this on many occasions, the chief example of which was sending His Son to die for these same lawbreakers. But that God does not act this way most of the time does not make Him negligent, for we have just said that to step in and prevent evil is effectively to keep people from being truly free. Here is the dilemma in a nutshell: how does God stop multi-thousands of hurtful acts every day and, at the exact same time, allow His creatures the freedom that makes them independent persons?

The free actions of created beings account for most of the pain in the world. Elton Trueblood asserts that moral evil "is far more serious than natural evil and yet it is the more easily understood." While physical catastrophes are far-reaching, "these are almost trivial in their effects when contrasted with the

---

5. For Nash's insightful discussion, see *Faith and Reason*, pp. 190-194.

unmerited suffering which comes as a result of the actions of wicked men."
Trueblood explains that mental torment is the worst sort of suffering and people cause far more torture and anguish on their victims than does nature.[6]

NATURAL EVIL

What about natural evils that seem to pit us against the very world on
which we live? On a regular basis, we hear of disasters that dot the globe, taking thousands of lives. Trueblood remarks: "Natural evil is far less important,
in the modern world, than moral evil, but it is harder to explain."[7]

Natural evil is more difficult to answer because it appears to proceed from
God's creation, and doesn't seem to be connected with the free will of creatures. So why did God create a world with so many obvious imperfections?
We have said that theists usually respond to the evil in the world by saying
that, in some sense, God allows it to achieve some greater good or to avert
some greater evil. So what positive consequences result from the presence of
natural evil?

Our reply to questions such as these will be arranged into three main categories.[8] It should be carefully noted that some of our responses (especially the
initial section) will also apply to moral evil.

Free Will

We have already said that the free choices of created beings account for the
majority of suffering in the world. Emotions such as pride, hatred, jealousy,
and greed provide much of the motivation persons need to perform heinous
acts, including the two categories that probably encompass the most massive
amounts of evil: war and crimes of all sorts, explicit and implicit. But incalcu-
lable (and largely unexposed) amounts of suffering result from our daily
choices – hurts that go unmentioned and perhaps unrecognized even by the
injured parties. Our very words are often meant to produce subtle stings in

---

6. David Elton Trueblood, *Philosophy of Religion* (New York: Harper and
Brothers, 1957), p. 248.

7. *Ibid.*, p. 253.

8. In this categorization we follow Nash's outline, *Faith and Reason*, pp. 198-208.
However, we will diverge markedly at several points.

order to get our point across, or to keep another individual "in their place."

But there is another entire dimension to this problem that is often ignored in the theistic literature. The biblical witness is that Adam and Eve disobeyed God in the Garden of Eden, introducing human sin to the world (Gen 3; Rom 5:12-14). God responded to the disobedience, punishing the sin. Although believers are more familiar with the moral consequences, physical pain also resulted and the earth was no longer the same place it had been before (Gen 3:14-19).

But man's Fall was orchestrated by Satan, who had likewise chosen the option of sin at some earlier time.[9] This introduced both moral and natural evil from another angle, since Satan and his demons frequently chose to inflict much pain, including natural disasters. Geisler even argues the majority of natural evil may be explained in this manner.[10] We will return to this topic below.

So the biblical witness testifies that it is more than just the sin of human beings that introduced moral and other evils into the world. Satan and his demons also used their freedom to violate God's law. This is not a very popular topic among many of the philosophers who discuss this subject.[11] But for those who think there are reasons to accept the biblical testimony,[12] this adds an entirely new dimension to the subject of the free will of created beings.

So human beings, Satan, and his fallen angels are all part of the quandary known as the problem of evil. Yet, as we already said, this free will is actually a blessing in disguise. Apparently God concluded that it was better to create creatures with freedom, in spite of the results, than not to give His creation that right. Presumably, few would trade their right of free choice even for the pain in the world.

---

9. Compare Gen 3:1-5, 13-15 with Luke 10:18; 1 John 3:8; Rev 12:9; 20:2.

10. For some biblical samples, see Job 1:6-19; Mark 5:1-20; 2 Cor 12:7. Cf. Geisler, *Philosophy of Religion*, pp. 392-393.

11. While attempting to take man's vices solemnly, referring to them as the "most serious" kind of sin, Trueblood still talks about the account of Adam and Eve "according to the legendary story of Genesis" (p. 251).

12. See chapter 25 for an outlined case addressing the trustworthiness of the New Testament. In chapter 27 we discuss the authority of Jesus, based on the fact of His resurrection from the dead (chapter 26). For arguments from Jesus' authority to the inspiration of the Old Testament, see Robert P. Lightner, *The Saviour and the Scriptures* (Philadelphia: Presbyterian and Reformed Publishing Company, 1966); John W. Wenham, *Christ and the Bible* (Grand Rapids: Baker Book House, 1984).

Natural Law

The second category of goods comes from the existence of natural laws in the universe, a necessary condition for the fulfillment of both divine and human objectives. There are at least two aspects that we need to note concerning this state of affairs.

First, we live in a world that generally behaves according to prescribed principles, often spoken of as natural laws. Such is essential for free creatures to function in a normal manner. Further, regularity is also crucial when we discuss miracles as God's actions that are contrasted with the normal order of things.

But at this juncture, problems arise. The same sun that is needed for life on earth can also burn. Likewise, fire warms; it also consumes. Water is absolutely indispensable to existence as we know it, but water can also kill. Gravity is taken for granted, but tensions in the earth's crust can cause untold destruction. In another regard, it is important that pain serves us as a physical warning, but it obviously hurts even while it helps.

Brian Hebblethwaite makes a strong claim here:

> There may well be logically necessary conditions which make it impossible to create an ordered physical universe containing organic creatures without the possibility of accident and pain. This line of argument can be reinforced by our increased scientific knowledge of the laws of nature . . . .[13]

If this assessment is correct, then an ordered physical world absolutely requires the possibility of pain and suffering. Hebblethwaite adds, even more pointedly: "God can no more create a balance of nature without the death of individuals than he can create a square circle."[14]

The atheologian may inquire whether God could have created another sort of world, complete with different laws. But there are some important problems with such a suggestion. Initially, since most natural forces can potentially initiate both good and bad results, such a proposal would basically have to change the entire system as we know it. It is not even clear how such an enterprise could fulfill the desired conditions. While isolated suggestions about this or that difference might be helpful, we would have to address the entire uni-

---

13. Brian Hebblethwaite, *Evil, Suffering and Religion* (New York: Hawthorn Books, Inc., 1976), p. 73.
14. *Ibid.*

verse. It is doubtful that humans can even conceive of the necessary amount of transformation implicit in such a charge.

Additionally, the atheologian needs to go beyond the previous formulation and show how such an alternative world would actually increase the resulting good. Perhaps it is the case that to whisk away the potential suffering also significantly curtails the quality of life and growth as persons (see the next category below).

Not surprisingly, no atheologian has adequately shown how another world would have produced at least as much good and less evil at the same time. Since it appears that a finite mind could not even grasp the requirements of such an enterprise, it would seem that this makes the atheological challenge highly suspect, if not just plain impossible to prove.[15]

Some pose another question, and ask whether God couldn't intervene in order to either change the laws or thwart the evil before it occurs? This scenario would require a simply massive number of miracles – so many that natural law and its affects would be substantially averted. Further, it is still not at all clear that such a scenario would increase the achievable good in the world. But the most serious problem with the interventionist scheme would be a dual one – the regular suspension of natural law and the resulting alteration of free will, which we have said depends on a steady natural order. For example, in order to halt the results of the laws, God would actually be preventing the normal consequences of free acts. Once again, this would be to limit creaturely freedom. We would return to the previous problems.

Some frustrated critics might counter that at least God could act once in a while to help the situation. And many Christian theists agree – maintaining that this is exactly what God does do on certain occasions.[16] Hebblethwaite comments that if this world was the only possible way for God to create finite beings, then the theistic response has much explanatory power. And here we have a close similarity to the free will defense. Just as true freedom allows the possibility of a wrong choice, "so does finite free personal being require an ordered yet flexible environment in which to be rooted and nurtured . . . ."[17]

---

15. For a few of the theists who make these and other responses to this question, see Peterson, *Evil and the Christian God*, pp. 115-116; David Basinger, "Evil as Evidence Against God's Existence: Some Clarifications," *Modern Schoolman*, Volume 58 (1980-1981); Nash, *Faith and Reason*, pp. 202-204; Hebblethwaite, *Evil, Suffering and Religion*, pp. 73-74.

16. For a discussion of this last point, see chapter 29.

17. Hebblethwaite, *Evil, Suffering and Religion*, p. 75.

The second aspect of a natural law theodicy has already been introduced above. The biblical perspective is that Satan and his demons rebelled. Human beings made choices and experienced their own Fall some time later. Besides the moral repercussions of sin, physical pain also resulted (Gen 3:14-16) and the earth was changed, as well (3:17-19). Further, we have seen that Satan and his demons are capable of perpetrating much suffering, including the performance of natural disasters. While many philosophers oppose such references to Satan,[18] the key question concerns their basis.[19]

Much later after the Fall of Adam and Eve, the condition of life on the earth is described as having grown wicked, evil, corrupt, and filled with violence. So God judged the earth with the flood (Gen 6:5-13). Depending on one's view of how much of the earth was covered, there would definitely have been some far-reaching effects on the natural order.

So biblical theism contends not only that the world was created with natural laws, but that the introduction of moral evil effected other changes in nature. Thus, free will plays a vital role in natural, as well as moral, evil.

Soul-Making

A third category of goods that proceeds from the presence of evil in the universe argues that working through painful situations is one of the best ways for a human being to increase in virtue. Additionally, such growth is the foremost means of preparing for eternal fellowship with God. This position is perhaps most-developed in John Hick's "Irenaean theodicy." God's love for us "presupposes a 'real life' in which there are obstacles to be overcome, tasks to be performed, goals to be achieved, setbacks to be endured, problems to be solved, dangers to be met. . . . In this sense, life's challenges help to develop our characters."[20]

However, this view is definitely not synonymous with Hick's formulation.[21] Biblical insights teach some of the same truths, as well as other elements. Faith is refined in the fires of suffering (1 Pet 1:6-7; 5:7-10). Pain can serve as a moral warning (1 Cor 11:27-32; 2 Cor 12:7-10), although this is definitely

---

18. An example is found in *Ibid.*, pp. 45-48, 52-53, 70-71, 102.

19. See footnote number 11 above.

20. See Hick, *Evil and the God of Love*, p. 326.

21. Nash offers a few concise criticisms of Hick's view, *Faith and Reason*, p. 205, footnote 27.

not always its purpose. Suffering helps us to know how best to comfort others when they hurt (2 Cor 1:3-7).

One of the most satisfying aspects is that the believer's torment is not unrewarded. For the Christian, pain is reconciled in the future state. Paul even encourages us to get our minds off our suffering by concentrating on the benefits of eternal life (2 Cor 4:7-18). Peter gives similar encouragement: our knowledge of heaven brings joy even when we suffer for our faith (1 Pet 1:3-6). The author of Hebrews explains that this was a characteristic of believers down through the ages (11:32-40). The belief in eternal life for the Christian is not an isolated one, either. In the New Testament, this hope is firmly linked to the resurrection of Jesus, which is also central in some of the passages on suffering.[22]

One objection to the soul-making theodicy is that evil often does not have a positive outcome, but often overwhelms those caught in its clutches. Persons often respond in the opposite manner, or sometimes die suddenly with no chance to grow. This objection has a definite point – pain and evil often fail to provoke the ultimate reaction. However, a couple of responses are also in order. Our three major categories are certainly compatible with one another and are not meant to be utilized alone. As such, we definitely do not claim that each can (or is meant to) stand alone. Insights from all three should to be combined.[23]

Accordingly, we need to remind the critic that real freedom presupposes bad choices. Without such, the person is not truly free. Sometimes these unsatisfactory decisions lead to defeat, loss, and failure. The worst consequence is eternal separation from God.[24] Another objection is that senseless, gratuitous evil is far out of balance with any good that could possibly be attained. This is also a serious objection. In fact, we want to take an entire section to address this difficult question.

GRATUITOUS EVIL

Now we've worked our way to what is perhaps the most difficult issue of all. Many theists and atheists alike agree that there ought not be any cases of

---

22. For examples of the more than one dozen times where the believer's resurrection is linked to that of Jesus, see 1 Cor 15:20, 44-57; Phil 3:21; 1 John 3:2; cf. John 14:19; Acts 4:2. Jesus' resurrection is also the key in some of the apostolic advice concerning suffering (2 Cor 4:14; 1 Pet 1:3).

23. Nash, *Faith and Reason*, p. 199.

24. For a defense of the biblical teaching on Hell, see Habermas and Moreland, *Immortality*, Chapter 11.

purposeless suffering, or incidents where the type or amount exceeds what is absolutely necessary. Presumably, these scholars think that any evils beyond those which are imperative would not be compatible with the orthodox notion of God. This position even seems rather common-sensical to many. But interestingly, some theists find no problem with God allowing gratuitous evil! We will explore both of these major theistic responses.

While it is difficult to ascertain for sure, Geisler seems to argue against the presence of such evil. He says "only a theistic God can guarantee man that unnecessary evil will not occur." Later, he lists one of the essential propositions required of an adequate theodicy: "That the *total amount* of evil that does occur be no more than is necessary to the achievement of the overall plan to obtain the greatest good possible."[25]

Then Geisler goes on to argue several counter-points. (1) "No finite mind is in a position to press this point" about the large amounts or unequal distribution of evil. (2) Philosophical and historical evidences for a theistic world view argue "that the right amount of evil is being allowed to accomplish the greatest good." (3) "The theodicy suggested here does not require weighing exact amounts of evil or measuring the degree of distribution . . ." (4) Theism only needs to argue that there is more good than evil, not that the "most" good results.[26]

Those who take a stand against gratuitous evil often defend the cognate view that God carefully controls all things so that no more evils than necessary are permitted. On this view, sometimes called the doctrine of meticulous providence, no evil is ever meaningless.[27] In other words, God never allows a bit more evil than that which translates to actual good.

But a growing number of theists think that it is unnecessary to require such a doctrine. If what we have said above makes sense, then it is actually possible that God allows created beings to make free choices to the extent that great amounts of seemingly meaningless suffering occur.[28] We will explore this option.[29]

---

25. Geisler *Philosophy of Religion*, pp. 372, 373. Actually, it is not crucial to Geisler's following points whether he opts against gratuitous evil or not.

26. *Ibid.*, pp. 396-397.

27. Although he rejects this theory, see Nash's helpful summary, *Faith and Reason*, pp. 216-217.

28. It may appear to some that there is very little difference between the two theistic positions being contrasted here. Both think that the large amounts of evil in the world are quite real and both agree that there are reasons why it is allowed. Nash makes a distinction at this point which may be helpful to some. Those who allow

If much evil is due to free will, then won't creatures overstep their bounds on various occasions, even greatly so? We said earlier that many alternative options which are suggested at the expense of theism tend to limit human freedoms. Does the doctrine of meticulous providence do the same? In other words, if only "meaningful" evil is allowed and no more, does this not limit the range of choice? Would Hitler and Stalin still be free to perpetrate their atrocities? For God to step in and stop all gratuitous evil would be, on this view, to terminate a profound number of free choices.

But we have also said that orthodox Christianity has long asserted that God *has* acted in order to limit the range of evil and will do so again hereafter. The Incarnation is the chief example of this; Satan and death were defeated at the Cross. The future will witness Satan's final defeat. Does this prove meticulous providence? Only if it is thought that *all* gratuitous evil can thereby be explained. Otherwise, we are left with periodic interventions for which only God knows the reasons.

With regard to natural law, defenders of meticulous providence seem to contend that God constantly intervenes in nature to nullify the worst evils. To repeat, this limits the free decisions which depend on these laws. Further, if one decides that a natural law theodicy makes sense, then "it is difficult to see why the same laws of nature will not also produce instances of gratuitous natural evil."[30] To rephrase this last comment, if both goods and evils proceed from necessary natural laws, why must it be stopped at certain points? Lastly, the free will of Satan and his demons would have a direct bearing on the multiplicity of natural disasters and their effects, as we find in Scripture, as well.

Gratuitous evil is also related to soul-making. As much evil as some natural calamities produce, many grow through the experience or through one's involvement with it. This is *not* to say that these disasters always justify the growth, for on the view we are presently discussing, some evil has no such specific justification.[31] But the point here is that suffering can still produce further spiritual maturation.

---

gratuitous suffering think that specific instances of evil may not have corresponding *specific* reasons, yet the *overall* system is meaningful in allowing free choices, natural law, and spiritual growth (pp. 219-220).

29. See Nash, *Faith and Reason*, pp. 216-220 and Peterson's *Evil and the Christian God* for defenses of this view.

30. Nash, *Ibid.*, p. 219.

31. See footnote number 27 above.

CONCLUSION

In this chapter, we discussed the two basic sorts of evil: moral and natural. The first is to be laid at the doorstep of free created beings. To change the results of their choices in any significant way would be to impinge on the nature of their freedom. After all, it seems impossible to both guarantee truly free decisions and eradicate the evil consequences at the same time. As Trueblood states: "Evil is the price we pay for moral freedom."[32]

Natural evil (as well as moral evil) appears to result not only from free will, but also from the normal consequences of natural law, and for the purposes of spiritual growth. To change any of these, as one would have to in order to alter the resulting suffering, would be to deny crucial aspects of creaturely freedom and/or natural law. Further, it is arguably impossible for finite human beings to assess the amount of evil in the world and declare that it is ultimately unbalanced.[33]

The answer to whether gratuitous evil actually exists is not an easy one. Theists have answered the issue both ways. We think that the scales are somewhat tipped in favor of such pain, but we are not dogmatic on this subject. Nash summarizes it quite nicely: "God could not prevent gratuitous moral evils without seriously impairing moral freedom; he could not eliminate gratuitous natural evils that are a natural outcome of the world without imperiling other significant values."[34]

It is often said that the problem of pain and evil is the chief skeptical response to a theistic universe. But after surveying the overall picture, Nash declares that the victory on this question goes to theism.[35] Perhaps surprisingly, there are actually even serious problems with the claim that atheism gains from such a discussion. We will attempt to "put the shoe on the other foot" as we note some of the atheologian's predicaments in the next chapter.

---

32. Trueblood, p. 251.

33. DeWolf, *The Religious Revolt Against Reason*, p. 172; Young, *A Christian Approach to Philosophy*, pp. 169-173; Geisler, *Philosophy of Religion*, p. 396. We will return to this issue in chapter 22.

34. Nash, *Faith and Reason.*, p. 219.

35. *Ibid.*, p. 221.

Chapter Twenty
ATHEISM AND EVIL: A FATAL DILEMMA

INTRODUCTION: IMPORTANCE OF THE QUESTION

The world can certainly be a painful place to live. We can insulate our-selves from the daily reports, but we tend to hear and see them even when we do not desire it. We don't have to look very far – just to live in a world with others is to be involved. We are all distressed by the suffering we endure, and by what we observe around us. We are confronted by adversity and affliction – or it confronts us! – whether we call ourselves atheists, agnostics, panthe-ists, or theists. All of us labor under these burdens.

So far, we have treated the problem of pain and evil as if it affected theists alone. In particular, we have asked how such problems are consistent with belief in God. Theists just seem to take a defensive posture rather than go on the offensive when questioned about their faith. But in this chapter we want to turn the issue around. Strangely enough, atheists have their own conceptual problems with suffering – and several of them are major, indeed. We will look at some of the dilemmas here.

ARE THERE CONTRADICTIONS IN THEISM?

We have said that some atheologians, taking a harder line than their colleagues, hold that the orthodox concept of God is actually contradictory. They maintain that one or more of God's attributes conflicts with the presence of evil in the world. But is this actually the case? We will begin by distinguishing between two sorts of epistemological[1] predicaments: logical dilemmas and those that only appear to be so. Mavrodes refers to the first as a "hard" dilemma, one where the core beliefs are *logically incompatible* with each other. "Soft" dilemmas occur when someone falsely believes that these beliefs are irreconcilable.[2]

Based on a similar distinction, Nash addresses the atheologians' objection by summarizing Plantinga's "theistic set" as follows:

1. God exists.
2. God is omnipotent.
3. God is omniscient.
4. God is omnibenevolent.
5. God created the world.
   and
6. The world contains evil.[3]

Specifically, where is the contradiction in this "theistic set"? It would appear to be difficult to prove one here. Prominent atheologian J.L. Mackie actually admits "that there is no explicit contradiction between the statements that there is an omnipotent and wholly good god and that there is evil." Yet he thinks that if additional premises are added, the contradiction will become obvious. He suggests appending "the at least initially plausible premises" that an omnibenevolent being would eliminate evil as far as he can and that such a being has no limits.[4]

The theist might respond in a twofold manner. (1) There are apparently no direct contradictions in the theistic set above, at least according to Mackie. This is significant in itself. (2) The premises that the atheologian would like to add in order to force a contradiction also fail to do an adequate job, as we argued in the last chapter. We will briefly review some of our conclusions.

---

1. Epistemology is the area of philosophy that deals with how we know what we do, including various theories that claim to offer the best means of gaining such knowledge.

2. Mavrodes *Belief in God*, p. 106.

3. Nash, *Faith and Reason.*, p. 181. For further details, see Plantinga, *God, Freedom, and Evil*, Part 1.

4. Mackie, *The Miracle of Theism*, p. 150.

Using Mackie's examples, should God eliminate evil as far as He can? The theist might ask how such would be possible without limiting human freedom? Moreover, might such action actually have the negative consequence of reducing the good that results from the suffering? Further, and perhaps most difficult of all, how could finite beings ever know whether God *already* accomplishes just what Mackie suggests?

Or can an omnipotent God do anything, as per Mackie's second question? Orthodox theology has long insisted that there are things that even an omnipotent God cannot do – such as contradictory actions. So again, the issue concerns whether God could remove the evil without contradicting the free will of His creatures. We are right back at our earlier point. No one has shown how either of these options involves a contradiction.[5]

Nash mentions another possible atheological objection: couldn't God eliminate all the evil that He can without either forfeiting a greater good or allowing a greater evil? But once again, how could it ever be determined that this is not the very case we have at present? Arguing against the type or amount of evil in the world gets us back to the options entertained and dismissed in the last chapter. So this creative suggestion does not eliminate evil or otherwise cause us to reformulate our theistic set above, failing to do the job for the critic. In fact, Nash asserts that "our new proposition is totally consistent with the existence of evil in God's creation."[6]

Besides, as Mavrodes counters, the theist is certainly justified in offering a counter-argument to the existence of evil in God's universe. Mavrodes explicates it this way:

> If God is omnipotent and benevolent, then He cannot allow evil unless there is a justification for allowing it. But He obviously does allow it. Consequently, if He

---

5. Very interestingly, atheist William Rowe presents an influential argument against the theistic position, but still freely admits that there is no contradiction in theism. He even concludes that theists can *rationally* affirm their position. Cf. William L. Rowe, *Philosophy of Religion: An Introduction* (Belmont: Wadsworth Publishing Company, 1978), p. 94 with Nash's evaluation of it (*Faith and Reason*, pp. 212-215). C. Stephen Evans agrees with Nash that no one has proven a contradiction in theism at this point in his book, *Philosophy of Religion: Thinking About Faith* (Downers Grove: InterVarsity Press, 1982), p. 137. See chapter 19 above for many details concerning such atheological counter-arguments. Nash provides other problems for alternative formulations like Mackie's on pp. 183-186.

6. Nash, *Ibid.*, p. 186.

is omnipotent and benevolent, then He has a justification for allowing evil. He is benevolent and omnipotent. Therefore, He is justified in allowing evil.[7]

In other words, although atheologians are fond of juxtaposing the actual existence of evil over against the orthodox doctrine of God, theists can just as well counter with the above argument. The logical form of the first argument is no more valid than that of the second.[8] So atheologians reach a roadblock here. They have been unsuccessful in discovering the "missing premise" that would prove the theistic set stated above to be contradictory. Nash concludes the matter this way: "Even though atheologians have been claiming for decades that the theistic set is self-contradictory, none of them has yet produced the required missing proposition that will prove the claim . . . we are still waiting for him to show that his claim is true."[9]

EVIL IS POSITION- AND PERSON-RELATED

Most people speak of the quandary we are discussing in our last three chapters as *the* problem of pain and evil. Even most scholars appear to think of the overall subject as if it were primarily one, major issue. Our readers might even have noticed that, up until this point, that is how it has been discussed in this book, too. But while we have been satisfied until now to deal with the more general features, it is time to be more specific. The answers that one gives to the problem of evil largely depend on the perspective from which one is answering – the general world view and the specific "twists" contained in one's position, as well as one's personal outlook.

The first matter is nicely summarized by John Feinberg:

> The notion that there is one and only one theological/philosophical problem of evil is mistaken . . . 'the theological/philosophical problem of evil' does not refer to one problem, but to a series of problems that arise in regard to various theological positions as such positions are coupled with their respective normative ethical views.[10]

Then how are we to judge whether the problem of evil actually causes a predicament with regard to a particular view? Again, Feinberg is helpful. As

---

7. Mavrodes, p. 95.

8. It seems that Rowe allows a similar formulation to count toward the rationality of the theistic position. See footnote number 5 above.

9. *Ibid.*, pp. 186-187.

10. Feinberg, *Theologies and Evil*, pp. 147-148.

encountered within a particular philosophical or theological system, the presence of a dilemma "always" depends on the logical consistency of propositions internal to that view.[11] Accordingly, the problem of evil involves a host of issues, depending on the particular system of thought being addressed. In order to see if any specific position is adversely affected, one must view the charge against the logical consistency of the whole. Such is a question of internal congruity, especially since we already saw that there is no explicit contradiction in the theistic set. When such distinctions are made, it is entirely possible that certain theistic views will appear to be inconsistent, while others may pass the test just fine. Feinberg investigated eight theistic responses to evil and concluded that six of them were internally consistent.[12]

There is another significant consideration that follows from this perspective. The atheologian may continue to utilize the problem of evil to object to theistic systems (often without making any distinctions between them). But as long as a system links the notions of God's omnipotence, omniscience, and benevolence with the presence of evil in a way that is logically consistent, then the atheologian must object on other grounds.[13]

This last consideration is a crucial one. There is no explicit contradiction between theism and evil. Therefore, if the theistic system in question is internally consistent, then the atheologian must utilize a critique other than juxtaposing the problem of evil over against a specific species of theism. This potentially removes much of the sting of the atheological objection from pain and suffering.

But there is still another aspect to this situation. Not only must the matter of evil be evaluated against a specific theological system, but we can break the inquiry down even further. There appears to be a very personal feature in discussions on this subject. Not all sensitive, knowledgeable theists are bothered by the issues involved. In short, many just don't perceive the force of the objection.[14]

---

11. *Ibid.*, p. 148. Mavrodes responds similarly (pp. 105, 110).
12. *Ibid.*, p. 158.
13. *Ibid.*, p. 148.
14. I can illustrate this last thought with a personal reflection. I (Habermas) spent ten years as a skeptical believer with severe questions about the Christian faith, even being involved in heated debates with Christians. But during this time, the problem of evil never struck me as a very worthwhile complaint. While I was impressed with certain factual objections to Christianity, and brought these up regularly in my arguments, I thought that theists had too many possible ways to answer the presence of evil, and so I never used it.

While it is quite true that ones *feelings* on this subject are not determinative, this is *precisely* the point. The problem is not a conflict between logically irreconcilable positions, but one involving the beliefs and tastes of the individuals themselves.

George Mavrodes expands on this last suggestion, indicating that the issue of evil does not exist in a vacuum. There must be a person who thinks that there is a problem. However, just because someone experiences such a dilemma, this provides no logical reason to conclude that *someone else* ought to have the same problem. In short, the problem of suffering is person-related. The matter of pain and evil fails to involve any objective conflicts, and there is a strong subjective element.[15]

In fact, Mavrodes makes some rather direct comments on the logical nature of the dilemma. He says: ". . . one person's belief in a core that someone else takes to be inconsistent constitutes no dilemma for the believer."[16] Some skeptics will argue that the theist is simply avoiding a difficult quandary – that he is, in effect, "copping out" of the problem. But Mavrodes answers again:

> The important point is that the critic who makes a truth- or logic-oriented objection is not in a privileged position. . . . In particular, the fact that the critic is unconvinced by the theologian counts for no more than the fact that the theologian is unconvinced by the critic. Of course, the theological defender is almost uniformly charged with the burden of proof, while critics of his views are often thought to have no such obligation. But this is merely an accidental feature of the current state of culture and philosophy; it has no basis in logic and reason. In particular, if the claim that the problem of evil involves no real contradiction obligates its proponent to prove this claim, then the claim that the problem does involve a real contradiction should place an analogous obligation on its proponent.[17]

Thus we conclude this second consideration. There is no such thing as *the* problem of evil. There is only a dilemma in theological or philosophical systems that are internally inconsistent in terms of the logic involved. Further, in systems where there is no logical contradiction (of which there are probably a fair number), the issues are person-related. Some believers think they have a perfectly good response and will not be bothered by this problem at all. But the critic's lack of convincing counts nothing against the theistic position, any more than the believer not being convinced counts against the atheological

---

15. Mavrodes, pp. 101-104.
16. *Ibid.*, p. 103.
17. *Ibid.*, pp. 108-109.

position. This all seems to place the atheologian in the unenviable position of having to prove that there are *logical* conflicts in *every* theistic system.

RECOGNIZING EVIL

In spite of the two difficulties for the atheologian that we have already mentioned, perhaps the worst of their problems is an inherent dilemma in their own system. The charge was eloquently levelled by C.S. Lewis, as a telling argument against his own naturalism. How can atheists even question the existence of a Creator based on the pain and evil in the world? Since atheists seldom recognize the existence of any absolute right or wrong, they have no basis for identifying the presence of evil. Lewis explains it like this:

> My argument against God was that the universe seemed so cruel and unjust. But how had I got this idea of *just* and *unjust*? . . . Of course I could have given up my idea of justice by saying it was nothing but a private idea of my own. But if I did that, then my argument against God collapsed too – for the argument depended on saying that the world was really unjust, not simply that it did not happen to please my private fancies. Thus in the very act of trying to prove that God did not exist – in other words, that the whole of reality was senseless – I found I was forced to assume that one part of reality – namely my idea of justice – was full of sense. Consequently atheism turns out to be too simple.[18]

We need to expand upon Lewis' point a bit, for there appears to be a hidden assumption or two here. He is charging that the atheist has a very serious dilemma. If there is no absolute standard of right and wrong, as most atheists appear to believe, then the atheist has no right to utilize the presence of pain and evil in the world against the orthodox view of God. The reason is straightforward – in the absence of ethical absolutes, then even the real presence of profound suffering is not actually something that is objectively *wrong*. So while the pain would still be real (not an illusion) it is simply a reality devoid of any *ethical* consequences.

To say it another way, the atheist's objections to the suffering in the world amount to little more than their personal dissatisfaction with certain aspects of reality. In the absence of objective ethical standards, then Lewis appears to be correct: atheistic complaints to evil constitute some "private idea" of right and wrong, and evil is simply something that "did not happen to please my private

---

18. C.S. Lewis, *Mere Christianity* (New York: Macmillan, 1952), pp. 45-46. The italicized words are those of Lewis.

fancies," nothing more.

How might the atheist respond to this argument? One option is to assert that there really are ethical absolutes in the universe. But such an alternative is unpalatable to the majority of atheists.[19] Not only does it conflict with their widespread notions of human freedom and lack of objective values, but it seems to backfire into the major premise of the moral argument for God's existence (see next chapter). In brief, if absolute, objective ethical standards exist, then it is very difficult to explain them as being the result of chance evolution.

To summarize briefly, the atheist can only use the problem of evil to object to the orthodox conception of God if there is some standard by which to recognize the evil in the first place. Apart from such a standard, suffering is reduced to unfortunate feelings of dislike for the pain. On the other hand, if there *is* such an objective criterion, then the question must include the existence of such a measurement in a chance universe. In short, if evil objectively exists, then God would appear to exist as well, with some sort of relationship between such a Being and the evil.

THE THEISTIC WORLD VIEW VERSUS NATURALISM

The atheologian could very well make another sort of response to the dilemma we just outlined for her. It could be asserted that atheists *don't have* to recognize objective values in order to advance the issue of evil against Christian theism. Rather, they can raise the problem from *within* theism as an *internal* problem for this world view to solve, since it *does* recognize an absolute standard of right and wrong.

Here's another way to look at the objection. We said above that the question of evil is an internal matter of consistency within a system, and this

---

19. The humanists who signed the First Manifesto in 1933 explained: "Humanism asserts that the nature of the universe depicted by modern science makes unacceptable any supernatural or cosmic guarantees of human values." Those who endorsed the Humanist Manifesto II in 1973 said: "We affirm that moral values derive their source from human experience. Ethics is autonomous and situational . . . . Human life has meaning because we create and develop our futures." Paul Kurtz, *Humanist Manifestoes I and II* (Buffalo: Prometheus Press, 1973). For these quotations and other details, see Norman L. Geisler, "The Collapse of Modern Atheism" in *The Intellectuals Speak Out About God*, edited by Roy Abraham Varghese (Chicago: Regnery Gateway, 1984), pp. 129-152.

response questions that coherence. To say it popularly, the atheologian basically issues the challenge to stage the contest in the theistic ball park, since she cannot play in her own.

The theistic reply might first be to point out that, at worst, she is in the same place where she began two chapters ago. Thus the atheological response *doesn't change anything*. It only reasserts the former position, which we have answered in much depth. In short, God allows evil for the greater goods that are potentially achieved, particularly regarding creaturely free will, natural laws, and soul-making.

Then theists might assert, as we did above, that the atheologian has not been successful in pointing out any actual contradictions in the theistic system. Further, the atheologian must also specify which theistic perspective she is referring to, since this is only a problem for systems that are susceptible to the criticism and for individuals who "feel the crunch."

But there is still another reply that will put the issue in a broader context. If the atheologian insists on playing in the theistic ball park (since the atheologian has, in effect, no home field!), then we need to look at the two starting line-ups. It is seldom recognized that naturalism, *per se*, offers comparatively few positive arguments *in favor* of its position. The naturalist primarily features the problem of evil and *responses to* contrary positions. As Trueblood asserts concerning the case against God's existence, "The chief negative evidences constitute the problem of evil."[20]

But naturalists cannot even offer evil as an argument that *favors* their position, since they cannot officially recognize its nature. Thus, if we are correct here, naturalism is largely a world view that must resort to objecting to theist's arguments (including proposing evil as an internal problem) rather than supporting their own system. From the outset of the "ball game," this severely limits their offensive "punch."

On the other hand, theism (and Christian theism in particular) can offer a multitude of arguments in its favor. Some of these evidences have been included in this book. The existence of God (Parts One and Two), the origin of life (chapter 15), the trustworthiness of the New Testament (chapter 26), the historicity of Jesus' resurrection (chapter 27), the uniqueness of Jesus Christ (chapter 28), and God's personal involvement with His people (chapter 30)

---

20. Trueblood, p. 231.

are some examples. Other theistic evidences might include a carefully constructed case from fulfilled prophecies of various types,[21] and several arguments for life after death.[22]

Now here's the point of analyzing the naturalistic and theistic "starting line-ups." While we have said that the former relies chiefly on critiques of opposing positions, theism offers *both* numerous positive arguments in its favor, as well as excellent critiques of naturalism itself.[23] There's nothing wrong with naturalists desiring to utilize evil in order to offer an internal critique of theism, but they cannot expect theists to play by naturalistic rules, since they have none by which to judge the existence of suffering.

Therefore, to play in the theistic ball park is fine, but naturalists must be prepared to view evil as an internal problem for theism. But as such, the problem must be viewed in light of the many arguments which both evidence theism and argue against naturalism. In other words, it is certainly true that evil exists, sometimes in great quantities. And we don't always know why we suffer (chapter 22). But it is also true that this is a universe where God exists, and where He created life, predicted the future, directed the writing of the New Testament, sent His unique Son Jesus Christ, raised Him from the dead, gets personally involved with His people, and offers them eternal life in His glorious, eternal Kingdom.[24]

To see all this from a different angle, it is undeniable that suffering and evil really exist. But it is comforting to know that it also happens in a universe where God raised Jesus from the dead, confirming His unique message. Therefore, even when we don't know why certain things happen as they do, we still have the assurance that there is a reason for all of it. This is what we mean by playing in the theistic ball park. Evil cannot be taken in isolation from the other relevant data, and that data explain evil much easier than evil can explain away all the evidence.

---

21. For example, see Robert C. Newman, Editor, *The Evidence of Prophecy: Fulfilled Prediction as a Testimony to the Truth of Christianity* (Hatfield: Interdisciplinary Biblical Research Institute, 1988). Many of the authors of this volume are trained in some aspect of both science and Scripture studies.

22. See Habermas and Moreland, *Immortality*, Chapters 1-6.

23. For the latter, see chapters 3 and 10 here, plus the entire volume edited by Varghese, *Intellectuals Speak Out About God*, for a scientific, philosophical, and theological reaction against naturalism from a wide variety of perspectives.

24. For an argument from Jesus' resurrection to the Christian theistic model of heaven, see Habermas and Moreland, Chapters 9-10.

CONCLUSION

In this chapter we went on the "offensive" in favor of the theistic answer to the problem of evil. This is a seldom-used tactic, but is well warranted by the evidence. Strangely enough, naturalism has plenty of problems with the suffering in the world. We addressed four such predicaments. In the end, we even think that their struggles prove to be fatal.

First, no contradictions in the theistic set have yet been proven. Atheologians have tried to do so, but have not generated the missing premise that would prove that theism is internally inconsistent. In fact, in addition to other responses, theists are always able to reply that since God does have certain attributes, there *must* be an adequate reason for the evil in the world.

Second, atheologians have generally failed to recognize that there is no single problem of evil. Separate theistic systems respond differently to the various issues. Moreover, these are not external difficulties, but internal ones, affecting the consistency of a particular perspective. Additionally, suffering is a subjective, person-related issue; it bothers some theists, but not others. Just because critics are still not convinced does not count against theism any more than the reverse counts against naturalism.

Third, naturalists are not able to raise the objection concerning evil either from their own system or as an argument in favor of naturalism. The reason for this is that naturalists who do not recognize the objectivity of ethical values have no basis from which to protest the presence of suffering. From their viewpoint, it is only an unfortunate consequence of life. While they may not like it, their own system does not allow them to recognize any objective complaints to lay at the theist's feet.

The seemingly few naturalists who do accept objective values have the greater problem of explaining this phenomenon in a chance universe, especially since it is the major premise in the moral argument for God's existence. Thus, it would appear that, if evil really exists, so does God.

Some atheologians have therefore been satisfied to offer evil as an internal critique of theism, pointing out that its views are inconsistent. But, fourth, we argued that such an internal charge does not exist in a vacuum, but must be evaluated along with the distinctive evidences for theism. It is a contest between world views. And it is easier to explain evil by the arguments for Christianity than it is for evil to eliminate all of these excellent evidences.

This last point has interesting implications. Whereas theists seldom deny the reality of evil, admitting it along with all the other evidences, naturalists must deny virtually all (or perhaps even all) of the major evidences for a theistic universe.[25] This is another indication of the untenable nature of this world view.

---

25. For this last argument in more developed form, see Gary R. Habermas, "Paradigm Shift: A Challenge to Naturalism," *Bibliotheca Sacra*, Volume 146, number 584 (October-December, 1989), pp. 437-450.

Chapter Twenty-One
THE MORAL
ARGUMENT FOR GOD'S EXISTENCE

INTRODUCTION: IMPORTANCE OF THE QUESTION

Pain and evil are unquestionably real. On the one hand, suffering seems to be an actual part of the fabric of the universe as we know it, although it was not always so. We appear to experience life's agonies on a daily basis, both in our own lives and through the descriptions of others. To say that heartache and misery are rampant in our world is not an exaggeration. Even the initial reaction of the believer is often to cry out to God to ask "Why?" as if we knew no other response.

But on the other hand, we have seen in the last few chapters that there is an entirely different side to evil. We argued that God allows it for the greater goods that are accomplished through it, chiefly the free will of created beings, the need for the laws of nature, and the possibility of soul-making, ending in the gift of eternal life. Without these benefits, life would not exist as we know it.

Further, atheists have even worse problems with evil. One of these is relevant to this chapter. We saw that the very quandary of suffering itself requires the knowledge of absolute ethical values. Otherwise, there can be no objective recognition of evil and one must be satisfied to make nothing more than statements of personal preference.[1] But atheists generally do not acknowledge the

---

1. In other words, the atheist can object to evil in personal terms, such as by

necessary moral standard to even identify the presence of objective evil in the world. This is why they cannot launch their protests from their own world view. Instead, they can only raise the issue as an internal feature of theistic systems.

In this chapter we will take the next step and argue in detail what we hinted in the last chapter. The recognition of both evil and a moral code signify God's existence. For those few atheists who do recognize a moral standard, their naturalistic, chance universe fails to provide any adequate reason for such absolute morality. While it is true that theists can recognize the objective presence of evil, this may be a blessing in disguise. They can also rest in the knowledge that the ability to do so indicates that God exists, as well.

ATTEMPTS TO CONSTRUCT A MORAL ARGUMENT

There have been numerous noteworthy attempts which generally argue that there is an objective moral code of right and wrong and that such requires God as its Source. Such efforts are usually said to have originated with Immanuel Kant (d. 1804), one of the most influential philosophers ever. While Kant actually opposed the construction of any proofs for God's existence, he also thought that God was a postulate of practical reason, which he took to be a rational or reflective faith that centered in ethical concerns.[2]

For Kant, the highest good (or *summum bonum*) resided in the merger of one's moral duty and happiness. But the pursuit of such is obtainable only on the assumption that the individual person is immortal, having an eternity to progress morally. While this cannot be demonstrated, it "is an inseparable corollary of an *a priori* unconditionally valid practical law."[3] But this requires

---

saying, "I don't like suffering." But this is not a moral judgment, unless the atheist accepts an objective standard of right and wrong. Without it, how would one know the difference between evil and non-evil?

2. Immanuel Kant, *Critique of Practical Reason*, translated by Lewis White Beck, third edition (New York: Macmillan, 1993), pp. 132-133. For another of his treatments on this subject, see Immanuel Kant, *Religion Within the Limits of Reason Alone*, translated by Theodore M. Greene and Hoyt H. Hudson (New York: Harper and Row, 1960), pp. 3-6, 129-138, 142-151.

3. Kant says that there is "an infinitely enduring existence and personality of the same rational being; this is called the immortality of the soul." Later he says, "Only endless progress from lower to higher stages of moral perfection is possible to a rational but finite being." See *Critique of Practical Reason*, Book II, Chapter II, Section IV, especially p. 129.

another truth: we "must postulate the existence of God as necessarily belong-
ing to the possibility of the highest good."[4] All of this is ultimately based on
the presence of morality and our pursuit of it. Kant concludes that "it is morally necessary to assume the existence of God."[5]

Early this century, Hastings Rashdall developed further the moral argument, making it a full-fledged evidence for the existence of God. In doing so,
his argument became a model for later thinkers. Rashdall argued that there
was an absolute moral law:

> The proposition that some things are right, others wrong . . . is an immediate
> datum or deliverance of consciousness. The truth is assented to, and acted upon,
> by men of all religions or none, by persons who hold most dissimilar views as
> to the ultimate nature of the Universe, and by men who profess to have no theo-
> ry of the Universe at all.[6]

Where, then, does such an absolute moral law exist? It cannot dwell "wholly and completely" in any individual person; neither can it "exist *in* material
things."[7] Absolute morality can only reside in a Mind "which is the source of
whatever is true in our moral judgments . . . a Mind whose thoughts are the
standard of truth and falsehood alike in Morality and in respect to all other
existence." In short, "objective Morality implies the belief in God."[8]

C.S. Lewis developed details of the moral argument beyond most other
scholars, spending a significant amount of time on objections to it.[9] He argued
that there must be a universal moral law or all disagreements and moral criticisms would be meaningless. Throughout our lives, we make constant reference to this moral standard. Its existence is indicated by two reasons. First,
there are striking similarities in the moral laws of different nations and cultures, and "you can recognize the same law running through them all."[10]

---

4. Kant, *Ibid.*, Section V, "The Existence of God as a Postulate of Pure Practical
Reason," p. 131.

5. *Ibid.*, p. 132.

6. Hastings Rashdall, *The Theory of Good and Evil*, Volume II (Oxford: The
Clarendon Press, 1907). Book III, Chapter I, sections IV and V, pp. 206-213, 219-220
are reproduced in John Hick, Editor, *The Existence of God* (New York: Macmillan,
1964), pp. 143-152. See p. 145 for this statement.

7. Rashdall, *Ibid.*, p. 149.

8. *Ibid.*, pp. 149-150.

9. C.S. Lewis, *Mere Christianity*, pp. 17-39.

10. *Ibid.*, p. 24. For a lengthy catalogue of these laws and their similarity from culture to culture (mostly ancient), see C.S. Lewis, *The Abolition of Man* (New York:
Macmillan, 1947), pp. 93-121.

Second, persons judge between the moralities of different cultures, as when much of the civilized world judged Hitler's Nazi morality.[11]

The moral law cannot be simply "herd instinct" or the stronger impulse would always win. Yet, humans often decide in favor of the "weaker" instinct, such as when one neglects the desire to save herself and runs back into a burning building in order to rescue someone else. We know it is right to protect lives whenever possible.

Neither can morality be something we only learn from our society but for which there is no absolute basis. Doubtless we learn morality, says Lewis, but, like the mathematical tables, they are independently true, as well. The two reasons mentioned above show that morality is more than just something our society says is true. Further, moral law is not another law of nature. The latter show what will probably happen, while the former dictate what we *ought* to do. There is a major difference.[12]

Lewis concludes that the moral law cannot be explained any other way except as being objectively binding. Such an absolute code demands an absolute Lawgiver who gave us the law and wants us to obey it.[13]

Elton Trueblood makes his own contribution to this topic. First, he provides a three-step moral argument for the existence of God. According to this scholar, (1) the "best evidence for ethical objectivity is . . . the fact that there is really a significant agreement in moral convictions, an agreement too great to be accounted for by coincidence." (2) Our moral experience, including various sorts of ethical judgments and arguments, is meaningless without an objective law. (3) This moral order requires a Divine Being.[14]

After dealing with the initial two points, he then examines the third. He poses an important question: why can't we just stop with the law itself; why must we proceed any further? Trueblood answers that the moral law cannot be accounted for as a natural law, for such laws are divorced from any moral notions. Neither can human beings explain it on their own, for we habitually experience the fact that we don't measure up to it. Likewise, the whole of human society cannot justify it in themselves, because "the group, as well as the individual, has sinned."[15]

11. Lewis, *Mere Christianity*, pp. 24-26.8
12. Lewis answers these objections in *Ibid.*, pp. 21-26.
13. *Ibid.*, pp. 31-39.
14. Trueblood, *Philosophy of Religion*, pp. 112-114.
15. *Ibid.*, p. 114.

Then Trueblood draws the following conclusion:

This means that the only locus of the moral law is a superhuman mind. That it must be a mind is clear when we realize that law has no meaning except for minds, and that it must be superhuman is clear when we realize that it cannot be ours. Therefore, the recognition of an objective moral law drives us to the belief in God, without whom that law would have no significant being. If we believe the law, we must also believe in the conditions which make the law possible.[16]

Lastly, Trueblood notes that the being behind the moral law must be personal, for only such a being could appreciate morality and give the law. Thus, the objective moral law "leads to a personal understanding of what is deepest in reality."[17]

As we might surmise from our analysis, many of these forms of the moral argument for God's existence also have similar characteristics. Some are more convincing than others, employing stronger premises and providing more support. We will return to this subject below, in order to evaluate the potency of the argument as a whole.

OBJECTIONS

Atheologians have raised various sorts of objections to the moral argument. Most of these center on the problem of evil, like those we addressed in the last three chapters, such as how God could allow suffering. But as we have said, atheologians who argue from the presence of evil have numerous problems. Most relevant to this chapter, they have to decide whether they are raising their objection from within their own system, or as an internal problem in theism. If the former, the point reverses against them, since they really cannot recognize evil unless they have a basis for objective right and wrong. But this, in turn, is the key premise in the moral argument for God's existence.

If the complaint questions the internal consistency of theism, it must oppose the many evidences for this perspective. But this is not enough. Naturalism must also single out and address the various types of theism, as well, since some are affected by certain objections, while others are immune to them. As a whole, we concluded that it was much easier to explain evil in a theistic context with its vast array of evidences, than it is to resolve the

---

16. *Ibid.*, p. 115.
17. *Ibid.*

problem from a naturalistic perspective with its distinct shortage of either direct evidence or the inability to recognize evil on its own grounds.

A few atheologians have advanced other objections. Betrand Russell repeats a classical question that has been voiced at least since Plato's *Euthyphro* when he asks where the moral law comes from. Does it proceed from God's fiat, or is it external to Him? If the former, it is arbitrary; if the latter, then God is even subject to it and then He is not the highest good.[18]

Initially, the theist may charge that this challenge commits the classic black/white fallacy of informal logic. The atheological objection allows only two options when others are possible, so it is an illegitimate protest. Additionally, classical theism usually answers that the moral law proceeds from God's nature, meaning that it is not external to Him, neither is it arbitrary. Thus, the moral law reflects His own perfect character. A third response admits that the moral law proceeds from God's will, but asserts that this does not make it arbitrary, since God's will is ultimate. Any of these responses, and especially the last two, nullify the atheological conjecture.[19]

One very instructive exchange on God's existence, including many details on the moral argument, occurred in a 1948 debate between the two eminent philosophers Bertrand Russell and F.C. Copleston.[20]

Interestingly, Russell did not repeat the objection just noted above. But he did defend his recognition of right and wrong apart from God: "I feel that some things are good and that other things are bad. I love the things that are good, that I think are good, and I hate the things that I think are bad."

Copleston responded by asking Russell about his basis for such a statement: "Yes, but what's your justification for distinguishing between good and bad . . . ?"

Russell responded in a rather surprising manner: "I don't have any justification any more than I have when I distinguish between blue and yellow."

Copleston pressed the issue again: " . . . so you distinguish good and bad by what faculty?"

"By my feelings" was all Russell said in his next response![21]

---

18. Bertrand Russell, *Why I Am Not a Christian* (New York: Simon and Schuster, 1957).

19. Cf. Geisler, *Philosophy of Religion*, pp. 124-125.

20. Originally aired on the British Broadcasting Corporation, the debate was later reproduced in Russell's *Why I Am Not a Christian*, and in John Hick's *The Existence of God*. Our references are taken from the latter text.

21. Russell and Copleston in Hick, p. 183.

The debate continued along these same lines, with Copleston questioning whether feelings were a sufficient guide for morality. Russell again said that they were, in the sense that blue and yellow were different: although he could not prove that something wasn't yellow, he simply accepted the majority view, not that of someone who was color-blind. In the same way, Russell thought that he could make an ethical decision and be satisfied that most people agreed with him. Copleston repeatedly asked whether there was any outside criterion or ground for arguing in this manner, and Russell told him he needed no more than the majority decision, as in the case of color perception.

After Russell affirmed his acceptance of at least a practical notion of moral obligation, Copleston said that the "vast majority of the human race will make, and always have made, some distinction between right and wrong." Then he continued, saying that such recognition is best explained by there being an author of the moral code recognized by most people.

At this point, Russell appeared to alter his tactics. He first replied that the moral law continually changed. Copleston countered that this was no argument against the actual existence of a universal moral law (see next section below). Russell again went on to another response, declaring that the law can arise from the teaching one receives from "one's parents or one's nurses." Copleston countered that even this ability to evaluate and criticize the moral law presupposed an objective standard for our actions.[22] The two philosophers left this subject moments later.

A couple of items ought to be noticed from this dialogue. Russell apparently did not think that the atheologian was only able to raise the question of evil from within the theistic system. Rather, he wanted to establish his own notion of right and wrong. But how did he justify this notion of value apart from some standard, especially when his agnosticism[23] presented no grounds for such recognition? Russell answered that he was able to recognize the difference between right and wrong by his feelings – just as he was able to distinguish blue from yellow. The color appeared to him a certain way and others generally agreed with him.

But here's the rub. The detection of colors and the recognition of proper behavior are not quite analogous. Morality is not something we perceive. But there are other, more serious, problems here. It is clear that Russell's notion of

22. *Ibid.*, pp. 184-189.
23. In the debate, Russell affirmed that he was defending the agnostic position, instead of atheism (p. 167).

morality is not grounded in any objective standard beyond man's majority recognition. So he falls prey to exactly the same critique we raised above: on what grounds, then, can he recognize the actual existence of pain and evil? It would appear that this scholar has no objective measuring-stick for suffering.

Moreover, if morality is also decided by feelings and confirmed by majority decision, we are certainly on very shaky grounds. Majority decisions are not binding, yet Russell acted as if such was a sufficient ethical basis. For example, what if the Nazis (an issue brought up by Copleston) convinced most others in the world that they were right to murder millions of people? Would it then be correct? If so, then we see the problem even more clearly. If not, then why not? Such actions were allowed in their country. How far must majority decisions extend?

Further, does Russell's analysis of the nature of morality properly account for the sense that most people seem to have that cold-blooded torture and murder are *intrinsically* wrong? This is perhaps why Nash comments on "the weakness of the countermoves" proposed by atheologians against the moral argument.[24] It certainly appears that Russell's case is doomed to failure.

A RECONSTRUCTED MORAL ARGUMENT

In our earlier survey, most of the versions of the moral argument have certain foundational concepts in common. At the same time, some scholars evidence key premises better than others. Here we will attempt to outline a single expression of the case for the existence of God based on the presence of objective morality in the world. We will add only one additional notion to the above efforts. Afterwards, we will provide a brief explanation of some of the major concepts.

1. An objective moral code exists.
   a. Such a rule is the basis for disputes and moral discussions.
   b. There is an amazing amount of agreement within different nations and cultures over what we might call the major crimes of force (such as murder, kidnapping, and rape).
   c. Moral judgment has been passed on certain cultures from the outside, as when much of the civilized world judged Hitler's Nazi regime.

---

24. Nash, *Faith and Reason*, p. 159. Nash concludes his treatment of the moral argument by asking, "Which world-view best explains our consciousness of the objective moral order?" (p. 161).

2. To give reasons for denying the existence of moral absolutes and/or hold that others ought to do the same is self-refuting.
3. The moral code cannot be explained by natural or human means.
   a. The code is not a law of nature, for nature makes no ethical judgments, neither does it distinguish between inanimate objects and life.
   b. The code was not created by a human being or by society as a whole, for this cannot:
      (1) answer 1-2 above (especially 1c and 2).
      (2) explain why we sometimes decide on options that are *not* in our best interests, or which may *not* preserve our lives (including feeling guilty when we don't choose such obligations).
      (3) do the best job of explaining why, individually and corporately, we usually realize we have failed to fulfill this moral code.
4. The creator of the moral code must be a personal, moral Legislator beyond man.
   a. Neither man nor society is the creator of the code.
   b. Moral laws have no meaning apart from minds.
   c. Only personal beings appreciate, originate, and enforce morality, or relate morally to other beings.
   d. The moral argument compliments other arguments earlier in this book, providing additional hints about this Legislator.

Perhaps a few comments are in order concerning this amalgamated moral argument. It would seem that 1a is difficult to deny. All of us explicitly or implicitly rely on moral laws to solve (or at least to shed light on) disputes and moral issues. Even Bertrand Russell thought that he knew the difference between good and bad, and he is not the only atheologian who would defend such a notion. Ed Miller states the point quite succinctly:

If we did not believe that there is an objective and unchanging foundation of moral values and ideals, then we would never bother to make such judgments, at least seriously. On the contrary, that we continue to exercise moral judgment, not only in reference to ourselves but also to others, is clear evidence that we do, in fact, take such judgments as counting for something and as being ultimately and objectively significant. In this way, it may be argued, it is self-contradictory (practically speaking) to make judgments of moral value and to deny at the same time that there is any objective basis of morality.[25]

As to why similar laws prohibiting the major crimes of force generally persist from culture to culture (1b), atheologians like Russell frequently object

---

25. Ed Miller, *God and Reason* (New York: Macmillan, 1972), p. 90, as quoted by Nash, p. 160.

that these laws also differ, or that they are not absolute, but change over the years. Copleston rightly objected that this does not disprove "the universality of the moral law." Russell did not object.[26]

Nash explains why Copleston is correct:

> So far as objective truth is concerned, absolutely nothing follows from the fact that two individuals or two cultures disagree over the morality of a particular action any more than that their disagreement over some nonethical issue might be thought to imply the absence of any objective truth in this nonethical case. When person A says that the world is flat and person B claims the world is round, it hardly follows that there is no objective truth about this issue.[27]

Of course, depending on its nature, evidence of change among different cultures and the absence of certain laws might count against 1b. But here is the key: we are not discussing each and every law that a culture may have, but only those major crimes of force that we outlined above. These appear to remain rather constant. The question, of course, is why this is the case. Nash writes, " . . . it is difficult to see what would justify the conclusion that in ethical disputes *no* beliefs are objectively and universally true."[28]

Perhaps 1c is even more evidentially interesting. What gives nations the right to interfere with other nations and cultures and judge that they have committed wrongs against mankind? Such was certainly the case, for example, at the post-World War II Nuremberg Trials. Here it was ruled, not just that the Nazi war criminals had transgressed international human rights, but that they were morally wrong.

Another debate on the subject of God's existence between two philosophers, theist Thomas B. Warren and imminent atheist Antony G.N. Flew, made these trials a central focus. Warren had to bring the subject up three times, imploring Flew to answer, before the latter would even respond to the subject, and then without touching the pithiest issues. In the course of their discussions, Flew admitted each of the following:

1. There is an objective moral law that requires human compliance. Flew specifically said: "I fully share Dr. Warren's outrage against the monstrosities of the Nazi era." Later he stated: "I agree with Dr. Warren that certain things are categorically right or wrong . . . " Then in a questionnaire, Flew answered

---

26. Russell and Copleston in Hick, p. 186.
27. Nash, *Faith and Reason*, p. 159.
28. *Ibid.*, p. 160. (The italics are Nash's.)

in the affirmative when asked whether, "In murdering six million Jewish men, women, and children the Nazis were guilty of real (objective) moral wrong." Likewise, he affirmed that he "would have had the objective moral obligation to die rather than join them [the Nazis] in the murder of men, women, and children."[29]

2. When asked what type of law the Nazis were guilty of violating, Flew answered "International Moral."[30]

Flew answered in the *negative* in response to the following statement: "The judges at Nuremberg would have been justified in concluding that, since the Nazis were obeying the law of their own land, the Nazis were *not* guilty of real (objective) moral wrong in torturing and/or murdering six million Jewish men, women, and children."[31]

To sum up briefly, Flew expressly and repeatedly affirmed the existence of objective moral laws, especially in regard to torture and murder. He insisted that the Nazis could *not* take refuge in their own laws which allowed such actions. Rather, he thought that the law that operated in this instance was international in nature. Whatever the character of this standard, it must be higher than that of any nation or people.

It would seem that Flew has a great moral dilemma of his own here, as a few questions will reveal. How does he derive his notion of objective moral law from his naturalistic universe? Why is this law so sacred that he would willingly die not to take part in the Nazi crimes? According to naturalism, why is human life sacred at all – why is life to be valued in such an objective way over non-life? These difficulties deserve far more attention than we can spend on them here, but perhaps the chief issue concerns the presence of this elusive, objective moral law in a universe without God and ultimate meaning, that exists as a product of mere chance. To me, it is simply amazing that influential atheologians like Russell and Flew would even admit such a law.

Additionally, based on naturalistic premises, on what basis does a law exist over and above national ordinances? Why does international law take precedence over a nation's right to govern itself? Flew's view that the Nazi war criminals violated international law even appears to be contrary to the procla-

---

29. Thomas B. Warren and Antony G.N. Flew, *The Warren-Flew Debate on the Existence of God* (Jonesboro: National Christian Press, 1977). Flew's four statements and answers are taken, respectively, from pp. 67, 70, 248, 250.

30. *Ibid.*, p. 248.

31. *Ibid.*, p. 250.

mation of Robert Jackson, the Nuremberg prosecutor. Jackson declared that, "There is a higher law which transcends the provincial and the transient."[32] While Jackson doesn't specify the nature of this law, that it transcends geography and time gives us a hint.

We have not defended statement 2 so far in this chapter, but it appears to be a devastating charge against naturalists. If atheologians think they have good reasons for holding that no moral absolutes exist and that others should agree with them, they are contradicting themselves. The claim that there are no moral absolutes is itself an absolute in the area of morals, if it is claimed that one *ought* to hold such a position.[33]

Another example of such a mistake occurs when one makes the common claim in sexual morality that "Anything is allowed between two, consenting adults." This is frequently meant as a counter-claim against moral absolutes, when, in fact, it affirms at least two – "consenting" and "adults." Is sex thereby morally permissible between a consenting adult and a *non-consenting* adult? Or, is sex allowed between an adult and a *baby*? So once again, to hold that there are good reasons for affirming the non-existence of moral absolutes and that others should agree is self-contradictory.

It would seem that few would deny 3a and hold that the moral code is one of nature's laws, since nature is devoid of ethical judgments and doesn't even differentiate life from non-life. Further, it is not even *wrong* to break a law of nature in the sense that we normally mean such a statement.

Statement 3b is probably the most disputed claim of all. But to say that our society or methods of education are sufficient to explain the moral code is not to do justice to the depths to which that law is ingrained in our very existence, as in 1a-c. And how do we even go about denying the existence of moral absolutes (point 2) in order to say that they are man-made?

Although it is true that we need pragmatic moral laws in order to live with one another peaceably, why is life to be valued at all? What is actually *wrong* with murder? We are disgusted at the very suggestion that all we need to do is change human laws and/or opinion in order to give approval to such heinous crimes. This should make us realize that the moral laws are *more* than just practical guides – we really *do* think that it is intrinsically wrong to murder

---

32. Robert Jackson as quoted by Warren, *Ibid.*, p. 41. Incidently, Warren's own answer to Flew's admissions is recorded on pages 75-76.

33. See J.P. Moreland, *Scaling the Secular City*, pp. 92, 244.

and torture others, as witnessed to by both Russell and Flew.

That is precisely why we think it is admirable to attempt to save a life, even at the possible expense of our own, as in 3b(2), as opposed to the more base desire to simply save our own life. Yet, we all witness to 3b(3) in our realization that we have fallen short of the ethical ideal, individually and as human beings. Few would claim that they had never broken a moral law.

Now we come to the crunch point of the argument. How could such an absolute moral standard originate in a naturalistic universe? It follows from all of this, then, that the Author of the moral code is beyond us (4a). This Legislator must have a mind, for otherwise the law would have no ultimate explanation or meaning (4b). This Source relates to us in a personal manner by appreciating, originating, and enforcing the code (4c). Last, our other arguments in Sections I and II of this volume provide some additional hints (4d).

CONCLUSION

In this chapter we outlined several versions of the moral argument for the existence of God. Then we dealt with some common objections to it. We concluded by piecing together an amalgamated case that appears to set forth its strongest features. We conclude that the moral argument is a probable pointer to God's existence. It is not a deductive proof, at least in the form we presented it. But it makes by far the most sense of the moral code recognized by theists, as well as by many atheologians.

At every turn in the discussion of moral values, the naturalistic position is weighed down with difficulties. It has the appearance of a drowning swimmer trying to keep its head above the water. If it concedes something on the one hand, it is condemned on the other. But if it fails to admit the point, it appears to be in even more trouble.[34] It is an understatement to say, at the very least, that naturalism is not even close to being the *best* explanation for the existence of our moral conscience.

---

34. Nowhere was this struggle more apparent than in the two debates involving Russell and Flew. Especially in the latter case, the skeptical position seemed to be on an uphill climb, at a loss to provide adequate explanations.

Chapter Twenty-Two
WHEN ALL ELSE FAILS

INTRODUCTION: IMPORTANCE OF THE QUESTION

Life is sometimes like a gigantic jigsaw puzzle. A single missing piece can keep us from seeing the overall picture, or that same segment can be the one that organizes the whole. So it is with the problem of pain and evil. We have spoken about the reality of suffering and why God allows it. We have argued that atheists have several major problems in this same area, and that the recognition of evil actually backfires into an argument for God's existence. These are certainly important considerations.

However, it is our contention that there is another response that needs to be considered – one that sheds light from a completely different perspective. This may possibly even be the key – the puzzle piece that ties the rest of the picture together. Moreover, it may well be the most emotionally satisfying of all the responses to this riddle of pain and suffering. When all is said and done, this is the truth that underlies all the others. It even relieves us from the burden of always having to know why something happened the way it did. In the end, to ignore it could be to tear the heart out of our answer.

THE CASE OF JOB

Job was an Old Testament believer who wrestled intently with the problem of his own misfortune. In fact, his name is almost synonymous with suffering.

On top of his pain, he couldn't understand God's silence toward him. He must have thought the situation lasted far too long. But through his trials, we are taught extraordinary truths that transformed Job's life and can illumine ours.

To summarize his case very briefly, Job was tested by Satan and numerous calamities befell him. His domestic animals were slain or carried off by marauders, who killed his servants, as well. Lastly, he learned that his children had been killed by a desert storm (Job 1:13-19).

Then phase two of the suffering came. Satan afflicted Job with personal sickness in the form of painful sores over his entire body (2:7-8). Job's wife suggested that he respond to his troubles by simply cursing God and dying (2:9). Still he refused to sin by charging God with fault in any of these disasters (1:20-22; 2:10).

Most of the book concerns Job's dialogue with his three friends, Eliphaz, Bildad and Zophar. But during these discussions, Job's complaint against God begins to surface. He blames God for his distress. Specifically, the idea that he suffered unjustly seemed to bother Job the most, and he states some of his grievances rather strongly. He charges that God denied him justice (27:2), oppressing him while being kind to the wicked (10:3). He also desires to face God so he can argue his case with Him (13:3, 21-22). All the while, the silence of God is one of the major issues – when Job called out for help, there was no response (19:7). He even requests God to leave him so he can have a little joy! (10:20-22).[1] Yet Job never gives up or loses hope. He voices his trust in God (13:15) and yearns to be with Him (19:25-27). He also was determined not to sin (27:3-4).

When Job's three friends stopped responding, a fourth person, Elihu, begins his own dialogue with Job. He articulates more truth than the other three friends, frequently speaking on God's behalf. Initially, Elihu is angry at Job for justifying himself at God's expense (32:1-2). Then he and Job converse over the next six chapters.

The beginning and ending of Job's story are well known. After all of his troubles, he is visited by the Lord Himself. When he repents of his arrogance and pride, Job is blessed by God more than he ever had been in the past. Yet, what transpires just before and during his confrontation with God, and the lessons he learns, are not as frequently recognized.

The apex of the entire Book of Job occurs when God Himself challenges

---

1. For other complaints, see Job 7:11; 10:13-14; 12:6; 14:19; 16:9.

him, giving him the audience he requested. (Maybe this is a bit of a warning to us to watch our demands!) In a sense, the confrontation takes the form of something like a final exam. God begins by telling Job that He will ask the questions for a change and Job could give the answers (38:1-3). After all, Job knew so much (38:4-5).

The first question on the Lord's examination must have immediately shown Job that he was in the wrong league! God quizzed Job on whether he could create the world (38:4-11)! Other inquiries concerned Job's ability to move the stars (38:31-33) and control the animal kingdom (Chapter 39). By this point, Job was beginning to understand how awesome God was, since He obviously handled all these details in the universe on a daily basis.

But these were not all of God's questions – His exam also included the hardest problem of all. He actually challenged Job to explain the very problem of evil that he had inquired about himself (Job 38:12-15; 40:8-14). Incredibly, God insisted that if Job could solve these matters, then the Lord of the universe would admit that Job could save himself (40:15).

By this time, Job had observed enough. He had already confessed that he had nothing left to say (40:3-5). After getting the meeting he desired, Job concluded by announcing his certainty that the Lord was omnipotent (42:1-2). This conclusion had already been proclaimed earlier by both Elihu and the Lord, perhaps before Job came to the same recognition.[2]

The conversations with Elihu and later with the Lord are literally packed with important lessons for Job to learn and heed.[3] (1) Job shouldn't assert his own righteousness against the Lord, especially in a rebellious and scornful manner (Job 32:2, 5-7; 40:4, 8; 42:5, 6). (2) God should not be blamed if He chooses to stay silent (34:29; 35:12-16). (3) Still, God responds in many ways even if these means are not perceived by men (33:14; 38:1ff.). (4) God is personally involved with human needs (34:21-22; 42:12).

(5) God should not to be condemned or blamed for the evil in the world; it is unthinkable that God would act unjustly (34:10, 12, 17; 38:12-15; 40:8-14). (6) Man shouldn't trust in his own knowledge (34:35; 37:5, 24; 38:2, 4, 18; 39:2; 42:3), but in God (35:14; cf. 42:1-6). (7) It is beneficial to follow God (34:9; 42:5ff.). (8) Wickedness is judged, but righteousness is rewarded (34:11; 36:16-17; 42:12). (9) God's works are incomprehensible (37:5, 23-24;

---

2. For some instances, see the related claims in Job 33:12; 36:26; 37:5, 23; 40:2.

3. Most of the following principles are repeated by both Elihu and God.

38:2-39). (10) God should be praised (36:24ff.; 37:14; 38:4ff.).

Job worked through his problems in a very personal, existential way. He didn't have the luxury of taking a theoretical, detached look at his dilemma – he had no other option but to live it. So what he learned in this matter could be quite instructive. What was his conclusion?

In the beginning of his ordeal, Job's major question concerned the reason why he suffered. Strangely, he never received an answer to that question – God didn't include it on His final exam. God did challenge Job more than once to solve the problem of pain and evil, but no answer is given. Maybe this tells us something important. Philip Yancey thinks that Job couldn't have understood the answer even if God gave it. For God to have explained the secret of evil to Job would be like attempting to teach Einstein to a clam![4]

Whatever the reason why no answer is given, one thing is clear. Job was satisfied in the end. Why? Because He realized that God could do anything, including take care of evil. After confessing God's omnipotence, Job confessed that the problem was with him – he questioned areas he did not understand (42:1-3). In light of the information he received in his "showdown" with the Lord, Job repented (42:6).

So Job made a specific decision. Based on what he learned about God, he knew he could trust Him in those things that he still did not know. He was satisfied even though he never learned the reason why he suffered. We ought not miss the fact that he made this decision while he was still tormented, before God blessed him (42:10-17).

There is a tremendous principle here for believers today to learn, as well. When the presence of pain and evil *can* be explained, so much the better. Scripture addresses many of these causes, as we have already seen. But even when we *cannot* figure it out, or when God is silent, we ought to trust Him, for we know enough about Him to do so. After all, we know we are finite, so why do we frequently act as if we were not? There is much in the universe that we cannot explain.

APPLYING JOB'S LESSON

Job's account is included in Scripture for the edification of believers. So what can we learn from this wise man's experiences? We also suffer, although

---

4. Philip Yancey, "When Bad Things Happen to Good People," *Christianity Today*, Volume 27, Number 12, August 5, 1983, p. 23.

seldom on the scale that Job did. Still, we wrestle with some of the same perennial quandaries: Why is pain a constant companion throughout life? Why are others allowed to inflict suffering upon us? How are we to handle the silence of God? Why doesn't He do something about it?

Job's conclusion can be ours, too. He confessed that his objections were due to his own ignorance (42:1-3). Unlike him, we may know the purpose of troubles that come our way. But then again, we may not always know why we suffer, either. It is on those occasions that Job's advice is best applied. The key is that the basis for Christianity is firm, as pointed out in this book. Therefore, what we know about God is sufficient in these matters to trust Him with those questions to which we don't know the answers. Thus, we know enough to trust Him whether we have an explanation for a particular situation or not.

Interestingly enough, we are far better off than was Job in terms of what we know about God. He knew a number of significant facts, but there can be little question that we know far more. Scripture is filled with His truths. So how do we actually apply this knowledge? We may approach tough situations with a method. We can first ask whether the conditions are such that we can ascertain why we are suffering.[5] Often the origin of the distress is evident. For example, in many cases the free will of other human beings is the cause for the pain.

But there will also be numerous times when we don't understand why things happen the way they do. To be honest, sometimes we wonder if God is still in control. On these occasions, we need to remind ourselves what we do know about God. Here's one way to do it: "I'm not sure why things are happening the way they are, but this is *still* the world where God raised His Son from the dead, thereby insuring eternal life. Therefore, I can trust God that there is a good answer to this situation even if I don't know what it is."[6]

But sometimes our questions and worries are more stubborn, so we need to be more forceful with ourselves. In such cases, we must focus on the factual issues. Here's a sample discussion between two Christians:

"I just can't understand why God is allowing this to happen to me. Sometimes I wonder if He really cares for me at all."

"But did God raise His Son Jesus from the dead?"

"What? Well yes, but that doesn't really help me when I wonder about my current predicament."

---

5. See chapter 19 for some of the major reasons why God allows suffering.

6. See chapter 26 on the outstanding historical evidence for the resurrection of Jesus.

"But it should. Please bear with me and answer me once again – do you really believe God raised Jesus Christ from the dead?"

"Sure I do, but . . . "

"Since you know that this is a world where God raised His Son, don't we also know that Christianity is true? So isn't God still in control?"

"Well, I guess I have no reason to think that He ever relinquished His rights to govern the world!"

"Then is it possible that, while you don't know why you are suffering, He does?"

"Well, certainly that's the case."

"Then since you *know* numerous truths about God, like His having raised Jesus, shouldn't you trust Him in those areas where you *don't* know all of the answers?"

Once again, here is the key: what we know about God is sufficient to trust Him in those things we don't know. Not only can such truth keep us focused on the most important matters in the Christian faith, but it can free us from the burden of always having to figure out exactly what God has in mind when people suffer. In fact, even the insinuation that we can or ought to know God's thoughts is ridiculous and violates clear biblical teachings. The facts are quite simple at this point: I am not God. So why do I insist so often on acting like I know everything? As George Mavrodes asserts, it isn't necessary to know *what* God's grounds for allowing evil are in order to have a reasonable faith that He *does*, in fact, have such grounds.[7]

Paul's advice for those who suffer is quite similar. He tells us to turn our thoughts away from our circumstances to the reality of eternal life, since God has guaranteed the latter by raising Jesus from the dead. The reason is definitely practical: our suffering is temporal, while our life in heaven goes on forever (2 Cor 4:14-18).[8]

Some will perhaps maintain that this teaching really isn't practical enough because it fails to reduce the level of their actual pain, which is the immediate problem. However, this reply fails for at least two reasons. First, eternal life is real and its very nature[9] signifies its priority in both thinking and acting. True, the suffering is also real. But Paul's advice is correct *even if* the pain is not thereby lessened, because eternal life is still ultimate reality, long after the

---

7. George Mavrodes, *Belief in God*, p. 93.

8. Seeking heaven above earth's concerns is what Habermas has termed the "top-down" perspective on life. See Gary R. Habermas, *Dealing with Doubt* (Chicago: Moody Press, 1990), Chapter 9. Cf. Habermas and Moreland, *Immortality*, Chapter 12.

9. The priority of eternal life comes from both its quality (it is far better than life

pain subsides. But second, Paul's suggestion *can* actually lessen the pain! A positive word from a medical doctor who informs us that our lingering sickness is not terminal often lessens our misery, since the emotional factor has been reduced. We leave the office already feeling better, even daring to think that we must be getting over our sickness. But we have not gotten better in just those few minutes! Rather, we feel better because we are convinced that we are not dying! Our emotions are soothed.

In a similar way, a proper perspective on eternal life can adjust the believer's thinking away from the immediate situation. We can gain the assurance that, at least ultimately, everything will turn out fine (especially in eternal terms!). Meditation on heaven allows us to refocus attention away from the pain, thereby lessening the emotional component. This is helpful, precisely since these same emotions frequently cause the most pain.

So now we're back to the lesson that Job learned. He unquestionably went through deep waters. He thought God had dealt with him unjustly. But the prodding of Elihu and especially the message of God Himself brought him back to his senses. In the end he confessed his errors and acknowledged that he had delved into matters that he did not understand. He finally realized that God could do all things. And he knew he could trust God to take care of the deep things of the universe, including the problem of evil.

CONCLUSION

Pain and evil are real. We certainly learn that much from Job! God allowed Satan to test this righteous man in order to discover his true allegiance. Job suffered greatly, and cried out against God. But he never abandoned his faith in the Almighty. He braved his anguish, the misleading counsel of his wife, and the bad advice of his three friends. In the end, he learned from his mistakes. As a result, he repented of his rebellion and confessed that the problem was his. Meredith Kline describes the finale this way: "The Creator's surpassing wisdom has been so effectively impressed on Job that he will not further dispute God's ways as he had once and again."[10]

---

on earth) and its quantity (it lasts far longer). For details on these two points, including the New Testament witness on the subject, see Habermas and Moreland, *Ibid.*, p. 263, footnote 32.

10. Meredith G. Kline, "Job," *The Wycliffe Bible Commentary*, edited by Charles F. Pfeiffer and Everett E. Harrison (Nashville: The Southwestern Company, 1962), p. 487.

So what may we glean from Job's experiences? Elton Trueblood summarizes very nicely:

> The essential point of these final speeches is that the problem is too great for the finite mind, that Job sees only a small segment of reality, and that his criticisms are accordingly inappropriate. . . . The point is that the humble worshipper *already* has abundant reason to believe in God in the full theistic sense. If, then, he runs into some difficulty, even a difficulty as great as the problem of evil, he does not, for that reason, give up his faith. *The reasons for his faith are so great that they can weather a few storms.* Religious insight makes us believe that there *is* a full solution of the problem of evil though we are too ignorant and dull to reach it.[11]

The theme of the Book of Job is that we are wrong to blame God with the world's problems, especially the realities of pain and evil. Rather, believers know enough about God to trust Him even in the matters that trouble us most. At least this gemstone should be acquired from this sacred writing. No other text deals with the topic of suffering so eloquently. Trueblood states that such a message "must always be a part" of any adequate treatment of the quandary of evil.[12] We add that it just might be the capstone on the entire subject.

Thus, a series of philosophical arguments isn't always the way to handle religious dilemmas (though such an approach is even used in Scripture). Here we have practical, down to earth advice about how to turn our thoughts away from our own questions to the Person and nature of God Almighty. We learn to place God and His Kingdom above the worries of earth (see Matt 6:19-34). And we learn that what we know concerning God should cause us to trust Him in what we don't understand.

After all, we were taught the same message from our Lord Himself. Jesus' resurrection from the dead reveals that God is still on the throne. But just three days earlier, wasn't the Son of God tortured and didn't He die a horrible death? Who could know more about pain than Him? We are even told that Jesus learned from His sufferings (Heb 5:8). Just shortly before He died, God's unique Son wondered why He had been forsaken. He also resigned Himself totally to the will of His Father. Shouldn't we who call Jesus Lord learn to do the same?

---

11. Trueblood, *Philosophy of Religion*, p. 244. (The italics are Trueblood's.)
12. *Ibid.*, p. 244.

Chapter Twenty-Three
SUMMARIES AND CONCLUSIONS

PART THREE
Chapter 18: "So Much Pain and Evil"

We have, indeed, dealt with a tough issue in Part Three of this volume. Before we could explain how ethics actually confirms and even argues for God's existence, we had to wade through some rough waters. The problem of pain and evil is generally said to be the most common objection to Christian theism. It seems that skeptics and Christians alike struggle with these matters. In this chapter we will briefly summarize the approach we took.

Different ways to explain the presence of suffering have been suggested. Some propose that evil is illusory. Others say that it disproves God's existence altogether. Another response is that we must modify the classical understanding of Him, typically by concluding that God is finite. In this case, He would like to do something about evil but simply isn't able to do so. The chief theistic response is that God exists, but allows evil either to gain some greater goods or to avoid some greater evils.

Chapter 19: "Why Does God Allow Suffering?"

So why does God allow pain and evil? Dividing this question into three parts appears to be a helpful strategy. First, moral evil results from the free choices that created beings make, whether explicitly or implicitly. Considering that war and crime ensue in such a manner helps us to understand that moral evil is the dominant variety of suffering.

The biblical answer is that moral evil follows from the exercise of the free will of God's creatures – not only the Fall of man, but Satan's rebellion, and that of his demons, as well.[1]

While atheologians sometimes propose alternate solutions that they think were open to God, it doesn't appear that any other possibilities can solve the problems in question. For example, to create free creatures who nevertheless cannot sin would seem to be a contradiction.

Second, natural evil was defined as that which results from nature – such as floods, earthquakes, or other physical disasters. Our threefold approach here was based on the free will defense, natural law, and soul-making. We have said that most evil results from the free choices of created beings. But Scripture testifies that the freedom of Satan and his minions can even be used to cause natural evil. But to change creaturely freedoms is to alter the nature of the freedom itself.

Much suffering comes from these natural disasters. But it seems that there is no way to change the character of the world without amending natural law or, once again, the freedoms involved. So much of what is required for living – water, sunlight, gravity – can also cause untold problems. Alternative explanations again fail to show how a better world would result. For example, if God intervened in order to stop only the worst evils, He would curtail much freedom and/or adjust nature's laws accordingly. Further, many theists argue that evil can develop one's character and teach us crucial truths in ways that nothing else can. Ultimately, the goal of this soul-making is eternal life in heaven.

Third, what about the difficult question of gratuitous evils – those that seem to be purposeless? We viewed two different positions: that theism really can't admit any aimless suffering and that the possibility of such is actually required in order to fulfill the nature of true freedom. At any rate, human beings are not fit judges of the *amount* of evil, so they are not able to decide that suffering is out of balance.

In short, the character of free choice, the laws of nature, and God's desire that we grow and develop both spiritually and morally best answer the question of why we suffer so much. But to alter the character of free will or to change nature's laws would be to affect the nature of sentient life as we know it. Other schemes have failed to produce viable alternatives.

---

1. We have said that this portion of our answer is not very popular in some circles, but we think that it is justified as part of the biblical world view that is taught in Scripture and which is justified by the data. We make a preliminary attempt to lay such a basis in Part Four.

Chapter 20: "Atheism and Evil: A Fatal Dilemma"

At this point in our discussion, theism went on the offensive. Atheologians themselves have at least four distinct and serious problems with the presence of evil. First, critics have been unsuccessful in their attempts to produce the contradiction in theism – *why can't* evil exist in a universe created by the God of orthodoxy? The lack of any logical incompatibility means that the problem of evil is not a hard dilemma but a soft one, to be solved *within* belief-systems. Besides, the theist can use the following argument, to which she has just as much right as the atheologian does to his: since God is omnipotent and omnibenevolent, then there is a justification for evil. God does allow evil. Therefore, there is justification for it.

Second, there is no such thing as *the* problem of evil. It depends on the position and the one holding it. Difficulties only exist in those theistic systems that are affected by certain objections, while others remain undisturbed. The fact that atheologians *are* vexed by the issues does not count against theism any more than the fact that many sensitive theists are honestly not bothered by the challenge to their faith counts against atheism.

Third, how can atheists even *recognize* the actual existence of evil? It would appear that they have a real dilemma here. Few atheists acknowledge the existence of absolute right and wrong. To do so would seem to beg for an answer to a crucial question: where does an objective ethical standard come from in a naturalistic universe? At this point, the atheologian gets too close to the moral argument for God's existence.

But *not* to admit such a moral standard gets the naturalist into more hot water: if she does not recognize the objectivity of ethical values, then no basis exists from which to protest the presence of suffering. Thus, if right and wrong don't objectively exist, then there are no grounds on which to recognize evil – it is only an unfortunate consequence of life that we don't enjoy. While atheists may not like it, their own system does not allow them to recognize any objective complaints to lay at the theist's feet. In short, it would appear that, if evil really exists, so does God.

But some atheologians have protested that they can object to theism apart from the recognition of any ethical standard. Rather, they are satisfied to follow the course we outlined earlier and offer evil as an *internal* critique of theism, pointing out that its views are inconsistent. But we said that such a strategy raises its own, serious problems for the atheologian.

Fourth, such an internal charge does not exist in a vacuum, but must be evaluated along with the whole of theism, including its distinctive evidences. This is a contest between world views. And frankly, it is easier to explain evil in accordance with the arguments for Christianity than it is for evil to eliminate all of these excellent evidences. Theists seldom deny the existence of evil, acknowledging it along with the other areas of confirmation. But naturalism must rely on its denials of *all* of the major evidences for a theistic universe. Here is another indication of the untenable nature of this latter position.

Chapter 21: "The Moral Argument for God's Existence"

At this point, we surveyed a number of earlier formulations of a moral argument for the existence of God, as well as objections to them. Then we attempted a positive statement of such an argument, based on three major pillars: (1) the existence of an objective moral code, (2) the self-refuting nature of naturalistic denials of this standard, and (3) the inability of physical or human alternative explanations. We explained and supported each of these areas, including sub-points.

Chapter 22: "When All Else Fails"

Last of all, we moved from philosophical arguments to some existential considerations from the Book of Job. Instead of staying in our "ivory tower" world, we studied perhaps the best known case of suffering of all time. What lessons did Job learn? He realized that he knew enough about God to trust Him in those things he did not understand – which included his pain, in particular.

Then we tried to apply this truth. How might believers today employ such a lesson in their own lives? Maybe the Incarnation is the key, especially since we are even told that Jesus learned obedience through His suffering (Heb 5:8)! Without question, Jesus experienced an incredible amount of affliction, including one of the most excruciatingly painful deaths known. Yet, on the cross, the Son of God still committed Himself to His Father (Luke 23:46). Later, the greatest event of all history took place: Jesus was raised from the dead.

Not only do we know far more about God than did Job, but we have records of the most influential Life of all time. We need to consciously confront our suffering with the question: "Is this still the world where Jesus was raised from the dead?" The point here is a straightforward one. If God raised Jesus, then eternal life is a fact and Christian theism is true.[2] This should make a real difference in our lives. As Paul says, suffering is temporary, while eternal life lasts forever (2 Cor 4:14-18). Believers need to grow in faith by focusing and refocusing on these truths precisely during their times of suffering. Pain is easier to accept when we, like Job, remember the truths that we know about God and recall that He is still in control. After all, we do not have His vantage point and need to trust Him. Moreover, the resurrection of Jesus reminds us that even death is not the end. Life is not as complicated when we know our final destination.

---

2. See chapters 26-28 for some of the details.

PART FOUR

Evidence
from History

Chapter Twenty-Four
HISTORY AND EVIDENCE

INTRODUCTION: IMPORTANCE OF THE QUESTION

History is not a subject that everyone likes. Many of us associate this discipline with hours spent studying for exams, memorizing names and dates. But history is much more than this. It also involves such undertakings as analyzing trends and various sorts of theories, as well as the actual process of gathering evidence in order to ascertain what happened in the past. In this chapter we will begin with a notion of history itself. Then we will view the method of historical investigation.[1]

A CONCEPT OF HISTORY

The term "history" is used variously by different scholars. No uniform definition is agreed upon by everyone, while numerous approaches and interpretations are commonly utilized.[2] It is not our purpose to treat these contemporary

---

1. For many of the details in this chapter plus more material on related subjects, see Gary R. Habermas, *Ancient Evidence for the Life of Jesus: Historical Records of His Death and Resurrection* (Nashville: Thomas Nelson, 1984), Chapter 1. (This volume was renamed *The Verdict of History: Conclusive Evidence for the Life of Jesus* in 1988.)

2. For some of these interpretations, see Patrick Gardiner, "The Philosophy of History" in the *International Encyclopedia of the Social Sciences*, edited by David L. Sills (New York: Macmillan and The Free Press, 1968), vol. 6, pp. 428-433.

notions. Still, there is at least some general agreement concerning the concept of history.

Historians generally recognize that their subject includes at least two major factors – the actual events in particular and the recording of these events. So this discipline is chiefly concerned with what has happened and how these events have been annotated and interpreted. This conception comprises the core understanding of history as it will be used in this book. Other elements are certainly involved, but these two major ideas are essential and recur most often, composing the foundation of historiography.

A couple of other factors are relevant to this discussion and should also be mentioned briefly. First, there is always a subjective factor involved whenever history is recorded. To give just one example, the historian must select the material that she will (and will not) present. The historical event itself is objective – generally we speak in terms of it occurring or not occurring. But the recording and interpreting of the event introduces subjective factors.

For W.H. Walsh, the subjectivity of the writer is certainly present, but it is not an overly serious roadblock to obtaining historical truth. This subjectivity must be allowed for, but its effects can be offset.[3] Our approach towards history ought to be one of caution, since we need to recognize this subjective bias and then make the proper allowances for it.[4]

Perhaps an example of this subjective factor would be helpful. In ancient history, the writings of Tacitus provide a case in point. It is known that this Roman historian was prejudiced in his writing, presenting an "aristocratic bias" and being convicted that moralizing was the "highest function" of history. Other times inaccuracies tarnish his text, as when he credits speeches to people who never gave them or incorrectly reports details in battle accounts. Moses Hadas maintains that the interpretations of Tacitus "must often be challenged" since he "could see only through his own lenses which were strongly colored."[5]

Does this mean that Tacitus must be rejected as a trustworthy source for ancient Roman history? Do these subjective elements found in his writings

---

3. W.H. Walsh, *Philosophy of History* (New York: Harper and Brothers, 1960), pp. 101, 103.

4. William Wand, *Christianity: A Historical Religion?* (Valley Forge: Judson Press, 1972), pp. 29, 31, 42; cf. Gardiner, pp. 432-433.

5. See Moses Hadas, "Introduction" to *The Complete Works of Tacitus* (New York: Random House, Inc., 1942), pp. IX-XIX.

invalidate the information that he seeks to impart to his readers? As strange as it may seem, Hadas paradoxically states that Tacitus was Rome's greatest historian.[6]

Then he explains:

One may well ask how trustworthy the resultant history is. A modern historian guilty of such faults would surely lose all credit . . . With allowance made for rhetorical embellishment customary in his day, and within the limits of distortion which his own views of morality and politics make inevitable, Tacitus never consciously sacrifices historical truth.[7]

Michael Grant illustrates how Tacitus is not an isolated case in ancient times. The Greek Herodotus blended legends and anecdotal material into his histories, while another Roman, Livy, allowed for the operation of omens. Even worse, both Livy and Tacitus are examples of ancient historians who wrote about events that took place long before their time, sometimes as much as five centuries earlier. The results indicate frequent inconsistencies and contradictions in these ancient writings.[8]

But modern historians do not despair about reconstructing ancient times. As Hadas explained, scholars can make allowance not only for the subjective facets involved in the recording and interpretation of events, but even for incorrect data. The reconstructing of ancient history relies on the ability of the scholar to determine the facts of the past in spite of these deterrents.[9]

We will employ some of these same principles when we investigate the resurrection of Jesus in chapter 26. Although we will ask about events that occurred many centuries ago, historical investigation is still capable of ascertaining objective data.

Second, history cannot reach a point where it is positive of its findings in all instances. As with physics, medicine, and other inductive disciplines, there is also a certain amount of dependence on probability in history, as well.[10] Ernest Nagel, for example, concedes that his deterministic view of history opposes the almost unanimous convictions of contemporary physicists. Such scientific conclusions have had an effect on historians, for the accepted

---

6. *Ibid.*, p. IX
7. *Ibid.*, XVII-XVIII.
8. Michael Grant, *Jesus: An Historian's Review of the Gospels* (New York: Charles Scribner's Sons, 1977), pp. 183-189.
9. Hadas, pp. XVII-XVIII; cf. Grant, *Ibid.*
10. Wand, pp. 51-52.

scientific view against a deterministic universe has helped to turn historians in the same direction.[11]

Nagel tabulates five primary reasons for the general rejection of historical determinism by so many historians today. First, there are no developmental laws or patterns in history. No principles or precepts exist that would determine certain outcomes in advance of their occurrence. Second, history cannot be predicted, in spite of frequently-repeated ideas to the contrary. Past events or other such data do not determine the future. The third argument concerns the appearance of novel events and configurations of new ideas that recur throughout history. Fourth, unexpected or chance events outside the ordinary are also a part of history. The fifth argument is the conflicting results that occur when one attempts to apply the concept of a deterministic world to the freedom and moral duty of human beings. Such freedom requires a creative aspect in history arising from human choice.

Some examples of Nagel's five points might be helpful. Who could have predicted the wide dissemination of views brought about by a novel culture from a war-like community in third century B.C. Macedonia? Or who could have anticipated the creative civilization that would grow from a barbaric peoples situated on the banks of the Tiber River that would finally emerge in the first century B.C.? These and other similar findings have convinced many historians to reject the deterministic view of history. Again, Nagel asserts that the opposition to determinism in modern physics has also been a key factor, exercising a direct influence on most historians.[12]

So historians generally recognize the necessity of couching conclusions in probabilistic terms. For Wand, we cannot be as sure of historical investigation as some have thought in the past. Our judgments must be made according to which facts are most likely in terms of the historical evidence.[13] Montgomery likewise opts for a critical investigation of the data, with the decision concerning the occurrence of a specific event being based upon the credibility of the evidence. In fact, probability is referred to as the only adequate guide for the historian.[14]

---

11. Ernest Nagel, "Determinism in History" in William Dray, Editor, *Philosophical Analysis and History* (New York: Harper and Row, 1966), p. 355.

12. *Ibid.*

13. Wand, pp. 25-27, 51-52, 156.

14. John Warwick Montgomery, *Where is History Going?* (Grand Rapids: Zondervan, 1969), pp. 71-74.

However, we must carefully note a critical detail of special importance. The concept of probability does not preclude our achieving certainty in matters of well-established historical findings. Events that are validated by careful historical research (and especially those established for long periods of time) in the absence of viable contrary findings are proven facts.

If additional data casts doubt on such an event, it might be necessary to reopen the investigation. But precluding such contrary material, the fact may be viewed as certain, or as provisional proof. For instance, we need not doubt the death of Julius Caesar by assassination, Napoleon's defeat at Waterloo, or the election of Abraham Lincoln as the sixteenth president of the United States of America. These facts are well-established at this time and thus proven to be certain.

It has not been our purpose to deal exhaustively with the concept of history.[15] Yet, a contemporary treatment of the subject ought to include at least these components. We will refer to history as both the occurrence of past events, as well as the recording and interpreting of them. Recognizing the inevitable influence of a subjective element when history is written, allowance must be made for it in order for objective data to be obtained. Realizing also that history deals with probabilities, we need to ascertain as nearly as possible those facts that best fit the data.

As is the case with probabilities and uncertainties, any event is possible. Such is the nature of inductive studies. Therefore, events ought not be ruled out (either scientifically or historically) before they are researched. A thorough investigation of the evidence is required. Events that are firmly established by historical investigation may be regarded as certain, proven by the available data.[16]

HISTORICAL RESEARCH AND INVESTIGATION

The occurrence of past events can usually be discovered (within a certain

---

15. For a more complete treatment, see Earle E. Cairns, *God and Man in Time* (Grand Rapids: Baker Book House, 1979), pp. 11-29.

16. The careful reader will note that we are not using "proof" in the sense of apodictic certainty such as that achieved in certain types of mathematics and deductive logic, but in the sense of other sorts of inductive studies. For details, see Gary R. Habermas, "Probability Calculus, Proof and Christian Apologetics," *The Simon Greenleaf Review of Law and Religion*, Volume VIII (1988-1989), pp. 57-88.

probability) by a careful investigation of the facts. These former events are only accessible by a study of the available historical evidence. Although the historian usually did not personally participate in what she is studying (assuming she wasn't originally there), she can inspect the relevant data such as the eyewitnesses, written documents, and various other records, structures, and archaeological finds. Upon such confirmation the historian must build her case. Such tools comprise the working principles of historical research.[17]

Of course, what the existing data reveal is not automatically accepted as true, especially if there are conflicts in the testimony. The historian has the job of critically investigating the available sources in order to ascertain as closely as possible their accuracy. Results can be obtained by determining which conclusions best fit the evidence. The historian builds on such groundwork.[18] We therefore decide on the evidence at hand – choosing the most probable conclusion.

Historical data must be available if the historian is to investigate the past in such a manner. These sources are often divided into two types: primary and secondary. Primary sources "are underived, firsthand, or contemporary with the event," and are much more crucial.[19] They may consist of eyewitness testimony given in various forms.

Secondary material witnesses to primary sources, directed to past persons and events. These may take the form of works like textbooks, monographs, edited volumes, and syllabi. As such, they help elucidate and expand the previously existing materials.

Primary sources consist of both literary and non-literary remains. The former include written documents, either official or unofficial. Pliny the Younger's famous correspondence, penned while he was a Roman governor in Asia Minor during the early second century A.D., is an example of writings

---

17. Walsh, p. 18. Some illuminating examples of historical investigations of the past are supplied by Delbruck's methods of determining how ancient battles were fought in the times of the Greek and Roman empires. By examining the historical data, Delbruck successfully obtained information such as the size of the opposing armies, how they actually maneuvered, and other facets of specific battles in ancient times. For instance, see Edward M. Earle, Editor, *Makers of Modern Strategy* (Princeton: Princeton University Press, 1943), especially pp. 264-268 for Delbruck's historical techniques.

18. Walsh, pp. 18-19.

19. Cairns, *God and Man in Time*, p. 34. For further details regarding our following discussion, see Cairns, pp. 33-42, although we will diverge at certain points.

composed by a state official or representative. An unofficial primary document would include informal works of a firsthand nature, such as books, newspapers, journals, or periodicals. Julius Caesar's account of his battles in Gaul, written before his rule in first century B.C. Rome, is an example.

Documents written by eyewitnesses or that reflect their influence are, of course, extremely important in historical study, whenever they are available. Examples of such eyewitness sources are provided by American interest in the 1950's and 60's in published interviews with still-living Civil War veterans.[20] Literary remains in the form of inscriptions on stone, metal, or other materials (termed epigraphy) are also available in some cases.

Primary non-literary remains include material such as recordings obtained directly from eyewitness interviews, oral tradition, photographs, and archaeological artifacts. Eyewitness testimony using recorded interviews obviously cannot extend much over 100 years, at the most. Tradition, whether oral or written, sometimes reaches back into antiquity, with sources such as reports, legends, heroic stories, and ballads. Reliable traditions grounded in eyewitness testimony would be an important source. On the other hand, Americans are acquainted with George Washington and the cherry tree or the exploits of Davy Crockett. The weakness with this sort of tradition is that it must be trustworthy and not simply hearsay or storytelling.

Archaeological artifacts can be quite valuable as witnesses to our past. Remains like architecture, monuments, grave sites, burial chambers, furniture, art work, clothes, coins, tools, or other implements can often help determine both historical backgrounds and events. For example, Jewish burial chambers have actually revealed very specific data concerning burial customs, human physical characteristics, and varieties of death inflicted by enemies. Excavations of Qumran near the Dead Sea have uncovered not only the scrolls themselves, but also numerous facts from about the time of Jesus regarding the ascetic and communal lifestyle of the sectarian Essenes. Uncovering Greek cities such as Athens, Corinth, and Ephesus have provided invaluable evidence concerning the art, religious beliefs, and lifestyle of these ancient cultures.

The gathering of the primary and secondary sources does not complete the study; neither does the historian automatically conclude that such a collection

---

20. See Otto Eisenschiml and Ralph Newman, *Eyewitness: The Civil War as We Lived It* (New York: Grosset and Dunlap, 1956).

of data is synonymous with the facts themselves. Rather, these sources must be organized and subjected to criticism before conclusions can be drawn.[21] In the case of written documents, for example, both external and internal historical criticism is implemented.

External criticism is applied for the purpose of checking the writing itself and is divided into two parts. Higher criticism assesses the authenticity of the document regarding elements such as its background, authorship, date of writing, place of composition, the audience, and reason for writing. Further, is the text reliable? Does it bear signs of corresponding to fact? Lower criticism concerns the question of whether we essentially have the text as it was originally composed. It involves questions of manuscript evidence: the dates of existing copies, their comparison to the original, and the presence of any documentary interpolations or omissions. *Internal* factors are also helpful in assessing a document's reliability. They include the competence and character of the author, as well as his ability to separate facts from feeling, opinion, or other subjective distortion.

If the sources are unwritten, criticism could take such forms as the use of dating methods, other scientific testing procedures such as chemical analysis, and comparisons to relevant written accounts. The testing of eyewitness interviews and oral tradition would follow lines of criticism closer to those used for documentary sources, complete with external and internal phases, including authorship, the date of the testimony, its credibility, and whether it has been modified by time or circumstances.

After the historian gathers her materials, organizes them, and applies external and internal criticism, she is ready to prepare and formulate her conclusions. The results should conform to all the known data and provide the most comprehensive and probable judgment on the issues. The outcome is then open to careful scrutiny from other scholars, which should prompt the cautious historian to be able to defend the results, based on the factual data available.

CONCLUSION

We began by maintaining that a concept of history includes at least the events themselves and the records of these occurrences. Additionally, there is

---

21. For details of Cairns' treatment, see *Ibid.*, Chapter 2.

always a subjective element in reporting the past and conclusions from this discipline must be couched in probabilistic terms. When proper procedures are followed, the objective data of history can be uncovered within these parameters.

But some historians have attempted to disallow the objective knowledge of history. They argue that the interpreter's biases, the inability to observe history directly, and the need for an overall interpretive framework militates against the discovery of objective data.[22] Of course, a major question here concerns the meaning of the term "objective." We pointed out above that *absolute* certainty in history is not possible. Further, there is no direct observation or complete knowledge of the events themselves. Moreover, one's world view definitely plays a part in the process, too.[23]

But in this chapter we have outlined how the historian's methods and tools, especially the use of primary sources, are still able to achieve accurate knowledge of the past. Most historians agree with this conclusion. Cairns summarizes as follows:

> Through scientific study of his artifacts and documents, the historian can be reasonably certain concerning an event. . . . There is a surprising amount of consensus among historians on the basic facts and on many conclusions about the past.[24]

These preliminary considerations will especially lay the groundwork for our discussions of the New Testament (chapter 25) and the resurrection of Jesus (chapter 26). Some may question the historical study of miracles. But if it is claimed that such an event actually occurred in history, then that portion of the claim can be investigated. To reject miracles in an a priori manner is improper. The lack of an omniscient vantage point, the scientific emphasis on probabilities, and the use of inductive methodology all validate this conclusion.[25] In this final section of the book, we will attempt to ascertain what the historical data reveal with regard to Christianity.

---

22. Such is the case in Charles Beard, "That Noble Dream," in *The Varieties of History*, edited by Fritz Stein (Cleveland: The World Publishing Company, 1956).

23. For a detailed discussion of many of these issues, see Norman Geisler, *Christian Apologetics* (Grand Rapids: Baker Book House, 1976), Chapter 15.

24. Cairns, *God and Man in Time*, p. 97.

25. For more details here, see Habermas, *Ancient Evidence for the Life of Jesus*, pp. 23-27: "Historical Research and Miracle Claims."

Chapter Twenty-Five
THE NEW TESTAMENT

INTRODUCTION: IMPORTANCE OF THE QUESTION

Maybe you've had a fairly common experience while "talking religion" with someone. You were making progress explaining some important concept, when the other individual broke your train of thought with a challenge: "Why should I believe that? I don't accept the Bible as an authority."

Integral to a treatment of the historicity of Jesus Christ is the condition of the New Testament text. We looked at some of the key tests for a written document in the last chapter. Who are the authors of the books? Are they credible witnesses? When did they write? Do the documents present a trustworthy picture of the Founder of Christianity? Are there any ways to check individual passages? Do we have the essential texts that the authors composed?

We propose a threefold approach to this subject characterized by our moving from general to specific information. The first two steps will be presented in this chapter, with the third coming in the next. All three stages combine in our overall strategy. Initially, we will begin with the more general question of whether the texts as a whole are reliable. How does the New Testament measure up to other ancient documents in terms of manuscript numbers and their dates? Are there any outside criteria that help to determine its truthfulness?

Next, we will briefly address the issues of authorship and date of writing. What criteria can be used to determine who wrote a particular book? What is the date of the original material? Can we know whether the writer was in a good position to know the subject he addresses?

Last, do standards exist by which we can ascertain the reliability of individual historical passages? In other words, even apart from the entire book itself, are there additional reasons for thinking that specific texts present trustworthy information? We will concentrate on some specific verses in the next chapter in order to provide an example of this final step.

We can illustrate this threefold approach in the following diagram. We will be working from the bottom up, progressing to greater levels of specificity:

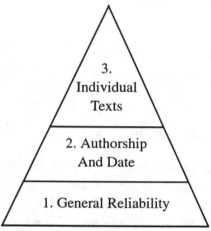

Before we begin, two cautions need to be stated. First, we are not really addressing the subject of the inspiration of Scripture here, although we will provide a few hints.[1] Rather, our entire discussion is more concerned with the reliability of the New Testament – is it a trustworthy document? In particular, do we have accurate data concerning Jesus?

Second, it is absolutely impossible in the scope of one chapter to detail the various arguments in what is an incredibly detailed subject; more than one book could easily be filled with relevant material. Instead, we intend to give an overview of the issues involved, indicating directions the interested reader might take. Footnotes will furnish additional sources and ideas. We will work on tiers one and two in this chapter.

Then, we will single out a sample text in the next chapter. This will illustrate further the procedure we just suggested. Our selected passage is 1 Corinthians 15:1-11, an indispensable discussion of the central doctrines in

---

1. For a common approach to the subject, see chapter 29, footnote 1.

Christianity: the gospel of the death, burial, and resurrection of Jesus Christ. Are there special, independent reasons to support the historicity of these words? We will turn now to our tri-leveled investigation.

GENERAL RELIABILITY

Before turning to more specific questions like authorship and date of writing, we need to examine the general case for the accuracy of the New Testament. Since we no longer possess the original writings, can we still determine what the texts said? Are there any extra-biblical documents or archaeological discoveries that provide widespread confirmation of the historical accounts?

In order to reconstruct the books as they were written by the original authors, ancient copies are indispensable. Theoretically, the more manuscripts we have, the better we are able to compare them in order to determine the correct textual readings, especially in light of the variant readings that exist.[2] But other factors besides number alone are also crucial. In general, the earlier manuscripts are usually preferred. Additionally, the wide geographical distribution of the copies and the textual "family" to which a copy belongs also assist in determining the particular reading.[3]

The New Testament is easily the best attested ancient work in several areas: the number of existing manuscripts, the time gap between writing and the earliest copies, and the completeness of the books. Ancient classical works have far fewer manuscripts – twenty entire or partial copies would be an excellent number. By comparison, the New Testament has over 5000 full or partial Greek manuscripts. Texts in other languages would add thousands more to this number.[4]

---

2. Variant readings concern the differences in the reproductions of an author's work. We are *not* referring here to the author's original composition. In spite of their number, the variants in the copies of the New Testament are largely trivial and actually concern an extremely small number of readings – less than one percent of the whole. For details, see Norman L. Geisler and William E. Nix, *A General Introduction to the Bible* (Chicago: Moody Press, 1968), pp. 365-367.

3. On utilizing manuscript copies to determine the original biblical text, see *Ibid*, Chapter 26.

4. See F.F. Bruce *The New Testament Documents: Are They Reliable?* (Grand Rapids: Eerdmans, 1967), especially p. 16; John A. T. Robinson, *Can We Trust the New Testament?* (Grand Rapids: Eerdmans, 1977), especially p. 36; cf. Craig Blomberg, *The Historical Reliability of the Gospels* (Downers Grove: InterVarsity Press, 1987).

Such a large amount of copies provides the New Testament with a much better means of ascertaining the original text. The closest competitor is Homer's *Iliad*, attested by 600 copies, a truly exceptional quantity. But while this Greek classic has far fewer manuscripts and is shorter than the New Testament, there is still, perhaps surprisingly, about 25 times more doubt about its original wording![5]

One of the most important issues concerns the date between the author's original writing and the earliest copies. For ancient classical works, a gap of 700 years would be minimal. The interval significantly lengthens to 1,300 or more years in a number of important cases. By comparison, the Chester Beatty Papyri and Bodmer Papyri contain most of the New Testament and are dated about 100-150 years after its completion. An entire copy of the New Testament (Codex Sinaiticus) and a nearly complete manuscript (Codex Vaticanus) date only about 250 years after the original autographs. Early dates for these copies help to insure the authenticity of the New Testament text.[6]

Further, we have the entire canonical New Testament, but this is not so with all ancient works. For example, of Livy's 142 books of Roman history, 107 books have been lost. Only four and a half of Tacitus' original fourteen books of Roman *Histories* remain and only ten full and two partial books exist of Tacitus' sixteen books of *Annals*. This is also a factor in establishing the authenticity of the biblical writings.[7]

So there is simply outstanding manuscript evidence for the New Testament documents. This is widely admitted, even by critical scholars. As John A.T. Robinson clearly and succinctly states on this topic: ". . . the wealth of manuscripts, and above all the narrow interval of time between the writing and the earliest extant copies, make it by far the best attested text of any ancient writing in the world."[8]

---

5. The relevant statistics are provided by Geisler and Nix, pp. 366-367.

6. Bruce, pp. 16-18; Robinson, pp. 36-37; Henri Daniel-Rops, Editor, *The Sources for the Life of Christ* (New York: Hawthorn Books, Inc., 1962), Chapter IV (by Daniel-Rops), pp. 41-42. We must remember that the excellent number and variety of New Testament manuscripts insures the nature of the original text even over this short time span between the New Testament and the earliest copies.

7. Bruce, p. 16; Robinson, pp. 37-38.

8. Robinson, *Can We Trust the New Testament?* p. 36. Well-known philosophical atheist Antony Flew agrees. See Gary R. Habermas and Antony G.N. Flew, *Did Jesus Rise from the Dead? The Resurrection Debate*, edited by Terry L. Miethe (San Francisco: Harper and Row, 1987), p. 66.

But after all, good manuscripts do not necessarily guarantee truthful accounts, although they assist an argument in that direction. What other data support the general reliability of the New Testament texts? Do we have any outside corroboration? In particular, we need to focus on sources for the life of Jesus, since He is the Center of Christianity and will be our primary thrust in the next two chapters.

We have a fairly large listing of data about Jesus from outside the pages of the New Testament, which corroborate the picture from the Gospels. Some of this information comes from non-Christian writers, including ancient historians like Tacitus, Suetonius, and Thallus. Jewish sources such as the Talmud and Josephus are also helpful. Government officials like Pliny the Younger and two Caesars (Trajan and Hadrian) provide details about early Christian beliefs and practices. The Greek Lucian and the Syrian Mara Bar-Serapion also speak about Jesus. Gnostic writings such as The Gospel of Truth, The Gospel of Thomas, and The Treatise on Resurrection claim to give us a theological look at Jesus, often from a non-orthodox viewpoint.[9]

Altogether, seventeen non-Christian writings record almost 50 different details concerning the life, teachings, death, and resurrection of Jesus, as well as particulars about the early church. This information comes from about 20-150 years after Jesus' death, which is considered early in terms of ancient historiography. The most widely-recorded fact is Jesus' death, mentioned in eleven different texts. Tacitus, for example, reports that Jesus was executed during the reign of Caesar Tiberius, under procurator Pontius Pilate.[10]

Also reported by these non-Christian sources are Jesus' disciples, His miracles, His fulfilling prophecy as well as being a prophet Himself, and the belief that He was Deity. Furthermore, He is called a good teacher and philosopher whose message included the need for a faith conversion, denial of the gods, the brotherhood of believers, and immortality. He was crucified for blasphemy, later rising from the dead. His disciples were changed into men who proclaimed Jesus and His teachings.

Another category of information comes from archeological artifacts, although little of this information directly concerns Jesus. Luke's record of

---

9. For details, see Habermas, *The Verdict of History* (Nashville: Thomas Nelson, 1984, 1988), especially Chapter IV. See also R.T. France, *The Evidence for Jesus* (Downers Grove: InterVarsity Press, 1986) and F.F. Bruce, *Jesus and Christian Origins Outside the New Testament* (Grand Rapids: Eerdmans, 1974).

10. Tacitus, *Annals*, 15:44.

Caesar Augustus' census is illumined by an ancient Latin inscription called the *Titulus Venetus*. Background information helps us to understand more about the cities, towns, coinage, and languages spoken in first century Palestine. The Bethesda and Siloam pools, foundations of Herod's temple, the possible location of Pilate's Praetorium (or headquarters), and at least the general vicinity of Golgotha and the garden tomb all enlighten the reader of the Gospels.

A Latin plaque refers to "Pontius Pilatus, Prefect of Judaea." The Nazareth Decree, issued as an "ordinance of Caesar," gives a strict warning against grave robbing, threatening death to those who fail to comply with the command. Most scholars agree that it was circulated by Claudius between A.D. 41-54. A highly debated subject, the Shroud of Turin possibly provides some rather detailed information about Jesus.[11] Although not strictly archaeological, A.N. Sherwin-White has provided a wealth of background information corroborating the details of the trial of Jesus.[12]

The New Testament even contains important sayings about Jesus that predate the books in which they are included. These creeds provide the clearest example of the data that was preached in the earliest years after Jesus' death, before the first canonical volumes were written. Paul, for example, clearly explains on various occasions that he is repeating teachings that have been given to him.[13]

These early creedal statements report Jesus' birth as a human being, His preaching, and that people believed in Him. Numerous details about the Last Supper are related, as well as Jesus' standing before Pilate and making His confession. He died, was resurrected, and appeared to His followers. He ascended to heaven and was glorified.[14] One of these reports will be discussed at length in the next chapter.

---

11. For details, see Habermas, *The Verdict of History*, Chapter VII; France, Chapter 4; Bruce, Chapter XI.

12. A.N. Sherwin-White, *Roman Society and Roman Law in the New Testament* (Oxford: Oxford University Press, 1963; Grand Rapids: Baker Book House, 1978), Lecture Two. Cf. pp. 162-171 on Luke's census.

13. See especially 1 Cor 11:23; 15:3; cf. also Phil 2:6-11; 2 Ti 2:11; Luke 1:1-4. Additionally, the early preaching in Acts (2:14-39; 3:12-26; 4:8-12; 5:29-32; 10:34-43; 13:16-41) includes many elements of the earliest apostolic message.

14. "Creeds" which relate this material are found in Lk. 24:34; Rom. 1:3-4; 4:25; 10:9; 1 Cor 11:23ff.; 15:3ff.; Phil 2:6-11; 1 Tim 2:6; 3:16; 6:13; 2 Tim 2:8; 1 Pet 3:18; 1 John 4:2. See previous footnote for details from the Book of Acts. For a discussion, see Habermas, *The Verdict of History*, Chapter V.

Last, Christian sources outside the New Testament also report numerous facts from the life of Jesus. The writings we will use are quite early, dating from the end of the first century to the middle of the second. They report numerous details regarding Jesus' birth and family, His baptism, and His apostles. His miracles and fulfilled prophecy are celebrated. We are told that His major theme was the Gospel of the Kingdom of God, which He passed on to His disciples so they could give it to others. Many details are reported about His death by crucifixion at the hands of Pilate and Herod. But Jesus was raised from the dead and appeared to His disciples, who we are told actually touched Him. The resurrection proved Jesus' message. He also ascended to heaven.[15]

There is a surprising array of pre- and extra-New Testament sources for the life of Jesus Christ. We briefly outlined four sorts of reports: non-Christian, archaeological, creedal, and Christian. A total of over 100 different items from the life, teachings, death, resurrection of Jesus and early church beliefs are included! Almost all of these can be learned without even opening the pages of the Bible.

It should be clearly understood that we are in no way hinting that these sources should stand by themselves or that they are stronger than the New Testament data itself. This should be clear from the remainder of this chapter and the next one.

Rather, the point here is that there is a surprising amount of data that corroborates the overall picture of Jesus in the Gospels. This is not to say that there are no other questions, or that we can verify the entire Christian message in this manner. But the available manuscript evidence, extra-biblical sources, and limited archeological information points to the conclusion that we are on strong grounds when we report that we have no initial reason to doubt the general picture of Jesus that we have in the Gospels. Now we will turn to more specific, and even stronger, data.

AUTHORSHIP AND DATE

Another crucial issue concerns the authors of the books that are significant

---

15. For the testimonies of Clement of Rome, Ignatius, and The Epistle of Barnabas, see J.B. Lightfoot, Editor and translator, *The Apostolic Fathers* (Grand Rapids: Baker Book House, 1891, 1956). For a discussion of these and other early sources, see Habermas, *Ibid.*, Chapter VI.

for our study of the historicity of Jesus. For example, are the Gospels written by those in good position to know the data? As we mentioned above, we cannot argue the case for these books here. But we will attempt to provide some direction for such a study before we zero in on a specific text where Paul makes some notable historical claims.

The evidence strongly indicates that the Gospels and Acts were under the control of eyewitness testimony, as recognized by a number of critical scholars.[16] For instance, it is often thought that the author of the second gospel is John Mark, who recorded the testimony of Peter, an apostle and eyewitness.[17] It is popular to name Luke as the author of both the third gospel and the Book of Acts, which provides further firsthand testimony since Luke tells us that he collected information from eyewitnesses (Luke 1:1-4).[18]

The authorship of Matthew is probably viewed as the hardest puzzle. Some critical scholars take Matthew to be the compiler of the Q document,[19] thereby providing eyewitness testimony.[20] The reason for the renewed interest in the fourth Gospel is partly because it is often linked closely with the eyewitness

16. Archibald M. Hunter, *Bible and Gospel* (Philadelphia: The Westminster Press, 1969), pp. 29-32; Daniel-Rops, pp. 21, 38, 50-85; Francois Amiot, "Jesus, An Historical Person," in Daniel-Rops, p. 10; Robert M. Grant, *An Historical Introduction to the New Testament* (London: Collins, 1963), pp. 180; cf. pp. 199-200.

17. C.E.B. Cranfield, *The Gospel According to Mark* (Cambridge: Cambridge University Press, 1963), pp. 5-6; A.M. Hunter, *The Gospel According to St. Mark* (London: SCM Press LTD, 1953), pp. 16-17; A. M. Hunter, *Introducing the New Testament*, Second Edition, Revised (Philadelphia: The Westminster Press, 1957), pp. 41-43; Robert M. Grant, p. 119; Bruce, *The New Testament Documents*, pp. 35-37; R.A. Cole, *The Gospel According to St. Mark* (Grand Rapids: Eerdmans, 1970), pp. 28-50; John Drane, *Introducing the New Testament* (San Francisco: Harper and Row, 1986), pp. 181-182.

18. Norval Geldenhuys, *Commentary on the Gospel of Luke* (Grand Rapids: Eerdmans, 1972), pp. 15-22; E.J. Tinsley, *The Gospel According to Luke* (Cambridge: Cambridge University Press, 1965), pp. 2-4; C.F.D. Moule, *Christ's Messengers: Studies in Acts of the Apostles* (New York: Association Press, 1957), pp. 10-13; Hunter, *Introducing the New Testament*, pp. 49-50; William Hamilton, *The Modern Reader's Guide to Matthew and Luke* (New York: Association Press, 1957), p. 14; Robert Grant, pp. 134-135; F. F. Bruce, *Commentary on the Book of Acts* (Grand Rapids: Eerdmans, 1971), p. 19; Bruce, *The New Testament Documents*, pp. 41-44; Ray Summers, *Commentary on Luke* (Waco: Word Books, 1972), pp. 8-10.

19. The Q document ("Quelle") is a major source thought by some to lie behind the Synoptic Gospels.

20. Hunter, *Introducing the New Testament*, pp. 55-56; Robert Grant, p. 129; Bruce, *The New Testament Documents*, pp. 39-40; cf. Drane, p. 191.

testimony of the apostle John as its major source.[21]

Although we will not specifically discuss the dates of the Gospels and Acts, critical scholars generally assign them somewhere between A.D. 60-100, or about 30-70 years after the death of Jesus. This is well within the time span when memoirs and other eyewitness accounts are written.[22]

These conclusions by critical theologians concern the eyewitness and even apostolic testimony behind the Gospels and Acts. As such, these are valuable indications that the authors were in good position to ascertain the trustworthiness of the information they provided concerning Jesus Christ. A.M. Hunter declares that there are several reasons for knowing that the Gospels are reliable. (1) The earliest Christians very carefully preserved the tradition of Jesus' life and teachings. (2) The Gospels incorporate eyewitness testimony, bringing us close to the known facts about Jesus. (3) The gospel authors were apparently honest reporters. (4) Jesus is presented virtually the same way throughout the four Gospels.[23]

But even beyond our consideration of the authorship of the Gospels, France makes a worthwhile assertion. While he thinks that a plausible case can be made for the four traditional authors, he actually argues that "Authorship . . . is not a major factor in our assessment of the reliability of the gospels."[24] France insists that we judge the Gospels by the same criteria used in ancient historiography. In this discipline, authorship is not as important as two other factors: the Gospels are the earliest sources for Jesus and the nature of the tradition behind them causes us to treat them seriously.[25]

---

21. Raymond E. Brown, *The Gospel According to John*, The Anchor Bible (Garden City: Doubleday and Company, Inc., 1966), Volume I, Chapter VII; Raymond E. Brown, *New Testament Essays* (Milwaukee: The Bruce Publishing Company, 1965), pp. 129-131; Leon Morris, *The Gospel According to John* (Grand Rapids: Eerdmans, 1971), pp. 8-35; R.V.G. Tasker, *The Gospel According to St. John* (Grand Rapids: Eerdman, 1968), pp. 11-20; Hunter, *Introducing the New Testament*, pp. 61-63; Robert Grant, p. 160; William Hamilton, *The Modern Reader's Guide to John* (New York: Association Press, 1959), pp. 13-15; Robinson, p. 83; Bruce, *The New Testament Documents*, pp. 48-49; Drane, pp. 196-197.

22. The sources in footnotes 15-20 above contain numerous discussions of the dates of these texts and the interested reader may consult them. Regarding an example of collecting eyewitness testimony over a period of time that is longer that what we are discussing here, see Eisenschiml and Newman, *Eyewitness: The Civil War as We Lived It*, cited in chapter 24.

23. Details are found in Hunter, *Bible and Gospel*, pp. 32-37.

24. France, p. 124.

25. *Ibid.*, pp. 122-125.

France is right about at least one thing. In general, ancient historians do not view the Gospels as non-historical propaganda, as some would have us think. They usually take them seriously, as decent sources for information concerning Jesus, opposing the more radical versions of criticism of many contemporary New Testament scholars. In fact, after their own investigation of the data, ancient historians frequently find an adequate basis for history in the New Testament. Sherwin-White levelled the following indictment at recent biblical scholarship:

> So, it is astonishing that while Graeco-Roman historians have been growing in confidence, the twentieth-century study of the Gospel narratives, starting from no less promising material, has taken so gloomy a turn in the development of form-criticism . . . that the historical Christ is unknowable and the history of his mission cannot be written. This seems very curious.[26]

Thus Sherwin-White asserts that the same standards commonly applied to ancient non-religious history can also be employed with the New Testament records, resulting in the emergence of a factual account. Another ancient historian, Michael Grant, likewise applies normal historical techniques to the New Testament and concludes that much can be known about the historical Jesus. Grant specifically rejects the methodology of the radical theologians.[27]

Here an objection is often heard. We are sometimes told that the New Testament authors cannot be compared to ancient, non-religious writers, since the latter recorded history while the former allowed their religious beliefs to significantly color their record.

Sherwin-White and Grant provide numerous responses to this charge. (1) Several prominent writers in antiquity composed works quite similar in their intent to that of the Gospels. As a matter of fact, the Gospel authors "would have applauded" these ancient efforts, yet the latter are well recognized as historical.[28] (2) Literature like the radical critics believe the Gospels to be is nonexistent in ancient times. Sherwin-White asserts, "We are not acquainted with this type of writing in ancient historiography."[29]

(3) The Gospels are dated quite close to the time period that they record, while ancient writers often describe events that took place centuries earlier. Still, modern historians are able to successfully reconstruct the events even from these

---

26. Sherwin-White, p. 187.
27. Michael Grant, *Jesus*, especially pp. 175-184, 198-201.
28. *Ibid.*, p. 182
29. Sherwin-White, p. 189.

ancient periods of time. (4) Ancient histories sometimes "disagree amongst themselves in the widest possible fashion," but the facts can still be ascertained.[30]

(5) Contemporary theologians are often satisfied just to explore the experiences of the earliest disciples, but historians look for adequate causes behind these experiences. (6) New Testament writings such as the Book of Acts are confirmed by external historical information. (7) Even the principles of radical criticism do not preclude the discovery of history in the Gospels. Although the primary interest of the Gospel writers was spiritual, there is no good reason why they would pervert the historical in the process. Both aspects are important and complementary.

Sherwin-White and Grant are examples of historians who have pointed out some of the many weaknesses in the critical methods of contemporary theologians. Both scholars conclude that if the same criteria used with other ancient writings are applied to the New Testament, we can derive an historical basis for the life and teachings of Jesus.[31]

So it is perhaps true that the Gospels may be established on grounds apart from authorship, as is done with other ancient documents. On the other hand, we don't understand how authorship is still not "a major factor" in the discussion.[32] At the very least, knowing that the writer is in a position to be trustworthy would significantly strengthen one's case for the historicity of Jesus.

As an example of applying our strategy, we will now single out the Book of 1 Corinthians for consideration, addressing the issues of authorship and the date of composition. In the next section we will address the specifics of a single text from this writing that is crucial to the discussion of the resurrection.

Critical scholars rarely doubt the Pauline authorship of 1 Corinthians. Clarence Tucker Craig even goes as far as to say the following about this writing: "It is unnecessary to discuss the authenticity of the letter . . . . No letter has better external testimony than this one."[33]

Most commentaries agree with Craig, usually glossing over the issue of

---

30. *Ibid.*, p. 187.

31. For more complete data concerning these points of critique, see Sherwin-White, *Ibid.*, pp. 186-193 and Grant, especially pp. 180-184, 199-200.

32. As France maintains on p. 124.

33. Clarence Tucker Craig, "Introduction and Exegesis of I Corinthians," *The Interpreter's Bible*, edited by George Arthur Buttrick (New York: Abingdon-Cokesbury Press, 1953), Volume X, p. 13. After a few other comments, Craig adds, ". . . it is well established that a corpus of Pauline letters circulated widely by the first half of the second century and contained our letter . . . ."

authorship altogether. S. Lewis Johnson goes a bit further than many when he gives the matter some succinct attention: "The external and internal evidences for the Pauline authorship of the letter are so strong that it is really unnecessary to give the matter more than cursory attention." Treating the second subject, he elaborates briefly: "The internal evidences – of style, vocabulary, and content – harmonize with what is known of both Paul and Corinth. This is a genuine product of Paul the Apostle."[34]

Paul's epistles were regularly cited from the end of the First Century to the initial decade of the Second Century. At least three writers of this period knew his books well. Clement of Rome (ca. A.D. 95-96), Ignatius (ca. A.D. 107), and Polycarp (ca. A.D. 110) either quote from or refer to 12 of the 13 letters traditionally credited to Paul, with Philemon being the only exception. The other 12 epistles are either referred to or quoted almost 90 times! Of this number, 1 Corinthians is mentioned over 30 times, easily the most references to any one of Paul's letters.[35] Moreover, Clement clearly states his view concerning the authenticity of this book: "Take up the epistle of the blessed Paul the Apostle" (47). Such early citations are certainly significant and show why 1 Corinthians is so well received.

Scholars are equally agreed that Paul first visited Corinth about A.D. 50 (cf. Acts 18:1-18a). His first epistle to them was written about A.D. 54-57.[36] This would mean that the book was penned approximately 25 years after Jesus' death.[37] We are on solid grounds when we accept 1 Corinthians as the writing of the Apostle Paul, being composed not long after the death of Jesus. In the next chapter we will provide additional criteria which indicate that Paul

---

34. S. Lewis Johnson, Jr., "I Corinthians," *The Wycliffe Bible Commentary*, (Nashville: Southwestern, 1962), p. 1228.

35. The interested reader may consult Lightfoot's above edition of *The Apostolic Fathers* for such references, since citations of Scripture are printed in italics and esily detected. For the actual figures in this paragraph, I am indebted to an unpublished essay by one of my graduate students, Kevin Smith ("References to Paul by Ignatius, Polycarp, and Clement," April 30, 1992).

36. Compare Craig, p. 13; Johnson, pp. 1227-1228; Donald Guthrie, *New Testament Introduction*, Revised Edition (Downers Grove: InterVarsity Press, 1990), pp. 457-459; Merrill C. Tenney, *New Testament Survey*, Revised Edition (Grand Rapids: Eerdmans, 1961), pp. 295-296; Hunter, *Introducing the New Testament*, pp. 97, 105.

37. For our purposes, it is a moot point whether 1 or 2 Corinthians contains parts of other earlier letters by Paul to this church. Concerning the issue, see the sources in the previous footnote. Cf. Drane, pp. 313-314.

is an authoritative source for the data he records. We think that detailed studies of the Gospels and Acts would also establish apostolic eyewitnesses as either the authors or chief sources behind the writers of these volumes, as well.

CONCLUSION

We stated in this chapter that there are definite steps we might take to confirm the veracity of the New Testament texts. More specifically, we are interested in the historical passages that comment on particulars in the life of Jesus. We proposed treating this process in three stages. First, we gave a brief overview of the general trustworthiness of the New Testament, concluding that we have both more and earlier manuscript evidence than for any other writing of antiquity. Additionally, pre- and extra-New Testament data of various sorts provides a rough outline of the major facets of Jesus' life, confirming the Gospel data.

Second, we briefly addressed the subject of the authorship and date of the relevant texts, hinting where a case for the Gospels and Acts might go. Then we provided specifics on the Book of 1 Corinthians, detailing why critical scholars are so unanimous in ascribing the work to the Apostle Paul, about 25 years after the death of Jesus.

The final stage of our case will be completed in the next chapter.[38] We will concentrate on a single text in an effort to show how there can be additional reasons for thinking that we have trustworthy information about Jesus. There our chief subject will be His death and resurrection.

---

38. See "An Early Christian Report" in chapter 26.

Chapter Twenty-Six
THE RESURRECTION OF JESUS

INTRODUCTION: IMPORTANCE OF THE QUESTION

Imagine what must have been the first thought to occur to the women when they arrived at the tomb of Jesus on resurrection morning. Experiencing despair and feeling despondent, they may have discussed the death of Jesus among themselves. Perhaps they divulged their shattered dreams and their crushed hopes. Maybe one of the women reminded the others that they had a job to do, finishing the burial process, begging the others not even to discuss recent events. It was most certainly a painful situation for all of them.

One other thing for sure – no one expected Jesus to rise from the dead. This was strictly a business trip; the women brought spices to prove it. So picture their total surprise when they looked up and saw the huge stone rolled away from the door of the tomb! What a conversation stopper! Furthermore, the body was missing! What a flood of conflicting thoughts must have rushed into their minds. What happened to their Lord?

The Gospels tell us that the women were immediately confused by the data. They were "afraid yet filled with joy" (Matt 28:9, NIV). When the disciples heard, they were even less willing to believe. Other possibilities crossed their minds. After all – and here we can readily identify with them – a resurrection would be a pretty awesome thing!

THE RESURRECTION AND CURRENT THOUGHT

The critical stance on Jesus' resurrection has shifted substantially in recent decades, in a perhaps unexpected, positive direction. The naturalistic theories[1] of the Nineteenth Century older, liberal theologians are rarely held in current studies. Rather, contemporary thinkers have approached this issue in a markedly different manner.

After applying the techniques of various sorts of critical investigation, non-evangelical scholars differ on how many of the reported facts concerning the death and resurrection of Jesus ought to be recognized as historical. However, there is an amazing unanimity concerning a certain core amount of data. In other words, there are a minimal number of events generally agreed to be facts by practically all critical scholars who deal with this topic, whatever their school of thought or discipline. Critical theologians, exegetes, historians, and philosophers who study this subject usually accept this factual basis. Virtually all scholars consider at least eleven events to be knowable history, while perhaps most include a twelfth, as well.

(1) Jesus died due to the severity of crucifixion and (2) was then buried. (3) His death caused the disciples to lose hope and experience despair. (4) Although not recognized to the same degree as the other findings here, most scholars seem to hold that the tomb in which Jesus was buried was found empty just a few days later.

Critical scholars even acknowledge that (5) the disciples then had real experiences that they believed were literal appearances of the risen Jesus. (6) These experiences transformed the disciples from apprehensive followers who were afraid to identify with Jesus into bold proclaimers of His death and resurrection, even being willing to die for this belief. (7) This resurrection message was central in early Christian preaching and (8) was especially proclaimed in Jerusalem, where Jesus had died shortly before.

Accordingly, (9) the Christian church was established and grew, (10) featuring Sunday as the primary day of worship. (11) James, the skeptical brother of Jesus, was converted when he believed he also saw the resurrected Jesus. (12) Saul of Tarsus, the famous persecutor of the church, became a Christian a couple of years later after an experience that he, similarly, believed to be an

---

1. These alternative schemes are produced by substituting some normal occurrence(s) for the belief in the literal resurrection. It's as if the critic fills in the following blank: "Jesus didn't rise from the dead. What really happened was _____."

appearance of the risen Jesus.[2]

At least these historical facts are crucial in a contemporary investigation of Jesus' resurrection. Except for the empty tomb, almost all critical scholars who explore this subject agree that these are a minimal amount of knowable historical facts. Additional data is also readily accepted, depending on the investigator in question. However, it isn't the amazing amount of agreement that is most important here. It is far more crucial that historical research *confirms* each of these facts.

Therefore, any conclusion concerning the historicity of Jesus' resurrection should adequately account for these details. The most pivotal fact here, recognized as historical by virtually all scholars, is this: the original disciples had experiences that they thought were appearances of the risen Jesus. This conclusion especially follows from a critical examination of the data, not from the consensus of views. A fascinating result is the current popularity of varying critical positions that accept and support the facticity of Jesus' resurrection.

NATURALISTIC THEORIES

We will now outline the broad parameters of an apologetic for Jesus' resurrection, supported by three major sets of arguments. First, naturalistic, alternative theories have failed to explain away this event. Each hypothesis that would seek to explain the resurrection in other than the usual manner is refuted by several key objections and is thus disproven by the known historical facts. Combinations of theories suffer the same fate.[3]

---

2. For more skeptical persons, a further move can be made. Frequently, I (Habermas) have randomly singled four of the facts from this list (numbers 1, 5, 6, and 12), sometimes adding a fifth (either number 3 or 7), in order to show the strength of the case for the resurrection. For the factual basis for each of these minimal facts, how they can be developed into perhaps the strongest basis for each of these minimal facts, how they can be developed into perhaps the strongest case of all in favor of the resurrection, and a sampling of more than 30 contemporary scholars from different disciplines who admit their facticity, see Gary R. Habermas and J.P. Moreland, *Immortality: The Other Side of Death* (Nashville: Thomas Nelson, 1992), pp. 69-72, 246-247, footnote 69.

3. We are simply unable to deal with each of these naturalistic theories and their refutations in this essay. For details, see Gary Habermas, *The Resurrection of Jesus: A Rational Inquiry* (Ann Arbor: University Microfilms, 1976), especially pp. 114-171. For a more succinct treatment, see Habermas and Moreland, *Immortality*, pp. 55-65. An older classic that is still of much value is James Orr, *The Resurrection of Jesus* (Grand Rapids: Zondervan, 1908, 1965).

One interesting illustration of the fate of the naturalistic theories is that they were disproven in the Nineteenth Century by the liberals themselves, by whom these hypotheses were popularized. These scholars refuted each other's theories and dismissed them one by one, leaving no viable options.

Instances of this phenomenon are helpful. Albert Schweitzer, in his epic survey of the liberal lives of Jesus, dismissed Reimarus' fraud theory and listed no proponents of this view since 1768.[4] David Strauss administered the death blow to the swoon theory advanced by such critics as Friedrich Schleiermacher, Karl Venturini, and Heinrich Paulus.[5] Turning the tables, Schleiermacher and Paulus criticized the hallucination theory, later popularized by Strauss. The major decimation of the hallucination theory resulted from the writings of Theodor Keim.[6] Further, Otto Pfleiderer criticized his own inclinations toward the legendary or mythological theory, even admitting that it did not explain Jesus' resurrection.[7]

So Nineteenth Century liberals systematically decimated each others' alternative theories on an individual basis, showing their deficiencies in terms of the historical facts. Twentieth Century critical scholars reacted somewhat differently, usually rejecting naturalistic theories wholesale, judging that they are incapable of explaining the known data. This is a typical practice of recent schools of thought.

For example, Karl Barth declares that each of these theories is confronted by many inconsistencies, concluding that "today we rightly turn up our nose at this."[8] Raymond Brown likewise explains that Twentieth Century critical scholars have rejected these hypotheses, asserting that they are no longer considered respectable. Contemporary thinkers, he adds, ignore these alternative

---

4. Albert Schweitzer, *The Quest of the Historical Jesus*, translated by W. Montgomery (New York: Macmillan, 1906, 1968), pp. 21-23.

5. David Strauss, *A New Life of Jesus* (London: Williams and Norgate, 1879), Volume I, p. 412. See also Schweitzer's assertion that Strauss disproved such rationalistic theses (*Ibid.*, p. 56).

6. Friedrich Schleiermacher, *The Christian Faith*, edited by H. R. Mackintosh and J. S. Stewart (New York: Harper and Row, 1963), Volume 2, p. 420; Schweitzer, pp. 54-55, 211-214; Orr, pp. 27, 219-231.

7. Otto Pfleiderer, *Early Christian Conception of Christ* (London: Williams and Norgate, 1905), pp. 152-159.

8. Karl Barth, *The Doctrine of Reconciliation*, Volume 4, Part I of *Church Dogmatics*, edited by G. W. Bromiley and T. F. Torrance (Edinburgh: T. and T. Clark, 1956), p. 340.

views, as well as any popularized renditions of them.[9]

Besides Barth and Brown, rejections of these hypotheses come from critical scholars as dissimilar as Paul Tillich, Gunther Bornkamm, Ulrich Wilckens, John A.T. Robinson, Wolfhart Pannenberg, and A.M. Hunter, among others.[10] Critical scholars such as these have pronounced a significant epitaph on the failure of these naturalistic theories.

EVIDENCES FOR THE RESURRECTION

The second set of arguments supporting Jesus' resurrection as an historical event consists of a number of positive evidences, ten of which will be enumerated here. Each of these has been taken from the list of recognized historical facts previously listed. This means that the factual basis for these evidences is admitted by the vast majority of contemporary scholars. We will only be able to state these arguments with very little elaboration.

The foremost evidence for Jesus' resurrection is (1) the disciples' eyewitness experiences, that they believed were literal appearances of the risen Jesus. Naturalistic hypotheses have not explained these incidents and additional facts corroborate this eyewitness testimony. (2) As a result, these eyewitnesses were transformed from timid believers into bold witnesses who were even willing to die for their convictions. (3) They declared the resurrection immediately, (4) with this being the very center of the apostolic message. (5) Most scholars would agree that Jesus' burial tomb was found empty. Each of these evidences requires an adequate explanation.

Further, the disciples broadcasted this message in the city of Jerusalem itself, where Jesus had recently died. (6) But in repeated confrontations, the Jewish authorities could not disprove their message in spite of having both the

---

9. Raymond Brown, "The Resurrection and Biblical Criticism," *Commonweal*, Volume 87 (November 24, 1967), especially p. 233.

10. Paul Tillich, *Systematic Theology* (Chicago: The University of Chicago Press, 1971), Volume 2, especially p. 136; Günther Bornkamm, *Jesus of Nazareth*, translated by Irene and Fraser McLuskey with James M. Robinson (New York: Harper and Row, 1960), pp. 181-185; Ulrich Wilckens, *Resurrection*, translated by A. M. Stewart (Edinburgh: Saint Andrews Press, 1977), pp. 117-119; John A.T. Robinson, *Can We Trust the New Testament?* pp. 123-125; Wolfhart Pannenberg, *Jesus – God and Man*, translated by Lewis L. Wilkens and Duane Priebe (Philadelphia: Westminster Press, 1968), pp. 88-97; A.M. Hunter, *Bible and Gospel*, p. 111.

power and the motivation to do so. Additionally, (7) the very existence of the Christian church, organized by monotheistic, Law-abiding Jews who nonetheless (8) worshiped on Sunday in order to commemorate the resurrection, both demand historical causes as well.

Two further facts that potently argue for the historicity of the resurrection are that two skeptics, (9) James and (10) Paul, became Christians after experiencing what they also believed were appearances of the risen Jesus. In a challenging statement, Reginald Fuller concludes that even if the appearance to James had not been recorded by Paul (1 Cor 15:7), such would still have to be proposed in order to account for both James' conversion and his subsequent promotion to the authoritative position of leader of the Jerusalem church.[11] This is even more emphatically the case with Paul's conversion.[12]

In light of the failure of the naturalistic theories, this minimum of ten evidences provides a powerful case for the historicity of Jesus' resurrection. Additionally, it is significant that each of these evidences was based on an ascertainable historical fact that is recognized as such even by critical scholars.[13]

To be more succinct, when the early and eyewitness experiences of the disciples, James and Paul are considered, along with their corresponding transformations and the content of their central message,[14] the historical resurrection is shown for what it is: the best explanation for the facts. This is especially the case in the absence of viable alternative theories. Therefore, it may be concluded that Jesus' resurrection is an event of history. But we will proceed beyond this basis to an additional two sets of arguments to further strengthen this case.

---

11. Reginald Fuller, *The Formation of the Resurrection Narratives* (New York: Macmillan, 1971), p. 37.

12. *Ibid.*, pp. 37, 46-47.

13. As mentioned earlier, the empty tomb is the lone exception here. Although not unanimously accepted, perhaps a majority of recent scholars still recognize it as historical. See Robert H. Stein, "Was the Tomb Really Empty?" *The Journal of the Evangelical Theological Society*, Volume 20 (March 1977), pp. 23-29. See also the sources listed below.

14. This does not even include the report of the more than five hundred people who claimed to have seen the risen Jesus at once, concerning whom Paul pointed out that most were still alive and therefore could be questioned (1 Cor 15:6).

AN EARLY CHRISTIAN REPORT

Contemporary approaches to the historicity of the resurrection have taken some new paths.[15] The center of attention has been the text in 1 Corinthians 15:3ff., where virtually all scholars agree that Paul recorded another ancient creed(s) like those discussed in the previous chapter. This report on the death and resurrection of Jesus is actually much earlier than the book in which it is recorded. We already pointed out that Paul wrote this epistle about A.D. 55-57.

Numerous considerations show that this material is traditional and earlier than the date of Paul's writing. He utilizes the technical terms "delivered" and "received," which signify the imparting of oral tradition. The parallelism and stylized content, the non-Pauline words, sentence structure, diction, and the possibility of an Aramaic original add to this conclusion. Further indications of traditional material include the Aramaic name Cephas (see the parallel in Luke 24:34), the threefold usage of "and that" (like Aramaic and Mishnaic Hebrew means of narration), and the two references to the Scriptures being fulfilled.[16]

How much earlier is this material than the Book of 1 Corinthians? Critical scholars generally agree that this report has an extremely early origin. Joachim Jeremias designates it "the earliest tradition of all."[17] Wilckens declares that it "indubitably goes back to the oldest phase of all in the history of primitive Christianity."[18] Most typically, scholars date Paul's reception of

---

15. This portion is a somewhat revised version of Section I of the author's article, "Jesus' Resurrection and Contemporary Criticism: An Apologetic (Part II)," *Criswell Theological Review*, Volume 4 (1990), pp. 373-385.

16. In particular, see Fuller, 9ff.; Pinchas Lapide, *The Resurrection of Jesus: A Jewish Perspective* (Minneapolis: Augsberg Publishing House, 1983), pp. 97-99. See also Raymond Brown, *The Virginal Conception and Bodily Resurrection of Jesus* (New York: Paulist Press, 1973), pp. 81, 92; Robinson, p. 125; Paul Van Buren, *The Secular Meaning of the Gospel* (New York: Macmillan,1963), pp. 126-27; Rudolf Bultmann, *Theology of the New Testament*, translated by Kendrick Grobel (New York: Charles Scribner's Sons,1951, 1955), Vol. I, p. 296; cf. Willi Marxsen, *The Resurrection of Jesus of Nazareth*, translated by Margaret Kohl (Philadelphia: Fortress Press, 1970), p. 80; Bornkamm, p. 182; Joachim Jeremias, "Easter: The Earliest Tradition and the Earliest Interpretation,"translated by J. Bowden, *New Testament Theology* (New York: Charles Scribner's Sons, 1971), p. 306.

17. Jeremias, *Ibid.*, p. 306.

18. Wilckens, p. 2.

this formula to two to eight years after the crucifixion itself, or from about A.D. 32-38.[19] Most of those who comment on the issue hold that Paul most likely received this material shortly after his conversion during his visit to Jerusalem with Peter and James, who are included in the list of appearances (1 Cor 15:5; 7; Gal 1:18-19).[20]

We are given a hint in Galatians 1:18 that might confirm this scenario. In reference to his lengthy visit with Peter shortly after his conversion, Paul's use of the term *historeo* may indicate an investigative inquiry. William Farmer argues that this word in context signifies Paul's acting as an examiner or as an observer of Peter.[21] Additionally, the immediate context both before and after Paul's description of this trip to Jerusalem indicates that his topic is the nature

---

19. For some of the many critical scholars who accept such a dating, see Hans Grass, *Ostergeschehen und Osterberichte*, Second Edition (Gottingen: Vandenhoeck und Ruprecht, 1962), p. 96; Oscar Cullmann, *The Early Church: Studies in Early Christian History and Theology*, edited by A.J.B. Higgins (Philadelphia: Westminster Press, 1966), pp. 65-66; Leonard Goppelt, "The Eastern Kerygma in the New Testament," *The Easter Message Today* (New York: Thomas Nelson, 1964), p. 36; Pannenberg, p. 90; Fuller, pp.10, 14, 28, 48; C.H. Dodd, *The Apostolic Preaching and Its Developments* (Grand Rapids: Baker Books, 1980), p. 16; A.M. Hunter, *Jesus: Lord and Saviour* (Grand Rapids: Eerdmans, 1976), p. 100; Brown, *The Virginal Conception and Bodily Resurrection of Jesus*, p. 81; Thomas Sheehan, *First Coming: How the Kingdom of God Became Christianity* (New York: Random House, 1986), pp. 110, 118; G.E. Ladd, *I Believe in the Resurrection of Jesus* (Grand Rapids: Eerdmans, 1975), p. 105. Hans Kung dates this "creedal" statement from A.D. 35-45 in his book *On Being a Christian* (Garden City: Doubleday and Company, Inc., 1976), p. 348. Norman Perrin believes that the date is no later than A.D. 50, but he does not undertake a closer approximation. See Norman Perrin, *The Resurrection According to Matthew, Mark and Luke* (Philadelphia: Fortress Press, 1977), p. 79. Gerald O'Collins attests that he is not aware of any scholar who places the date for Paul's reception of this material after the A.D. 40's. See O'Collins, *What are They Saying About the Resurrection?* (NewYork: Paulist Press, 1978), p. 112. It should be very carefully noted that our major conclusions would still follow, even with a some-what later date for this "creed."

20. According to Goppelt, scholars generally recognize that this creed's original form is Palestinian in nature (p. 36). For those scholars who generally favor the Jerusalem scenario we just outlined, see the list in footnote number 19. Grass is an exception, opting for Damascus as the locale, necessitating an even earlier date (p. 96), whereas Kung, Perrin, and Sheehan do not seem to answer this question in their immediate contexts.

21. William R. Farmer, "Peter and Paul, and the Tradition Concerning 'The Lord's Supper' in I Cor. 11:23-25," *Criswell Theological Review*, Volume 2 (1987), especially pp. 122-130. On the apostolic, Petrine nature of this "creed," see pp. 135-138.

of the Gospel (Gal 1:11-17; 2:1-10). In the latter reference, Paul checked the content of his Gospel preaching with the other apostles fourteen years later, a message that explicitly included the resurrection (1 Cor 15:1-4).[22]

As a result of the early dating and apostolic source, this ancient formula is an invaluable report of the original eyewitnesses' experiences. German historian Hans von Campenhausen declares about this pre-Pauline material: "This account meets all the demands of historical reliability that could possibly be made of such a text."[23] A.M. Hunter repeats this assessment.[24] After discussing this creed, C.H. Dodd states emphatically:

> The date, therefore, at which Paul received the fundamentals of the Gospel cannot well be later than some seven years after the death of Jesus Christ. It may be earlier, and, indeed, we must assume some knowledge of the tenets of Christianity in Paul even before his conversion.[25]

Dodd follows this statement with a challenge to anyone who would make the dubious charge that Paul was mistaken regarding the content and apostolic nature of the Gospel message. They must bear the burden of proof.[26]

Here we need to make one of the most vital points of this entire chapter. Our conclusion concerning this creedal material does *not* rest on knowing the actual date when and the precise location where Paul received it. For any who doubt the reliability of this data, there is still an excellent foundation for the assertion that Paul's report is authoritative. There are at least five weighty indications that the *content* of this Gospel "creed" (and probably the actual words) is early and apostolic in nature, whether it came from Paul's trip to Jerusalem in the mid-30s A.D. or not.

(1) Paul tells us that he is recording a list of eyewitness appearances of

---

22. It may be objected that Paul explicitly says in Gal 1:11-17 that he did not receive his message of the Gospel from any man, including other apostles. But such an interpretation would contradict Paul's own words. In the above text, he is speaking specifically of his initial and direct call by the Lord, where he was given the Gospel message before he ever met another apostle. Otherwise, why did he need to inquire of Peter in the first place? Additionally, he makes it equally clear that he later consulted with the other apostles *specifically* to ascertain if his Gospel message was correct (Gal 2:2). Therefore, to say that he never checked with any other apostle on this subject is to miss his point.

23. Hans von Campenhausen, "The Events of Easter and the Empty Tomb," *Tradition and Life in the Early Church* (Philadelphia: Fortress Press, 1968), p. 44.

24. Hunter, *Jesus: Lord and Saviour*, p. 100.

25. Dodd, p. 16.

26. *Ibid.*

Jesus to the disciples and that this material was passed on to him (1 Cor 15:3-7). This creed is stylized in its structure, which is one of numerous indications of its formal, authoritative status in the early church. (2) Paul is the eyewitness, apostolic source behind his own resurrection appearance recorded in verse 8.

(3) Paul declares that all of the other apostles were currently preaching the same message concerning Jesus' appearances (1 Cor 15:11, 14, 15). (4) Paul specifically checked the nature of the Gospel content (that included the resurrection) with the apostolic leadership and was told that his teaching was accurate (Gal 1:11-2:1-10). Comparatively few, if any, contemporary scholars hold that Paul was totally mistaken at all four of these junctures.

(5) Additionally, this basic information is further corroborated by the early creedal material contained in Acts, which testifies to several important details concerning Jesus' resurrection and His appearances.[27] In almost every one of these texts, a chief idea is that the disciples were "witnesses" of Jesus' coming to them after His death.[28]

Here we have five forceful reasons for concluding that this traditional data is apostolic, eyewitness, and authoritative.[29] The pre-Pauline report of Jesus' resurrection appearances, the appearance to him, the attendant data about the other apostles, along with the report in Galatians and the primitive texts in Acts, all clearly link the eyewitness content of the Gospel with its proclamation.[30] The evidence shows that the participants actually saw the risen Jesus, both individually and in groups.

---

27. For this theme, see the early confessions in Acts 2:22-33;3:14-15, 26; 4:10; 5:30; 10:39-43; 13:27-37.

28. This theme surfaces in Acts 2:32; 3:15; 5:32; 10:41; 13:31. In at least the last two texts, group appearances of Jesus are in view. See Dodd's extended and influential discussion of these passages (pp. 17-31); cf. Drane, p. 99.

29. When dealing with the resurrection appearances of Jesus, critics respect more than just the creedal reports in 1 Cor 15:3ff. and Acts 2-5, 10, 13. After an analytical study of the Gospels, Dodd shows that these writings contain several reports that rely on early tradition. He insists that the appearances recorded in Matt 28:8-10, 16-20; John 20:19-21, and, to a lesser extent, Luke 24:36-49, are also based on early material. He states that even the other Gospel accounts of Jesus' resurrection appearances lack the mythical tendencies often found in some types of ancient literature and likewise merit careful consideration in a study of this subject. C.H. Dodd, "The Appearances of the Risen Christ: An Essay in Form-Criticism of the Gospels," *More New Testament Studies* (Grand Rapids: Eerdmans, 1968).

30. This section of the chapter functions as the third step outlined in the previous

THE VISUAL NATURE OF JESUS' APPEARANCES

The dozen historical facts listed earlier in this chapter can be established on critical grounds and are almost always recognized as historical even by a wide range of non-evangelical scholars. This limited amount of data has performed several tasks for us in this chapter. They are capable of arguing decisively against each of the naturalistic theories, although we were not able to pursue details here.

These basic, known facts also provide some of the strongest evidences for the resurrection of Jesus. The disciples' early and eyewitness experiences have not been explained away on alternative grounds. They were transformed into persons who were even willing to die for their faith. Paul reported that the risen Jesus appeared to him, and that James the brother of Jesus saw Him, too. Both men were radically converted as a result. The resurrection was the very center of the earliest church preaching. None of this was disproven by the ancient enemies of the church. The evidences for the empty tomb[31] are also noteworthy. So the critically ascertained, historical data verify the reports that the disciples witnessed Jesus' resurrection appearances, all in the absence of viable alternative hypotheses.

Another major advantage of this limited number of facts is that it allows us to focus on and address directly the *nature* of these post-resurrection experiences. Most critical scholars conclude that the disciples' perceptions were visual in nature, for no other conclusion satisfies all of the information. Historian Michael Grant thinks that an analysis will actually "prove" that the earliest witnesses were convinced that they had seen the risen Jesus.[32] Carl

---

chapter on the New Testament. So we wish to add that the Gospel accounts of the resurrection appearances should also be utilized as records of what the eyewitnesses actually saw. For examples of arguments for each of the specific resurrection texts in the Gospels, see William Lane Craig, *Assessing the New Testament Evidence for the Historicity of the Resurrection of Jesus* (Lewiston: The Edward Mellen Press, 1989); Grant Osborne, *The Resurrection Narratives: A Redactional Study* (Grand Rapids: Baker Book House, 1984).

31. Again, this report is not as unanimously accepted as the other facts. For additional defenses of the empty tomb besides those of von Campenhausen and Stein, listed above, see Edward L. Bode, *The First Easter Morning* (Rome: Biblical Institute Press, 1970), pp. 155-75; William Lane Craig, "The Empty Tomb of Jesus," *Gospel Perspectives: Studies of History and Tradition in the Four Gospels*, edited by R. T. France and D. Wenham (Sheffield: JSOT Press, 1981), Volume II, pp. 173-200.

32. Michael Grant, *Jesus*, p. 176.

Braaten insists that even contemporary skeptics agree with the conclusion that the early believers thought the Easter appearances were real events in space and time.[33] Reginald Fuller labels the disciples' belief in the risen Jesus "one of the indisputable facts of history." Then Fuller declares that the certainty that the disciples had some sort of visionary experiences "is a fact upon which both believer and unbeliever may agree."[34]

Wolfhart Pannenberg summarizes the issue like this: "Few scholars, even few rather critical scholars, doubt that there had been visionary experiences."[35] So the next question is, can hallucinations (or other subjective theories) explain these facts? Pannenberg explains that such a response is a very unlikely one,[36] and numerous other critical scholars regularly cite their agreement with him.[37] Why are such suppositions rejected by most of these intellectuals?

Even a brief critique of hypotheses involving hallucinations (or similar responses) is sufficient to reveal significant ways in which it fails noticeably in its attempt to explain away the data. Hallucinations are private events, but Jesus appeared to groups of people.[38] Moreover, the disciples despaired after the death of Jesus, contrary to the required hallucinatory mood of expectation and hope. Further, Jesus appeared to a variety of persons, at several times and

---

33. Carl Braaten, *History and Hermeneutics* (Philadelphia:Westminster Press, 1966), p. 78.

34. Reginald H. Fuller, *The Foundations of New Testament Christology* (New York: Charles Scribner's Sons, 1965), p. 142.

35. Wolfhart Pannenberg, "The Historicity of the Resurrection: The Identity of Christ," *The Intellectuals Speak Out About God*, p. 260.

36. *Ibid.*, pp. 260-261. For a far more technical treatment of some of the many problems here, see especially Pannenberg, *Jesus – God and Man*, pp. 94-97.

37. For examples of such scholars, see Tillich, vol. II, especially p. 156; Grass, p. 96; Barth, p. 340; Jeremias, p. 302; Brown, "The Resurrection and Biblical Criticism," p. 233; Bornkamm, p. 185; Lapide, pp. 124-126; Fuller, *The Formation of the Resurrection Narratives*, pp. 46-49; Robinson, pp. 123-125; A.M. Ramsay, *The Resurrection of Christ* (London: Collins, 1961), pp. 41, 49-50; Neville Clark, *Interpreting the Resurrection* (Philadelphia: Westminster Press, 1967), pp. 100-101.

38. Clinical psychologist Gary R. Collins said the following in personal correspondence to Habermas (21 February 1977):

> Hallucinations are individual occurrences. By their very nature only one person can see a given hallucination at a time. They certainly are not something which can be seen by a group of people. Neither is it possible that one person could somehow induce an hallucination in somebody else. Since an hallucination exists only in this subjective, personal sense, it is obvious that others cannot witness it.

places. That all of these people were simultaneously candidates for hallucinations significantly stretches our reason.

Additionally, what about Jesus' brother James? And don't forget Paul, either! Did these two skeptics also desire to visualize the risen Jesus? Continuing, such theses say nothing about the empty tomb, so we need another theory there.[39] As Pannenberg concludes with regard to such objections, "These explanations have failed to date."[40]

We can succinctly summarize our chief point from this section of the chapter. The known historical data overwhelmingly dictate that the disciples saw something that they concluded were appearances of the risen Jesus. Yet, the facts disprove hypotheses depending on hallucinations or other subjective explanations. So the core elements of the original disciples' experiences definitely indicate that they witnessed actual appearances of the risen Jesus.

James D.G. Dunn indicates that there is a widespread consensus among contemporary, critical theologians of this conclusion: Jesus appeared to His disciples, and not just as a spirit.[41] Here we must *carefully* reiterate: this is true not simply because critics say it is, but because *the facts dictate this conclusion.* Thus, while critical conclusions are helpful, the most crucial consideration is that the *factual data demonstrate* that Jesus appeared to His disciples after His death.

CONCLUSION

Our arguments have been based on a *limited number* of knowable historical facts and *verified by critical procedures.* Therefore, contemporary scholars should not spurn such evidence by referring to "discrepancies" in the New Testament texts or to its general "unreliability." While critical claims of this nature are problematic on other grounds not addressed here, we have concluded that Jesus' resurrection appearances can be historically demonstrated *based*

---

39. For other details, see Gary R. Habermas, *The Resurrection of Jesus: A Rational Inquiry*, pp. 127-145. A much briefer critique, including additional critical questions, is found in Habermas and Moreland, *Immortality*, pp. 60-61.

40. Pannenberg, *Jesus – God and Man*, p. 96.

41. James D.G. Dunn, *The Evidence for Jesus* (Philadelphia: Westminster Press, 1985), pp. 73-75. Critical scholars usually believe that Jesus really appeared in some rather undefined, but non-physical, fashion. For a treatment of this view, including reasons for bodily appearances of Jesus, see Habermas and Moreland, Chapter 9.

only on a limited amount of critically recognized historical facts.

Nor should critics cite the sometimes popular slogan that "something" occurred to the disciples that is indescribable, because of covert naturalistic premises. Neither should the nature of history itself or the "legendary character" or "cloudiness" of the New Testament texts be allowed to oppose these conclusions. Similarly, we should not be satisfied with the opinion that Jesus continues to live on through His teachings, but not literally. As we have said, these and other related views are challenged by *the historically ascertainable data admitted by virtually all scholars.* These historical grounds are adequate to demonstrate the literal resurrection appearances of Jesus.

Let's look at this from a different angle. Critics are fond of simply stating what they believe we *cannot* know concerning the New Testament accounts. In short, they would do better to concentrate on what *can* be determined from these texts. The factual basis indicates that Jesus' resurrection is by far the best historical explanation of this data. While questions may remain concerning other New Testament topics, even a limited number of determined facts are satisfactory to show that the same Jesus who had died by crucifixion shortly before later appeared to His followers.

Most critical scholars maintain either that the resurrection can be accepted by faith as an actual event or that some sort of appearances (abstract or bodily) need to be postulated as historical realities.[42] Although we have not addressed the actual characteristics of Jesus' resurrection body, we hold that the combined testimony of the New Testament is that Jesus rose in a transformed body that was nevertheless literal and physical. This is the report of the earliest eyewitnesses.

We outlined several sets of arguments for Jesus' resurrection, based on a limited number of facts established as historical and recognized as such by virtually all scholars. Naturalistic alternative theories have failed to disprove this event. Positive evidences, along with the early pre-Pauline traditional material, and the early preaching in Acts, further corroborate this conclusion. Data such as this decisively vindicate the reported, visual claims of the earliest eyewitnesses: Jesus was raised from the dead and literally appeared to a number of His followers, both individually and in groups.

---

42. For a survey of contemporary opinion on this issue, see Gary R. Habermas, "Jesus' Resurrection and Contemporary Criticism: An Apologetic," *Criswell Theological Review*, Volume 4 (1989), pp. 160-172.

Chapter Twenty-Seven
THE UNIQUENESS OF JESUS

INTRODUCTION: IMPORTANCE OF THE QUESTION

Have you ever encountered an incredible set of occurrences but didn't know how to "classify" them in your mind because they didn't fit any meaningful pattern in your experience? Conversely, have you ever come across the sort of key that organizes other events, giving meaning to them?

More than in the past, technology has made our world grow "smaller." Of course, we are not speaking in physical terms, but of our contact with peoples and cultures that we perhaps have never noticed before. One of the areas that we have come to recognize is the various sacred beliefs held by those in the world around us. It seems that there are a lot of religious claims "floating" around and even "messianic pretenders" who gather followers to themselves.

Often these teachers make striking religious statements that we can't easily classify because they don't fit our theological categories. Maybe we notice contradictions in their teachings or lifestyle – perhaps they make a wrong prediction or live by a vastly different standard than that of their devotees. But there is another feature we come to associate with religious claims, too. The one doing the talking seldom backs it up with evidence. We tend to be more impressed when someone "puts their money where their mouth is."

In the Person of Jesus, deeds match words. We just saw that He was literally raised from the dead in time-space history. This occurrence was indeed a
key event that shocked those who heard of it. Now we will ask a question in
reverse. Did His previous teachings and actions corresponded to this grand
event? Seen from another angle, did the resurrection give new meaning to His
religious claims?

THE RESURRECTION AND THE ACTION OF GOD

The resurrection does not stand alone. It is neither an isolated event without
meaning nor a brute fact of history pregnant with significance apart from any
other data. The reason this occurrence is so noteworthy is because it is linked
to the most singular Life that ever walked the face of this planet. This grand
event happened to Jesus, Who made simply incredible claims about Himself
and His world.

There are at least two different ways to tie the resurrection to the uniqueness of Jesus.[1] First, a prospective argument can be constructed that moves
from the existence of God forward to the resurrection. We have supported
many arguments for God's existence and attributes in this volume. In a theistic
universe, the resurrection of Jesus is an event that is not only consistent with
God's attributes, but even requires them. For examples, the resurrection
requires great knowledge and power, as well as being an orderly occurrence.
We would argue that God is omniscient, omnipotent, and efficient.

Antony Flew, an eminent philosophical atheist, even agrees that if God's
existence were known, the general line of this argument from God to the resurrection would follow. Flew declares: "Certainly given some beliefs about God,
the occurrence of the resurrection does become enormously more likely."[2]

We think that there is far more than enough evidence to establish God's
existence.[3] Accordingly, the resurrection follows from such a basis as an act

---

1. For the following argument in extended form, see Gary R. Habermas, *The
Resurrection of Jesus: An Apologetic* (Grand Rapids: Baker Book House, 1980;
Lanham: University Press of America, 1984), Chapters 1-5. A vastly edited form
appears in Habermas and Flew, *Did Jesus Rise from the Dead?*, pp. 39-42.

2. Antony G.N. Flew, personal correspondence with Terry L. Miethe, 1 April
1985.

3. On this first point, see the chapters above, as well as the debate between Terry
Miethe and Antony Flew, *Does God Exist? A Believer and Atheist Debate* (San
Francisco: Harper-Collins, Publishers, 1991).

that requires God's intervention.[4] In fact, this book up through the last chapter may even be construed as an extended form of this initial approach.

JESUS' UNIQUE CLAIMS

Second, today we can basically only look back at the claims of Jesus in a retrospective manner.[5] In a post-Easter sense, we generally view His pre-cross teachings through the lens of the cross and resurrection. Interestingly, this is also the way that most of the earliest Christian believers understood His claims. For the majority of them, the resurrection is the event that verified His assertions.

What did Jesus teach about Himself? For one thing, He claimed[6] to have a special relationship to the God of the universe. This is admitted in some sense by most critical scholars in recent times. According to Bultmann, Jesus taught that His person, deeds, and message signalled the inbreaking of God's Kingdom.[7]

Jesus not only taught that He had a unique relationship with God, but that He was actually Deity. There are at least four major indications of this. First, Jesus' own self-designations reveal His self-consciousness. He claimed the messianic title of the heavenly, pre-existent, divine Son of Man, and even maintained that He was God's Son.[8] Some critics have attempted to question

---

4. See Habermas, *The Resurrection of Jesus: An Apologetic*, Chapter 2.

5. In the scope of this chapter we will only be able to provide an outline in this section of what we have termed the retrospective argument. Our footnotes will suggest other sources that may interest readers who choose to pursue the relevant issues in more detail.

6. There is more than one way to ascertain the nature of Jesus' claims. One is to utilize the results of critical methodology, building on that minimalistic foundation, like we did in our last chapter on the resurrection. We will do much of this here, as well, especially in the footnotes. Critical conclusions will serve as sort of a lowest common denominator. A second way to establish Jesus' message is to begin by addressing the reliability of the New Testament, like we did in chapter 25. For further details related to such an approach, see Craig Blomberg, *The Historical Reliability of the Gospels*; Norman Anderson, *The Teaching of Jesus* (Downers Grove: InterVarsity Press, 1983); R.T. France, *The Evidence for Jesus*, as well as the sources listed below.

7. Bultmann, *Theology of the New Testament*, Vol. I, especially pp. 7-9.

8. For examples of some especially insightful texts, see Mark 2:10-11; 12:1-11; 13:32; 14:61-64; Matthew 11:25-27. This is an intricate topic and it is difficult to handle it briefly. For the uses of these and other titles in Scripture and their meanings, see I.H. Marshall, *The Origins of New Testament Christology*, Updated Edition (London: InterVarsity Press, 1990); Oscar Cullmann, *The Christology of the New Testament*,

whether Jesus really referred to Himself by using either the title Son of Man[9] or the concept of Son of God,[10] but the evidence soundly disproves them.

---

translated by Shirley C. Guthrie and Charles A.M. Hall (Philadelphia: Westminster Press, 1963); Donald Guthrie, *New Testament Theology* (Downers Grove: InterVarsity Press, 1981), especially pp. 270-291, 301-321. For more succinct treatments, see the following articles in the *Evangelical Dictionary of Theology*, edited by Walter A. Elwell (Grand Rapids: Baker Book House, 1984): Robert H. Stein, "Jesus Christ," pp. 582-585; Gary T. Burke, "Son of God," pp. 1032-1034; and Royce G. Gruenler, "Son of Man," pp. 1034-1036. We will make extensive use of these sources in the next two footnotes.

   9. For those who prefer a few technical details, Stein answers the more radical objection that Jesus never referred to Himself as the Son of Man (*Ibid.*, p. 584):

   . . . such attempts founder on the fact that this title is found in all the Gospel strata (Mark, Q, M, L, and John) and satisfies perfectly the "criterion of dissimilarity," which states that if a saying or title like this could not have arisen out of Judaism or out of the early church, it must be authentic.

   Regarding the second point, the church could not have invented the title of Son of Man for Jesus. It *never* designates Jesus in such a manner in any of the epistles. In the Gospels, it is Jesus' favorite self-designation, yet the title is not applied to Him by others except when referring to His own usage. Outside the Gospels, it only appears in Acts 7:56 and Rev 1:13, both times referring to the heavenly, exalted Jesus.

   In other words, how could the church have originated the title Son of Man as Jesus' favorite self-description, when basically the church itself does not even refer to Him in this manner? Cullmann asserts that this question is "completely inexplicable" by the critical thesis (*Ibid.*, p. 155).

   On the other hand, while Judaism definitely had such a concept at this general time, it would not, of course, have given Jesus such a title. But as we just saw, neither did the church assign the concept to Him. As Cullmann concludes, the only option that makes sense is that the Gospels correctly preserve the truth that Jesus used it of Himself (*Ibid.*, p. 155). Stein adds that those who deny the authenticity of this title do so on *a priori* grounds (before the facts are examined), not on exegetical ones (*Ibid.*, p. 584). Gruenler agrees here (p. 1035).

   Once it is known that Son of Man is Jesus' self-designation, the next question is whether He meant it to include His own Deity. In Mark 2:1-12 Jesus declared that the Son of Man had the authority to forgive sin, directly in the face of the Jewish leaders who claimed that such was a prerogative of God alone. (See the next point in our main text for pertinent details.) Another example comes from one of the three classic categories of Jesus' Son of Man sayings: His future coming and exaltation. Jesus linked this title with the claim that He was also the divine Son of God, which precipitated the final Jewish charge of blasphemy and lead to His execution (Mark 14:61-63). (See footnote 10 and the main text for other decisive particulars on this last point.)

   Accordingly, scholars have declared that Jesus' use of Son of Man includes His Deity as the heavenly, pre-existent, glorified divine figure of Dan 7:14. Cullmann summarizes: " . . . by means of this very term Jesus spoke of his divine heavenly character" (*Ibid.*, p. 162; cf. pp. 142, 151). See also Stein, *Ibid.*, p. 584; Guthrie, p. 280; Marshall, p. 68; Gruenler, p. 1035.

   10. Regarding those who question whether Jesus referred to Himself by the Son of

Additionally, Jesus used the name *Abba* to refer to God, a word that is translated as "Father" or even "Daddy." This identification has been a central focus in contemporary studies and is another claim of a unique familial relationship with God. Joachim Jeremias summarizes the matter this way:

> Abba . . . is . . . an authentic and original utterance of Jesus, and that this Abba implies the claim of a unique revelation and a unique authority . . . . We are confronted with something new and unheard of which breaks through the limits of Judaism.[11]

God concept, Stein agrees with many scholars when he states that Mark 13:32 "must be authentic, for no one in the church would have created a saying such as this in which the Son of God claims to be ignorant as to the time of the end" (Stein, *Ibid.*, p. 583). Guthrie agrees: " . . . it is impossible to suppose that a saying so Christologically embarrassing should have been invented. There is no strong reason to question its authenticity . . ." (Guthrie, p. 794, footnote 14; see also p. 308). Likewise Cullmann: "On the other hand, it is questionable whether the early Church could have invented a saying of Jesus which in this way limits his unity with the Father at such an important point" (*Ibid.*, pp. 288-289).

Most scholars think that Matthew 11:25-27 (cf. Luke 10:21-22) is the key reference expressing Jesus' self-consciousness about being the Son of God. Guthrie concludes that this passage "seems to include the unique filial relation between Jesus and God. There can be no doubt that Jesus was conscious of that relationship" (Guthrie, p. 307). Cullmann states that this text "points to Jesus' omniscience . . ." (*Ibid.*, p. 288). Marshall thinks that " . . . Jesus is applying 'a son' to himself, and is thus making an implicit claim to a unique relationship with God" (Marshall, p. 115; cf. also p. 123).

Again, does this title include Jesus' understanding that He was Deity? While John refers to Jesus as the only-begotten Son of God (for *monogenes*, see 1:16, 18; 3:16, 18), Jesus referred to God as *Abba* (Mk. 14:36), also denoting that unique filial relationship (see textual discussion directly below). Further, Matthew 11:27 depicts the uniqueness of the Son and His relationship to God. Last, Mark 14:61-64 provides additional insight into the meaning Jesus gave to this title, which the Jewish priests understood as nothing short of blasphemy. Other significant texts are Mark 12:1-11 and the baptismal, temptation, and transfiguration passages in the Synoptics, in each of which sonship is prominent.

Accordingly, Cullmann asserts that "Jesus' consciousness of being the Son of God refers both to his person and to his work: his work of salvation and revelation shows that the Father and the Son are one" (*Ibid.*, p. 290). Therefore, the Jews respond to Jesus' own self-consciousness and "correctly interpret Jesus' claim to be 'Son' as identification with God . . . ." (Cullmann, *Ibid.*, p. 302; cf. p. 270). Marshall points out that the title Son of God involves the concept of Deity, which emerged in the church "as the inescapable corollary of Jesus' position" (Marshall, pp. 129, cf. 123). Burke remarks that "Jesus conceived of his divine sonship as unique and unparalleled" (p. 1033). Others agree that Son of God involves one of Jesus' claims to be Deity (Guthrie, p. 306; Stein, *Ibid.*, p. 583).

11. Joachim Jeremias, *The Central Message of the New Testament* (Philadelphia: Fortress Press, 1965), p. 30.

Many scholars agree on the significance of this intimate way of referring to the God of the universe. It provides us with additional insight into Jesus' notion of His own Person. Speaking of Jesus' use of *Abba*, Guthrie states that "the evidence supports most strongly the view that Jesus was conscious of a relationship to his Father which was unique."[12]

Second, Jesus claimed authority unlike the founders of the world religions. Other religious personages basically said, in effect, that they would show their followers the right path, or the way of salvation. But Jesus didn't only teach the means to achieving salvation – He taught that He *was* salvation.[13] Jesus, in His own Person, confronted others with God's message and presence. Their response to Him would determine their destiny.[14] Jesus also claimed that he could forgive sin (Mark 2:1-12). This caused the Jewish critics to charge Him with blasphemy, since only God could pardon transgressions. But Jesus responded by asserting that His healing miracle proved that He could do so.

Again, recent scholars often agree on the significance of this situation. Concerning Jesus' forgiving of sins, Marshall states that "We have here a fact about the conduct of Jesus which is beyond critical cavil."[15] Guthrie explains: "Jesus as Son of man was exercising authority which he himself knew was legitimate only for God."[16] Cullmann adds: "this meant a conscious identification with God . . . ."[17]

Third, Jesus' actions were consistent with His claims. For example, He fulfilled Old Testament prophecy, showing Himself to be God's Messiah. Perhaps surprisingly, a number of critical scholars have viewed very seriously Isaiah 53 and the concept of Jesus as God's Suffering Servant.[18] We would

---

12. Guthrie, p. 304. Marshall speaks similarly, also including Jesus' term "Amen" in the discussion of His consciousness of His own unique position (p. 46).

13. See Mark 2:17; 8:34-38; 10:45; Matt 19:28-29; Luke 19:10; John 10:10.

14. Contemporary scholars recognize this emphasis in Jesus' teaching. Cf. Fuller, *The Foundations of the New Testament Christology,* pp. 105-106; Bultmann, *Theology of the New Testament,* Vol. I, pp. 7-9. We are not asserting that these two authors accept the ontological Deity of Jesus, only that they recognized Jesus' claim to authority. Marshall, who does not reject the ontological Deity of Jesus (pp. 128-129), agrees on the significance of Jesus' call to salvation: "Response to Jesus was the qualification for entering the kingdom and receiving its benefits." That Jesus spoke in such an authoritative manner is "beyond dispute" (p. 50).

15. Marshall, p. 50.

16. Guthrie, p. 280.

17. Cullmann, p. 282.

18. Martin Hengel, *The Atonement,* translated by J. Bowden (Philadelphia: Fortress Press, 1981); Cullmann, Chapter 3; Jeremias, *The Central Message of the New*

argue that the clearest case from the Old Testament would be one that lists perhaps a dozen messianic prophecies that both sufficiently answer critical objections and were still clearly fulfilled by Jesus.

Other actions of Jesus included His miracles. Ancient historian Edwin Yamauchi argues that Jesus is the only major religious founder for Whom there is early, eyewitness testimony for His miracles.[19] In a recent debate on "The Historical Foundations of Christianity," the two skeptical scholars even admitted that the evidence indicates that Jesus performed miracles.[20]

The awe-inspiring nature of genuine miracles is that they tend to point beyond themselves to the confirmation of some message, usually of a religious nature.[21] Jesus taught that His miracles evidenced His claims. In particular, He identified the resurrection as the major sign that His claims were true.[22] So according to Jesus, rising from the dead would be the chief indication of His unique connection with God, among other teachings.

A fourth indicator of the distinctive nature of Jesus' teachings concerning His Deity is the reactions that others had toward Him. In Mark 14:61-64, the major provocation for Jesus' death was His perceived blasphemy. When the High Priest asked the question, "Are you the Messiah, the Son of God?" He replied, "I am." The Jewish leaders called off the proceedings at that point and declared that they had sufficient evidence to condemn Jesus to die.[23] On the

---

Testament, pp. 31-50; Vincent Taylor, *The Atonement in New Testament Teaching*, Third Edition (London: The Epworth Press, 1963), p. 5.

19. Edwin Yamauchi, *Jesus, Zoroaster, Socrates, Buddha, Muhammad*, Revised Edition (Downers Grove: InterVarsity Press, 1972), p. 40; cf. pp. 6-7.

20. In a debate series entitled, "Christianity Challenges the University: An International Conference of Atheists and Theists," Howard Kee and Robert M. Price argued for the skeptical position in this debate on the New Testament. They were opposed by evangelicals E. Earl Ellis and R.T. France. The series took place in Dallas, Texas, on February 7-10, 1985, with this particular debate occurring on February 9.

21. Richard Swinburne explains that this is a common component in the notion of a miracle. See Swinburne, *The Concept of Miracle* (New York: Macmillan and St. Martin's Press, 1970), pp. 7-10.

22. Examples are found in Mark 2:1-12; Matt 11:1-6; 12:38-40; 16:1-4; Luke 11:20; John 5:36-37; 10:25, 38; 11:41-42; 14:11; 15:24. On the historicity of Jesus' predictions of His resurrection, see Habermas, *The Resurrection of Jesus: An Apologetic*, pp. 63-67.

23. We already noted above that this text also provides some of the clearest insight into Jesus' self-consciousness concerning His own nature.

other hand, most critical scholars recognize that the New Testament writers applied the title of God to Jesus.[24]

A new twist on Jesus' self-consciousness has recently been argued by Royce Gruenler. Utilizing only a minimalistic list of Jesus' evidenced sayings as assembled (and accepted) by radical New Testament critics themselves, one can still prove that Jesus was conscious of His own Deity. In other words, even using nothing more than the synoptic Gospel passages that contain no explicit Christological utterances and which critics almost unanimously believe to preserve the authentic words of Jesus, we still find that He claimed divine authority. Therefore, there is no good reason to differentiate between the Jesus of the minimal authentic sayings and the Jesus who makes the lofty claims found in all four Gospels. Jesus claimed divine prerogatives in both instances.[25]

These are some of the things that Jesus both said and did. It is true that anybody can claim whatever they want, but the facts show that Jesus did more than just make all sorts of lofty declarations. He led an exemplary, sinless life.[26] He also fulfilled Old Testament prophecy and performed miracles. Then He was raised from the dead. Yes, Jesus certainly did more than just make claims!

In brief, Jesus both made unique assertions about Himself and was uniquely raised from the dead. It is reasonable to assert that He would best be able to explain the purpose behind His resurrection and His testimony is that this event served as the major sign that His world view had been verified by an act

---

24. Bultmann, *Theology of the New Testament*, Vol. I, p. 129; Fuller, *Foundations of New Testament Christology*, pp. 208, 248-249; Cullmann, Chapter 11; Raymond E. Brown, *Jesus – God and Man* (Milwaukee: The Bruce Publishing Company, 1967), Chapter One.

25. See Royce Gordon Gruenler, *New Approaches to Jesus and the Gospels: A Phenomenological and Exegetical Study of Synoptic Christology* (Grand Rapids: Baker Book House, 1982). Gruenler remarks that even the Gospel of John is no exception here. Jesus makes no explicit claims in John which are inconsistent with what is known from His implicit claims that are derived from the minimalistic data discussed above.

26. We did not discuss this topic in this chapter, but it deserves some attention. One kind of evidence provided by Jesus was His character and the type of life that He lived. See Norman L. Geisler, *Christian Apologetics*, pp. 344-345. Geisler makes the point well on page 344:

Simply living a sinless life, as difficult as that would be, would not necessarily prove someone is God. However, if someone both claims to be God and offers a sinless life as evidence, that is an entirely different matter.

of God. The only time it can be shown that a resurrection in a glorified body literally took place in history,[27] it occurred to the only person who made such claims concerning His own deity and His distinct authority, as well as doing the sorts of things that Jesus did.

Pannenberg argues that Jesus' actions and teachings put Him in God's place. As a result, the Jews judged that He was a blasphemer. After the resurrection, this event was interpreted by many others in the First Century context as God's vindication of Jesus and His teachings.[28] He wasn't mistaken after all!

CONCLUSION

Jesus' entire career was actually characterized by His incredible theological claims and His extraordinary life. His said He had a unique relationship with the God of the universe, even referring to Him as His Father (or "Daddy") and Himself as Son. He also called Himself the Son of Man. He affirmed His Person even in the context of repeated Jewish charges of blasphemy and, finally, their sentence of death. He taught that He was the only way to God. He said He had the authority to forgive sins, which His critics properly identified as a prerogative of God alone. He fulfilled Old Testament prophecy and performed miracles. Jesus' literal resurrection from the dead adds the final significance to the truthfulness of these claims.

Jesus' personal theistic world view is largely expressed by the various aspects of these distinctive theological claims and teachings. Although the particulars cannot be defended here, much of Jesus' preaching, especially concerning the centrality of the Kingdom of God, is distinctive, even in the field of comparative religion.[29]

Contemporary critical scholars often recognize a number of these elements from Jesus' career. As Stephen Neill summarizes in his acclaimed study of the world religions, intellectuals can take the Gospels as critically as they like, but these writings still reveal the singular nature of Jesus' message:

> . . . Jesus is not the least like anyone else who has ever lived. The things he says about God are not the same as the sayings of any other religious teacher. The

---

27. See Gary R. Habermas, "Resurrection Claims in Non-Christian Religions," *Religious Studies*, Volume 25, pp. 167-177.

28. Pannenberg, *Jesus: God and Man*, pp. 67-68.

29. See Habermas and Moreland, *Immortality*, Chapter 9 and Habermas, *The Resurrection of Jesus: An Apologetic*, Chapters 4-5.

claims he makes for himself are not the same as those that have been made by any other religious teacher.[30]

Add to these teachings the nature of miracles in general and Jesus' teachings concerning the confirmatory value of His miracles in particular. Most significantly, the evidence shows not only that Jesus was raised from the dead in a glorified body, but that it is the only justified resurrection claim in all of history. Thus, the only time that a resurrection is known to have happened, it occurred to the only person who made such unique religious claims. The warranted conclusion is that Jesus' basic teachings were verified. In short, His unique claims were ultimately validated by the miraculous nature of His resurrection from the dead.[31]

Maybe an illustration will help us to grasp this point better. If we picked up the newspaper today and saw an article that proclaimed that a man, John Doe, came back to life after being pronounced dead at the local hospital, we might be amused. "Another one of those near-death experiences," we might think, making a mental note of the story. But what if the same paper contained an article declaring that scholars had found indisputable proof that the Islamic prophet Muhammad had been raised from the dead?[32]

Which article would you probably be more interested in reading? Which one might make you more nervous? For many Christians, the article about Muhammad would more likely get their attention because they would immediately recognize the implicit challenge to the uniqueness of Jesus Christ. In other words, John Doe has no distinctive religious teachings to back up the strange event that just happened. Besides, near-death experiences are common. But even if they couldn't put their apprehension into words, Christians would likely make the connection between the claimed resurrection of

---

30. Stephen Neill, *Christian Faith and Other Faiths*, Second Edition (Oxford: Oxford University Press, 1970), p. 233. See also J.N.D. Anderson, *Christianity and World Religions: The Challenge of Pluralism* (Downers Grove: InterVarsity Press, 1984); Stephen Neill, *The Supremacy of Jesus* (Downers Grove: InterVarsity Press, 1984).

31. We are chiefly concerned here with the theological claims that Jesus made in reference to Himself. We do not deny that there are religious or philosophical parallels, for instance, to certain of Jesus' moral teachings. But this should even be expected in light of the moral conscience given to all persons (Rom 2:14-15).

32. This is only an illustration. Not only do Muslims not teach such a doctrine, but we pointed out above that Jesus' is the only resurrection claim that can be historically established.

Muhammad and the nature of the Islamic prophet's religious teachings. Many Christians would presumably want to see if the declaration that he was raised from the dead carried any weight.

The key here is that we are more impressed when religious teachings are backed up. But with Jesus, we have a far more special case. He made unique claims – not just ones that were different from those of other teachers. Then He was uniquely raised from the dead. Now here's a truly singular situation in the history of religion.

Similar arrangements of the data have impressed many of today's renowned scholars. Swinburne agrees that a number of the claims surrounding Jesus are rather unique among the world's major theistic religions and that extraordinary miraculous events are potentially a means of evidencing such teachings.[33] Pannenberg declares that the relatedness of Jesus' declarations to his resurrection provides confirmation of His mission and death.[34] Even atheist Antony Flew agrees that if the resurrection actually occurred, naturalists would have to be open to Jesus' teachings concerning the Christian theistic world view, including Jesus' own Deity, even if it meant changing one's naturalism![35]

In short, Jesus taught what no other man taught, and He did what no other man did. Then He was raised from the dead, a one-of-a-kind historical event. The resurrection of Jesus Christ is not a "brute fact" of history that stands alone. In conjunction with the unique claims of Jesus, His resurrection shows that what He taught is true.[36]

---

33. Richard Swinburne, *The Existence of God* (Oxford: Oxford University Press, 1979), pp. 222, 225-226, 233-234, 241-243.

34. Pannenberg, *Jesus: God and Man*, p.73; Pannenberg in Varghese, pp. 263-264.

35. Habermas and Flew, pp. 49-50; cf. p. 3.

36. For this entire argument in extended form, see Habermas, *The Resurrection of Jesus: An Apologetic*, Chapters 1-5.

Chapter Twenty-Eight
THE SILENCE OF GOD

INTRODUCTION: IMPORTANCE OF THE QUESTION

How many times have you puzzled over God's silence? Maybe you prayed about something very important to you – even agonized over it – and wondered why nothing happened. Perhaps you thought you prayed according to all of the biblical conditions, and you still did not receive the answer you sought.

After following the line of argument in this book so far, maybe you now have another question. If God truly exists and if Christianity is true, then this complicates the issue of God's silence even further. Doesn't the Bible say that all the hairs of our heads are numbered and that God is intimately involved with our needs? Then why does it seem that He doesn't always meet these heartfelt needs? In the next chapter, we will pursue the cognate topic of the ways we can know that God is personal.

Doubts certainly occur when God does not act in the way that we think He should. The frequency of these questions in everyday life just complicates the issue. In this chapter, we are interested not so much in why all this seems to be the case, but how we respond when we think that God has let us down. Initially, we will view several passages of Scripture where similar questions are posed. Then we will investigate some of Abraham's struggles with his own doubts about God. How did this man of faith handle his own conflicts? A crucially important set of principles emerge when we grapple with this problem.[1]

When believers raise the question of God's silence, it is frequently viewed as a contemporary problem. After all, when we contrast our concern with the biblical accounts, doesn't God almost always answer? To frame the question more clearly, God *used* to act more frequently, but He no longer does so. Surprisingly, Scripture clearly shows that believers in both testaments have struggled with this exact same issue. While this knowledge is comforting, what can be learned from saints who deal with this question is even more instructive.[2]

BIBLICAL SAMPLES

Numerous times in Scripture believers cry out to God for assistance. Yet God does not answer as the person desired. This even appears to be a fairly common experience in biblical times. We frequently hear reports of God's silence.

One common grievance among contemporary Christians is this: "My prayers don't get through to God; it seems that they just bounce off the ceiling." We find a similar complaint in Lamentations 3:44. It is claimed in poetical terminology that God covered Himself with a cloud so Israel's prayers could not get through. The problem was the nation's sin (3:42).

David realized that one's personal sin also keeps an individual's prayers from being answered (Ps 66:18). Then in another passage, David speaks of his prayers returning to him unanswered, just like Christians today protest. This time he was apparently unaware of the reason, and it affected him emotionally (Ps 35:13-14).

Perhaps the most stunning of these Old Testament passages occurs in Psalm 44, a text that doesn't seem to get much attention. We are told that God stopped giving Israel victories over their enemies as He had done in the past, now disgracing His people before their foes (vv. 1-16). Yet the psalmist claims that the Jews had done nothing to deserve God's judgment (vv. 17-22). The

---

1. A longer version of this chapter occurs in Habermas, *Dealing with Doubt* (Chapter 6).

2. This chapter is not primarily concerned with the biblical *conditions* for answered prayer. Rather, how does a believer react when she thinks that prayers are not being answered, even if all the conditions have been met? In particular, what lessons can be learned through this experience? (But see footnote 6 below as well.)

writer concludes with this stinging rebuke in verses 23-24:

> Awake, O Lord! Why do you sleep?
> Rouse yourself! Do not reject us forever.
> Why do you hide your face
> and forget our misery and oppression?

Wow! God is accused of breaking promises, sleeping on the job, and forgetting about His people! What a charge against the sovereign God!

In a much less biting text, the writer in Psalm 74:9 gives another report on God's inactivity. He was neither working miraculous signs nor sending prophets among His people. God had not spoken and no one was sure how long His silence would last. Still another example is found in Isaiah 57:11. Here the Lord Himself proclaims that He had "long been silent" towards His people.

Texts like these might shock those today who express the seemingly common Christian attitude that God was active throughout the biblical period but is doing comparatively little at present.[3] But in addition to these separate passages, there are several periods of time in Scripture where God was silent.

One very interesting text is Daniel 10:10-14. Daniel had been fasting and mourning for a period of three weeks (10:2-3). In answer to his situation, an angel visited him. Interestingly, we are told that God heard Daniel's words and sent the angel on the first day of his petition. However, the messenger didn't get there very quickly – he was delayed during the three weeks by spiritual warfare! The angel Michael was then sent to assist the first angel. After being freed, the latter came to Daniel to explain the Lord's message to him (10:10-14).

There are several interesting features here. The answer to Daniel's prayer was actually decreed, but it got delayed. More specifically, Satan's forces hindered God's reply, with the answer not being manifest for some time. While we are not told of Daniel's response, he could presumably have considered his prayer to be unanswered. After all, he prayed diligently for three weeks, even mourning and fasting, but without response. Believers today are at least tempted to consider their prayers unanswered if nothing happens in a relatively short time. Yet it is possible that something similar occurs on certain

---

3. In the next chapter, we will address the issue of how believers can know that God is active in today's world.

occasions. God may already have responded even when we do not witness the answer immediately.

A major example of God's silence occurs between the Old and New Testaments. We hear comparatively little about the so-called 400 silent years between the last of the minor prophets and the birth of Christ. But what if we had been one of the Jews living in that time period? It might have provoked some emotional dilemmas. We might very well have wondered why we had not heard from the Lord for several generations.

This may actually have been the most unnerving of the periods of silence – 400 long years! Had God forgotten His people? Had He ever been angry for this length of time? Why would there be no communication during the interval directly following the centuries of Hebrew prophets? Would the Messiah foretold by God's messengers ever appear?

But then, just as Scripture witnesses that the darkest night is still followed by a new morning of rejoicing (Ps 30:5), the Jews who lived during these "dark ages" did not realize that the coming of the Messiah would be just around the corner. The central event in history effectively broke the silence of those many years. Ironically, the Incarnation reveals God's most personal involvement with His people – and it came after perhaps the most intense duration of silence. This is a lesson, indeed!

Such times are also found in the New Testament. The major instance is Jesus' own prayers in the Garden of Gethsemane. Suffering deep distress and anguish to the extent of sweating drops of blood, Jesus requested that His Father allow the coming events to be bypassed. Nonetheless, Jesus prayed that the Father's will would be done rather than His own. Certainly the portions of the prayers requesting the Father's will was accomplished, but not the earlier appeal avoiding the immediate future (Matt 26:36-43; Mark 14:33-36; Luke 22:39-44). Here Jesus was tempted like us, including suffering distraught emotions, yet without sinning (Heb 4:15).

Paul also discovered that God does not always act according to our will. This apostle prayed three times that God would remove an apparent physical problem, but all without success. Yet Paul learned the lesson that Jesus already knew, that the Father's will is preferable to ours (2 Cor 12:7-10).

In the Book of Revelation, we have another example of Christians who appear impatient with God for not acting more quickly. Believers who had been slain for their Christian testimony wondered how long God would linger before avenging their deaths. But they were told that it was necessary for them to wait a little longer until more of their comrades joined them (Rev 6:9-11). This is another instance where prayer was answered, but delayed.

These biblical cases signify that God does not always answer prayers or otherwise act in just the way believers think He should. Sometimes specific periods of silence ensue before the answer appears. On other occasions, there is a negative answer. It is simply a fact that believers have struggled with these matters throughout Scripture, rather than just in modern times. Many biblical saints presumably even lived their entire lives during one of the silent periods when God did not send revelation. But beyond the helpful knowledge that this was so, we need to ask what we can learn from these dilemmas. Are there any helpful truths that can assist us today? How did believers in Scripture react to the same conditions? How did they cope with them?

In Chapter 22 we already took an extended look at the example of Job. Here is perhaps the best known case of extreme suffering mixed with God's silence, at least at the outset. It was as if Job simply wanted to know why he was going through such pain, but couldn't get an answer. Then all of a sudden, God confronted him and challenged his misconceptions. In the process, Job realized several key truths about God's nature. In the end, Job unquestionably agreed that God was vindicated (not that the Lord needed Job's agreement!).

One of the ways God challenged Job was by asking him if he could explain or control pain and evil. And this saint realized that he couldn't do it. But he also learned that God could be trusted with the answer. The bottom line for Job was this: although there was much he *didn't* understand about God, he still decided to rely on Him in light of those things he *did* know about Him.

Another key lesson for us to learn is that Job's faith grew in the midst of his extraordinary struggles. He worked through his trials, learning the secret of allowing his conflict to make him a much stronger person. He also realized that what he knew about God meant that, *whatever* happened, God was still in control and it would all work out. Believers today have far more knowledge about God than did Job. True, we don't know everything. But since God raised Jesus from the dead and thereby guaranteed heaven for us, we can learn to trust Him in other matters.

THE CASE OF ABRAHAM

Scripture calls Abraham a man of faith. Yet, believe it or not, he definitely wrestled with his own trust in God and perhaps also with the issue of God's silence. In the process, he learned some great truths that we will attempt to apply to our contemporary questions. Hopefully, his victory can greatly assist us in our own struggles.

To set the scene just briefly, God spoke to Abraham (when his name was still Abram) and called him to take his family from his homeland and move them west to Canaan. Abraham was promised that a great nation would come from him there and that they would, in turn, be the source of blessing for all the peoples of the earth (Gen 12:1-3). So Abraham and his family left, and, after several incidents, settled in the land of Canaan. There he and his wife Sarah lived and later died. God greatly blessed his family and he became the father of the Israelites through Isaac his son and Jacob, his grandson.

Abraham was characterized as a man of faith. It is doubtful that anyone in Scripture is known better by that description. The writer of Hebrews notes several of the accomplishments that came from trusting God. From the outset, he responded to God and migrated to Canaan, even though he did not know where he was going (Heb 11:8-10). He likewise believed God's promise that he and Sarah would have a child, even though they were both quite elderly. To make matters worse, Sarah was childless. But Abraham's faith that God was trustworthy allowed him to be the father of a great nation (11:11-12).

Then when God commanded Abraham to sacrifice his own son Isaac, Abraham was willing because he believed God's word and trusted His promises. God would raise his son from the dead if that was the way He wanted it (11:17-19). In brief, Abraham lived his life by faith; God honored that and blessed him (cf. Jas 2:21-24). "But how can we ever compare Abraham to ourselves?" some may ask. "Why would he ever have reason to question God's leading? After all, didn't Abraham speak directly to God basically whenever he wanted to do so? And wasn't God always there to communicate with Him? It's not the same for us."

However, upon examining the texts, we find that Abraham may also have struggled with the question of God's silence, in spite of our modern conceptions of their relationship. For example, as Genesis 16 closes, Abraham is 86 years old (16:16). As far as we know, the next time God spoke to him was thirteen years later when Abraham was 99 years old (Gen 17:1)!

It is difficult to be dogmatic here, but it is at least possible that God did not communicate with him during this time frame. Neither does it appear that God conversed with Abraham throughout his life on a weekly or even a yearly basis. There may have been gaps, perhaps even sizeable ones. Most Christians today would probably say that God has communicated with them more than once in the last thirteen years!

Nonetheless, Abraham was a man of great faith. This does not mean that God expected him to believe in a vacuum, however. Abraham was given warrant for his trust. God spoke to him and this must have been quite convincing. Then there was the rather mysterious time when Abraham asked God how he might *know* that Canaan would be given to him (Gen 15:8). The Lord responded that he could know this truth *for certain*, utilizing a supernatural manifestation in order to make a covenant with Abraham (15:13-21). Faith does not exclude good grounds for belief. Abraham exercised an extraordinary amount of faith, without which the outstanding events in his life would not have been possible.

In spite of all this, Abraham still experienced several troublesome moments. Job questioned God about the suffering he was undergoing. Strangely enough, Abraham also struggled, specifically in regard to his faith. We just mentioned Abraham's need for assurance, resulting in a supernatural revelation (Gen 15:8-21). On two other occasions, Abraham concealed the identity of Sarah in order to save his own life (12:10-20; 20:1-18). But if he really believed God would raise a great nation from him, why should he be fearful for his life, as we are told he was (10:12-13; 20:11)?

Then when Sarah still hadn't delivered a child, she convinced Abraham to bear a son (Ishmael) by her servant Hagar, in spite of God's promises (16:1-16). Moreover, when the Lord repeated the promise that Abraham would have a child by Sarah, he literally laughed in God's face (17:15-17), as Sarah would do later (18:10-15)![4] Where was that faith we heard so much about?

Seriously, none of this is meant to denigrate Abraham's faith. These episodes were spread over twenty-five years,[5] and no human being lives a perfectly consistent life. On the whole, Abraham regularly acted in faith, never allowing unbelief to master him.

So what happened in Abraham's life to overcome his doubts about God's promises? The apostle Paul utilizes Abraham as his example even in the midst of these momentary lapses. When he could have just given up and ignored God's call, Abraham chose to believe instead. When a child was promised, he

---

4. On this point, see Lynn Anderson, *If I Really Believe, Why Do I Have These Doubts?* (Minneapolis: Bethany House, 1992), pp. 72-80.

5. Compare Genesis 12:4 with 21:5.

did not react in unbelief even though all the medical data opposed it. Abraham did not give up or cease to believe; his faith was actually strengthened (Rom 4:18-25). So here is his secret: Abraham not only exercised faith, but his faith grew as he trusted God more and more, one step at a time, even after failures.

Imagine a faith that actually grows even when the pressures of life are the greatest! Yet that was Abraham's experience. And like Job, the primary reason is that he concluded that God was trustworthy; what he already knew about Him was enough to trust Him in unknown areas (Rom 4:20-21). So Abraham was strengthened even during trying times because He trusted God. Believers today can also let their faith grow precisely during the times when it is under the harshest attack.

CONCLUSION

A perennial question among believers concerns the perception that God is often silent when His people call on Him. There are many reasons why prayer may not be answered like believers expect. Yet we said at the outset that this chapter is not primarily concerned with *why* prayers are not answered but *how* believers respond when they *think* that they have not been.[6]

Believers often question God's silence. But we saw that there is no dichotomy between biblical times and today. Such a thesis simply is not supported by the facts. God answers many prayers according to the requests. But not only do believers still wonder why other petitions are not answered similarly, but we even seem to forget the times when God *does* respond, sometimes in spectacular fashion!

Using the experiences of Job (in chapter 22) and Abraham, we found that some believers grow even during tough times. Similarly, believers today can also resolve to trust the Lord further, even thriving *during* times of uncertainty. Perhaps the key principle here is that we know enough about God in other

---

6. Perhaps it should still be helpful to give a brief list of some of the biblical conditions for answered prayer. Most of these factors are personal in nature: confessing one's sin (Ps 66:18; 1 John 1:9), exercising faith (Mark 11:24; Jas 1:5-8), being obedient (John 15:7; 1 John 3:22), and praying in Jesus' name (John 14:13-14; 15:16; 16:23). However, not everything is up to us. We are also told to pray according to God's will (1 John 5:14-15). Further, Scripture even states that individual prayers sometimes went unanswered when the nation of Israel functioned in a state of sin (Lam 3:42-44; cf. Isa 57:11), which may have a parallel even today.

crucial areas to trust Him even in those instances where we cannot figure things out completely. After all, I may not know why things happen as they do, but this is still a world where God raised Jesus from the dead and believers still have eternal life. So why do I have to know all the answers right now?

Practicing the truth is crucial here: we need to exercise our faith precisely during our times of doubt. How do we do this? Directly affirming our belief in God by prayer or meditation is one such idea. Praising God is another avenue in redirecting our thoughts toward Him. Still another helpful practice is to list our answers to prayer as they occur, thereby providing a ready record for times when we experience such difficulties. Questions like those addressed in this chapter, in general, tend to be more emotional in nature,[7] so lists of answered prayer are helpful in confronting the untruths that we tell ourselves. As Job and Abraham discovered, we can also witness the growth of our own faith and the corresponding lessening of doubt's grip on our lives.

7. On the strength of emotional doubt and some possible remedies, see Habermas, *Dealing With Doubt*, Chapter 4. For more suggestions on increasing our faith during our times of struggle, see pp. 93-112.

Chapter Twenty-Nine
OUR PERSONAL GOD

Introduction: Importance of the Question
Classic Indications of God's Involvement
Contemporary Indications of God's Involvement
Conclusion

INTRODUCTION: IMPORTANCE OF THE QUESTION

Orthodox Christianity has always held that God is personally involved in the lives of believers. But what are the indications that this is really so? How does everyday life reveal this great truth? How about those moments when we wonder if this is really the case? Do you sometimes puzzle over this subject, questioning what you have to do to "get hold" of God? Could there be more to practicing the Christian life that we've previously experienced, something that allows us to be more aware of God's presence?

In the previous chapter we attempted to put a related concern in perspective. We maintained that it is not a fair assessment to say that God answered more prayers in biblical times than He does today. The truth of the matter is that there is no proof that this issue has changed significantly since earlier times. God frequently answers prayers just the way we petition Him and sometimes does not. But times of silence have been reported throughout Scripture as well, literally from Genesis to Revelation. Sometimes these times are lengthy. On the other hand, countless numbers of believers attest that God has answered their prayers, and often very specific ones.

In this chapter, we propose a twofold approach. We want to offer both classic and contemporary indications that God is involved in our lives, making Himself known to us. We only caution the reader that we will not be able to remain long on any of the topics, but will point the interested student to extended treatments.

CLASSIC INDICATIONS OF GOD'S INVOLVEMENT

Throughout Scripture, God revealed Himself in several important ways. There never seems to be any question that He was involved in the lives of His people. We will briefly list a number of means by which He showed Himself to be personal.

(1) We should not lose sight of the fact that Scripture itself is an indication that God is interested in us. A few chapters ago, we addressed the subject of the reliability of the New Testament. If we additionally discover a basis for the inspiration of these texts,[1] then we have ascertained that God has sent us His personal instructions for our lives (2 Tim 3:16). According to 2 Peter 1:21, the nature of the inspiration process involves direct interaction between God and the writer. In the words of John Wenham:

> So then, starting with belief in the incarnation and a very general belief in the historical truth of the Gospels, we have found ourselves apparently compelled to accept our Lord's view of Scripture. According to his teaching God so guided the authors that the words they wrote were his words. We have seen that this applies not only to the Old Testament, but also in principle to the New.[2]

(2) Fulfilled prophecy is another indication that God is particularly involved in the process of human history. That He not only predicts the future but also brings it to pass shows that He is interested in both daily occurrences on earth and the long term direction of history.[3]

---

1. The most common argument proceeds from a trustworthy New Testament text to a study of the words of Jesus, to determine the proper notion of inspiration. See John Wenham, *Christ and the Bible*, Chapters 1, 5; Robert P. Lightner, *The Saviour and the Scriptures*; Geisler, *Christian Apologetics*, Chapters 16, 18; Guthrie, *New Testament Theology*, Chapter 10.

2. Wenham, p. 187.

3. For example, the city and nation prophecies throughout many of the prophetic books of the Old Testament reveal numerous details that were minutely fulfilled, sometimes against great odds. For examples, see the predictions concerning Tyre (Ezek 26:1-16), Gaza and Ashkelon (Amos 1:6-8; Jer 47:1-7; Zeph 2:4-7; Ezek 25:15-16), Babylon (Isa 13:1-22, 14:4-23; Jer 51:1-64), Samaria (Hos 13:16; Mic 1:5-9), Edom – Petra, Dedan, and Teman (Isa 34:5-15; Jer 49:17-22; Ezek 25:12-14; Obad), and the kingdoms of Babylon, Medo-Persia, Greece, and Rome (Dan 7). For details on the fulfillments of these prophecies, see Floyd E. Hamilton, *The Basis of the Christian Faith: A Modern Defense of the Christian Religion* (New York: Harper and Row, Publishers, 1964), pp. 308-324; Peter W. Stoner and Robert C. Newman, *Science Speaks: Scientific Proof of the Accuracy of Prophecy and the Bible* (Chicago: Moody Press, 1968), Chapter 2. There is also the entire topic of Messianic prophecy, but that point will overlap with our discussion of the Incarnation below.

(3) Another type of intervention involves the times God worked miracles in history, both corporate and personal. Cases of the former include the crossing of the Red Sea (Exod 14) or Elijah's confrontation with Baal's prophets (1 Kings 18:16-40). It is sometimes said that the three great periods of miraculous intervention in Scripture are during the lives of Moses, Elijah and Elisha, and Jesus and His apostles. Many of the personal healings occurred in these instances. In general, the purpose of a miracle is to teach or confirm a message, further indicating God's interest in our existence and needs.

(4) Other times, God visited His people directly, again displaying His attention. He walked with Abraham (Gen 18) and revealed Himself to Moses (Exod 3-4:17). The entire nation of Israel perceived His presence in the pillar of cloud and fire (Exod 13:21-22), and again at the giving of the Ten Commandments (Exod 19:16-20). King Nebuchadnezzar watched as Daniel's three friends were unharmed by his fire, being joined by a fourth Person (Dan 3:19-30). Although such occasions were not common, they were nonetheless retold throughout the centuries, providing a basis for the belief that God periodically intervened in a very personal fashion on behalf of His people.

(5) Without question, the major indication that God is personally involved with us is the Incarnation of Jesus. We have already pursued a number of the relevant details in two previous chapters. Briefly, how could God show His intentions any more clearly than by becoming a Man, identifying with the human condition and needs? Jesus walked on the earth for more than thirty years, experiencing human life, including its suffering and its temptations (Heb 2:18; 4:15). His tortuous death by crucifixion graphically portrays the heights of God's interest in us, sharing our pain for the purpose of providing the possibility of redemption. His resurrection foreshadows the future state of the believer. This is the all-time, prime example of love and concern (John 15:13). In no other religion has God become Man in such a unique, one-time embodiment, identifying with our needs.

These are some of the chief indications from Scripture that God is personal, continually involved in the plight of human existence. Some erroneously think that clues such as those above are limited to Scriptural times alone. But we will now point out ways in which God is still active today, never ceasing to relate to us personally.

CONTEMPORARY INDICATIONS OF GOD'S INVOLVEMENT

It seems that many Christians conclude that God is basically inactive today, at least compared to biblical times. Such an opinion is potentially dangerous, affecting our world view at several points. For example, this is one of the avenues to Christian doubt. Further, why wouldn't God continue to show His interest in such a manner? Doesn't Scripture say He still controls the future and will answer prayers? In this section, we will propose a number of ways in which God is still actively involved with us. Some correspond to the biblical categories we have just discussed. Once again, we will only be able to outline our responses.

(1) God has predicted the future (see above), and any fulfillments that occur today are relevant to our topic. This is not the place to discuss the intricacies of various schools of prophecy, but we will simply draw a single important conclusion. Even the different approaches to eschatology customarily share the sense of significance concerning key events like the nationhood of Israel in 1948.[4] So our point is that, depending on the view one takes, the contemporary fulfillment of prophecy evidences God's ongoing involvement with humankind.

(2) Both in Scripture as well as today, countless thousands of believers attest to God's answers to prayer. God's replies to Moses (Exod 8:8-13) and King Hezekiah (2 Kings 20:1-11) provide examples of this phenomenon. Contemporary answers to prayer also reveal that God often hears us, and acts in accordance with our requests.

(3) Further, and often in conjunction with the previous point, God healed needy individuals in biblical times.[5] Even today, there are numerous documented (and actually quite extraordinary) cases of healings.[6] Although there

---

4. For overviews of this, as well as related issues (including differing eschatological perspectives), see John F. Walvoord, *Israel in Prophecy* (Grand Rapids: Zondervan, 1962); Charles L. Feinberg, Editor, *Focus on Prophecy* (Westwood: Fleming H. Revell Company, 1964); Guthrie, Chapter 8.

5. Of the dozens of examples, see 1 Kings 17:8-24; 2 Kings 4:8-37; 5:1-19; Matt 9:1-8; Mark 6:30-44; Acts 3:1-10.

6. Rodney Clapp describes himself as one who has never been successful getting answers to prayers for extraordinary sorts of healing. Still, he records a couple of amazing, documented examples. See Clapp's article, "Faith Healing: A Look at What's Happening," *Christianity Today*, Volume 27, No. 18, December 2, 1983 and Volume 27, No. 19, December 16, 1983. In the latter issue, also see his article "One Who Took Up Her Bed and Walked."

Compare the incredible account in Mark Buntain, with Ron Hembree and Doug Brendel, *Miracle in the Mirror* (Minneapolis: Bethany House, 1981), especially chapters 18-19. Pat Robertson has compiled a number of remarkable miracle accounts,

are various conceptions of how this ought to occur,[7] these methods are not contradictory. Such activity shows that God still concerns Himself with the needs of individuals.

(4) In recent evangelical writings,[8] there has been a new interest in pursuing the "Christian disciplines," which are various kinds of practices in the Christian life performed in order to bring the believer into closer fellowship with the God of the universe. Dallas Willard explains the purpose of the disciplines:

> We need an understanding that can guide us into constant interaction with the Kingdom of God as a real part of our daily lives, an *ongoing spiritual presence* that is at the same time a *psychological reality* .... We will establish, strengthen, and elaborate on this one insight: *Full participation in the life of God's Kingdom and in the vivid companionship of Christ comes to us only through appropriate exercise in the disciplines for the life in the spirit.*[9]

A number of the disciplines, such as meditation, prayer, fasting, solitude, and worship aim especially at our relationship with our Lord.[10] Meditation, in particular, seems to be most suited to our purposes. After speaking of the

---

some of which are documented with film footage and medical records. See Robertson (with William Proctor), *Beyond Reason: How Miracles Can Change Your Life* (Toronto: Bantam Books, 1984).

A former professor of philosophy has recently written an unpublished manuscript on apologetics. After establishing a strict definition of "type A" miracles where the events are "so immediate and extraordinary" that they will only admit of a supernatural explanation, he documents quite a number of contemporary cases of such clearly documented events.

7. Some prefer quiet church meetings or private times where the needy are remembered in specific prayers. Others send elders to anoint the sick with oil and pray over them. Still others, however, call the sick to the front of the church. Our point here is that God is not limited by our methods and still works in various situations.

8. Some of the best known volumes on the subject are as follows: Dallas Willard, *The Spirit of the Disciplines* (San Francisco: Harper and Row, 1988); Richard J. Foster, *Celebration of Discipline: The Path to Spiritual Growth*, Revised Edition (San Francisco: Harper and Row, 1988); Richard J. Foster, *Freedom of Simplicity* (San Francisco: Harper and Row, 1981); see also John Caldwell, *Intimacy with God: Christian Disciplines for Spiritual Growth* (Joplin: College Press, 1992).

9. The italics are Willard's, *Ibid.*, pp. xi, 26. Foster agrees, speaking about the disciplines: "We have only one thing to do, namely, to experience a life of relationship and intimacy with God . . . ." (*Celebration of Discipline*, p. 4).

10. For details on these practices, see Foster, *Celebration of Discipline*, Chapters 2-4, 6, 11; Willard, Chapter 9. For most believers, this is probably new territory and the reader could well disagree with some of the assertions made in these writings. So one needs to interact prayerfully and biblically with the various ideas.

Lord's desire to commune with us in the deepest confines of our heart, Foster says: "Meditation opens the door . . . the aim is to bring this living reality into all of life. . . . You will see meditation as communication between the Lover and the one beloved."[11]

Perhaps Christians don't experience the presence of the Lord as much as they would like because they don't take the time to practice the spiritual exercises commanded in Scripture. Meditation, along with the other disciplines, teaches us to cultivate a living relationship with the God of the universe.[12]

(5) If C.S. Lewis is right, God even woos unbelievers to Himself with joy, a technical term which Lewis defines as an intense inward longing or desire where the craving itself is a delight. This sensation "in the pit of the stomach" often surfaces as we hear a moving piece of music, read a poem or a piece of mythology, or see an emotionally moving photograph. Lewis expresses his view that this longing is not for anything on earth, although many mistakenly think so. Rather, we want something beyond – joy betrays our desire for heaven (cf. Eccl 3:11).[13] As Lewis states: "There have been times when I think we do not desire heaven but more often I find myself wondering whether, in our heart of hearts, we have ever desired anything else."[14]

(6) For the believer, God also speaks to our hearts in another manner – by the witness of the Holy Spirit. This is a difficult subject to pursue briefly, but various New Testament texts[15] seem to declare at least this minimum: the

---

11. Foster, *Ibid.*, pp. 20, 23.

12. We should carefully note, however, that biblical meditation differs markedly from varieties found in Eastern religious traditions such as Hinduism and Buddhism. The Bible teaches that we should fill our minds *with* God's truth, as opposed to attempting to empty it. Further, biblical methods do not teach believers to deny oneself in the process, as is common in the Eastern traditions. For more on meditation, see: Calvin Miller, *Transcendental Hesitation: A Biblical Appraisal of TM and Eastern Mysticism* (Grand Rapids: Zondervan, 1977); Thomas McCormick and Sharon Fish, *Meditation: A Practical Guide to a Spiritual Discipline* (Downers Grove: InterVarsity Press, 1983).

13. For two of the places where C.S. Lewis comments on the subject of joy, see his volumes *Surprised by Joy: The Shape of My Early Life* (New York: Harcourt, Brace, Jovanovich, 1955), pp. 16-18, 165-170, 238); *The Pilgrim's Regress: An Allegorical Apology for Christianity, Reason, and Romanticism* (New York: Bantam Books, 1943), Preface to the Third Edition, pp. ix-xiii. Cf. Peter Kreeft's excellent development of this theme in *Heaven: The Heart's Deepest Longing* (San Francisco: Harper and Row, 1980).

14. C.S. Lewis, *The Problem of Pain*, p. 145.

15. The chief passage is Rom 8:16; compare Gal 4:6-7; 1 John 3:24; 4:13.

Holy Spirit provides direct confirmation that the believer is a child of God. This testimony is not a feeling and it cannot be proven; neither is it an evidence for Christianity. Yet, proof is not the point here at all. We are interested in the value of the Holy Spirit's witness in terms of the Christian's sense that God is personal. We might say it this way: apologetics establishes the truth of Christianity; the witness of the Holy Spirit persuades believers that they are participating in that reality.[16]

(7) We mentioned above that God has, on a number of occasions in Scripture, intervened directly in human affairs. Some argue that this remains the case today, as well, while others will question these claims. No doubt, this is a enigmatic question and it is difficult to know how to "classify" the information. There is certainly room here for differing opinions. But some interesting data exist, nonetheless.

For instance, Don Richardson has recorded numerous accounts where missionaries have encountered peoples who seemed to be specially prepared for the Gospel by what they claimed was a revelation from God. In one case, a Gedeo man of Ethiopia prayed that God would reveal Himself to his people. He began having visions that "two white-skinned strangers" would come and build shelters like his people had never seen before within sight of a sycamore tree near one of their villages. He was informed that these two men would bring a message from God. Several "soothsayers" in the tribe added other details. The missionaries appeared eight years later, coming to the exact town the visionaries had predicted, stopping under the same sycamore tree! Thousands of the Gedeo people turned to God as a result.[17]

Another sort of example comes from the literally thousands of people who have reported near-death experiences. A number of Christians claim to have seen Jesus personally during one of these episodes.[18] While we cannot verify

16. For details concerning both this point and the larger issue, see Bernard Ramm, *The Witness of the Spirit* (Grand Rapids: Eerdmans, 1959); Habermas, *Dealing With Doubt*, Chapter 8 ("The Testimony of the Holy Spirit").

17. Don Richardson, *Eternity in their Hearts*, Revised Edition (Ventura: Regal Books, 1984). This account is found on pp. 54-56.

18. One such personal account is by psychiatrist George G. Ritchie (with Elizabeth Sherrill), *Return from Tomorrow* (Waco: Word Books, 1978). Other examples include Petti Wagner, *Murdered Heiress . . . Living Witness* (Shreveport: Huntington House, Inc., 1984); Weldon Metcalf, "I Saw Christ's Face," *The United Brethren*, Volume 90, Number 9, September, 1975, pp. 15, 20; Coral Ridge Ministries, "From Death's Door to Heaven's Gate," *Impact*, November, 1992, p. 1.

the heavenly scenery reported in such sightings, there is an incredibly large amount of data for NDE's in general, and for the reality of human consciousness extending beyond clinical death.[19] Is it still possible that some of these Christians really saw Jesus, remained in His presence for a short while, and even communicated with Him?

So whether believers speak about the classic or the contemporary indications that God is personal, there simply are a number of manifestations of His interaction with and care for us. This is the case even if one has differences over some of our suggested categories.[20] God meets our needs and sends direction for our lives.

CONCLUSION

Life provides many hints that the God Who exists is personal. In biblical times, He inspired numerous writers to compose Scripture, predicted the future, and performed miracles. Once in a while He even intervened directly. But His greatest self-revelation was the Incarnation of His Son, Jesus Christ.

To hear some Christians talk, however, the days of God's activity have ended. One can almost get the idea that God is seldom very involved with us any longer. But we have argued that this view does not accord with either the biblical prescription for the Christian life or Christian experience. Most believers think that prophecy is still being fulfilled today. Answers to prayer and healing show God's interest in daily affairs. Practicing the other disciplines taught in Scripture, such as meditation, increase our realization of God's continuing presence. Unbelievers are wooed by God, while believers receive the witness of the Holy Spirit. Some even think that God continues to communicate in other personal ways today, as well.

---

19. Four categories of evidence for NDEs are presented in Habermas and Moreland, *Immortality*, Chapters 5-6. For world view considerations inevitably raised by such accounts, including our reasons for claiming that we cannot evidentially determine the nature of the heavenly portion of such encounters, see pages 90-94. But this hesitancy on the other-worldly segments of the reports should not be confused with our conclusion that other aspects of the NDE data do present strong evidence for what we term minimalistic life after death.

20. There are even some variations here between the two authors of this volume. But our point is that this is fine. We think that part of the job of Christian philosophers and theologians is simply to present *possible* scenarios, multiplying the potential options that believers have, even if they are not always accepted by everyone.

To be sure, not everyone will agree that each of the categories in our contemporary list is a legitimate avenue in which to see God's involvement in human lives. But given the biblical context, these are certainly defensible, as are others. Our list was not exhaustive. Although it is not our point in this chapter to argue in any detail for these signs of God's activity, several of them are accompanied by evidence on their behalf.

God has left a number of hints not only that He exists, but that He both has been and continues to be interested in our lives and needs. Then why do believers constantly wonder about this subject? This ongoing inquiry indicates that there are still several practical lessons for us to learn.

(1) As we saw in the last chapter, we often phrase the problem incorrectly. Even in biblical times, we learn that God did not always answer prayers the way believers sought. Some of the best-known saints struggled with this. Then we are surprisingly told on a number of occasions that there were times when God was silent, often for long periods.

In cases where we don't understand, the truths learned by Job (chapter 22) and Abraham (this chapter) are also instructive: we know enough about God to trust Him in the things we don't understand. This is a message that involves both reason and faith. What we *do* know is based on a solid foundation – far more than Job or Abraham had. But when we *don't* understand, we still ought to trust the God we know. After all, we are not omniscient and we should recognize our own limitations.

But there are more answers for our questions. (2) Our classical and contemporary lists above reveal a wide variety of "clues" that God has left for us, indicating some of His personal activities. We have no good reason to conclude that God has left us alone in the universe. So it must be that we have the very human tendency to exhibit selective memory. Sometimes we remember what we think God *hasn't* done, while conveniently forgetting the many things we have witnessed that He *has* done. Or maybe it is just the case that we have never before realized how many ways God acts in our lives. Further, we need to open our eyes to His works in the lives of others, too.

But there is at least one other conclusion we should draw. (3) The lists we have presented do more than just answer a common question about God's interest in us. It might become obvious that believers need to *cultivate* their relationship with the Lord. Examples are not difficult to find. We must correct the false impressions that we have about God's concern for us. Periodically listing answers to prayers, or even keeping charts of our requests, are excellent ways to remember how God has acted. We really do need to meditate deeply on the truths we are taught in Scripture. Practicing some of the other biblical disciplines provides a means of obeying God's call to such tasks, besides cultivating additional avenues to fellowship with God.

We will close with a question to help us focus. Where would our relationship with our husband, wife, or another loved one be if we gave them as much time and attention as we do our Lord? We must frankly acknowledge that we are responsible for our relationship with the Lord, too. What have we done to deepen our fellowship? Correcting our misconceptions, reviewing what God has done throughout history, and cultivating our present walk with the Lord might provide part of the answer we seek.

Chapter Thirty
SUMMARIES AND CONCLUSIONS

PART FOUR

In the three previous sections of this book, we've explored a number of philosophical, scientific, and ethical indications that this is a theistic universe. But of course, there are many varieties of theism in the world, more than one of which would be equally delighted over some of the material that we presented. So in the last section, a question of a different sort arose: is there evidence that favors any of the particular theisms? In other words, how do we choose between the various concepts of God? Generally, the data we studied were historical in nature.

Chapter 24: "History and Evidence"

Initially, we outlined a concept of historiography, emphasizing the actual event and the recording of it. Since we must deal not only with what happened but with the human accounts of it, a subjective element is involved. Further, we can only know events according to probability. Still, we explained how objective knowledge of historical occurrences was still achievable as the historian used tools such as eyewitness interviews, written documents, other existing records, structures, or various sorts of archaeological finds. To this data we must apply both external and internal criticism.

This is an indispensable portion of the process of writing history. These concepts, in turn, provided a foundation for our final section, laying the groundwork for the remaining chapters. Does Christianity, with all of its exclusive and miraculous claims, feature an historical underpinning? We wanted to find out, warning that we could not disallow supernatural claims on *a priori* grounds. We need to see where the evidence leads.

Chapter 25: "The New Testament"

Our initial area of investigation was the New Testament. We did not ask whether these writings were inspired, but whether they lined up well as trustworthy historical documents. We proposed a threefold approach, progressing from the general reliability of the New Testament and its record of the life of Jesus, in particular, to questions of authorship and date, to the issue of specific texts. Accordingly, we investigated several relevant areas of corroboration.

The New Testament text is known from the existence of numerous early manuscript copies. Comparing these texts to copies of other ancient, classical writings, we reported that the New Testament had no rivals in terms of the large number of manuscripts or the time gap between the earliest copies and the originals. Further, none of the books have missing sections or shortened endings, as is so often the case with other ancient writings. While this does not prove that the texts are necessarily truthful, it does show that we have what the initial writers intended – we have a reliable record of their words.

The life of Jesus is obviously the central focus of the New Testament. Do we have a faithful record of His teachings and actions? Both external and internal sources argue that we do, indeed, have trustworthy testimony concerning Him. Without even opening the pages of the Bible, ancient *non-Christian* writings from about A.D. 50-180 record almost 50 different details concerning Jesus' life, teachings, death, and even His resurrection, as well as some of the earliest Christian beliefs. Christian sources *outside* the New Testament add many extra facts to this list. Together, these two sorts of information, along with some relevant details from archaeology, agree on dozens of different facts, many of which are attested by both Christian and secular writers!

However, the earliest and most critically respected data is ironically derived, not from these outside sources, but from the New Testament itself. Contained in these writings there are numerous short, pithy summary comments that address areas of central concern to early believers. By far the most common topic is the Gospel of the death and resurrection of Jesus, but other areas are also mentioned. What makes them so valuable is that literary and other analyses reveal that these creeds actually pre-date the books in which they are written, and the content is traceable to apostolic teaching. One of these texts (1 Cor 15:ff.) provides an invaluable report of eyewitness testimony concerning the resurrection appearances of Jesus (see below).

None of these sources for the life of Jesus contradicts the Gospels in any way. Rather, they augment the canonical texts and provide both external and internal documentation, confirming the reliability of the appropriate areas of the New Testament. So whether we speak of the condition of the New Testament manuscripts or corroboration for the life of Jesus, Christians are on strong grounds.

From here we progressed to the topics of authorship and time of writing. We began by outlining a case for the early date and apostolic authority behind the Gospels and Acts, pointing the interested reader to additional sources. Then, in light of the special part some of its testimony would play in the next chapter, we paid special attention to the Book of 1 Corinthians, arguing for its Pauline authorship and traditional date. The third and final subject of evidencing a specific text would remain until the next chapter.

Chapter 26: "The Resurrection of Jesus"

With such a basic background, we turned to the subject of the resurrection of Jesus, beginning by outlining twelve historical facts that can be ascertained from the available information. Additionally, these facts are recognized by virtually all critical scholars who address this topic.

From this starting point, the known data are sufficient to refute the naturalistic theories that are meant to question the resurrection. Each of these alternative views can be disproven by the facts. Further, ten evidences which demonstrate the resurrection were derived from these same historical details.

But we didn't stop there. Going further, we returned to the last stage of our earlier threefold topic, which called for investigating the veracity of specific New Testament texts. As an example, we chose the testimony in 1 Cor 15:3ff. for Jesus' resurrection appearances. Paul explains that this information is not his own, and the most popular conclusion is that he received it directly from Peter and James in Jerusalem about A.D. 35. Regardless of the exact details here, we listed numerous other arguments for the veracity of Paul's eyewitness report of the appearances of the risen Jesus.

All of this data argue that the disciples really had visual experiences. Many critical scholars even agree that this is undeniable. However, hallucinations or other subjective encounters fail to explain these eyewitness reports. So the evidence we are left with indicates that Jesus was literally raised from the dead. Whatever else the critic believes about the New Testament, he would do well to deal *specifically* with the facts that lead us to this conclusion.

Chapter 27: "The Uniqueness of Jesus"

Accordingly, what does all of this tell us about Jesus' world view? First, we argued prospectively that since this is a theistic universe,[1] the resurrection of Jesus is an event that can best be understood as an act of God. The connection between God and this awesome miracle is the fact that a creative act such as Jesus' resurrection in a glorified body appears to require attributes that only God has, such as omnipotence and omniscience. Further, the resurrection is an orderly event that crowned the life of Jesus.

Second, we argued retrospectively that the resurrection confirmed the claims that Jesus made concerning Himself – such as His Deity and His intro-duction of God's plan of salvation. He made the incredible declarations that He was the Son of Man and the Son of God. He even referred to the God of the universe as *Abba*, which is translated "Father" or even "Daddy." He said that He had the authority to forgive sins and asserted that He was the only way of salvation. Further, He performed miracles and fulfilled prophecy. His teachings on these subjects were clear. In fact, He was finally crucified for His assertions to be Deity, since He claimed such a unique relationship to God.

In other words, not only is Jesus Christ the sole Person ever to be raised from the dead in a glorified body, but He also made unique claims, especially pertaining to Himself and the nature of salvation. Moreover, no one would better understand the relation between these teachings and the resurrection than Jesus Himself, and He taught that the latter confirmed His message. In short, Jesus was a singular Individual in human history. The only Person who was raised from the dead never to die again is the same One who made these unique claims. In Him, teaching and event are united. As a result, His theistic world view was shown to be verified by an act of God. If we want to know

---

1. This, of course, was our central argument in the first three sections of this book, so we are on solid ground here.

which form of theism is true, we need to study the teachings of Jesus.

Chapter 28: "The Silence of God"

The New Testament clearly portrays a personal God Who is involved with our daily needs. Here two questions arise. How do we account for God's periodic silence? In what ways does God show Himself to be personal? In our last two chapters we pursued these cognate questions.

To answer the first of these questions, we surveyed a number of biblical texts where the author also struggled with the issue of God's silence. Perhaps surprisingly, we found that there is no dichotomy between biblical times, when it seems like God always answered prayer, and the present. Even throughout Scripture, God did not always act as others thought He should. There were even long periods when He was silent.

Abraham is one of the major examples of a believer who frequently struggled in spite of God's contact with him. But he grew in faith and is repeatedly cited in the New Testament as a grand example of such, even though his trust clearly faltered at times. Like Job,[2] Abraham learned that what he knew about God was sufficient to trust Him in those areas that he did not always understand. We need to practice this lesson ourselves during times of doubt.

Chapter 29: "Our Personal God"

The answer to the second question also comes from a study of Scripture, which supplies many hints that God is personal. He inspired the writers of Scripture, predicted the future, and performed miracles. Sometimes He intervened directly. Undoubtedly, His greatest amount of involvement occurred with the Incarnation of His Son, Jesus Christ.

Today, many believers appear to have the opinion that God is seldom involved with us. Yet, this seems to oppose both Scripture and Christian experience. Many of these same believers think that prophecy is still being fulfilled today and will continue to be so in the future. Multiple answers to

---

2. See our extended treatment of Job's struggles in chapter 22. His lessons are also very helpful with our two questions here.

prayer and cases of actual healing show God's concern about our daily affairs. Practicing other spiritual disciplines taught in Scripture, such as meditation and fasting, increase our realization of God's continuing presence. Further, unbelievers are enticed by God, and believers are taught by the Holy Spirit. Some Christians even reason that God continues to personally communicate today in additional ways.

Not everyone agrees that all of the categories in the latter list are proper paths by which God's involvement is seen in human lives. But given the biblical witness, these items are at least defensible. Perhaps others are, as well; our list was not meant to be exhaustive.

So where do we go from here? How may we best conclude our volume? The God of Scripture has left us with a number of indications of His existence. But this is not some sterile truth about a God Who is not interested in us. He has shown Himself to be personal during biblical times and continues to be involved with our lives and needs at present. There is more than just theoretical truth for us to learn here, although such is certainly important in its own right. Some intensely practical lessons follow, as well. First, we must remember not to phrase the problem incorrectly, which causes unneeded problems. Even in Scripture, God was frequently silent, often for long intervals, and did not answer prayers the way believers sought. Some great saints struggled with this matter.

At those times when we still don't understand why things happen as they do, the truths learned by Job and Abraham continue to be instructive. What we *do* know about God is established on solid grounds – with far more content than these Old Testament saints had. We even know that God raised His Son from the dead and that heaven awaits us. So we have all the more justification to trust the God we know during those times when we *don't* understand our plight. And we need to remember our place in the universe, too. Only God is omniscient; we should recognize our own limitations.

Second, both our biblical and contemporary lists reveal a wide variety of clues that God has left for us, manifesting His personal involvement in our lives. God has not abandoned us in the universe. Our thoughts to the contrary often seem to be based on faulty biblical scenarios. Other times the problem is a very selective memory: we recall what we think God *hasn't* done, while conveniently forgetting the many things where we have witnessed what He *has* done. We think that this practice often keeps us from celebrating the many ways God acts in our lives.

Third, the fact that God is personal indicates that believers need to *enrich* their relationship with Him. Examples are readily available. We should meditate deeply on scriptural truth, correcting the false impressions that we have about God. Periodically we should list the answers to our prayers in order to remember what God has done for us. Practicing some of the biblical disciplines is a matter of obedience, in addition to availing ourselves of other means of drawing close to God.

In short, believers need to spend more quality time with their Lord. As we asked in the last chapter, what kind of relationship would we have with our husband, wife, or another loved one if we treated them to the same amount of time and attention as we do with our Lord? What have we done to develop our fellowship with God? Revising our misunderstandings, reviewing what God has done specifically for us, and improving our present relationship with the Lord might both help us to know firsthand that He is personal, as well as deepening our fellowship with Him.

Appendix A

YES, IT IS AN UGLY WORLD!

Yes, Atheist, let me be one of the first Christians to be totally honest with you. It is an ugly world out there! No question about it. In the third part of this book, "Evidence from Ethics," we have defended the case that only Christianity has an ultimate answer to the problem of the evil in our world. But I must admit the real tragedy of it all is that very often the world is made such an ugly place by Christians who do more than their share to be intellectually dishonest, who lack personal integrity, and who can be cursedly meaner that their atheist counterparts.[1]

By these "bad" Christians I do not mean people who profess to be Christians but never "darken the door of a church" – except, of course, on Easter and Christmas. Sometimes it is exactly those Christians who "profess" their Christianity the loudest; on television, in pulpits across the land, and in their church pews; who are the most dishonest, righteously indignant – when they themselves have no righteousness with which to be indignant about anything – and vindictive; who give Christianity a bad name.

I have seen these very "fundamentalistic," legalistic Christians be far worse to their own brothers and sisters than any atheist or secular "corporate monster."[2] These "Christians" wear the label of every denomination or religious

---

1. Yet, in "total honesty" I must quickly add that I know atheists and theists alike who are like this. "Bad" professing Christians do not have a corner on these "decidedly unbecoming-of-a-human" traits.

2. I have worked for secular corporations and found them often surprisingly humane and ethical. I am aware that they can often be just the opposite. One of my sayings, which I believe to be generally true, is: "They will have a job for you as long as they need you, but not one second longer." But before we jump to conclusions, in

group. Most ironically (and very sadly), they often claim to be the only Christians in the world. I probably should not give you this information, but if you are an atheist, and you want to see one just attend church board meetings at random. In all likelihood, you will run across many which will reinforce your opinions about Christians being "two-faced," and hypocritical.

Part of the reason many Christians – even famous ones – are like this is that American Christianity has imbibed the success ethic of 20th century America which stands clearly and forcefully in opposition to the Christian ethic. Unfortunately, many Christians do not see this! We are judged as successful by what we *do* not by who we *are*. We are judged to be successes by how much *money* we make, *power* we have, by what *others* think of us.

But for Jesus "successful" was synonymous with being "faithful," to Him and our fellows; by *being* a certain way, not by *doing* anything as such! Now to be sure, *being* something means we will strive to act with integrity, that is with love, joy, peace, etc. (Gal 5:22-23), but the "being" is the *essential* basis for the "doing."

I know one of the chief lieutenants of one of the most famous television "evangelists" quite well who told me that what really mattered – the unquestionable bottom line – to this prominent evangelist was "nickels and numbers." The whole ministry was *pervaded* by the "bigger is greater" success syndrome! Thank the Lord that many are seeing through this subtle evil. It is the "being" that *makes us* a success! The "doing", e.g., bigger numbers, more money, more more more *never* make us successes; any more than does the perceived lack of it in the eyes of others make us *failures*. Very often, Fundamentalists are so devoid of ethical principle, so deceitful and deceiving that they can make the truth into a lie!

Let me relate to you the story of a friend of mine[3] who grew up in a Christian home and in a very conservative Christian grade and high school. He now, as a result of his Christian school experience, claims to be an atheist. His mother told me that he: "had been turned-off to Christianity by the judgmental, legalistic attitudes he was subjected to in the Christian school which

---

my experience, this is just as true of Christian organizations as it is of secular ones!

3. I believe him to have great integrity. In a letter to me discussing this matter in part, and telling me to feel free to use his name (which I decided not to do), he said: "While I know that you would disagree with me, I have to say, in utmost honesty, that facing a firing squad would, for me, be a far more attractive alternative to ever returning to the church."

he attended for eleven years." His mother went on to say:

> Our son _____ was an extremely sensitive child, and being our first, we did not recognize this extreme sensitivity. He knew we supported the school since it was staffed by "Christians" and when disturbing incidents occurred he just kept most of them to himself, always feeling that he was "bad" or "wrong" because he disagreed. He . . . [was] always very obedient, always getting the highest marks on behavior, respect and courtesy. One teacher even told us he was "too good." He tried so hard to be that perfect person which the school required, we required and he felt that God required – until finally he just gave up – realizing that it was impossible to achieve. . . . In spite of his progress . . . his greatest fear (and even terror) is ever becoming a Christian, which he still associates with judgmental legalism, and even worse, psychological abuse."[4]

Here is part of what the son said to me in a letter:

> Dear Dr. Miethe: Thank you for the letters and article . . . you sent . . . which I have had the pleasure of reading. It is most admirable that you have chosen to speak out against the corruption and hypocrisy . . . . It is particularly refreshing to discover someone with a Christian point of view, who nonetheless understands and condemns the abominations which the fundamentalist religious movements continue to perpetrate. I have noticed that most bigots and dogmatists, when confronted with their folly, frequently resort to slandering those who question them.
>
> As one who has a keen interest in social and political currents, I have in recent years become increasingly concerned about the personality cults, dogmatism, bigotry, and blind devotion which seem to be such an essential part of contemporary fundamentalist thought. I find it astounding that television ministers such as . . . still have such a devoted following despite the obvious fraud these [are] based on. Even more alarming is the thirst for power and control many of these television ministers seem to possess, and which has found an exponent in the so-called New Right and Reconstructionist movements.
>
> An amazing parallel can be drawn between the last days of Rome leading to the ascent of the Dark Ages and the state of Western man's society today – a dogmatic, oppressive, superstitious approach to religion, runaway materialism, an unquenchable thirst for wealth and power, irresponsible use of technology, an emphasis on conformity and contempt for individuality, ethnocentrisms and vulgar nationalisms, refusal of social responsibility, incompetent leadership and cultural superficiality. I sincerely believe that if a new dark age is to be avoided, drastic changes must be made in Western Man's thinking.
>
> Fundamentalism is yet another symptom of the degenerate nature of the Western world. Fortunately, many Christians, such as yourself, are becoming aware of this problem within modern religious thought. The fundamentalists I encountered during my days at _____ Christian School have never been rivaled in their intolerance by any social/ideological group I have ever encoun-

---

4. Letter to me dated 12 September 1988.

tered (save, perhaps, a couple of obscure Marxist-Leninist sects).

I know that many of my criticisms of fundamentalism as well as the culture that allowed its proliferation would be dismissed by many as the typical pessimism and skepticism of most twentieth century nihilist-existentialists but I do feel that these negative social trends are to be expected when humans abandon their reason, their sense of individuality and sociality and their personal faith in favor of external controls and blind self-alienation. Thank you once again for the letters and best wishes for the future. Most Sincerely, _____.[5]

I could not agree with my atheist friend more. Most unfortunately, often it is the Christians who seem to be most intolerant.

The stories – which I have since confirmed – which this young man tells are like the worst horror stories one can imagine. He tells stories of faculty being "dictatorial and self-righteous and of hypocrisy and overt radicalism" that was common in the Christian school. He had a teacher that told the class "if we did not seek God's will for our lives we could possibly lose a relative or even a body part as some sort of divine punishment . . . . " In a Bible class, his biology teacher (who also taught Bible) told the class: "I don't have anything against blacks, I think everybody should own one."[6] This teacher "frequently castigated anyone who disagreed with his own opinions." Another teacher "insisted that the boys cross their legs in the manner in which girls usually cross theirs, as the masculine way was too revealing" and said: " . . . that no true Christian child would talk in the hall." You can imagine the guilt trip this puts on young people! Yet, I have heard a great number of similar stories from Christian young people!

As absurd as these incidents are, they do not compare with some things said and done by a number of speakers during chapel services. The examples are too numerous to relate. One chapel speaker "shouted and screamed and did all the things a good evangelist is supposed to do. He advocated the death penalty for homosexuality, saying he felt like going on a 'queer hunt' and that

---

5. Letter to me dated 29 September 1988.

6. "You cannot be a racist and a Christian! To use the cross, the ultimate symbol of divine love, as a symbol of human hate is unthinkable," and "Racism is truly one of the worst sins possible. It is one of the most visible forms of godlessness. It is symptomatic of the disease of self-love which is at enmity with the Gospel message. The central principle of the Christian life is denial of self to reach out in love and service to God and all of His creation. The cross is the very symbol of death to sin and self. Therefore a racist is, in real terms, one of whom Paul speaks when he says, 'they are enemies of the cross of Christ' (Philippians 3:18)!" Both statements quoted from Terry L. Miethe's *Reflections*, Volume Two.

we should 'fry' homosexuals." After taking all he could for all those years my friend transferred to a public school. Of his experience in the Christian school, and of the transfer, he says:

> I had become so disillusioned and confused that I very nearly had a nervous breakdown and began using drugs to escape the pressure I was under. From my conversion to Christianity at age four until I was around fourteen, I had always been a believing and practicing Christian. I prayed and read the Bible often and I occasionally tried to "witness" to my peers. I wholeheartedly accepted fundamentalist doctrine. However, as more and more hypocrisy and radicalism were unveiled before me, I came to realize that I had been greatly deceived. I had always been told that public schools were a disgrace, but when I began to attend public schools, I found that the teachers were committed and professional, that the students were more well-behaved than they were at _____ Christian School, and that public schools had no more drugs than [my "Christian" school] did. The quality of education at [the public school] was much better than it was at [the Christian school]. I came to understand that it was not "the people of the world" who had the problem, but rather the "believers." In time, I decided to abandon fundamentalist practice, as I realized that it was based primarily on hypocrisy and deceit. Most "Christians" I knew really had more in common with the Pharisees who killed Christ.[7]

Why have I belabored the point? If (as the old saying goes) "I had a nickel for every" young person I have personally known in my ministry who has been driven from the church by the church "I would be a rich man today."

Certainly, the point is not that all Christian schools are like the one referred to above. Some are very excellent schools. But in my experience, the story related above is all too common. I have known several churches, and other Christian institutions, which do more to turn sensitive, intelligent people with integrity "off" than "on" to Christ and Christianity! What a tragedy!

Further, I have personally known dozens of people (even in the middle of a southern fundamentalist culture) who would become Christians readily if they did not think doing so meant "kissing your brains good-bye." Unfortunately, this was the opinion they received by watching television evangelists and the Christians associated with them which these atheists knew in their community. Perhaps, it would be more accurate to refer to them as "agnostics with integrity."

But let me remind you, Atheist, "truth" is not decided on the basis of whether the one who claims to believe it, practices it or not. "Truth" is

---

7. Letter to "The Executive Committee of his Christian school dated 29 September 1986.

decided on the basis of an honest appraisal of the evidence! I beg you –
implore you – to spend the rest of your life seeking the truth, always being
willing to re-examine the evidence. As I hope, and assert, I am willing to do.
And, I politely remind you that none of us knows how much time we have on
this earth. This is *not* meant to be a "scare tactic," but only a reminder of reality.

There is a wonderful loving God who *loves you* so very much that He died
for you and who will accept you just as you are! In John 3:16, Jesus says:
"For God so loved the world, that He gave his only begotten Son, that whoever believes in Him should not perish, but have eternal life." [NASB]
Remember, in reality, the Bible is a great love story. A love story about a God
who loves us and woos us even when we shake our fists in His face!

Do not let me, or other Christians, who may not be at times what we should
be, be stumbling blocks in your path to truth and happiness, to God!
Diligently search the evidence and I believe you will find a loving God who is
bigger than all of the ugliness we experience in our world, ugliness – in all
truth – to which we all, Christians and atheists, contribute at times.

Appendix B

THE CHRISTIAN AND DEBATE[1]

Many Christians do not think debate is important *or* valid. "Why waste your time debating," because: (1) "Debating never changes anyone's mind, especially that of the debater." Or, (2) "Debating is sacrilegious because as Christians *we* know the truth and should never question only accept what we already know." Both positions, as we will see, are seriously flawed.

It is important to point out that "debating" and "arguing" are *not* the same! As a freshman at a major state university, I quickly learned there were three subjects you should not argue because you could never win. Everyone agreed – at least tacitly – that they were of such a nature and there was evidence for many differing opinions, as to almost preclude the possibility of any kind of real agreement. In the mid sixties, as now, behind this statement was the assumption that truth was relative. The subjects were: politics, sex, and religion. Yet, in our free time about all we did was to argue – yes – politics, sex, and religion. A poignant Latin phrase comes to mind: *de asini umbra disceptare*. Disraeli, in his novel *Sybil*, freely rendered the Latin as "little things affect little minds." How true. Perhaps Disraeli was more "refined" than either the Romans or we were as university freshman. Though "politics, sex, and religion" are certainly not "little things," they can be rendered thus when "argued" by "little minds."

Well, if debate and argument are not the same, what is the difference? To answer this question we need to look at "debate" as it is now practiced and as it was practiced in the eighteenth century. Of course, everyone recognizes that

1. This material on "The Christian and Debate" originally appeared in abbreviated form in *The LodeStar Review*.

the "staged confrontations" we witness in the name of "presidential debates" are not debates at all! They are, at best, forums where the two candidates get half of the allotted time to state their positions in a pabulum form that would starve a baby!

Today, in our colleges and universities, debate as it is practiced often has more to do with style than content. Student debaters are taught to "make points," to destroy, make fun of the opponent, to use any tactic that will help one *win*. If, along the way, one happens to have the better information, facts, "truth" to support the "performance" then fine, but *do* everything – use any tactic – possible to win! If this is what "debate" is all about, then I agree that "debating never changes anyone's mind, especially that of the debater." "Debate" practiced thus is really not meant to "change anyone's mind," but only to appear to win an argument.

But the eighteenth century had a great tradition of real "debate." "Debate" was an honored method for "getting all the facts on the table," for pursuing the breadth and depth of a subject in an attempt to discern the *truth of a matter*! Proponent and opponent alike were interested, not in making points, but honestly presenting the very best evidence for what they believed to be true. Such debates were important events in shaping thought, the course of discussion in the future, and eventually public opinion on a subject. These debates could go on for hours and involve several days. They were often then printed in a book which also advanced the pursuit of truth. This view of debate can be as important today as it was then, if practiced with intelligence and integrity!

If, as a Christian you are going to engage in debate, permit me to give you some important advice regarding "method." *First*, – and one of the two *most* important aspects – *do your homework*: prepare, prepare, prepare *and* prepare. There *must* be no exception to this rule! When I was debating a very famous Roman Catholic Archbishop, I went with a well prepared manuscript intending to "shed more light than heat" on the subject and to answer important questions regarding the topic that had either not been raised before or answered adequately. This debate was to be repeated twice in two days to different audiences. The second day it was taped for public T.V. On the second day my "opponent" the Archbishop started by apologizing to our audience for his erroneous preconceived opinions about me and said he was going to abbreviate his remarks so Dr. Miethe would have more time to speak! What a compliment.

Second, as best you can, know your audience. This is not as hard as you might expect. You should at least have a good idea by the nature of the occasion, where you asked to debate, and by whom – in general – what type of audience you will be addressing. If you misjudge this some, it will not be a serious matter *if you have prepared very well* because you can modify your presentation according to the needs of the situation. Do you want to speak to your supporters in the audience, your opponent, or those people in the audience who are against your position? My contention is that you should try to speak to all three. "How" (articulation and personality) you present your message is as important as "what" you say.

Third, ask yourself what it is you want to accomplish in the debate. Do you want to show clearly the differences in the two positions – assuming there are only two and, as a Christian, you should have the integrity to admit the true situation in this regard – or build on the commonalties? Actually, in reality this can be a false dilemma. As Christians, we should always try to do both for an accurate statement of the evidence will show both are usually true.

Fourth, and equal with preparation, *be gracious*, Christian! I have known several famous Christian debaters who won the "argument," but lost the "debate"! – They had the best content *and* the worst personality. Consequently, the audience went away with more emotional sympathy for the atheist opponent, and therefore for his position! We *can* often build bridges even as we clarify differences.

True, you most probably will not "win" over your opponents in the audience or your actual opponent just because of one debate. But you can give your supporters in the audience, who may know some of the opponents, material so they can continue the debate in the gracious manner with which you began it. You may also be able to make a "friend" out of your opponent for the future which may be of inestimable value!

Once, while driving my good friend (and "world famous" atheist philosopher) Antony G.N. Flew around, he said to me: "Terry, why should I believe a man when he speaks to me about heavenly things, if I cannot believe him when he speaks to me about earthly things?" Christians, above all others, must have integrity when they speak about, or *do*, anything! I have been involved in debating Tony Flew twice and we have built a friendship which I value highly.[2] Tony is one of the finest, most ethical men I have ever met! He is simply wrong, I believe, in holding that God does not exist. I hope and pray that my friendship will be used to honor and glorify my Lord in Tony's life.

Christians should be involved in debate because we have a scriptural mandate to be out there in the market place (Acts 17:17-34), to serve as salt, light and leaven (Matt 5:13-16, 13:33), to give an answer for the hope that is in us (1 Pet 3:15), to set forth our case (Isa 41:21). (The answer to the second reason in the first paragraph regarding why we should not debate.) And, we must debate with great preparation, intellectual honesty, personal integrity, and simple graciousness. It should never be that the atheist is found to be *more of any of these* than his Christian opponent!

---

2. See Terry L. Miethe, Editor, *Did Jesus Rise from the Dead? The Resurrection Debate*, Gary Habermas and Antony Flew (San Francisco: Harper & Row, 1987) and Terry L. Miethe & Antony G.N. Flew, *Does God Exist? A Believer and an Atheist Debate* (San Francisco: Harper Collins, 1991).

Bibliography

"A good Booke is the pretious life-blood of a mafter fpirit, imbalm'd and trea-fur'd up on purpofe to a life beyond life."[1]

John Milton (1608-1674), *Areopagitica*

"A good book is the purest essence of a human soul."

Thomas Carlyle (1795-1881)
Speech in support of the London Library, 1840

"A good book is of much value and a great companion – a great book is worth its weight in gold!" (19 Nov. 1981)

Terry L. Miethe, *Reflections,* Volume Two, 1983

Adler, Mortimer J., and Charles Van Doren. *How to Think About God: A Guide for the 20th-Century Pagan.* New York: Collier Books, Macmillan Publishing Co., 1980.

_____. *How to Read a Book.* Revised and updated edition. New York: Simon & Schuster, 1992.

Adams, Robert. "Moral Arguments for Theistic Belief," in *Rationality and Religious Belief,* edited by C. F. Delany. Notre Dame, IN: University of Notre Dame Press, 1979, pp. 116-40.

Anderson, J. N. D. *Christianity: The Witness of History.* Downers Grove: InterVarsity Press, 1970.

_____. *Christianity and World Religions: The Challenge of Pluralism.* Downers Grove: InterVarsity Press, 1984.

---

1. This is carved in Old English above the entrance to the Reading Room of the New York Public Library. Or as we would write it in today's English: "A good book is the precious life-blood of a master spirit, embalmed and treasured up on purpose to a life beyond life."

Anderson, Lynn. *If I Really Believe, Why Do I Have These Doubts?* Minneapolis: Bethany House, 1992.

Anderson, Norman. *The Teaching of Jesus.* Downers Grove: InterVarsity Press, 1983.

Aquinas, St. Thomas. *Summa Theologica.* Translated by the Fathers of the English Dominican Province. London: Burns, Oates and Washbourne, 1920.

_____. *Summa Contra Gentiles.* Translated by Vernon J. Bourke and others. New York: Doubleday & Company, 1956-7.

Athearn, Clarence R. *The Religious Education of Alexander Campbell.* St. Louis: The Bethany Press, 1928.

Ayer, A. J. *Language, Truth and Logic.* Second Edition. London: Gollanoz, 1946.

_____. *The Central Questions of Philosophy.* London: Penguin Books, 1973.

Bado, Walter, S.J. "What is God? An Essay in Learned Ignorance." *The Modern Schoolman* 42 (1964), pp. 3-32.

Barth, Karl. *The Doctrine of Reconciliation* 4, Part I of *Church Dogmatics.* Edinburgh: T & T Clark, 1956

_____. *.Anselm: Fides Quaerens Intellectum* (Faith in Search of Understanding). English Translation by I. W. Robertson. Cleveland: Meridian Books, 1962.

Basinger, David. "Evil as Evidence Against God's Existence: Some Clarifications." *Modern Schoolman* 58 (1980-1981).

Beard, Charles. "That Noble Dream," in *The Varieties of History.* Edited by Fritz Stein. Cleveland: World Publishing Company, 1956.

Berman, David. *A History of Atheism in Britain: From Hobbes to Russell.* London and New York: Croun Helm, 1988.

Bertocci, Peter A. *An Introduction to the Philosophy of Religion.* New York: Prentice-Hall, 1951.

Bethell, Tom. "Darwin's Mistake." *Harper's Magazine* (February, 1976) pp. 70-74.

_____. "Agnostic Evolutionists: The Taxonomic Case Against Darwin." *Harper's Magazine* (February, 1985), pp. 49-61.

Blomberg, Craig. *The Historical Reliability of the Gospels.* Downers Grove: InterVarsity Press, 1987.

Bode, E. L. *The First Easter Morning.* Rome: Biblical Institute Press, 1970.

Bonansea, Bernardino M. "The Impossibility of Creation from Eternity According to St. Bonaventure." *Proceedings of the American Catholic Philosophical Association* 48 (1974), pp. 121-135.

Borne, E. *Atheism.* New York: Hawthorn Books, 1961.

Bornkamm, Günther. *Jesus of Nazareth.* Translated by Irene and Fraser McLuskey with James M. Robinson. New York: Harper and Row, 1960.

Bourke, Vernon J. *Augustine's Quest for Wisdom: Life and Philosophy of the Bishop of Hippo.* Milwaukee: The Bruce Publishing Company, 1945.

_____. *The Pocket Aquinas.* New York: Washington Square Press, 1960.

_____. *Will in Western Thought: An Historico-Critical Survey.* New York: Sheed and Ward, 1964.

_____. *Aquinas' Search for Wisdom.* Milwaukee: Bruce, 1965.

Bowden, J. *New Testament Thology.* New York: Charles Scribner's Sons, 1971.

Braaten, Carl. *History and Hermeneutics.* Philadelphia: Westminster, 1966.

Brightman, Edgar S. *A Philosophy of Religion.* New York: Prentice-Hall, 1940.

Brown, Colin. *Philosophy and the Christian Faith.* Chicago: InterVarsity Press, 1969.

Brown, Delwin, Ralph E. James and Gene Reeves, Editors. *Process Philosophy and Christian Thought.* Indianapolis: Bobbs-Merrill Company, Inc., 1971.

Brown, Patterson. "Infinite Causal Regression." *The Philosophical Review* 35 (1966), pp. 510-525; and later published in *Aquinas: A Collection of Critical Essays*, edited by Anthony Kenny. Notre Dame, IN: University of Notre Dame Press, 1976, pp. 214-236.

Brown, Raymond E. *New Testament Essays.* Milwaukee: Bruce Publishing Company, 1965.

_____. *The Gospel According to John*, The Anchor Bible. Garden City, NY: Doubleday and Company, Inc., 1966.

_____. *Jesus—God And Man.* Milwaukee: Bruce Publishing Company, 1967.

_____. "The Resurrection and Biblical Criticism." *Commonweal* 87. (Nov. 24, 1967).

_____. *The Virginal Conception and Bodily Resurrection of Jesus.* New York: Paulist Press, 1973.

Bruce, F. F. *The New Testament Documents: Are They Reliable?* 5th Revised Edition. Grand Rapids: Eerdmans, 1960.

_____. *Commentary on the Book of Acts.* Grand Rapids: Eerdmans, 1971.

_____. *Jesus and Christian Origins Outside the New Testament.* Grand Rapids: Eerdmans, 1974.

Buell, Jon A. and O. Quentin Hyder. *Jesus: God, Ghost or Guru?* Grand Rapids: Zondervan, 1978.

Bultmann, Rudolf. *Theology of the New Testament.* Translated by Kendrick Grobel. New York: Charles Scribner's Sons, 1951, 1955.

Buntain, Mark with Ron Hembree and Doug Brendel. *Miracle in the Mirror.* Minneapolis: Bethany House, 1981.

Burtt, E. A. *The Metaphysical Foundations of Modern Physical Science.* London: Routledge and Kegan Paul Limited, 1932.

Burrill, Donald R, Editor. *The Cosmological Arguments: A Spectrum of Opinion.* Garden City, NY: Doubleday Anchor, 1967.

Butler, Joseph. *The Analogy of Religion,* in *The Works of Joseph Butler.* Edited by W. E. Gladstone. Oxford: Clarendon Press, 1896. *The Analogy of Religion* was first published in 1736.

Cairns, Earle E. *God and Man in Time.* Grand Rapids: Baker, 1979.

Caldecott, Alfred. *The Philosophy of Religion in England and America.* London: Methuen & Co., 1901.

Caldwell, John. *Intimacy with God: Christian Disciplines for Spiritual Growth.* Joplin: College Press, 1992.

Campenhausen, Hans von. *Tradition and Life in the Early Church.* Philadelphia: Fortress Press, 1968.

Campbell, George. *A Dissertation on Miracles.* London: T. Tegg & Son, 1762; Reprinted in 1834.

Camus, Albert. *The Plague.* Translated by S. Gilbert. New York: Random House, Inc., 1948.

Chandler, Russell. *Racing Toward 2001: The Forces Shaping America's Religious Future.* Grand Rapids: Zondervan and San Francisco: Harper, 1992.

Chapman, Colin. *The Case for Christianity.* Grand Rapids: Eerdmans, 1981.

Chenu, M.D. *Toward Understanding St. Thomas.* Chicago: Henry Regnery, 1964.

Clapp, Rodney. "Faith Healing: A Look at What's Coming. " *Christianity Today* 27 (December 2, 1983); 27(December 16, 1983).

Clark, Neville. *Interpreting the Resurrection.* Philadelphia: Westminster, 1967.

Clark, Gordon H. *The Philosophy of Science and Belief in God.* Nutley, NJ: Graig, 1964.

Clarke, Bowman L. *Language and Natural Theology.* The Hague: Mouton & Co., 1966.

Clarke, W. Norris. "How the Philosopher Can Give Meaning to Language About God," in *The Idea of God*, E.H. Madden, R. Handy, and M. Farber, eds. Springfield, IL: Charles C. Thomas, 1968.

Cole, R. A. *The Gospel According to St. Mark*. Grand Rapids: Eerdmans, 1970.

Collins, James. *A History of Modern European Philosophy*. Milwaukee: Bruce,1954.

_____. *God in Modern Philosophy*. Chicago: Henry Regnery, 1959.

_____. "Philosophy and Religion." *Great Ideas Today*. Edited by Robert Hutchins and Mortimer J. Adler. Chicago: Encyclopaedia Britannica, Inc., 1962, pp. 314-372.

Continuum. Winter issue (1976), Number 5, devoted to the contemporary experience of God.

Copleston, Frederick. *A History of Philosophy*. Volume 5: "Modern Philosophy: The British Philosphers, Part II Berkeley to Hume. Garden City, NY: Image Books, 1964.

Craig, Clarence Tucker. "Introduction and Exegesis of I Corinthians. " *The Interpreter's Bible*. Edited by George Arthur Buttrick. New York: Abingdon-Cokesbury, 1953.

Craig, William Lane. *The Existence of God and the Beginnings of the Universe*. San Bernardino: Here's Life Publishers, Inc, 1979.

_____. *The Cosmological Argument: from Plato to Leibniz*. New York: Barnes and Noble, 1980.

_____. "Philosophical and Scientific Pointers to Creation ex Nihilo." *Journal of the American Scientific Affiliation* 32 (1980), pp. 5-13.

_____. *The Son Rises*. Chicago: Moody, 1981.

_____. "The Empty Tomb of Jesus." *Gospel Perspectives: Studies of History and Tradition in the Four Gospels*. Edited by R. T. France and D. Wenham. Sheffield: JSOT Press, 1981.

_____. *Apologletics: An Introduction*. Chicago: Moody, 1984.

_____. "Professor Mackie and the Kalam Cosmological Argument." *Religious Studies* 20 (1985), pp. 367-375.

_____. *The Only Wise God: The Compatibility of Divine Foreknowledge and Human Freedom*. Grand Rapids: Baker, 1987.

_____. *Assessing the New Testament Evidence for the Historicity of the Resurrection of Jesus*. Lewiston: Edward Mellen Press, 1989.

Cranfield, C. E. B. *The Gospel According to Mark.* Cambridge: Cambridge University Press, 1963.

Cullmann, Oscar. *The Christology of the New Testament.* Translated by Shirley C. Guthrie and Charles A. M. Hall. Philadelphia: Westminster, 1963.

_____. *The Early Church: Studies in Early Christian History and Theology.* Edited by A. J. B. Higgins. Philadelphia: Westminster, 1966.

Daniel-Rops, Henri, Editor. *The Sources for the Life of Christ.* New York: Hawthorn Books, Inc., 1962.

Daniélou, J. *God and the Ways of Knowing.* Cleveland: Meridian Books, 1957.

Davies, Brian. *An Introduction to the Philosophy of Religion.* Oxford: Oxford University Press, 1982.

Davies, Paul. *God and the New Physics* (New York: Simon and Schuster, 1983).

_____. "The Anthropic Principle." *Science Digest* (October, 1983).

De Lubac, Henri. *The Discovery of God.* New York: P.J. Kennedy and Sons, 1960, especially chapters 1-3.

DeWolf, L. Harold. *The Religious Revolt Against Reason.* New York: Harper & Brothers, 1949.

Dietl, Paul J. "On Miracles." *American Philosophical Quarterly* 5 (1968), pp. 130-134.

Dirscherl, D, Editor. *Speaking of God.* Milwaukee: Bruce, 1967.

Dodd, C. H. *More New Testament Studies.* Grand Rapids: Eerdmans, 1968.

_____. *The Apostolic Preaching and Its Developments.* Grand Rapids: Baker, 1980.

Drane, John. *Introducing the New Testament.* San Francisco: Harper and Row, 1986.

Dunn, James D. G. *The Evidence for Jesus.* Philadelphia: Westminster, 1985.

Durbin, Bill Jr. "How It All Began: Why Can't Evangelical Scientists Agree?" *Christianity Today.* (August, 1988). pp. 31-44.

Earle, Edward M., Editor. *Makers of Modern Strategy.* Princeton: Princeton University Press, 1943.

Eddington, Sir Arthur Stanley. *Science and the Unseen World.* London: Allen and Unwin, 1919.

Eisenschiml, Otto and Ralph Newman. *Eyewitness: The Civil War as We Lived It.* New York: Grosset and Dunlap, 1956.

Ellis, E. Earle. "Dating the New Testament." *New Testament Studies* 26 (July, 1980), pp. 487-502.

Elwell, Walter A. , Editor. *Evangelical Dictionary of Theology.* Grand Rapids: Baker, 1984.

Empson, William. *Milton's God.* Revised Edition. London: Chatto and Windus, 1965.

Eslick, Leonard James. "What is the Starting Point of Metaphysics?" *The Modern Schoolman* 34 (May, 1957), pp. 247-263.

_____. "The Real Distinction: Reply to Professor Reese." *The Modern Schoolman* 37 (1961), pp. 149-160.

_____. "Toward a Metaphysics of Creation," *Metaphysical Investigations: A Selection of Lectures Delivered Before the Philosophers' Club of St. Louis University,* 1964.

_____. "The Empirical Foundations of Metaphysics." *Proceedings of the St. Louis University Philosophy Club,* 1966. Later published as: "The Negative Judgment of Separation: A Reply to Father Burrell." *The Modern Schoolman* 44 (Nov., 1966), pp. 35-46.

_____. "Omnipotence: The Meanings of Power." *The New Scholasticism* 42 (Spring, 1968), pp. 289-292.

_____. "From the World to God: The Cosmological Argument." *The Modern Schoolman* 60 (1983), p. 153.

Evans, C. Stephen. *Subjectivity and Religious Belief.* Grand Rapids: Eerdmans, 1978.

_____. *Philosophy of Religion: Thinking About Faith.* Downers Grove: InterVarsity Press, 1982.

Fabro, Cornelio. *God in Exile: A Study of the Internal Dynamics of Modern Atheism from its Roots in the Cartesian Cogito to the Present Day.* Westminister and New York: Newman Press, 1968.

Fairbairn, Andrew M. *The Philosophy of the Christian Religion.* New York: Hodder & Stoughton, 1902.

Farmer, William R. "Peter and Paul, and the Tradition Concerning 'The Lord's Supper' in I Corinthians 11:23-25." *Criswell Theological Review* 2 (1987).

Feinberg, John S. *Theologies and Evil.* Washington, DC: University Press of America, 1979.

Ferguson, Sinclair B., David F. Wright, and J.I. Packer, Editors. *New Dictionary of Theology.* Leicester, England: InterVarsity, 1988.

Ferré, Frederick. *Basic Modern Philosophy of Religion.* New York: Charles Scribner's Sons, 1967.

Ferré, Nels F. S. *Faith and Reason*. New York: Harper & Brothers, 1946.

Fischer, David Hackett. *Historians' Fallacies: Toward a Logic of Historical Thought*. New York: Harper Torchbooks, 1970.

Fisher, George Park. *Manual of Christian Evidences*. New York: Scribner's, 1899.

Flew, Antony G.N. "Theology and Falsification," and "Divine Omnipotence and Human Freedom," in *New Essays in Philosophical Theology* edited by Antony Flew and Alasdair MacIntyre. New York: Macmillan, 1955, pp. 96-99.

_____ and Alasdair MacIntyre. *New Essays in Philosophical Theology*. London: SCM Press, 1955.

_____. *Hume's Philosophy of Belief*. London: Routledge and Kegan Paul, 1961.

_____, Editor. *Body, Mind, and Death*. New York: Macmillian, 1964.

_____. *God and Philosophy*. New York: Dell Publishing Co., Inc, 1966.

_____. " 'Theology and Falsification' in Retrospect" in M. L. Diamond and T. V. Litzenburg *The Logic of God: Theology and Verification*. Indianapolis: Bobbs-Merrill, 1975.

_____. *A Rational Animal: and other Philosophical Essays on the Nature of Man*. Oxford: Clarendon Press, 1978.

_____. *God, Freedom and Immortality*. Buffalo: Prometheus, 1984. Reissue of a book first published in 1976 as *The Presumption of Atheism*.

_____. *God: A Philosophical Critique*. La Salle, IL: Open Court, 1984. Reissue of a book first published in 1966 as *God and Philosophy*.

_____. *The Logic of Mortality*. Oxford: Basil Blackwell, 1987.

_____. *David Hume: Philosopher of Moral Science*. Oxford: Basil Blackwell, 1988.

Foster, Richard J. *Freedom of Simplicity*. San Francisco: Harper and Row, 1981.

_____. *Celebration of Discipline: The Path to Spiritual Growth*. Revised Edition. San Francisco: Harper and Row, 1988.

France, R. T. *The Living God*. Downers Grove: InterVarsity Press, 1970.

_____. *The Evidence for Jesus*. Downers Grove: InterVarsity Press, 1986.

Fuller, Reginald H. *The Foundations of New Testament Christology*. New York: Charles Scribner's Sons, 1965.

_____. *The Formation of the Resurrection Narratives*. New York: Macmillan, 1971.

Gange, Robert A. *Origins and Destiny.* Waco: Word Books, 1986.

Gardiner, Patrick. "The Philosophy of History." *The International Encyclopedia of the Social Sciences* 6. Edited by David L. Sills. New York: Macmillan and The Free Press, 1968.

Garrigou-Lagrange, R. *God, His Existence and Nature.* St. Louis: St. Louis University Press, 1934, especially Appendix.

Geach, P T. *God and the Soul.* London: Routledge and Kegan Paul, 1969.

Geisler, Norman L. and William E. Nix. *A General Introduction to the Bible.* Chicago: Moody, 1968.

_____. *Philosophy of Religion.* Grand Rapids: Zondervan, 1974.

_____. "Process Theology" in *Tensions in Contemporary Theology.* Second Edition. Edited by Stanley N. Gundry and Alan F. Johnson. Grand Rapids: Baker, 1976.

_____. *Christian Apologetics.* Grand Rapids: Baker, 1976.

_____. *The Roots of Evil.* Grand Rapids: Zondervan, 1978.

_____. *Miracles and Modern Thought.* Grand Rapids: Zondervan, 1982.

Geldenhuys, Norval. *Commentary on the Gospel of Luke.* Grand Rapids: Eerdmans, 1972.

Gerstner, John H. *Reasons For Faith.* Grand Rapids: Baker, 1967.

Gilby, Thomas. *St. Thomas Aquinas Philosophical Texts.* London: Oxford University Press, 1951.

Gilson, Etienne. *Christianity and Philosophy.* London: Sheed and Ward, 1939, especially pp. 77-102.

_____. *Being and Some Philosophers.* Toronto: Pontifical Institute of Mediaeval Studies, 1949, especially pp. 160-182.

_____. *The Philosphy of St. Thomas Aquinas.* Authorized Translation from the Third Revised and Enlarged Editon of "Le Thomisme." New York: (Originally by Random House, now available from) Dorset Press, 1956.

_____. "The Idea of God and the Difficulties of Atheism." *Philosophy Today* 13 (Fall, 1969), pp. 174-205. Reprinted from *The Great Ideas Today 1969,* M. J. Adler and R. M. Hutchins, eds. Chicago: Encyclopaedia Britannica, Inc, 1969.

Goppelt, Leonard. "The Eastern Kerygma in the New Testament." *The Easter Message Today.* New York: Thomas Nelson, 1964.

Grant, Michael. *Jesus: An Historian's Review of the Gospels.* New York: Charles Scribner's Sons, 1977.

Grant, Robert M. *An Historical Introduction to the New Testament.* London: Collins, 1963.

Grass, Hans. *Ostergeschehen und Osterberichte.* Second Edition. Göttingen: Vanderhoeck und Ruprecht, 1962.

Green, Michael. *Runaway World.* Downers Grove: InterVarsity Press, 1986.

Green, Ronald M. *Religious Reason: The Rational and Moral Basis of Religious Belief.* New York: Oxford University Press, 1978.

Greig, J.Y.T. *The Letters of David Hume.* Oxford: Oxford University Press, 1932.

Gruenler, Royce Gordon. *New Approaches to Jesus and the Gospels: A Phenomenological and Exegetical Study of Synoptic Christology.* Grand Rapids: Baker, 1982.

Gunn, James E. "Observations in Cosmology: The Shape of Space and Totality of Time." *The Great Ideas Today 1979*, M.J. Adler, ed. Chicago: Encyclopaedia Britannica, Inc. 1979.

Guthrie, Donald. *New Testament Introduction.* Revised Edition. Downers Grove: InterVarsity Press, 1990.

Habermas, Gary R. *The Resurrection of Jesus: A Rational Inquiry.* Ann Arbor: University Microfilms, Inc., 1976.

_____. *The Resurrection of Jesus: An Apologetic.* Grand Rapids: Baker, 1980; Lanham, MD: University Press of America, 1984.

_____. "Skepticism: Hume." *Biblical Errancy: An Analysis of Its Philosophical Roots.* Edited by Norman L. Geisler. Grand Rapids: Zondervan, 1981.

_____ and Kenneth E. Stevenson. *Verdict on the Shroud: Evidence for the Death and Resurrection of Jesus.* Ann Arbor: Servant Books, 1981; Wayne, PA: Dell Publishing Company,1981.

_____. "Averroës, Rationalism, and the Leap of Faith." *Shalom: Essays in Honor of Dr. Charles H. Shaw.* Edited by Eugene J. Mayhew. Farmington Hills, MI: William Tyndale College Press, 1983.

_____. "Resurrection of Christ." *Evangelical Dictionary of Theology.* Edited by Walter Elwell. Grand Rapids: Baker, 1983.

_____. "Knowing that Jesus' Resurrection Occurred: A Response to Stephen Davis." *Faith and Philosophy* 2 (July, 1985), pp. 295-302.

_____. *The Verdict of History: Conclusive Evidence for the Life of Jesus.* Nashville: Thomas Nelson, 1988. Originally published (1984) under the title: *Ancient Evidence for the Life of Jesus: Historical Records of His Death and Resurrection.*

_____. "Resurrection Claims in Non-Christian Religions." *Religious Studies* 25 (1989), pp. 167-177.

_____. "Paradigm Shift: A Challenge to Naturalism." *Bibliotheca Sacra* 146 (Oct.-Dec., 1989), pp. 437-450.

_____. "Jesus' Resurrection and Contemporary Criticism: An Apologetic." *Criswell Theological Review* 4.1 (Fall, 1989), pp. 159-174. Part 2 of this article is in Volume 4, No. 2.

_____. *Dealing With Doubt*. Chicago: Moody, 1990.

_____ and Kenneth E. Stevenson. *The Shroud and the Controversy: Science, Skepticsm, and the Search for Authenticity*. Nashville: Thomas Nelson, 1990.

_____. "The Jesus Christ of History." *Student Leadership Journal* (Formerly *His*). (Fall, 1990), p. 10.

_____. "An Appraisal of the Leap of Faith." *Michigan Theological Journal* 2 (1991), pp. 82-96.

_____. "The Resurrection of Jesus and Contemporary Scholarship: A Review Essay." *Bulletin of the Evangelical Philosophical Society* 14 (1991).

_____. "The Recent Evangelical Debate on the Bodily Resurrection of Jesus: A Review Article." *Journal of the Evangelical Theological Society* 33 (Sept., 1991), pp. 375-378.

_____ and J. P. Moreland. *Immortality: The Other Side of Death*. Nashville: Thomas Nelson, 1992.

_____. "The Early Christian Belief in the Resurrection of Jesus: A Response to Thomas Sheehan." *Michigan Theological Journal* 3 (1992), pp. 105-127.

_____. "A Plea for the Practical Application of Christian Philosophy." *Living Your Faith: Closing the Gap Between Mind and Heart* by Terry L. Miethe. (See entry below.)

Hackett, Stuart C. *The Resurrection of Theism: Prolegomena to Christian Apology*. Second Edition. Grand Rapids: Baker, 1982.

Hadas, Moses. "Introduction." *The Complete Works of Tacitus*. New York: Random House, Inc., 1942.

Hamilton, Floyd. *The Basis of the Christian Faith: A Modern Defense of the Christian Religion*. New York: Harper and Row, 1964.

Hamilton, William. *The Modern Reader's Guide to Matthew and Luke*. New York: Association Press, 1957.

_____. *The Modern Reader's Guide to John*. New York: Association Press, 1959.

Harris, Samuel. *The Philosophical Basis of Theism.* New York: Charles Scribner's Sons, 1883.

Hartshorne, Charles and William L. Reese *Philosophers Speak of God.* Chicago: University of Chicago Press, 1953.

_____. *The Logic of Perfection.* LaSalle, IL: Open Court, 1962.

_____. *Anselm's Discovery.* LaSalle, IL: Open Court, 1965.

_____. *Creative Synthesis and Philosophic Method.* LaSalle, IL: Open Court, 1970.

_____. *Omnipotence and Other Theological Mistakes.* Albany: State University of New York Press, 1984.

Hayek, F. A. *Studies in Philosophy, Politics and Economics.* London: Routledge and Kegan Paul, 1967.

_____. *Law, Legislation and Liberty: Volume I Rules and Order.* Chicago and London: University of Chicago Press and Routledge, 1973.

Hawking, Stephen W. "The Limits of Space and Time," in *The Great Ideas Today 1979*, M.J. Adler, ed. Chicago: Encyclopaedia Britannica, Inc., 1979.

Hebblethwaite, Brian. *Evil, Suffering and Religion.* New York: Hawthorn Books, Inc., 1976.

Heisenberg, Werner. *Philosophic Problems of Nuclear Science.* New York: Pantheon Books, Inc., 1952.

_____. *Physics and Philosophy: The Revolution in Modern Science.* New York: Harper & Brothers, 1958.

Helm, Paul, Editor. *Divine Commands and Morality.* New York: Oxford University Press, 1981.

Hengel, Martin. *The Atonement.* Translated by J. Bowden. Philadelphia: Fortress Press, 1981.

Hick, John, Editor. *The Existence of God.* New York: Macmillan, 1964.

_____. *Evil and the God of Love.* Revised Edition. San Francisco: Harper and Row, 1977. Originally published in 1966 with Macmillan. Holland, R. F. "The Miraculous," *American Philosophical Quarterly* 2 (1965), pp. 43-51.

_____. and A.C. McGill, Editors. *The Many-faced Argument.* Recent Studies on the Ontological Argument for the Existence of God. New York: Macmillan, 1967.

Holmes, Arthur F. *Philosophy: A Christian Perspective, An Introductory Essay.* Downers Grove: InterVarsity Press, 1975.

Hübner, Kurt. *Critique of Scientific Reason.* Translated by Paul R. Dixon and Hollis M. Dixon. Chicago: University of Chicago Press, 1983.

Hume, David. *Hume's Dialogues Concerning Natural Religion.* Second Edition. Edited by N. Kemp Smith. Edinburgh: Nelson, n.d.

_____. *An Enquiry Concerning Human Understanding.* Edited by Antony Flew. LaSalle, IL: Open Court, 1988. Originally published in 1748.

Hunter, Archibald M. *The Gospel According to St. Mark.* London: SCM Press LTD, 1953.

_____. *Introducing the New Testament.* Second Edition. Revised. Philadelphia: Westminster, 1957.

_____. *Bible and Gospel.* Philadelphia: Westminster, 1969.

_____. *Jesus: Lord and Saviour.* Grand Rapids: Eerdmans, 1976.

Jaki, Stanley L. *Brain, Mind and Computers.* New York: Herder and Herder, 1966.

_____. *The Road of Science and the Ways to God.* Chicago: University of Chicago Press, 1978.

_____. *Cosmos and Creator.* Edinburgh: Scottish Academic Press, 1981; Chicago: Regnery Gateway, 1982.

_____. *Angels, Apes and Man.* La Salle, IL: Sherwood Sugden and Company, 1983.

_____. "From Scientific Cosmology to Created Universe," in *The Intellectuals Speak Out About God*, pp. 61-78, reprinted from *The Irish Astronomical Journal* 15 (March 1982), pp. 253-62.

Jastrow, Robert. *God and the Astronomers.* New York: W.W. Norton & Co., 1978.

Jeremias, Joachim. *The Central Message of the New Testament.* Philadelphia: Fortress Press, 1965.

Johnson. O. A. "God and St. Anselm." *The Journal of Religion* 45 (1965), pp. 326-334.

Johnson, S. Lewis, Jr. "I Corinthians." *The Wycliffe Bible Commentary.* Edited by Charles F. Pfeiffer and Everett E. Harrison. Nashville: The Southwestern Company, 1962.

Kant, Immanuel. *Religion Within the Limits of Reason Alone.* Translated by Theodore M. Greene. New York: Harper and Row, 1960.

_____. *Critique of Practical Reason.* Translated by Lewis White Beck. Third Edition. New York: Macmillan, 1993.

Kaufmann, Walter. *The Faith of a Heretic*. New York: Anchor Books, 1963.

_____. *Nietzsche: Philosopher, Psychologist, Antichrist*. New York: Meridian Books, 1966.

Kerkut, G. A. "Implications of Evolution," *International Series on Monographs on Pure and Applied Biology*, Vol. 4. New York: Pergamon Press, 1960.

Keyser, Leander S. *A System of Christian Evidences*. Tenth Edition, Revised. Burlington, IA: The Lutheran Literary Board, 1950.

Kim, Seyoon. *The Origin of Paul's Gospel*. Grand Rapids: Eerdmans, 1982.

Kline, Meredith G. "Job." *The Wycliffe Bible Commentary*. Edited by Charles F. Pfeiffer and Everett E. Harrison. Nashville: The Southwestern Company, 1962.

Knudson, Albert C. *The Doctrine of Redemption*. New York: Abingdon-Cokesbury, 1933.

Klubertanz, George P. *Introduction to The Philosophy of Being*. Second Edition. New York: Appleton-Century-Crofts, 1963.

Kreeft, Peter. *Heaven: The Heart's Deepest Longing*. San Francisco: Harper and Row, 1980.

_____. *Socrates Meets Jesus: History's Great Questioner Confronts the Claims of Christ*. Downers Grove: InterVarsity Press, 1987. Dedicated to Terry Miethe and Gary Habermas.

Kübler-Ross, Elisabeth. *On Death and Dying*. New York: Macmillan, 1969.

Küng, Hans. *On Being a Christian*. Garden City, NY: Doubleday, Inc., 1976.

_____. *Does God Exist? An Answer for Today*. Translated by Edward Quinn. Garden City, NY: Doubleday, 1980.

_____. *Eternal Life? Life After Death as a Medical, Philosophical, and Theological Problem*. Translated by Edward Quinn. Garden City, NY: Doubleday, 1984.

Kurtz, Paul. *Humanist Manifestoes I and II*. Buffalo: Prometheus, 1973.

Ladd, George E. *I Believe in the Resurrection of Jesus*. Grand Rapids: Eerdmans, 1975.

Lacroix, J. *The Meaning of Atheism*. New York: Macmillan, 1965.

Lapide, Pinchas. *The Resurrection of Jesus: A Jewish Perspective*. Minneapolis: Augsburg Publishing House, 1983.

Laudan, Larry. *Progress and Its Problems: Toward a Theory of Scientific Growth*. Berkeley: University of California Press, 1977.

Lavelle, Louis. *Evil and Suffering*. Translated by Bernard Murchland, C.S.C. New York: Macmillan, 1940.

LeFevre, Perry. *Philosophical Resources for Christian Thought*. New York: Abingdon, 1968.

Lewis, C.S. *The Pilgrim's Regress: An Allegorical Apology for Christianity, Reason, and Romanticism*. New York: Bantam Books, 1943.

_____. *The Abolition of Man*. New York: Macmillan, 1947.

_____. *Miracles: A Preliminary Study*. New York: Macmillan, 1947.

_____. *Surprised By Joy: The Shape of My Early Life*. New York: Harcourt, Brace, Jovanovich, 1955.

_____. "On Obstinacy in Belief," in *The World's Last Night and Other Essays*. New York: Brace Jovanovich, 1955.

_____. *Mere Christianity*. New York: Macmillan, 1960.

_____. *The Problem of Pain*. The intellectual problem raised by human suffering examined with sympathy and realism. New York: Macmillan, 1962.

_____. *God in the Dock: Essays on Theology and Ethics*. Grand Rapids: Eerdmans, 1970.

Lightfoot, J. B., Editor and translator. *The Apostolic Fathers*. Grand Rapids: Baker, 1891, 1956.

Lightner, Robert P. *The Saviour and the Scriptures*. Philadelphia: Presbyterian and Reformed Publishing Company, 1966.

Locke, John. *An Essay Concerning Human Understanding*. The Clarendon Edition of the Works of John Locke. Edited with an Introduction, Critical Apparatus and Glossary by Peter H. Nidditch. Oxford: Clarendon Press, 1975. Locke's work first published in 1690.

Lonergan, Bernard J. F. *Philosophy of God, and Theology*. Philadelphia: Westminster, 1973.

Lubac, H. de. *The Discovery of God*. New York: Kennedy and Sons, 1960.

Lucas, J. R. *The Freedom of the Will*. Oxford: Clarendon Press, 1970.

Luther, Martin. *The Bondage of the Will*. Translated by J. I. Packer and O. R. Johnson. London: J. Clarke, 1957.

MacKay, Donald M. *Human Science and Human Dignity*. Downers Grove: InterVarsity Press, 1979.

_____. *Science and the Quest for Meaning*. Grand Rapids: Eerdmans, 1982.

Mackie, J. L. "Evil and Omnipotence." *Mind*. XLIV. Number 254. (1955).

——————. *The Miracle of Theism*. Oxford: Clarendon Press, 1982.

Madden, Edward H. and Peter H. Hare. *Evil and the Concept of God*. Springfield, IL: Charles C. Thomas Publishers, 1968.

Maritain, Jacques. *Range of Reason*. New York: Charles Scribner's Sons, 1952, especially chapters 7-8.

——————. *Approaches to God*. New York: Harper & Brothers, 1954.

Marshall, I. Howard. *Kept by the Power of God*. Minneapolis: Bethany House, 1969.

——————. *I Believe in the Historical Jesus*. Grand Rapids: Eerdmans, 1977. In the "I Believe" series.

——————. *The Origins of New Testament Christology*. Updated Edition. London: InterVarsity Press, 1990.

Marxsen, Willi. *The Resurrection of Jesus of Nazareth*. Translated by Margaret Kohl. Philadelphia: Fortress Press, 1970.

Mascall, E.L. *He Who Is*. New York: Longmans, Green and Co., 1943.

——————. *Existence and Analogy*. London: Longmans, Green and Co., 1949, especially pp. 74-75,86-89,124, 143-147.

Matson, W. I. *The Existence of God*. Ithaca: Cornell University Press, 1965.

Mavrodes, George I. *Belief in God: A Study in the Epistemology of Religion*. Washington, DC: University Press of America, 1970.

McCormick, Thomas and Sharon Fish. *Meditation: A Practical Guide to a Spiritual Discipline*. Downers Grove: InterVarsity Press, 1983.

McInerny, Ralph M, Editor. *New Themes in Christian Philosophy*. Notre Dame, IN: University of Notre Dame Press, 1968.

——————. "Can God Be Named by Us?" *The Review of Metaphysics* 32 (September, 1978).

McIntyre, C.T., Editor. *God, History, and Historians*. New York: Oxford University Press, 1977.

McKloskey, H. J. "God and Evil. " *The Philosophical Quarterly* (April, 1960).

McPherson, Thomas. *The Argument from Design*. London: Macmillan, 1972.

Metcalf, Weldon. "I Saw Christ's Face." *The United Brethren* 90 (September, 1975).

Miethe, Terry L. *The Metaphysics of Leonard James Eslick: His Philosophy of God*. Ann Arbor: University Microflims, Inc, 1976.

_____. "The Ontological Argument: A Research Bibliography." *The Modern Schoolman* Vol. 54 (2 January 1977), pp. 148-166.

_____. "The Cosmological Argument: A Research Bibliography." *The New Scholasticism* Vol. 52, 2 (Spring, 1978), pp. 285-305.

_____, and Vernon J. Bourke. *Thomistic Bibliography, 1940-1978*. Westport, CT: Greenwood Press, 1980. 341 pages.

_____. "Atheism: Nietzsche," in *Biblical Errancy: An Analysis of its Philosophical Roots*. Grand Rapids: Zondervan, 1981, pp. 130-160.

_____. *Augustinian Bibliography, 1970-1980: With Essays on the Fundamentals of Augustinian Scholarship*. Westport, CT: Greenwood Press, 1982. 241 pages.

_____. *The Philosophy and Social Ethics of Alexander Campbell: From the Context of American Religious Thought, 1800-1866*. Ann Arbor: University Microflims, Inc, 1984.

_____. *The Christian's Guide to Following Jesus*. Minneapolis: Bethany House, 1984.

_____, Editor, Gary R. Habermas, and Antony G.N. Flew. *Did Jesus Rise From the Dead? The Resurrection Debate*. San Francisco: Harper and Row, 1987.

_____. *The Compact Dictionary of Doctrinal Words*. Minneapolis: Bethany House, 1988.

_____. Apologist's Corner: "The Christian and Debate." *The LodeStar Review* (November, 1988), p. 2.

_____. "The Universal Power of the Atonement," in *The Grace of God/The Will of Man*. Edited by C. Pinnock. Grand Rapids: Zondervan, 1989, pp. 71-96.

_____ and Antony G.N. Flew. *Does God Exist? A Believer and an Atheist Debate*. San Francisco: Harper Collins, 1991.

_____. "The Writings of Vernon J. Bourke." *The Modern Schoolman* 69 (March/May, 1992), pp. 499-509.

_____. *Living Your Faith: Closing the Gap Between Mind and Heart*. Joplin: College Press Publishing, 1993.

_____. "Agony: Key to Christian Victory." *Restoration Quarterly* 35 (1993).

Mill, John S. *Three Essays on Religion*. Third Edition. London: Longman, Green, Reader and Dyer, 1874.

Miller, Calvin. *Transcendental Hesitation: A Biblical Appraisal of TM and Eastern Mysticism*. Grand Rapids: Zondervan, 1977.

Miller, E.L. *Questions That Matter: An Introduction to Philosophy*. New York: McGraw-Hill, 1984, pp. 254-263.

Miller, Ed. *God and Reason*. New York: Macmillan, 1972.

Mitchell, Basil, Editor. *Faith and Logic: Oxford Essays in Philosophical Theology*. London: George Allen & Unwin LTD, 1957.

_____. *Morality: Religious and Secular*. Oxford: Clarendon Press, 1980.

_____. *How To Play Theological Ping-Pong: Essays on Faith & Reason*. Grand Rapids: Eerdmans, 1990.

Mitton, C. Leslie. *Jesus: The Fact Behind the Faith*. Grand Rapids: Eerdmans, 1974.

Montgomery, John Warwick. *History and Christianity*. Downers Grove: InterVarsity Press, 1964.

_____. "Inspiration and Inerrancy: A New Departure." *Evangelical Theological Society Bulletin* 8 (Spring, 1965), pp. 45-75. Also reprinted in *The Suicide of Christian Theology*, pp. 314-355.

_____. *The Suicide of Christian Theology*. Minneapolis: Bethany House, 1970.

_____. *Where Is History Going?* Minneapolis: Bethany House, 1972.

_____. *The Shape of the Past*. Minneapolis: Bethany House, 1975.

_____. *Faith Founded on Fact*. Nashville: Thomas Nelson, 1978.

Moody, Jr., Raymond A. *Life After Life*. New York: Bantam Books, 1975.

Moreland, J.P. *Scaling the Secular City: A Defense of Christianity*. Grand Rapids: Baker, 1987.

Morris, Henry M. *Scientific Creationism*. El Cajon, CA: Master, 1974.

_____ and Gary Parker. *What Is Creation Science?* San Diego: Creation-Life Publishers, 1982.

_____. *The Biblical Basis for Modern Science*. Grand Rapids: Baker, 1984.

Morris, Leon. *The Gospel According to John*. Grand Rapids: Eerdmans, 1968.

Morrison, A. Cressy. *Man Does Not Stand Alone*. Revised. New York: Revell & Co, 1944.

Mosley, A. W. "Historical Reporting in the Ancient World." *New Testament Studies* 12 (October, 1965), pp. 10-26.

Moule, C. F. D. *Christ's Messengers: Studies in Acts of the Apostles*. New York: Association Press, 1957.

_____. *The Phenomenon of the New Testament*. London: SCM, 1967.

_____. *The Origin of Christology*. Cambridge: Cambridge University Press, 1977.

_____. *The Birth of the New Testament*. 3rd Revised Edition. San Francisco: Harper and Row, 1981.

Mullins, E. Y. *Why Is Christianity True? Christian Evidences*. Philadelphia: The American Baptist Publication Society, 1905.

Murray, John Courtney. *The Problem of God: Yesterday and Today*. New Haven: Yale University Press, 1964, especially chapter 2.

Nagel, Ernest. "Determinism in History," in *Philosophical Analysis and History*. Edited by William Dray. New York: Harper and Row, 1966.

Nash, Ronald H. *Faith & Reason: Searching for a Rational Faith*. Grand Rapids: Zondervan, 1988.

_____. *Worldviews in Conflict: Choosing Christianity in a World of Ideas*. Grand Rapids: Zondervan, 1992.

Neill, Stephen. *Christian Faith and Other Faiths*. Second Edition. Oxford: Oxford University Press, 1970.

_____. *The Supremacy of Jesus*. Downers Grove: InterVarsity Press, 1984.

Neville, Robert C. *God the Creator: On the Transcendence and Presence of God*. Chicago: University of Chicago Press, 1968.

Newman, John Henry. *An Essay in Aid of a Grammar of Assent*. London: Longmans, Green & Co., 1939 (first edition, London, 1870).

Newman, Robert C., Editor. *The Evidence of Prophecy: Fulfilled Prediction as a Testimony to the Truth of Christianity*. Hatfield: Interdisciplinary Biblical Research Institute, 1988.

Newton-Smith, W. H. *The Rationality of Science*. International Library of Philosophy. Boston: Routledge and Kegan Paul, 1981.

O'Collins, Gerald. *What Are They Saying About the Resurrection?* New York: Paulist Press, 1978.

Ogden, Schubert M. *The Reality of God and Other Essays*. New York: Harper and Row, 1964.

_____. *Faith and Freedom: Toward a Theology of Liberation*. Nashville: Abingdon, 1979.

Orr, James. *The Resurrection of Jesus*. Grand Rapids: Zondervan, 1908, 1965.

Osborne, Grant. *The Resurrection Narratives: A Redactional Study.* Grand Rapids: Baker, 1984.

Owen, H. P. *The Moral Argument for Christian Theism.* London: Allen and Unwin, 1965.

Pannenberg, Wolfhart. *Jesus—God and Man.* Translated by Lewis L. Wilkens and Duane Priebe. Philadelphia: Westminster, 1968.

_____. *Theology and the Philosophy of Science.* Translated by Francis McDonagh. Philadelphia: Westminster, 1976.

_____. "Response to the Debate" in Gary Habermas and Antony Flew's *Did Jesus Rise From the Dead? The Resurrection Debate.* Edited by Terry L. Miethe. San Francisco: Harper and Row, 1987, pp. 125-135.

_____. *Metaphysics and the Idea of God.* Grand Rapids: Eerdmans, 1990.

Parker, Francis H. "The Realistic Position in Religion," in *Religion in Philosophical and Cultural Perspective.* Edited by Clayton Feaver, *et al.* Princeton: Van Nostrand Company, Inc, 1967.

Pascal, Blaise. *Pensées.* Arranged by Louis Lafuma and Translated by J. Warmington. London: J. M. Dent and Sons, 1960.

Peacocke, A. R. *Creation and the World of Science.* Oxford: Oxford University Press, 1979.

_____, Editor. *The Sciences and Theology in the Twentieth Century.* Notre Dame: University of Notre Dame Press, 1981.

Peirce, C. S. *Collected Papers.* Cambridge, MA: Harvard University Press, 1934 onwards.

Perrin, Norman. *The Resurrection According to Matthew, Mark and Luke.* Philadelphia: Fortress Press, 1977.

Peterson, Michael L. *Evil and the Christian God.* Grand Rapids: Baker, 1974.

Pfleiderer, Otto. *Early Christian Conception of Christ.* London: Williams and Norgate, 1905.

Pike, Nelson. *God and Evil.* Englewood Cliffs, NJ: Prentice-Hall, 1964.

Pinnock, Clark H. *Set Forth Your Case: An Examination of Christianity's Credentials.* Nutley, NJ: Craig Press, 1967.

_____, Editor. *Grace Unlimited.* Minneapolis: Bethany House, 1975.

_____. *Reason Enough: A Case for the Christian Faith.* Downers Grove: InterVarsity Press, 1980.

_____, Editor. *The Grace of God / The Will of Man.* Grand Rapids: Zondervan, 1989.

Plantinga, Alvin, Editor. *The Ontological Argument: from St. Anselm to Contemporary Philosophers.* Garden City, NY: Doubleday Anchor, 1965.

_____. *God and Other Minds. A Study of the Rational Justification of Belief in God.* Ithaca, NY: Cornell University Press, 1967.

_____. *God, Freedom, and Evil.* New York: Harper and Row, 1974.

_____. *God, Freedom, and Evil.* Grand Rapids: Eerdmans, 1974. Reproduction of Harper and Row Edition.

Plato. *Gorgias.* Translated by W. C. Helmhold. Indianapolis: The Bobbs-Merrill Co., 1952.

_____. *Plato: The Collected Dialogues.* Edited by Edith Hamilton and Huntington Cairns. Princeton: Princeton University Press, 1961.

Plotinus. *Plotinus: The Enneads.* Translated by Stephen MacKenna. London: Faber and Faber, Ltd., 1956.

Purtill, Richard L. *Reason to Believe.* Grand Rapids: Eerdmans, 1974.

_____. "Proofs of Miracles and Miracles as Proofs." *Christian Scholars Review* 6, No. 1 (1976), pp. 39-51.

_____. "Flew and the Free Will Defense." *Religious Studies* 13 (1977), pp. 477-483.

_____. *Thinking About Religion: A Philosophical Introduction to Religion.* Englewood Cliffs, NJ: Prentice Hall, 1978.

_____. *C.S. Lewis's Case for the Christian Faith.* San Francisco: Harper and Row, 1985.

Radhakrishnan, Sarvepalli and Charles A. Moore. *A Source Book in Indian Philosophy.* Princeton: Princeton University Press, 1957.

Ramm, Bernard. *Protestant Christian Evidences.* Chicago: Moody, 1953.

_____. *The Christian View of Science and Scripture.* Grand Rapids: Eerdmans, 1954.

_____. *The Witness of the Spirit.* Grand Rapids: Eerdmans, 1959.

Rashdall, Hastings. *The Theory of Good and Evil.* Volume II. Oxford: Clarendon Press, 1907.

Reichenbach, Bruce R. *The Cosmological Argument: A Reassessment.* Springfield, IL: Charles C. Thomas Publishers, 1972.

Reid, J. K. S. *Christian Apologetics*. Grand Rapids: Eerdmans, 1969.

Rice, Richard. *God's Foreknowledge and Man's Free Will*. Minneapolis: Bethany House, 1980.

Richardson, Don. *Eternity in Their Hearts*. Revised Edition. Ventura: Regal Books, 1984.

Ritchie, George G. with Elizabeth Sherrill. *Return from Tomorrow*. Waco: Word Books, 1978.

Robertson, Pat with William Proctor. *Beyond Reason: How Miracles Can Change Your Life*. Toronto: Bantam Books, 1984.

Robinson, John A. T. *Redating the New Testament*. Philadelphia: Westminister, 1976.

_____. *Can We Trust the New Testament?* Grand Rapids: Eerdmans, 1977.

Rowe, William L. "The Cosmological Argument." *Nous* 5 (1971), pp. 49-61.

_____. *The Cosmological Argument*. Princeton, NJ: Princeton University Press, 1975.

_____. *Philosophy of Religion: An Introduction*. Belmont: Wadsworth Publishing Company, 1982.

Royce, Josiah. *The Conception of God: An Address Before the Union*. New York: Macmillan, 1902 (first edition, Berkeley, California, 1895).

Russell, Bertrund. *Why I am Not a Christian*. New York: Simon and Schuster, 1957.

Schleiermacher, Friedrich. *The Christian Faith*. Edited by H. R. Mackintosh and J. S. Stewart. New York: Harper and Row, 1963.

Schweitzer, Albert. *The Quest for the Historical Jesus*. Translated by W. Montgomery. New York: Macmillan, 1906, 1968.

Sheehan, Thomas. *First Coming: How the Kingdom of God Became Christianity*. New York: Random House, 1986.

Sherwin-White, A. N. *Roman Society and Roman Law in the New Testament*. Oxford: Oxford University Press, 1963.

Sillem, Edward. *Ways of Thinking About God*. New York: Sheed and Ward, 1961, especially pp. 118-133, 136-9, 160-65.

Silvester, Hugh. *Arguing with God*. Downers Grove: InterVarsity Press, 1971.

Six, J. E. *L'athéisme dans la vie et la culture contemporaines*. 2 vols. Paris: Desclée, 1967-68.

Smart, Ninian. *Philosophers and Religious Truth*. London: SCM, 1964. Chapter two is an answer to the criticism that miracles are unscientific.

Smith, Gerard and L. H. Kendzierski. *The Philosophy of Being*. New York: Macmillan. Christian Wisdom Series, 1961.

Smith, John E. *Reason and God*. Encounters of Philosophy with Religion. New Haven: Yale Univeristy Press, 1967.

_____. *Experience and God*. New York: Oxford University Press, 1968.

Sontag, Frederick. *God, Why Did You Do that*? Philadephia: Westminister, 1970.

Sowell, Thomas. *Knowledge and Decisions*. New York: Basic, 1980.

Stearns, J. Brenton. "On the Impossibility of God's Knowing That He Does Not Exist." *The Journal of Religion* 46 (1966), pp. 1-8.

Stein, Robert H. "Was the Tomb Really Empty?" *The Journal of the Evangelical Theological Society* 20 (March 1977). Grand Rapids: Baker, 1978.

Stephen, Leslie. *English Thought in the Eighteenth Century*. Third Edition. London: Murrary, 1902.

Stoner, Peter W. and Robert C. Newman. *Science Speaks: Scientific Proof of the Accuracy of Prophecy and the Bible*. Chicago: Moody, 1968.

Strauss, David. *A New Life of Jesus*. Volume I. London: Williams and Norgate, 1879.

Summers, Ray. *Commentary on Luke*. Waco: Word Books, 1972.

Swinburne, Richard. *The Concept of Miracle*. London: Macmillan, 1970.

_____. *The Coherence of Theism*. Clarendon Library of Logic and Philosophy. Oxford: Oxford University Press, 1977.

_____. *The Existence of God*. Oxford: Clarendon Press, 1979.

_____. *Faith and Reason*. Oxford: Clarendon Press, 1981.

_____. *The Evolution of the Soul*. Oxford: Clarendon Press, 1986.

_____. "Natural Evil. " *American Philosophical Quarterly* 15.

Taylor, Alfred Edward. *Does God Exist*? New York: Macmillan, 1947 (first edition, 1945).

Taylor, Richard. *Metaphysics*. Englewood Cliffs, NJ: Prentice-Hall, 1974.

Taylor, Vincent. *The Atonement in New Testament Teaching*. Third Edtion. London: The Epworth Press, 1963.

Tennant, F. R. *Miracle and Its Philosophical Presuppositions*. Cambridge: Cambridge University Press, 1925.

_____. *Philosophical Theology*, Vol. 2, *The World, the Soul, and God*. Cambridge: Cambridge University Press, 1956.

Tenney, Merril C. *New Testament Survey*. Revised Edition. Grand Rapids: Eerdmans, 1961.

_____. *The Reality of the Resurrection*. New York: Harper and Row, 1963.

Thaxton, Charles B., Walter L. Bradley, and Roger L. Olsen. *The Mystery of Life's Origin: Reassessing Current Theories*. New York: Philosophical Library, 1984.

Thompson, Matthew. *The Problem of Good in the Problem of Evil*. A Thesis submitted to and accepted by the Faculty of Arts of the University of Birmingham, England, 1989.

Thompson, Samuel M. *A Modern Philosophy of Religion*. Chicago: Henry Regnery, 1955.

Thurman, L. Duane. *How to Think About Evolution*. 2nd Edition. Downers Grove: InterVarsity Press, 1978.

Tillich, Paul. *Systematic Theology*. Chicago: University of Chicago Press, 1971.

Tinsley, E. J. *The Gospel According to Luke*. Cambridge: Cambridge University Press, 1965.

Toulmin, Stephen. "Arthur Koestler's Theodicy." *Encounter* 52 (Feburary, 1979).

Trueblood, David Elton. *Philosophy of Religion*. New York: Harper and Row, 1957.

Valecky, L. C. "Flew on Aquinas." *Philosophy* 43 (1968), pp. 213-230.

Van Buren, Paul. *The Secular Meaning of the Gospel*. New York: Macmillan, 1963.

Van Frassen, Bas C. *The Scientific Image*. Oxford: Clarendon Press, 1980.

Varghese, Roy Abraham, Editor. *The Intellectuals Speak Out About God*. Chicago: Regnery Gateway, Inc, 1984.

Walsh, W. H. *Philosophy of History*. New York: Harper & Brothers, 1960.

Wand, William. *Christianity: A Historical Religion?* Valley Forge: Judson Press, 1972.

Warren, Thomas B. and Antony G. N. Flew. *The Warren-Flew Debate on the Existence of God*. Jonesboro: National Christian Press, 1977.

Weinberg, Steven. *The First Three Minutes: A Modern View of the Origin of the Universe*. New York: Basic Books, Inc., 1977.

Wenham. John W. *The Goodness of God*. Downers Grove: InterVarsity Press, 1974.

_____. *Easter Enigma: Are the Resurrection Accounts in Conflict?* Grand Rapids: Zondervan, 1984.

_____. *Christ and the Bible*. Grand Rapids: Baker, 1984.

Whately, Richard. *Historical Doubts Relative to Napoleon Bonaparte*. New York: Robert Caster, 1849. (Satirizes Hume's attack on miracles, claiming that Hume's views would eliminate historical knowledge of other unique and non-miraculous events.)

White, Morton G. (1970) "The Analytic and the Synthetic: An Untenable Dualism." *Analyticity*. Edited by J. F. Harris, Jr. and R. H. Severens. Chicago: Quadrangle Books, pp. 75-91.

Wilckens, Ulrich. *Resurrection*. Translated by A. M. Stewart. Edinburgh: Saint Andrews Press, 1977.

Wilder-Smith, A.E. *Man's Origin, Man's Destiny*. Wheaton, IL: Harold Shaw Publishers, 1968. Currently published with Bethany House Publishers.

_____. *The Creation of Life*. Wheaton, IL: Harold Shaw Publishers, 1970.

_____. *The Natural Sciences Know Nothing of Evolution*. Costa Mesa, CA: T.W.F.T. Publishers, 1981.

_____. *The Scientific Alternative to Neo-Darwinian Evolutionary Theory: Information Sources and Structures*. Costa Mesa, CA: T.W.F.T. Publishers, 1987.

Willard, Dallas. *The Spirit of the Disciplines*. San Francisco: Harper and Row, 1988.

Wisdom, John. *Philosophy and Psychoanalysis*. Oxford: Basil Blackwell, 1953.

Wolter, Allan B. "An Oxford Dialogue on Language and Metaphysics I." *The Review of Metaphysics* 31 (June, 1978).

_____. "An Oxford Dialogue on Language and Metaphysics II." *The Review of Metaphysics* 32 (December, 1978).

Wright, Christopher J. *An Eye For an Eye: The Place of Old Testament Ethics Today*. Downers Grove: InterVarsity Press, 1983.

Yamauchi, Edwin. *Jesus, Zoroaster, Socrates, Buddha, Muhammad*. Revised Edition. Downers Grove: InterVarsity Press, 1972.

Yancey, Philip. "When Bad Things Happen to Good People," *Christianity Today* 27 (August 5, 1983).

Yockey, Hubert P. "A Calculation of the Probability of Spontaneous Biogenesis by Information Theory." *Journal of Theoretical Biology* 67 (1977), pp. 377-398.

_____. "Self Organization Origin of Life Scenarios and Information Theory." *Journal of Theoretical Biology* 91 (1981), pp. 13-31.

Young, Warren C. *A Christian Approach to Philosophy*. Grand Rapids: Baker, 1954, 1957.

ABOUT THE AUTHORS

Terry L. Miethe is Provost and Honored Professor of Philosophy, Theology, and History at Emmanuel College, Oxford. He is currently a postdoctoral fellow in History at Christ Church, the University of Oxford, England. Dr. Miethe holds the A.B., with honors, from Lincoln Christian College; the M.A., with honors, from Trinity Evangelical Divinity School; the M.Div. from McCormick Theological Seminary; the Ph.D. in Philosophy, Phi Beta Kappa, from St. Louis University; and the A.M. and Ph.D. in Social Ethics and Theology from the University of Southern California. He is a member of eight scholastic honor societies in History, Psychology, Classical Languages, English, Philosophy, including Phi Beta Kappa and Alpha Sigma Nu. Dr. Miethe has written or edited fifteen books, including works on Augustine and Aquinas; *The New Christian's Guide to Following Jesus* (1984), *A Christian's Guide to Faith and Reason* (1987), *The Compact Dictionary of Doctrinal Words* (1988), *Does God Exist? A Believer and an Atheist Debate* (1991) with Antony Flew, *Living Your Faith: Closing the Gap Between Mind & Heart* (1993), and edited *Did Jesus Rise From the Dead? The Resurrection Debate* (1987). Dr. Miethe's books have been translated into German, Spanish, and Russian. He has also written dozens of articles.

Gary R. Habermas is honored Professor of Religion and Philosophy at Emmanuel College, Oxford. Dr. Habermas holds the B.R.E. from William Tyndale College, the M.A. in Philosophical Theology from the University of Detroit, the Ph.D. in History and Philosophy of Religion from Michigan State University, and the earned D.D. in Theology from Emmanuel College, Oxford. Dr. Habermas has written ten books, including: *The Resurrection of Jesus: A Rational Inquiry* (1976), *The Resurrection of Jesus: An Apologetic* (1980), *Did Jesus Rise from the Dead: The Resurrection Debate* (1987) with Antony Flew, *Verdict of History* (1984, 1988, British edition 1990), *Dealing with Doubt* (1990), *Immortality: The Other Side of Death* (1992) with J.P. Moreland. Dr. Habermas' books have been published in eleven foreign editions and translated into French, Spanish, Portuguese, Italian, Swedish, Norwegian, and Danish. He has also written dozens of articles, both scholarly and popular, in journals and periodicals such as: *Religious Studies, Faith and Philosophy, Catholic Digest, Bibliotheca Sacra, Journal of the Evangelical Theological Society, Saturday Evening Post,* and *International Christian Digest.*